T0369589

From Deep Learning to Rational Machines

From Deep Learning to Rational Machines

What the History of Philosophy Can Teach Us about the Future of Artificial Intelligence

CAMERON J. BUCKNER

OXFORD
UNIVERSITY PRESS

Oxford University Press is a department of the University of Oxford. It furthers
the University's objective of excellence in research, scholarship, and education
by publishing worldwide. Oxford is a registered trade mark of Oxford University
Press in the UK and certain other countries.

Published in the United States of America by Oxford University Press
198 Madison Avenue, New York, NY 10016, United States of America.

Library of Congress Cataloging-in-Publication Data
Names: Buckner, Cameron J., author.
Title: From deep learning to rational machines : what the history of
philosophy can teach us about the future of artifical intelligence /
Cameron J. Buckner.
Description: New York, NY : Oxford University Press, [2024] |
Includes bibliographical references and index.
Identifiers: LCCN 2023022566 (print) | LCCN 2023022567 (ebook) |
ISBN 9780197653302 (hardback) | ISBN 9780197653326 (epub) |
ISBN 9780197653319 (ebook other) | ISBN 9780197653333 (ebook)
Subjects: LCSH: Machine learning—Philosophy.
Classification: LCC Q325.5 .B83 2024 (print) | LCC Q325.5 (ebook) |
DDC 006.3/1—dc23/eng/20230927
LC record available at https://lccn.loc.gov/2023022566
LC ebook record available at https://lccn.loc.gov/2023022567

DOI: 10.1093/oso/9780197653302.001.0001

Printed by Sheridan Books, Inc., United States of America

This book is dedicated to my grandfather, Roland J. Melinsky, whom we lost to COVID-19 during this book's composition. He was the best human being I've ever met.

Contents

Preface

Trying to write a book about the philosophical implications of deep learning today is a bit like trying to saddle a mustang at full gallop. I started planning this book back in 2015, when it became clear that deep neural networks had fundamentally changed the game in computer vision. Despite having a professional interest in artificial intelligence (AI) and the philosophical implications of artificial neural networks for most of my adult life, I had assumed that we were still decades away from achieving the degree of success that AlexNet and its successors delivered on image labeling tasks. Then just as I'd begun to feel like I understood the basic principles that account for the success of deep convolutional neural networks like AlexNet on computer vision, I realized that I was already several years behind on an entirely different and equally exciting new neural network architecture, generative adversarial networks, that were reaching similarly astounding degrees of performance on image generation tasks. This sense of being perpetually in arrears recurred yet again with the ascendency of transformers on language tasks in 2018. It became clear to me, at least, that deep learning was much more than a one-trick pony, that it would be the workhorse of AI for years to come.

Though the importance of deep learning is today widely appreciated, the debate over its philosophical implications still seems trapped between implausible extremes—either deep learning agents are about to achieve singularity into a world-spanning superintelligence that will leave behind its puny human creators, or they are nothing more than enormous, ramshackle piles of statistical operations with little relevance to genuine intelligence. Relatedly, prognostications about deep learning's future prospects seemed hobbled by simplistic interpretations of philosophical positions that are seen to inspire such enthusiasm or skepticism. Enthusiasts of deep learning regularly don the mantle of empiricism, echoing Aristotle's conviction that abstract knowledge can be derived from sensory experience, whereas deep learning's critics favor Plato's nativist contention that the source of abstract knowledge is to be found in an innate mental endowment. The names of well-known philosophers of Western Europe like Locke, Descartes, Leibniz, Hume, Berkeley, and Kant regularly appear in works by computer scientists, psychologists, and neuroscientists seeking to understand deep learning's implications. Unfortunately, however, the subtle and elegant views of these philosophers are often pressed into simplistic molds to serve extreme predictions, often leading potentially fruitful interdisciplinary dialogue to end in frustration and talking past one another.

In fact, I think a great deal is to be gained by using influential works from the history of philosophy to contextualize the structure and achievements of deep learning's complex menagerie of network architectures. Philosophers might see how these architectures implement some of the empiricists' most ambitious speculations about the mind's operations, and scientists can benefit from empiricism's comprehensive roadmap of the rational mind—replete with a rich set of goals, challenges, and guideposts that can explain what specific achievements and failures in deep learning imply about the nature of rationality or intelligence. Unfortunately, these benefits can only be obtained by rolling up our sleeves and getting into the nitty gritty of both the philosophical positions and the computational models—and by setting aside simplistic extremes for a subtler continuum of views on the origins of rationality and abstract knowledge.

The most glaring misrepresentation found in the present debate is the claim—usually made by nativists—that empiricists believe that the mind begins with virtually no structure whatsoever. In fact, nearly every major empiricist was a faculty psychologist—that is, they believed that rational learning depends upon a complex interplay among active mental faculties, such as perception, memory, imagination, attention, and sympathy. Also obscured in these debates is the fact that deep learning research is already well on its way to modeling many of these active faculties, to great effect. The central thread of the book thus ties the philosophical history of empiricist faculty psychology to the details of these engineering achievements, hopefully bringing into focus how these engineering achievements add up to steady and consistent progress toward modeling the rational mind, while also clarifying how much remains to be done to realize fully human-like AI. Though this book is based upon my previously published work on these topics, at least 80 percent of it reflects new research.

In Chapter 1, I outline the terms for a useful debate between empiricist and nativist perspectives on deep learning. I describe how major theorists both historical and contemporary fit onto a continuum of views between radical empiricism and radical nativism, suggesting that the most empirically plausible options today will be more moderate. I outline a particular version of moderate empiricism that I develop and defend throughout the book, which I dub the Domain General Modular Architecture (DoGMA). I outline success conditions for a defense of the DoGMA, based in recent philosophy of science, focusing on the goal of modeling how rational faculties actually operate in a human-like cognitive architecture. In Chapter 2, I review methodological considerations relevant to gauging the success of the DoGMA's defense. I motivate a choice to focus on rationality rather than intelligence, given concerns about the history of psychometric research from which many intelligence-based approaches descend. I consider biases that could distort the evaluation such as anthropomorphism and anthropocentrism. I particularly focus on the way that nativist assumptions may be supported by a problematic bias that I have termed "anthropofabulation," which combines anthropocentrism with confabulation about the superiority of average human performance.

The remaining chapters of the book adopt a "philosopher of the week" format, zooming in on the views of a historical empiricist who had a particularly interesting and useful theory of a faculty, and then showing how some of their most ambitious ideas about that faculty have been realized in recent deep learning research. In Chapter 3, I focus on John Locke's views on the faculty of perception. Locke proposed several forms of perceptual abstraction in his attempts to explain how we acquired general category representations from interaction with their examples, and I illustrate how some of his ideas have been realized in deep convolutional neural networks, the kind of architecture behind AlexNet.

In Chapter 4, I focus on the views of the Ibn Sina (Avicenna) on memory. Ibn Sina had an interesting take on the role that affect plays in memory, enabling the faculty to serve a pivotal role in reinforcement learning and rational decision-making. I tie Ibn Sina's ideas about memory to successful models in deep learning that make use of deep reinforcement learning, such as DeepMind's Episodic Controller architecture, which can play Atari games at superhuman levels of performance.

In Chapter 5, I explore David Hume's views on the faculty of imagination. Hume had a particularly rich and ambitious take on imagination as a kind of mental laboratory in which new composite ideas could be created by fusing together old ideas in creative ways. I explain how Hume's theory, if successful, could rebut some of the most serious objections raised against empiricism by critics like Jerry Fodor. I then discuss how generative adversarial networks can be seen to realize some of Hume's most speculative and ambitious ideas. I also discuss more recent and powerful generative architectures, such as those behind DALL-E 2 and MidJourney. I review how such architectures can be modified to favor novelty in their outputs to model more human-like kinds of creativity and can even be used to create simulated input for offline learning or complex planning for future outcomes, as is found in DeepMind's Imagination-Augmented Agents (I2A) architecture.

In Chapter 6, I review William James's theory of attention. I review the diversity of roles and functions that have been ascribed to attention by cognitive psychology and argue that James's theory has the best chance of explaining how a single faculty could play all of these roles. I explain how James's view fits particularly well with predictive approaches which are on the ascendancy in machine learning. I explain how a mechanism called "self-attention" operates in transformer architectures, which have demonstrated so much success on language processing tasks such as automated translation, document summary, and the creation of human-like essays and articles. I also make a case that attention will need to play an important role in modeling cognitive control in order to regulate and coordinate the operations of the other faculties.

In Chapter 7, I discuss Sophie de Grouchy's views on social cognition and morality. De Grouchy had a particularly interesting empiricist take on the origins of empathy in the earliest experiences of infancy. I argue that research on artificial social cognition is in danger of taking on board too many rationalist assumptions and heading down blind alleys, and I suggest that accurate modeling of human-like moral and social cognition will require backtracking to develop better models of human-like emotional reactions and learning curricula to hone them if we can hope to better recapitulate the formative social interactions of infancy and childhood that are required to bootstrap a human-like faculty of empathy. I review a variety of early moves in these directions from areas of research like affective computing and artificial rearing studies.

The questions that arise in exploring these topics are neither simply engineering challenges nor purely philosophical conundrums; to create deeply rational machines will require us to both understand the nature of rationality itself and muster the engineering skill to demonstrate that our philosophical mantras can be turned into practical engineering success. "If you can't make one," pressed my favorite philosopher Fred Dretske (perhaps paraphrasing Richard Feynman, both of whom had a background in engineering), "then you don't know how it works." I have always wanted to understand the rational mind, so let us explore the details to see what can be built.

Acknowledgments

This book has benefitted from generous feedback from dozens of thoughtful friends and colleagues across the cognitive sciences, across many speaking engagements, online reading groups, social media interactions, and workshop discussions. In alphabetical order, I thank in particular Darren Abramson, Colin Allen, Mariam Aly, Mel Andrews, Jessica Andrews-Hanna, Olivia Bailey, Yuri Balashov, David Barack, Anthony Beavers, Juan Pablo Bermudez, Ned Block, Ali Boyle, Felipe De Brigard, Rosa Cao, Max Cappuccio, David Chalmers, Amit Chaturvedi, Lucy Cheke, Mazviita Chirimuuta, Ron Chrisley, Hayley Clatterbuck, David Colaco, L. Conkleton, Katie Creel, Matt Crosby, Mike Dacey, Tamas Demeter, Guy Dove, Zoe Drayson, Sina Fazelpour, Elmo Feiten, Chaz Firestone, Jim Garson, Justin Garson, Konstantin Genin, Javier Gómez-Lavín, Thomas Grote, Marcello Guarini, Marta Halina, Bryce Heubner, Linus Huang, Zach Irving, Michael Jacovides, Krešimir Josić, Brett Karlan, Bob Kentridge, Jackson Kernion, Phillip Kieval, Daniel Kirchner, Alexander Klein, Colin Klein, John Krakauer, Thomas Krödel, Peter Langland-Hassan, Neil Van Leeuwen, S. Matthew Liao, Grace Lindsay, Tal Linzen, Zachary Lipton, Robert Long, Edouard Machery, Corey Maley, Pete Mandik, Manolo Martinez, Joseph McCaffrey, Jay McClelland, Tom McCoy, Marcin Miłkowski, Raphaël Millière, Dmitri Mollo, Talia Morag, Jorge Morales, Jennifer Nagel, Thi Nguyen, Ankit Patel, Mary Peterson, Alessio Plebe, Charles Rathkopf, Ali Rezaei, Susanne Riehemann, J. Brendan Ritchie, Sarah Robins, Anna-Mari Rusanen, Bruce Rushing, Susanna Schellenberg, Tobias Schlicht, Eric Schliesser, Nick Shea, Henry Shevlin, Neil Sinhababu, Susan G. Sterrett, Catherine Stinson, Pär Sundström, Kathryn Tabb, Lisa Miracchi Titus, Alfredo Vernazzani, Martin Wally Wallace, Jonathan Weinberg, Evan Westra, Isaac Wiegman, Rasmus Winther, and Xin Hui Yong (and deep apologies to anyone I forgot to thank . . . it's been a wild few years).

I am grateful in particular to Gualtiero Piccinini for thorough comments on two drafts of this manuscript. I would also like to thank my developmental editor, Molly Gage, for two thorough passes through the entire manuscript (I asked her not to hold back with tough love, and she delivered). I am grateful to OpenAI and AnthropicAI for granting me access to experimental tools. I thank in particular Evan Morikawa for the cover art image, which was generated by DALL-E 2 to the prompt "A painting of the philosophy of artificial intelligence." I am also grateful for the "Philosophy and Cognitive Science of Deep Learning Reading Group" for helping me stay up-to-date on the newest developments in machine learning research, and the "Association Association" for helping me understand the oldest developments in associative learning theory, and to the students enrolled in the two incarnations of my "Philosophy of Deep Learning" seminar for voluminous feedback.

I also thank the National Science Foundation for a Scholar's Grant (#2020585), which supported the research behind this monograph, and the Leverhulme Centre for the Future of Intelligence and Clare Hall at the University of Cambridge for supporting me with a fellowship during the summer of 2022.

Note on Abbreviated Citations
to Historical Works

Citations to Aristotle

Free online editions at http://classics.mit.edu/Browse/browse-Aristotle.html
Citations to Aristotle will mention work (e.g., *De Anima*), Book, and Bekker numbers.

Citations to Locke

Free online editions at https://www.gutenberg.org/

E

Locke, J. 1690. *An Essay Concerning Human Understanding.* Edited by P. H. Nidditch. Oxford: Oxford University Press, 1979.
   Note: Citations to the *Essay* will include Book.Chapter.Paragraph numbers in BigRoman.smallroman.arabic format (e.g. II.ii.2).

Citations to Hume

Free online editions at https://davidhume.org/

T

A Treatise of Human Nature. Edited by D. F. Norton and M. J. Norton. Oxford: Clarendon, 2007.

Note: citations to the *Treatise* will include Book.Part.Section. Paragraph numbers in Arabic numerals followed by SBN numbers.

EHU

An Enquiry Concerning Human Understanding. Edited by T. L. Beauchamp. Oxford: Clarendon, 2000.

Note: citations to the *Enquiry* will include Book.Part.Section numbers in Arabic numerals followed by SBN numbers.

Citations to Ibn Sina (Avicenna)

There is no canonical collection of Ibn Sina's works, complicating citation. Unless otherwise noted, references to Ibn Sina's works will be to a translation by Rahman:

Rahman, Fazlur (trans.) (1952). *Avicenna's Psychology*. Westport, CT : Hyperion.

Note: Citations will mention the Arabic name of the original work (e.g. *Najāt*).

Citations to James

PP

James, W. (1890). *The Principles of Psychology, Vol 1*. New York: Henry Holt and Co. https://doi.org/10.1037/10538-000

Citations to De Grouchy

All citations to De Grouchy are to the recent edition translated by Sandrine Bergès:

De Grouchy, S. Sophie de Grouchy's "Letters on Sympathy": A Critical Engagement with Adam Smith's "The Theory of Moral Sentiments." Translated and edited by Sandrine Bergès and edited by Eric Schliesser. Oxford New Histories of Philosophy. New York: Oxford University Press.

Note: Citations to De Grouchy will include Letter number in Roman numerals.

1

Moderate Empiricism and Machine Learning

Instead of trying to produce a programme to simulate the adult mind, why not rather try to produce one which simulates the child's? If this were then subjected to an appropriate course of education one would obtain the adult brain. Presumably the child-brain is something like a note-book as one buys it from the stationers. Rather little mechanism and lots of blank sheets. . . . Our hope is that there is so little mechanism in the child-brain that something like it can be easily programmed.

—Alan M. Turing (1950:456)

1.1. Playing with fire? Nature versus nurture for computer science

In human inquiry, the introduction of a grand dichotomy—good versus evil, mortal versus divine, emotion versus reason—can take on the vital importance, as well as the attendant danger, of the discovery of fire. While such dichotomies support qualitative shifts in the reach of our theorizing, they are often quickly taken for granted, perhaps too quickly, as an elemental force governing the world and our place within it. The distinction between nature and nurture stands as a prime example. This opposition has animated the human intellect for thousands of years, motivating the systematic exploration of competing styles of theory in nearly every academic discipline. We tend to have strong intuitions as to whether human knowledge is produced by turning inward to unpack our innate mental endowment

From Deep Learning to Rational Machines. Cameron J. Buckner, Oxford University Press.
© Oxford University Press 2024. DOI: 10.1093/oso/9780197653302.003.0001

or by turning outward to interpret the cipher of experience, and the energy provided by these intuitions has powered a variety of scientific and technological innovations. As with other Promethean bargains, however, such advances are bought at the expense of new and persistent dangers. Vigorously rubbing these opposing intuitions against one another can generate friction without illumination, causing theorists to pursue a research program long after its empirical prospects have grown cold, or to lose sight of the details of one another's views in a haze of misunderstanding and exaggeration. And, of course, fires that grow too large can burn dangerously out of control. Lest we get singed, these distinctions must be continuously watched and carefully tended—particularly when a powerful new source of fuel is tossed into the flames.

We are now in the middle of just such a conflagration, and the new fuel source goes by the name of "deep learning." Indeed, funding and research for deep learning is currently blazing; as of 2023, every major tech company's marquee R&D group is focused on deep learning, with fierce bidding wars for top talent. Most issues of prestige publications like *Science* and *Nature* feature one of these groups' latest experiments. These publications report a series of transformative breakthroughs in artificial intelligence (AI), including systems that can recognize complex objects in natural photographs as well or better than humans; defeat human grandmasters in strategy games such as chess, Go, shoji, or Starcraft II; create novel pictures and bodies of text that are sometimes indistinguishable from those produced by humans; sift through the faintest radio echoes to discover new exoplanets orbiting stars thousands of light years away; crunch massive amounts of data generated by particle accelerators to try to find counterexamples to the Standard Model in physics; and predict how proteins will fold more accurately than human microbiologists who have devoted their lives to the task.[1]

---

[1] For details, see Baldi, Sadowski, and Whiteson (2014); T. Brown et al. (2020); Chowdhery et al. (2022); Jumper et al. (2021); Krizhevsky, Sutskever, and Hinton (2012); Ramesh et al. (2022); Shallue and Vanderburg (2018); Silver et al. (2017); and Vinyals et al. (2019).

In short, deep learning's current fortunes are white hot; but, as with all systems of knowledge acquisition, our expectations of its continued prosperity are shaped by our views on the nature-nurture dichotomy. Deep learning's current status and future development are therefore meaningfully informed by philosophical positions, particularly those on offer in the historically grounded but ongoing debate between empiricists and nativists. At first blush, this debate concerns the origins of human knowledge: empiricists hold that knowledge is derived from sensory experience, whereas nativists tend to be rationalists who instead prize our capacity to reason—usually driven by an innate theory of the world's basic structure and/or of rational minds—as the source of genuine knowledge.[2] When treated as an approach to AI, deep learning is already identified as a nurture-favoring, empiricist style of theory, though I argue that its achievements vindicate a moderately empiricist approach to cognition that is more nuanced and resourceful than the empiricism typically surveyed in evaluations of deep learning's potential. This moderately empiricist approach, legitimated by an investigation of the historical origins of the philosophical debate in the work of influential empiricist philosophers and the application of their views to the relationship between machine learning models and the mind, suggests that today's achievements in deep learning substantially increase the plausibility that rational cognition can be achieved—and is achieved, in humans, many animals, and, if we hope to succeed, artificial agents—without the aid of the innate theories or concepts usually recommended by the opposed, nature-favoring, rationalist faction of theorists.

While empiricist and nativists theorists fight over the past, present, and future of deep learning systems development, the current enthusiasm for empiricism in engineering and business threatens to burn out of control—though this particular strain of empiricism sometimes draws oxygen from a simplistic understanding of the relationship between the successes of deep learning systems and the way that

---

[2] To forestall confusion, the philosophical rationalism attributable to thinkers like Descartes, Leibniz, and Spinoza is not to be conflated with the new "rationalism" associated with blogs like LessWrong or Slate Star Codex, for which the traditional philosophical distinction is orthogonal.

humans and animals actually solve problems. Research is moving so rapidly that an influential deep learning publication can receive 20,000 citations by the time it is only two or three years old—many of those while it is available only on a preprint archive, meaning that it has not yet gone through the normal process of peer review by other academics who could skeptically assess its claims. Meanwhile, leading nativists are going hoarse calling for the fire brigade. These nativists worry that deep learning is being applied to a wide range of problems without a firm understanding of how or why it works, and that the solutions discovered by deep learning agents are brittle and do not generalize to new situations as well as the strategies deployed by humans and animals. Depending upon whether you ask empiricists or nativists, deep learning systems can either already process input data so effectively that they are at least slightly conscious and on the verge of achieving escape velocity into world-spanning superintelligence, or they can do little more than bludgeon problems with massive amounts of statistics and linear algebra that can imitate the outward appearance of human intelligence but, because they lack the underlying structure provided by the human mind's innate startup software, will never capture even the most basic aspects of human mentality.

Although deep learning can be understood in purely technical terms outside the nature-nurture dichotomy, and hence outside the empiricist-nativist debate, it is difficult to assess its prospects as a route to AI except through its light, with all its attendant prospects and perils. This debate, of course, has ancient historical origins, yet influential scientists frequently invoke its terms to explain and motivate their current views. For instance, in a front-page *Nature* article, a team from Google's DeepMind division pitched their AlphaZero system—which can easily defeat human grandmasters at the Chinese board game of Go, a game that is in some ways more complex than chess—as operating with a "tabula rasa" or blank slate algorithm (Silver et al. 2017). This empiricist metaphor entered the Western lexicon via Aristotle's *De Anima* (III, 429b–430a), which compares the human mind to the wax-covered tablets which the Greek academies used for notes; these tablets were "blanked" by heating them until the wax melted, smoothing the surface for reuse. The metaphor for the infant's mind became canonical through its repetition by a range of empiricist philosophers, from

Aristotle's inheritors Ibn Sina (Avicenna) and St. Thomas Aquinas (the latter of which summarized it with the Peripatetic Maxim, which states that "*nihil est in intellectu quod non sit prius in sensu*" or "nothing in the mind which is not first in the senses"—*De Veritate* 2.3.19), to the Early Modern empiricists John Locke and David Hume, with whom the view is today most commonly associated.[3]

Deep learning enthusiasts are not the only ones to summon the history of philosophy in this context. Contemporary nativists have also been eager to align the current debate with historical positions. In his critique of the AlphaZero paper, for example, the nativist psychologist Gary Marcus associates Silver et al.'s blank slate language with the views of Locke, who wrote that "all ideas come from sensation or reflection" (*E* II.ii.2). Marcus could just as well have linked it to Hume, who declared that "all our simple ideas in their first appearance are deriv'd from simple [sensory] impressions" (commonly referred to as his "Copy Principle"—*T* 1.1.1.7/4). Hume, however, is more frequently the target of Judea Pearl. One of the most influential living computer scientists and a frequent deep learning critic, Pearl has recently worried that deep learning theorists take as self-evident a "radical empiricism" according to which all knowledge "can be analyzed by examining patterns of conditional probabilities in the data" (2021).[4]

The history of philosophy certainly speaks to deep learning's achievements, but not in terms as simple as these interlocutors suggest. Where they see a stark dichotomy, Locke and Hume develop their keystone mantras into an elaborate empiricist theory of human

---

[3] Other philosophical traditions also have views which appear recognizably empiricist by the standards of this debate; for example, some of the Yogācāra Buddhist philosophers like Dharmakīrti are identified as empiricist by interpreters (Powers 1994; Tillemans 2021), and some have even wondered whether Western empiricists like Hume were influenced by exposure to Buddhist philosophy (Gopnik 2009). Other commentators, however, view such transcultural linkages with skepticism (Conze 1963; Montalvo 1999). At any rate, a very interesting book similar to this one could be written by drawing upon the faculty psychology in these alternative traditions to interpret and guide the development of deep learning. I am grateful to Amit Chaturvadi for drawing my attention to these potential parallels.

[4] In general, Pearl is less concerned here with the debate over nativism and antinativism in psychology than these other critics, and more engaged in the battle between skeptical Humean and realist approaches to causation in metaphysics and philosophy of science.

cognition that is more nuanced and flexible. In fact, most research in deep learning is motivated by a set of assumptions more consistent with these philosophers' less radical take on empiricism, and one of the main tasks of this book is to articulate exactly which version of empiricism is most supported by recent developments. Identifying and clarifying the moderately empiricist approach too often lost in the flashpoint debates can unlock untapped explanatory power, both for understanding deep learning's current methods and for charting the optimal course to future breakthroughs. The challenge is that as with political slogans, even the seemingly simple statements of the empiricist creed can mean different things to different constituencies. By putting in the interpretive work to understand them charitably, we can avoid talking past one another and direct evaluative efforts toward fruitful future research.

Unsurprisingly, even the most prominent nativists and empiricists today interpret the aforementioned slogans to imply quite different things. Nativist-leaning theorists tend to associate blank slates with the last great empiricist inferno, the behaviorist movement in American psychology, which reached the height of its power and then quickly dwindled to embers in the middle of the last century. Such theorists typically connect the empiricist blank slate with radically insufficient explanations for human learning. Steven Pinker articulates this perspective clearly in his book *The Blank Slate*. According to Pinker, today's empiricists have revived the doomed mission of the behaviorists, who "through most of the 20th century . . . tried to explain all of human behavior by appealing to a couple of simple mechanisms of association and conditioning" (Pinker 2003, p. 2).[5] Lake et al. also called out the "strong empiricism of modern connectionist models" which they identify with the "oversimplified behaviorism" that was "repudiated" by the cognitive revolution in the latter half of the twentieth century (2017, p. 4). This reported abrogation occurred when Noam Chomsky smothered behaviorism under a wave of his "Cartesian linguistics," which explicitly invoked the rationalist nativism of French philosopher René Descartes (Chomsky 1966) to inspire his arguments for an intricate set

---

[5] See also Childers, Hvorecký, and Meyer (2023), who also link deep learning to behaviorism; I defend a very different approach to linking deep learning to the history of the empiricist-rationalist debate.

of innate grammatical rules to explain human linguistic ability.[6] Marcus even formalizes this behaviorist interpretation of empiricism by defining cognition as a function ranging over four variables:

$$\text{cognition} = f(a, r, k, e)$$

where a = algorithms, r = representational formats, k = innate knowledge, and e = experience. Marcus's construal of the empiricist approach—which, as mentioned earlier, Marcus attributes to Locke—"would set k and r to zero, set a to some extremely minimal value (e.g., an operation for adjusting weights relative to reinforcement signals), and leave the rest to experience" (Marcus 2018b, p. 4).[7]

On this point, nativists practice something of the radical simplification they critique, by assuming that for the mind to be "blank" at birth, it must begin with virtually no innate structure at all. The more charitable nativist philosophers Laurence and Margolis (2015) have recently worried that summarizing current debates in cognitive science as the question of whether the mind has any innate structure whatsoever has the unfortunate consequence that "there aren't really any empiricists."[8] In reality, a completely structureless mind, like an inert mineral slab, would not learn anything by being subjected to any amount of stimulus. This seems to be something that nearly all influential empiricists have acknowledged. Back in the twilight of behaviorism's reign, the empiricist philosopher Willard van Orman Quine observed that even the most radical behaviorists, like John Watson and B. F. Skinner, were

---

[6] While also endorsing a rich package of "startup software" for the mind (which in their favored Bayesian models is typically programmed manually in symbolic form, including manually specified representational primitives and prior probability estimations) which they think should include components of Core Knowledge, Lake et al. (2017) are officially agnostic as to whether that software is innate or learned very early in childhood.

[7] What does "innate" mean here? An entire subarea of philosophy of science has burgeoned around the question of how best to define innateness (Ariew 1996; Griffiths and Machery 2008; Khalidi 2001, 2016, 2016; Mallon and Weinberg 2006; Mameli and Bateson 2006; Northcott and Piccinini 2018; Samuels 2004, 2007). For present purposes, we can proceed with a minimalist notion that implies at least "not learned" (Ritchie 2021).

[8] The empiricist-leaning developmental psychologist Linda Smith has also criticized this framing in her article, "Avoiding Associations When It's Behaviorism You Really Hate" (Smith 2000).

"knowingly and cheerfully up to [their] neck in innate mechanisms" (quoted in Laurence and Margolis 2015; Quine 1969:95–96): they must assume a rich array of biological needs, sensory mechanisms, attentional biases, and reflexive behaviors which could be associated with one another before even the simplest forms of associative learning could begin. The items on this list suit organisms to their evolutionary niches without appeal to innate knowledge structures, illustrating why a more detailed examination of empiricist-branded theorizing in both philosophy and computer science is required. A more systematic examination of the history of empiricist theorizing quickly reveals appeals to innate factors more expansive than this list. Thus, while Marcus's formalized model of empiricism is sharper than the empiricist mantras in its implications, it is also less useful, particularly if we aim for a charitable evaluation of deep learning's prospects.

The preceding illustration of the empiricist-nativist dichotomy, as it informs the development of deep learning systems, offers a paradigmatic example of the nature-nurture dichotomy's enduring influence on human thought. Both distinctions are too often resolved into stark binaries, whereas the debate is better represented in terms of subtle continuums and differences among styles of explanation. Although the persistence of the opposition between nature and nurture suggests an unsolvable philosophical riddle at the heart of knowledge acquisition, it can, with care, be of use to us. The same is true of the empiricist-nativist dichotomy. When interpreted with more attention to the history of philosophy and its precise context of application, it can encourage more useful and principled debates between distinct research methodologies.

In fact, in cases where scientists have taken pains to understand the debate's history, it can be seen to have fostered notable scientific discoveries of the last century, such as Albert Einstein's theory of special relativity or the very invention of the digital computer and artificial neural networks over which today's debates rage. The philosopher of science John Norton argues that Einstein's theory of special relativity was inspired by his participation in a reading group on Hume's *Treatise* around 1902–1903 with the mathematician Conrad Habicht and philosopher Maurice Solovine, from which Einstein obtained a deep regard for Hume's empiricism. In autobiographical notes from 1946, Einstein writes of his discovery of the relativity of simultaneity (to an inertial frame of reference) which undergirds special relativity that "this central point was decisively furthered, in my case, by the reading of David Hume's and Ernst Mach's philosophical writings" (quoted in Norton 2010). While rationalist philosophers like Immanuel Kant thought that absolute simultaneity was necessarily entailed by our a priori conception of spacetime, Einstein reasoned that if even these bedrock concepts were learned from experience, then there might be exceptions to them in extreme conditions, such as when objects travel at velocities approaching the speed of light.

Equally momentous achievements can be attributed to scientists listening to the nativist muse; the neuroscientist Grace Lindsay recounts how the early neural network pioneers McCulloch and Pitts (1943) idolized the rationalist philosopher Gottfried Leibniz, who theorized that the mind operates over an innate logical calculus from which all true propositions could be mechanically deduced (Lindsay 2021, Ch. 3). McCulloch and Pitts's idea that these complex logical and mathematical operations could be computed by large numbers of simple components organized in the right kind of network arrangement served as direct inspiration for both John von Neumann (1993) and Frank Rosenblatt (1958), whose works can be seen to have produced both the opposing research traditions responsible for the digital microprocessor architecture and deep neural networks (DNNs), respectively.

Here, I argue that the current incarnation of the nativist-empiricist debate in AI presents us with a similar golden opportunity, in which we might attempt one of the rarest feats of intellectual alchemy: the conversion of a timeless philosophical riddle into a testable empirical question. For, if we could apply the distinction to the deep learning debate without confusion or caricature, then we could simply build some artificial agents according to nativist principles, and other artificial agents according to empiricist principles, and see which ones are ultimately the most successful or human-like. Specifically, we can manually program the nativist systems with innate abstract knowledge, and endow empiricist systems with general capacities to learn abstract knowledge from sensory experience, and compare the performance of the systems on a range of important tasks. Crucially, however, the empiricists in this competition must be allowed more raw materials than Marcus's formal specification allows, if we aim to hold a fair and informative competition.

If we could accomplish this conversion, philosophers and computer scientists would both reap the rewards. On the philosophy side, empiricists have frequently been accused of appealing to magic at critical points in their theories of rational cognition. Locke and Hume, for example, often asserted that the mind performs some operation which allows it to extract some particular bit of abstract knowledge from experience but—given the scant understanding of the brain's operations available at the time—they could not explain how. Carefully examining the details of recent deep learning achievements might redeem some of the largest such promissory notes, by showing how physical systems built according to empiricist principles can actually perform these operations. Indexing the philosophical debate to these systems can further improve its clarity; where philosophical slogans are vague and subject to interpretation, computational models are precise, with all their assumptions exposed for philosophical scrutiny and empirical validation. Where successful, the plausibility of the empiricist approach to rational cognition substantially increases as a result. Of the benefits to computer science, philosophers have thought long and hard about the challenge of providing a complete approach to the human mind that is consistent with empiricist constraints, including how the mind's various components might interact and scale up to the highest forms of abstract knowledge and rational cognition. Deep learning is only now reaching for these heights in its modeling ambitions (e.g., Goyal and Bengio 2020), and so there may still yet be insights to mine from the history of empiricist philosophy that can be transmuted into the next engineering innovations.

To these ends, I here mount an interdisciplinary investigation into the prospects and implications of recent achievements in deep learning, combining insights from both computer science and philosophy. Doing so can both animate current engineering research with the warmth and wisdom of a classic philosophical debate, while simultaneously rendering the terms of that debate clearer than they have yet been in its long and distinguished history. Nevertheless, I know that such an interdisciplinary project is beset with its own distinctive risk. Richard Evans—an interdisciplinary researcher at DeepMind who has sought to create more powerful deep learning systems by augmenting them with logical maxims that he extracts from Kant's *Critique of Pure Reason* (including Kant's aforementioned maxim of simultaneity)— has issued a salutary warning for projects embarking under such ambitions:

> This is an interdisciplinary project and as such is in ever-present danger of falling between two stools, neither philosophically faithful to Kant's intentions nor contributing meaningfully to AI research. Kant himself provides: "the warning not to carry on at the same time two jobs which are very distinct in the way they are to be handled, for each of which a special talent is perhaps required, and the combination of which in one person produces only bunglers." [AK 4:388] The danger with an interdisciplinary project, part AI and part philosophy, is that both potential audiences are unsatisfied. (Evans 2020:18)

We must take Evans's (and Kant's) warning to heart. Yet we must also acknowledge that, in part because deep learning is implicated in the nature-nurture distinction, philosophers are particularly suited to undertake the project. Whatever our other bungles, we have experience tending to this particular fire. To proceed, however, we must discard stools altogether. We will be better able to gauge the current and future achievements of deep learning by instead building a more accommodating bench, with ample room for a spectrum of distinctive backgrounds and expertise. Given the intensity of the current discussion among theorists grappling with deep learning's potential, the most productive way forward involves lowering the debate's temperature until the smoke clears, and inviting theorists from a variety of backgrounds with distinctive expertise and a stake in deep learning's implications to work patiently through the details together.

1.2. How to simmer things down: From forms and slates to styles of learning

Thanks to rigorous investigation in several disciplines, today we know that nearly all knowledge originates from a combination of both innate and experiential factors. Both radical nativism and radical empiricism are, in short, false. Despite this, more nuanced expositions of the distinction between empiricism and nativism remain the exception and have been almost entirely absent from discussions over deep learning.[9] Without a better way to understand the substance of the distinction, the recognition of this ecumenical outcome carries, on both sides, the threat of obliteration. This may be why Locke and Hume's empiricist mantras are so frequently interpreted as shoring up a diametric opposition between empiricism and nativism. However, a closer examination of the history of empiricism suggests a more subtle continuum of views which can still support meaningful debates within the region of middle ground which remains empirically plausible. In fact, despite the allure of stark dichotomies, a historical review shows that empiricists, except for a few outliers, traditionally supposed that the mind begins with a significant amount of innate structure, and nativists typically acknowledged that most of the human mind's abstract knowledge is acquired through learning. We are more likely to generate insights relevant to both philosophy and computer science by wresting this moderation from extremism.

To begin, we can acknowledge that, contra the nativists reviewed earlier, the extremism of radical behaviorism was, from a historical perspective, just such an outlier. Rather than conflate all empiricist positions with behaviorism, we do well to follow further guidance provided by Laurence and Margolis (2012, 2015). According to their survey of historical and recent sources, it is more productive and widely applicable to construe the incarnations of the nativist-empiricist debate, both before and after behaviorism's heyday, in terms of two different styles of learning-based explanation:

> For contemporary theorists in philosophy and cognitive science, the disagreement revolves around the character of the innate psychological structures that underlie concept acquisition . . . According to

---

[9] The clearest examples one can find of such radical empiricism in the present debates are mostly found in grandstanding posts on social media sites; we should perhaps all let out a sigh of relief that figures like Descartes, Locke, and Berkeley did not have access to Twitter.

empiricist approaches, there are few if any innate concepts and concept acquisition is, by and large, governed by a small number of innate general-purpose cognitive systems being repeatedly engaged. . . .
The nativist approach, in contrast, holds that innate concepts and/
or innate special-purpose cognitive systems (of varying degrees of
specialization) play a key role in conceptual development, alongside
general-purpose cognitive systems. (2015, p. 4)

Radical behaviorists proscribed theorizing about inner mental
representations and faculties, because they worried that we could not
provide objective empirical evidence for their existence. This proscrip-
tion on theorizing about inner mental entities should be rejected, as it
was both by the empiricist philosophy that came before it and by most
deep learning theorists today. In fact, as glossed earlier, both sides
today agree that the mind begins with a significant amount of powerful
innate structure, that cognition involves complex interactions among
internal representations and faculties, and that the vast majority of
concepts are learned or acquired from experience. The two sides still
disagree, however, as to what exactly is innate. Nativists think that
domain-specific abstractions can only be efficiently derived from a
large number of innate, special-purpose concepts or learning systems
that evolution has tailored to particular kinds of problems, whereas
empiricists hold that general learning procedures can cooperate with a
smaller set of domain-general cognitive resources to solve a wide array
of problem types.[10]

Approaching matters this way places the weight of the distinction
between the nativist and empiricist approaches on a corresponding
distinction between domain-general and domain-specific cognitive
systems or representations. The contrast might, in turn, be indexed
to the range of inputs to which the innate resource responds: a highly

---

[10] The debate, as it stands today, mostly concerns the learning systems of the human
mind, or at least those of our closest primate relatives, and perhaps a few other successful evolutionary generalists whose cognition privileges power and flexibility, such
as dolphins and corvids. Some less flexible animals with more predictable niches, like
insects or amphibians, might have minds that are rigidly governed by just a few innate
representations and behaviors, without this implying that empiricism about human
knowledge or intelligence more generally is false or hopeless.

domain-specific innate resource will be triggered only by a few very precise kinds of stimulus or situation, whereas a highly domain-general resource can be flexibly applied to a wide range of stimuli or domains. For instance, an innate prey-detection module that only controls tongue-darting movements and is triggered only by flies is more domain-specific than an innate memory store, which can record any arbitrary experience. Paradigm examples of domain-specific psychological constructs are the "innate releasing mechanisms" proposed by the ethologist Konrad Lorenz. He explained these systems using a lock-key metaphor: evolution prepares organisms via innate stimulus patterns (the "sign stimulus"), which are uniquely suited to unlock behavioral responses adapted to provide fitness benefits in response to just those stimuli (Lorenz 1935; Ronacher 2019). An all-purpose memory store, by contrast, can perform its storage and retrieval functions on any arbitrary input.

At issue in the distinction between domain-general and domain specific cognitive systems is thus how inputs should be counted. Whereas the preceding tongue-darting example stands as a widely accepted illustrative starting point, we gain a better feel for the substance of the distinction by exploring a few specific nativist and empiricist views. Let us begin with nativism. Like empiricism, nativism can be understood as a continuum and manifests accordingly in more and less stringent forms. At the most radical end of the spectrum are the views of Plato and Jerry Fodor, according to which nearly every simple concept possessed by the mind is innate, including—as Fodor specifically adumbrated—the highly domain-specific concepts of CAR-BURETOR, BEATNIK, and QUARK (Fodor 1975; Laurence and Margolis 2015).[11] Further down the continuum, perhaps, come some of the

---

[11] I will here follow a common convention in this philosophical literature to put the names of concepts in small caps. Fodor's radical concept nativism is not actually as outrageous as it appears here, and he was probably trolling everyone to a significant degree in his bold claims that all these concepts are innate. All Fodor really means in saying that all these simple concepts are innate is that, if the mind has the kind of computational architecture he thinks it does, it needs to start with symbolic placeholders that could be triggered by the right experiences or linguistic labels, which later serve as pointers to files into which learning-based knowledge about the category can be collated. Later commentators have found ways to charitably salvage most of what Fodor says on the topic without endorsing his most absurd conclusions (Cowie 1998; Laurence and Margolis 2002; Sterelny 1989). As this is likely a prime example of a philosophical debate

most expansive drafts of Chomskyan linguistics, which posited potentially hundreds of innate grammatical principles and adjustable parameters thought to be common to all human languages—the "Universal Grammar"—to explain how human children efficiently home in on the precise grammar of their native language given limited experience (Chomsky 1986; Dąbrowska 2015; Lasnik and Lohndal 2010).[12] Most of these principles will only be activated by very specific kinds of grammatical structure, according to Chomsky, so this version of Universal Grammar appears to be a highly domain-specific, innate system.

Other nativists take inspiration from evolutionary psychology; Laurence and Margolis, for instance, sketch a still expansive but somewhat more biologically oriented list of special-purpose systems for dealing with "objects, physical causation, distance, movement, space, time, geometry, agency, goals, perception, emotions, thought, biological kinds, life stages, disease, tools, predators, prey, food, danger, sex, kinship, group membership, dominance, status, norms, morality, logic, and number" (Laurence and Margolis 2015:120). Laurence and Margolis think this list could implicate either innate concepts for each of these categories or innate learning modules specially tailored to acquire these concepts from experience. However, the key for them, and for other similarly situated nativists, is that the mind needs a rather elaborate and highly specialized array of start-up software to learn about these situations in a human-like way.

Other contemporary views that get labeled nativist tend toward the more domain-general side of the spectrum in their assumptions of innate endowments. Marcus himself puts in an order for a shorter list

---

that has generated at least as much friction as illumination (and Fodor himself recanted this extreme concept nativism in later works, sort of—Fodor 2008), I will not comment further on it here.

[12] There is substantial variability in the estimate of exactly how many principles and parameters are required to specify Universal Grammar in its most luxurious forms. In 1986, Chomsky suggested that it includes at least "X-bar theory, binding theory, case theory, theta theory, bounding theory . . . [as well as] certain overriding principles such as the projection principle, FI (full interpretation), and the principles of licensing" (Chomsky 1986:102). Fodor (2001) estimated about twenty parameters required to specify a grammar, and a wide variety of other estimates are available (Dąbrowska 2015).

of more domain-general mechanisms than Laurence and Margolis, and the Core Knowledge developmental psychologists like Spelke and Carey—favorites of more moderate nativists in AI like Mitchell (2019) and François Chollet (2019)—request only a handful of quite general innate concepts like OBJECT, AGENT, SOCIAL BEING, CAUSE, NUMBER, and SPACE (Carey and Spelke 1996; Spelke 1994). Regardless of how inputs are counted here, OBJECT and NUMBER almost surely apply to a wider range of stimuli and situations than DISEASE or KINSHIP, and they should count as more domain-general. Later versions of the Chomskyan program—after his adoption of "Minimalism" around the early 1990s—aim to reduce the list of innate language-specific principles to perhaps only one, a rule for joining together different kinds of structured representations, called "Merge" (Berwick and Chomsky 2016; Chomsky 1993). Most recently, Chomsky seems to have made peace with the possibility that Merge might usefully apply to a range of nonlinguistic domains as well, focusing instead on the conclusion that humans must have some kind of innate cognitive mechanism that allows us, and only us, to learn full-blown recursive language (Berwick and Chomsky 2017).

At this point, we can see that the gap between the nativist and empiricist positions has substantially narrowed—one referee's call of "slightly nativist" here could just as well be another's "mostly empiricist" there. But we should not let scorekeeping quibbles obscure the degree of consensus which has already emerged about the implausibility of the continuum's extremes.[13]

Turning to empiricism, it, too (as argued earlier), includes variations. However, empiricists generally aim to reduce the list of innate domain-specific learning mechanisms—and particularly those invoking innate concepts or ideas—into oblivion. Notably, the empiricist mantras of Locke and Hume referenced earlier only concern the origins of the mind's initial ideas or concepts (and their representational contents). From context, it is obvious that when Locke talks

---

[13] Pearl (2019) puts in perhaps the most modest requisition order of rationalist camp, insisting only upon rich mechanisms for representing and reasoning about the particularly broad domain of causation (some of which may be compatible with the domain-general approach to imagination that we will explore in later chapters).

about the mind being blank prior to experience, he refers only to its representational structures (its "ideas," in Lockean lingo), and not to its architecture or basic faculties. As the *Stanford Encyclopedia of Philosophy* entry on Locke ably puts it:

> While the mind may be a blank slate in regard to content, it is plain that Locke thinks we are born with a variety of faculties to receive and abilities to manipulate or process the content once we acquire it. Thus, for example, the mind can engage in three different types of action in putting simple ideas together ... In addition to these abilities, there are such faculties as memory which allow for the storing of ideas. (Uzgalis 2020)

Because it is necessary to distinguish this moderate empiricism from behaviorist construals, I hereafter refer to this doctrine as "origin empiricism." Importantly, origin empiricism does not prohibit the involvement of other active, innate factors in the process by which ideas are extracted from experience, or complex roles for previously acquired ideas in guiding the abstraction process; indeed, both Locke and Hume liberally invoke innate, general-purpose faculties like memory, imagination, and reflection as well as complex interactions among previously acquired ideas, even as they emphasize that the simple ideas from which these abstractions are crafted originate in sensations.[14]

In the context of AI, empiricist minimalism has been present since AI's prehistory, as evidenced from the quote by Turing with which this chapter began, which itself can be seen to channel the empiricist mantras of Locke and Hume. Yet, when nativists link historical empiricism to neural network modeling, they nonetheless tend to revert to reading empiricist figures as proto-behaviorists, despite behaviorism's aforementioned outlier status. This, in turn, leaves nativists stymied when empiricists appeal to innate faculties in their explanations of abstraction. For instance, when confronted by Hume's frequent appeal to an innate faculty of imagination, Fodor and Pylyshyn chide him for "cheating," because such faculties are something to which "qua

---

[14] For a useful discussion, see Millican (2009).

associationist [he] had, of course, no right" (1988:50, fn29). Such a charge saddles Hume with a tightly constrained view with little explanatory power; but Hume's Copy Principle, it is important to note, says only that "simple ideas in their first appearance" must be derived from experience. It does not say that general-purpose faculties, like the imagination, must be learned, as well. So long as Hume's imagination can do its job without invoking innate ideas, Hume is only "cheating" if we insist that the rules of bridge require him to sit out this round, when the printed invitation he sent us clearly proposed a game of spades. To put this another way: It is perhaps Fodor's reading of Hume that is out of order, rather than Hume's appeals to the imagination.[15]

Whereas many nativists like Fodor tend to interpret mantras like the Copy Principle quite literally—as though concepts are just identical duplications of sensory impressions—more charitable readers like Laurence and Margolis permit empiricists to appeal to psychological processes that do more than merely reproduce impressions when manufacturing the mind's ideas or concepts. This is why I follow Laurence and Margolis in holding that the more productive way to construe the debate, particularly in the context of the dispute over the future of AI, concerns only the number and domain specificity of the innate concepts and learning systems that must be manually programmed into the mind to achieve human-like learning and cognition.

In fact, recent DNN models, which offer a standard toolbox of transformational operations that can do powerful computational work without invoking any explicit innate concepts, suggest an alternative way to construe the empiricist spirit present in Hume and others. To wit, the mind might more creatively massage and manipulate information originating in the senses in crafting the mind's concepts or ideas.[16]

---

[15] For a systematic rebuttal of Fodor's reading of Hume, see Demeter (2021). For a book-length defense of the more constructive take on Hume's empiricism, see also Landy (2017).

[16] Recent empirical analyses of some of the most sophisticated deep learning architectures, transformers, suggest that there may be deep mathematical similarities between literal copying and some of the most abstract and impressive behaviors demonstrated by state-of-the-art deep networks, such as translation. As a team from the startup at AnthropicAI (which includes several philosophers) put it in their analysis of transformers:

We emphasize again that the attention heads that we described above simultaneously implement both the abstract behaviors that we described [. . . but] why do the same

While I think that empiricists like Locke and Hume all along supposed that empiricism was consistent with more than mere rote reproduction, for the sake of clarity and for the purpose of our investigation, I propose refining the Copy Principle, as the basic tenet of empiricism, into what I call the Transformation Principle:

COPY PRINCIPLE: "All our simple ideas in their first appearance are deriv'd from simple [sensory] impressions."

TRANSFORMATION PRINCIPLE: The mind's simple concepts (or conceptions) are in their first appearance derived from systematic, domain-general transformations of sensory impressions.[17]

The Transformation Principle makes explicit that empiricist learning methods include a variety of default operations that can alter the structure of their input through systematic transformations, such as those studied in topology. Initially, the default methods should be domain-general, in the sense that they are not innately keyed to a specific set of features in a particular domain (such as faces, tribal affiliations,

---

heads that inductively copy random text also exhibit these other behaviors? One hint is that these behaviors can be seen as "spiritually similar" to copying. Recall that where an induction head is defined as implementing a rule like [A][B] . . . [A] → [B], our empirically observed heads also do something like [A*][B*] . . . [A] → [B] where A* and B* are similar to A and B in some higher-level representation. There are several ways these similar behaviors could be connected. For example, note that the first behavior is a special case of the second, so perhaps induction heads are implementing a more general algorithm that reverts to the special case of copying when given a repeated sequence. Another possibility is that induction heads implement literal copying when they take a path through the residual stream that includes only them, but implement more abstract behaviors when they process the outputs of earlier layers that create more abstract representations (such as representations where the same word in English and French are embedded in the same place). (Olsson et al. 2022)

---

[17] I include "conceptions" here to emphasize that the representations described by the Transformation Principle can be subjective in nature; two agents can have different conceptions of the same target category, and the same agent can change their conception of that category over time. In philosophy, the Fregean tradition of talking about concepts requires them to be objective entities properly studied by logic rather than psychology, and I am here intentionally avoiding that philosophical baggage (Buckner 2018a; Gauker 2013; Machery 2009; Woodfield 1991). I do think there is good reason to maintain a tight relationship between subjective conceptions and objective reference, however; for a description of my full views on the relationship between conceptions and concepts in the context of representations in neural networks, see Buckner (2022).

or biological categories). According to empiricism, such domain-specific transformations can be derived by specializing these generic operations later, through learning. This refinement prepares us to appreciate what I take to be the biggest lesson to be derived from deep learning's achievements: that a generic set of hierarchical transformation methods can be trained to overcome a wide range of problems that until recently most vexed progress in more nativist-inspired AI. Switching to an idiom of transformation also drives home that the basic toolkit of empiricist methods is computationally much more powerful than the forms of elemental stimulus-response learning favored by radical behaviorism, such as classical and operant conditioning.

Resetting the debate over AI in these terms can bring clarity to recent disputes over the empiricist implications of prominent models. Without such a reset, insights into deep learning developments understood through the lens of origin empiricism will continue to be frustrated. Such obstruction was the consequence of Marcus's allegation that Silver et al. overinterpreted the empiricist implications of their Go victory for the AlphaZero system (Silver et al. 2017). In support of his charge, Marcus noted specifically that (1) AlphaZero relied on Monte Carlo Tree Search (MCTS) to explore the implications of possible moves, and (2) some of its neural network parameters (such as the size of convolutional layers) were specifically tuned to the game before training began.[18] Yet, according to the preceding argument, exploring moves using MCTS is consistent with origin empiricism if the mechanism is equally applicable to a wide range of other domains (whereas configuring AlphaGo's convolution parameters specifically to the game of Go is indeed more suspect). In similar spirit, Marcus, in a public debate with deep learning pioneer Yann LeCun at NYU in 2017, called out LeCun's own "most famous" and "greatly-valuable" work on deep convolutional neural networks as inconsistent with his empiricism because it involves "innately-embedding translational invariance," or the assumption that important properties tend to be conserved across variation along systematic input dimensions like size,

---

[18] In fairness, these parameters need to be set to some specific value, and it is not clear that the size of a convolutional layer can be translated into the kind of innate knowledge that rationalists have traditionally championed.

location, orientation, or duration (Marcus 2018b). Marcus brandished LeCun et al.'s (1989) description of translational invariance as "a priori knowledge of the task" as a revealing gotcha moment. But bias toward translational invariance is clearly consistent with origin empiricism if it is built into the model so as to allow it to be applied by default to a variety of other stimuli and tasks in nonspatial domains as well.[19]

Marcus interprets deep learning's recent trend toward more complex architectures and inductive biases as a vindication of rationalist nativism, but even Marcus must admit that these general-purpose, structure-based biases are a far cry from the more numerous and specific kinds of innate representations that nativists have traditionally recommended. Descartes and Leibniz, for example, supposed that basically all of Euclidean geometry was contained within our innate ideas of space (Janiak 2020, Ch. 5). However, a deep convolutional neural network (DCNN)'s bias toward translational invariance is at the same time more modest and more widely applicable than such innate geometry; it entails much less than the postulates of Euclidean geometry about the spatial domain, while at the same time applying much more broadly to any nonspatial data which exhibits the right kind of mathematical patterns.[20] It is crucial to acknowledge at this point that this is not a question of the original or primary evolutionary function of the bias; empiricists are free to agree that evolutionary considerations are important to understand the mind's organization—who today would deny that?—and that perhaps the demands of spatial reasoning posed an important fitness pressure that favored the brains of animals that imposed constraints on learning such as translational invariance. The

---

[19] Marcus emphasizes a point in this debate's Q&A exchange where LeCun seems to suggest that ideally, even translational invariance would be learned from experience. LeCun's point was likely that certain ways in which translational invariance is achieved in current DCNNs are biologically implausible and should be replaced by something with more fidelity to neural structure, if possible. In further clarifying comments, LeCun endorsed local connectivity as a biologically plausible structural parameter which would likely not need to be learned in later incarnations of deep neural networks. Readers are encouraged to watch the entire Q&A after the debate if interested in this issue: https://www.youtube.com/watch?v=vdWPQ6iAkT4 .

[20] Formally, it likely produces efficiency gains on any data patterns which exhibit a group-like structure (Achille and Soatto 2018; Bruna and Mallat 2011). Data patterns exhibiting group-like structure can be found far beyond the spatial domain.

central question for deep learning is rather how to best implement such biases in artificial systems.

The recent trend toward domain-general inductive biases thus reflects not the vindication of rationalist nativism, but rather the discovery that more flexible, domain-general, neurally inspired modeling methods can deliver dramatic performance gains on some of the same problems on which systems sporting domain-specific, manually encoded, symbolic versions of those assumptions had reliably and repeatedly failed. To understand this empirical and conceptual progress, it is more useful to focus on the way in which inductive biases are expressed in the mind. Nativists prefer to encode these inductive biases manually in a symbolic format that renders their interpretation transparent and constraints their application to a particular domain, whereas empiricists prefer to implement them using more global network structures that enable distinctive kinds of transformations—with extra points if those structures are "biologically plausible," with independent neuroanatomical support. The network theorists here emphasize that this latter approach applies the biases across a wider range of domains and situations, allowing domain-specific representations to emerge and connections to be drawn across very different kinds of inputs in potentially unpredictable and serendipitous ways. In short, domain-general inductive biases are critical to deep learning, regardless of philosophical allegiances. This explains why most deep learning theorists today not only do not hide their appeals to such domain-general inductive biases, as though they were embarrassing concessions to their nativist critics; they openly embrace them as the greatest achievements and future direction of their research program.

We see this in the dominant view at DeepMind—as expressed by senior figures like Demis Hassabis and Matthew Botvinick in the group's position papers (Botvinick et al. 2017; Hassabis et al. 2017)—which is more similar to the moderate origin empiricism recommended here.[21] In their response to Lake et al.'s (2017)

---

[21] James McClelland has also expressed this attitude in the work anticipating the current deep learning boom. Rogers and McClelland, for example, assert that "domain-general mechanisms can discover the sorts of domain-specific principles that are evident in the behavior of young children" (2004:369). He argues elsewhere that the transparent symbols and representations presumed by more nativist-friendly models are "abstractions that are sometimes useful but often misleading" and that the data they

Table 1.1 A List of Domain-General Inductive Biases Recommended by Goyal and Bengio (2020) to Allow DNN-Based Systems to Extract Domain-Specific Regularities across a Wide Variety of Domains

Inductive Bias	Corresponding Property
Distributed representations	Patterns of features
Convolution	Group equivariance
Deep architectures	Complex functions are composition of simpler functions
Graph neural networks	Equivariance over entities and relations
Recurrent links	Equivariance over time
Soft attention	Equivariance over permutations

criticisms, for example, they argue that AI should strive to design agents that can "learn and think for themselves" by eschewing "human hand engineering" and "representational structure" in favor of "larger-scale architectural and algorithmic factors" that allow agents to acquire domain-specific knowledge on their own (Botvinick et al. 2017). Yoshua Bengio—another central figure in deep learning—has endorsed the need for more complex neural network architectures featuring multiple structures that implement a set of domain-general inductive biases (Goyal and Bengio 2020; see Table 1.1). Among the relevant questions today is thus not whether empiricists are allowed any innate structure or architecture whatsoever, but rather how much domain-specific knowledge can be extracted from incoming sensory experience using biased domain-general transformation methods, and how much instead requires domain-specific programming—whether by genes into brains, or by computer scientists into silicon—before human-like learning and experience can even begin.[22]

are adduced to explain can be better accounted for in terms of "generic constraints that foster the discovery of structure, whatever that structure might be, across a range of domains and content types" (McClelland et al. 2010:353).

[22] Marcus, for example, says that the neural substrates for innate, domain-specific representational content "are consistently localized across individuals, suggesting an

While it might appear that both sides have already met in the middle, we should not lose sight of the fact that they still draw inspiration from different sources and recommend different methodologies for future AI progress. For example, the critical structure behind DCNNs was inspired by neuroanatomical research rather than nativist developmental psychology (Hubel and Wiesel 1967), and it was first implemented by neural network modelers who at least saw themselves as motivated by the tenets of empiricism (Fukushima and Miyake 1982). Many contemporary nativists, moreover, still want much more specific and expansive innate knowledge, and emphasize entirely different sources of evidence. Evans, for example, aims to endow deep learning agents with the principles of Kant's a priori intuition of space, or the "subjective condition of sensibility," recommending that DNN-based systems be supplemented with a set of at least six formal axioms of Prolog that he derives from Kant's First Critique (Evans 2020, Ch. 6); and Marcus still officially recommends "hybrid" systems that combine neural networks with manually programmed symbolic rules and knowledge structures extracted not from experience but from explicit theory in nativist developmental psychology. Thus, there remains a clear practical contrast in the research programs recommended by current empiricists and nativists, and deep learning's recent proclivity for general inductive biases is in no danger of sliding up a slippery slope to Platonic heaven.

1.3. From dichotomy to continuum

Regardless, reconceiving the current nativist and empiricist positions according to our earlier discussion allows for a more diverse spectrum of views to be arrayed along a continuum, and for individual theorists

---

important degree of genetic contribution to their neural organization"; and though they do not commit to the nativist option, Lake et al. (2017) specifically suggest that the mind may come "genetically programmed with mechanisms that amount to highly engineered cognitive representations or algorithms." Zador (2019) provides some arguments based on neuroscientific evidence as to why it is unlikely that any domain-specific knowledge could be genetically encoded in this way; it is much more likely that the genes specify more general wiring motifs that constrain the way neurons broadly self-organize, an approach which is consistent with the moderate empiricism defended in this book (for more discussion and examples, see Zaadnoordijk, Besold, and Cusack 2022).

to decide which region of the continuum best captures the organiza-tion of the intelligent or rational mind, given current empirical evi-dence. To further aid the reconception, however, we must specify its most radical opposing points in the current debate. On the one side, the radical empiricism that worries Marcus and Pearl finds expres-sion in the "Bitter Lesson," a widely circulated blog post written by DeepMind-affiliated researcher Rich Sutton in 2019.[23] According to Sutton, seventy years of AI research should cause us all to worry that "the only thing that matters in the long run is the leveraging of compu-tation" (Sutton 2019). According to this skeptical view, the program-ming of domain-specific knowledge that went into previous models was ultimately irrelevant and even counterproductive, as it hampered generalization to other tasks. The only thing that really improved per-formance in marquee AI achievements on this view, from Deep Blue to AlphaGo, was the application of more and more computation to larger and larger data sets. Even the largest deep learning models to date—GPT-3 with 175 billion parameters and a training set of over 40 billion tokens, or PaLM with 540 billion parameters—are thought by some to have fewer relevant parameters than the human brain, with its estimated 100 trillion adjustable synaptic connections (Hasson, Nastase, and Goldstein 2020). General intelligence will naturally arise, the student of the Bitter Lesson supposes, as soon as we stop trying to program human knowledge manually into machines in any form, and simply apply more data and computation to the solution of problems. This radical empiricism is fueled by recent results in "scaling research" on ever-larger networks and data sets; this research aims to show that qualitatively new forms of behavior can emerge by simply scaling up existing techniques to orders of magnitude more training or compu-tation (T. Brown et al. 2020). Though I do not think this is the right in-terpretation of the Bitter Lesson (or even the lesson recommended by Sutton), this extreme empiricist interpretation—when combined with the extreme nativist interpretation on the other side of the spectrum,

---

[23] DeepMind is itself a big tent, employing figures from quasi-rationalists like Richard Evans, who recommends a hybrid approach combining manually programmed Kantian assumptions about space, time, and causality with deep neural networks (Evans et al. 2020, 2021), to David Silver, who as we saw earlier invoked Locke in the attempt to es-chew human knowledge entirely in mastering the game of Go.

which might be indexed to the views of midcareer Chomsky or Fodor discussed earlier—will form a useful Scylla and Charybdis between which we can chart the development of the moderate origin empiricism defended in this book.[24]

When considering not only the continuum's radical terminal points but also its continuity, we might note that the degree of representational structure that has been manually programmed into AI systems forms a central axis along which methods in AI have swung to and fro over the past seven decades. In the 1960s and 1970s, under the direction of Chomsky and AI pioneers Allen Newell and Herbert Simon, the pendulum swung toward a high degree of manually programmed structure, finding its highest expression in the "expert systems" approach to AI (Newell and Simon 1976). On this approach—which John Haugeland (1985) famously dubbed "GOFAI," for good old-fashioned AI—progress was to be achieved by debriefing human experts in order to extract the abstract "heuristic" knowledge that allowed them to search efficiently for solutions to problems, and then manually program that knowledge into machines in the form of explicit rules and symbols (which, of course, they did not think was all innate; but they did not know how to create systems that could learn that heuristic knowledge for themselves).[25] IBM's Deep Blue, which bested Garry Kasparov in chess in 1997 (Campbell 1999), and its Watson system, which defeated human champion Ken Jennings at Jeopardy in 2011 (Ferrucci et al. 2010), were products of this tradition,[26] as is the Cyc system based at Cycorp in Austin, Texas, which can be seen as its most dogged and enduring exemplar (Matuszek et al. 2006). Today, however, most see the methodological pendulum as having swung sharply back toward minimal domain-specific programming, after Watson was sold off in parts, and Cyc relegated to database translation and other jobs more modest than the grand ambitions under which it embarked.

---

[24] A better interpretation of the Bitter Lesson is that the right structural tweaks in machine learning should be those that reward increases in computation and representational resources with increases in performance. This has become regarded by many machine learning researchers as a kind of heuristic for deciding whether some architectural innovation is likely to pay off.

[25] Some of Pearl's best-known research is in this tradition (Pearl 1984).

[26] Watson is known as a "hybrid" system in this context, as it integrates manually programmed symbolic knowledge with a variety of machine learning methods.

From this, we can align the continuum derived from the philosophical debate about the degree and domain specificity of innate knowledge to the corresponding methodological debate in AI regarding the number and specificity of symbolic knowledge representations to program manually into artificial minds (Fig. 1.1).[27]

1.4. Of faculties and fairness: Introducing the new empiricist DoGMA

To investigate usefully the similarities that unite and the differences that continue to divide moderate nativists and empiricists, it is necessary to rebut two specific aspects of the debate's common framing. First, I review the writings of the major empiricist philosophers, to emphasize their frequent appeals to faculty psychology. In other words, in eschewing innate ideas, these empiricists pushed the burden of deriving abstract concepts onto a set of active, general-purpose psychological faculties. Rational cognition on the empiricist model thus requires a cognitive architecture involving the cooperation of a variety of powerful innate faculties, such as perception, memory, imagination, attention, reflection, and sympathy/empathy. Not coincidentally, many recent breakthroughs in machine learning were obtained by adding computational modules implementing roles that philosophers and psychologists have attributed to one or another of these faculties. These interdisciplinary connections are often mentioned obliquely in computer science, but drawing them out and subjecting them to further scrutiny can provide further inspiration to machine learning modelers in the next round of innovation.

---

[27] The location of Bayesian modeling in Figure 1.1 is supported by a concern expressed by the generative linguist Norbert Hornstein of a Bayesian language-learning model in Perfors, Tenenbaum, and Regier (2011):

> "It is not clear how revelatory their conclusions are as their learning scenario assumes exactly the kind of richly structured domain specific innate hypothesis space the POS [poverty of the stimulus] generally aims to establish. So, if you are thinking that PTR gets you out from under rich domain specific innate structures, think again. Indeed if anything, PTR pack more into the innate hypothesis space than generativists typically do" (Hornstein 2012).

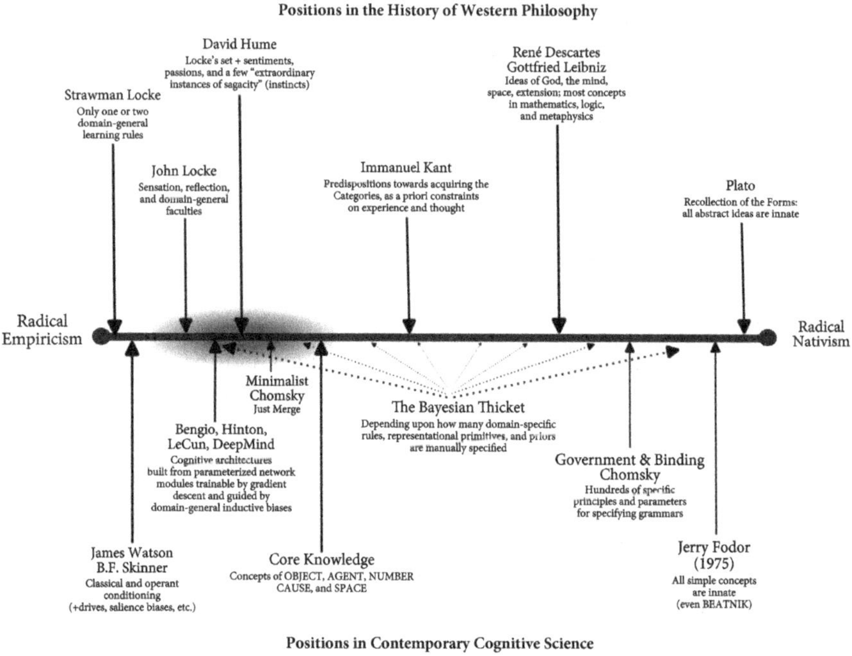

Positions in the History of Western Philosophy

David Hume
Locke's set + sentiments, passions, and a few "extraordinary instances of sagacity" (instincts)

René Descartes
Gottfried Leibniz
Ideas of God, the mind, space, extension; most concepts in mathematics, logic, and metaphysics

Strawman Locke
Only one or two domain-general learning rules

John Locke
Sensation, reflection, and domain-general faculties

Immanuel Kant
Predispositions towards acquiring the Categories, as a priori constraints on experience and thought

Plato
Recollection of the Forms: all abstract ideas are innate

Radical Empiricism

Radical Nativism

Minimalist Chomsky
Just Merge

The Bayesian Thicket
Depending upon how many domain-specific rules, representational primitives, and priors are manually specified

Bengio, Hinton, LeCun, DeepMind
Cognitive architectures built from parameterized network modules trainable by gradient descent and guided by domain-general inductive biases

Government & Binding Chomsky
Hundreds of specific principles and parameters for specifying grammars

James Watson
B.F. Skinner
Classical and operant conditioning (+drives, salience biases, etc.)

Core Knowledge
Concepts of OBJECT, AGENT, NUMBER CAUSE, and SPACE

Jerry Fodor
(1975)
All simple concepts are innate (even BEATNIK)

Positions in Contemporary Cognitive Science

Figure 1.1 The distribution of various thinkers and positions from the history of philosophy and contemporary cognitive science according to the dimension of the number and domain specificity of the innate ideas endorsed. The shaded left part of the continuum indicates the space of views which remain empirically plausible. It is hard to place Bayesian methods on such a continuum, as they can range from very domain-general to very domain-specific, with thousands of manually specified representational primitives and prior probability estimates. This difficulty is highlighted with the "Bayesian Thicket," which indicates that they range from some of the most empiricist to some of the most hypernativist options on offer today. To decide whether a Bayesian model is more empiricist or more nativist, one must scrutinize carefully the selection of learning rules, representational primitives, and prior probability estimations that went into its construction. (The same is true of neural networks, of course, though the inefficiency of manually specifying parameters in neural networks makes this a generally unpopular choice.)

Reviewing these ideas from the history of philosophy may be particularly useful to engineers at the present inflection point. Recent faculty-inspired network models have mostly been "one-offs," focused on only a single faculty like memory or imagination. However, we know that a full cognitive architecture will involve many such faculties interacting with one another and competing for shared resources. The competition will create new problems for deep learning modelers as they aim to bootstrap their architectures to higher forms of rational cognition. While engineers often focus on the next benchmark or technical tweak, philosophers often consider the big picture before the details, and thus have elaborated rich ideas about empiricist cognitive architecture that anticipate problems engineers will face in the next steps of building an artificial mind.

Second, in the interest of facilitating more even-handed interdisciplinary communication, I occasionally provide a counterweight to enthusiastic summaries of evidence for domain-specific innate structure imported by nativists from other areas of cognitive science. For example, Marcus, Mitchell, Lake et al., and Chollet write as though the empirical case for innate Core Knowledge in very young infants is almost incontrovertible. An even-handed appraisal would note that these positions are matters of active empirical debate in their respective disciplines, with a correspondingly distinguished list of empiricist developmental psychologists and biologists offering alternative—and I think often more compelling—accounts of the same empirical evidence. In many cases, I suggest, the nativists rely on an overly rosy or intellectualized view of the reliability, transparency, or robustness of distinctively human cognition and/or our current degree of empirical understanding of human uniqueness. In short, they often commit an error that I have dubbed "anthropofabulation," which combines anthropocentrism with a confabulated view of our own prowess (Buckner 2013). My empiricist counterassessments often invoke evidence impugning the reliability of human judgments and deflating our current level of understanding of introspection and "common sense." In short, while deep learning models frequently underperform expectations, human cognition is also fraught with embarrassing errors, and we should not let our inaccurately high opinions of ourselves or double standards bias our evaluation of artificial agents.

To render it more memorable, I dub the moderate empiricism endorsed here the "new empiricist DoGMA." This acronym captures the attitude that an empiricist (Do)main General Modular Architecture is the best hope for modeling rational cognition in AI.[28] The acronym's lexical meaning is also intended to serve as a Sword of Damocles hanging over our heads, as a warning against hubris. The name should constantly remind empiricists that the DoGMA must be viewed as an empirical hypothesis which should be retained only as long as it remains consistent with the balance of empirical evidence and continues to support a fruitful research program.

The DoGMA also notably treats faculty psychology with a realist attitude that is sometimes considered off-limits to empiricism. This may be seen to go against a standard reading of the faculty psychology of, at least, Locke and Hume. Millican (2009), for example, suggests that the frequent appeals to faculties made by these empiricists are merely a "way of speaking," ultimately shorthand for more basic associative operations. A famous passage in Locke that decries treating faculties as "so many distinct Agents" is often interpreted to support this view (E II.xxi.20). Demeter (2021) argues against this anti-realist reading of Hume's faculty psychology, suggesting that Hume intended to study the faculties from a third-person scientific perspective (in the way an anatomist would study internal organs), and that the comments from Locke and Hume which were interpreted as recommending an anti-realist attitude toward faculties were merely intended to contrast their approach to faculty psychology with the introspective approach to the faculties favored by the rationalists.[29] The empiricist reservations

---

[28] The acronym is a riff on the previous two dogmas of (logical) empiricism rejected by Quine—namely, the analytic-synthetic distinction (the idea that claims can be separated into those which are true by virtue of their meaning and those that are true by virtue of empirical facts) and semantic reductionism (the thesis that all empirically meaningful statements can be translated into sensory observation terms that would confirm or disconfirm them—Quine 1951).

[29] There are reasons to resist a simplistic approach to "mental anatomy" here, in that "mental organs" would likely need to share resources and interact with one another to a higher degree than physical organs. Neil van Leeuwen (2013:223) puts the worry in this way:

Perceptions, beliefs, emotions, mis-perceptions, rational inference systems, irrational biases, items in memory, etc. are all partial sources of novel ideas, so they are all potentially components of constructive imagination. Otherwise put, human imagination

about faculty psychology, on Demeter's reading, stem from rationalists such as Descartes treating the faculties like introspectible sources of distinctive evidence and mental powers, rather than like theoretical posits whose operations can only be uncovered through empirical observation and reasoning. As Demeter (2021) puts it:

> Faculties thus conceived are not intuitively accessible causal sources or postulates of some preconceived hypothesis in the framework of which experience is to be interpreted; they are conclusions of experimental reasoning, and their identity depends on whether the analysis of relevant observations is correct. (T 1.2.5.19) Instead of arguing *from* faculties, Hume argues *to* them; they are not the beginning but the aim of proper, experimental inquiry that reveals the characteristic activity of faculties (5364).

On this reading of Hume, the DoGMA is fully consistent and continuous with Hume's project. Faculties on this construal are like "mental organs" with distinctive operations to be uncovered by empirical reasoning, rather than by introspection or functional definition. The discovery of the critical aspects of those faculties that enable their distinctive operations— through DNN-based modeling—is a core aim of the DoGMA.

The DoGMA can be further characterized in terms of a negative and a positive side. The negative side prohibits appeal to innate ideas or concepts. The positive side commits us to derive domain-specific abstract knowledge from experience via the operation (and

is built out of components, many of which also serve other purposes; it's not a single "faculty." The great ancient anatomist Galen discovered multiple biological purposes for every bone he analyzed; I think something similar holds for the building blocks of imagination: abilities such as memory and perception serve both reality tracking and constructive imagination (more on this below). Imagination, in part, is the capacity to use them for more than one purpose.

Nevertheless, creating artificial systems that can model such a capacity requires endowing them with subsystems which have distinctively generative computational operations; an architecture with a perceptual recognition and a memory storage system will never be able to model these generative capabilities without further supplementation. Indeed, it has long been a refrain of empiricist faculty psychology, all the way back to Aristotle and Ibn Sina, that the faculties exist in a kind of hierarchy and that "higher" faculties will draw upon and in turn down-regulate lower faculties; this does not imply that each faculty lacks distinctive computational operations, which is the focus of the moderate empiricist modeling methodology recommended in this book.

cooperation) of active cognitive faculties embodying domain-general inductive biases. As a "to-do" list for machine learning, the DoGMA recommends that we model these faculties using architectures featuring multiple, semi-independent neural network modules characterized by distinctive wiring motifs or learning algorithms. My use of the term "module" here should be explicitly distinguished from Fodor's use of the term (Fodor 1983), as Fodorian modules are characteristically domain-specific and strictly informationally encapsulated; though the modules of the DoGMA share other properties in common with Fodor's list, such as performing their own distinctive operations, exhibiting a greater degree of internal than external information sharing, and possessing a fixed neural architecture.[30] These modules may, but need not, correspond to neuroanatomically distinct brain regions; indeed, we may expect that while these faculties perform distinct psychological functions, they compete for shared resources in the brain and their neural correlates might spatially overlap and even share many components.[31] Once articulated, we will find that the project of

---

[30] I thus invoke here a particularly weak notion of a "module," even by permissive recent standards (Robbins 2009). The notion invoked here is closest to that recommended by Carruthers (2006), though he also emphasizes the domain specificity that I here explicitly reject. I take no stance here on whether the mind is massively modular or also contains learned, domain-specific modules—I only here suggest that a useful way forward in deep learning research involves explicitly theorizing about computational models with distinctive operations that are more internally than externally connected and which implement roles attributed to domain-general psychological faculties in a coherent cognitive architecture.

[31] While I will introduce the faculties as distinct modules, we may decide upon reflection that one of the faculties can be reduced to a mode of or interaction among the others, or that the operations of two faculties are so intermingled that drawing a distinction between them would be artificial. Indeed, some theorists have argued that memory and imagination are merely two different aspects of the same faculty, or that attention is merely a mode of the other faculties (De Brigard 2014; Mole 2011a). Debates about the exact taxonomy of the faculties could reflect a healthy maturation of empiricist theorizing without threatening the basic point that empiricists can appeal to domain-general mental operations which exceed the most basic forms of associative learning. The DoGMA does stand in opposition to more radical forms of empiricism which seek to eliminate traditional faculty taxonomies entirely, such as the eliminativism recommended by neuroscientist Luiz Pessoa (Pessoa, Medina, and Desfilis 2022). While Pessoa suggests that the standard list of faculties derives from folk psychology and lacks convincing empirical support, I will here approach them more as solutions to computational problems faced by network-based approaches to rational cognition. It is an empirical discovery in computer science that network-based systems need mechanisms like distinct memory systems and attentional control to make decisions efficiently and flexibly in challenging environments.

modeling distinct faculties with distinct neural network architectures is already well underway in deep learning research, and that it is this moderate empiricist DoGMA—rather than behaviorism—which has inspired and is correspondingly bolstered by its recent achievements.

Even nativists and more radical empiricists who ultimately reject the DoGMA may benefit by considering its charitable characterization and defense. In fact, nativist-leaning readers may find more points of agreement with prominent deep learning theorists than they would have otherwise expected. For one, they may find many ideas traditionally championed by nativists—such as modularity (albeit, alas, not the domain-specific or massive flavors championed by Fodor 1983), model-based learning (albeit, alas, without innate concepts), and compositionality (albeit, alas, without unlimited productivity)— vindicated by the DoGMA. For another, most nativists may happily borrow from more powerful learning algorithms and architectures to integrate the recent achievements of deep learning into their own theories (as recommended even by critics such as Marcus). Charitable consideration of the DoGMA may even help nativists marshal empirical evidence as to exactly which ideas or concepts must be supposed innate. Thus, hopefully even nativists will see the value of systematically engaging with the considered, charitably construed views of the most influential empiricists.

I aim to show how prominent empiricist approaches are more reasonable and powerful than many have supposed, and I will consider the book a success if readers leave feeling that it is an open empirical question whether innate domain-specific structures are required for human-like AI, rather than being obviously required. Questioning the strength of the evidence for prominent nativist hypotheses like Core Knowledge is one route to this goal, but in the interests of space and novelty, I here focus on illustrating how much cognitive flexibility can be derived from domain-general structure in recent deep learning models, especially since much of this evidence is new to the debate and the pace of research has been so blisteringly fast.

Readers spoiling for a fight over the empirical support for nativism might be referred to a number of other works that critically evaluate it more directly (Christiansen and Chater 2016; Elman, Bates, and Johnson 1998; Griffiths and Tabery 2013; Mameli and Bateson 2006;

McClelland et al. 2010). However, it must be acknowledged by all parties that psychology's replication crisis has hit its developmental division hard, and even some prominent nativists in psychology have (admirably) admitted that their best-known empirical results and standard experimental practices have recently been called into question by systematic replication failures (Kampis et al. 2020; Kulke et al. 2018; Salvadori et al. 2015). A reform movement is currently underway in developmental psychology in particular (e.g., Frank et al. 2017; Oakes 2017; Rubio-Fernández 2019; The ManyBabies Consortium 2020); nativists may want to wait for the dust to settle there before insisting on specific components of Core Knowledge in their critiques of deep learning.

1.5. Of models and minds

To forestall some obvious worries about the aims of AI research as understood here, it will help to clarify the nature of the purported relationship between deep learning models and the human mind. I will not here be assuming or arguing for the position that current deep learning models themselves possess important mental properties like intelligence, cognition, rationality, or consciousness. Our ability to draw conclusions about the innate endowment of the intelligent or rational mind by examining current neural network models is immediately impeded by the fact that these systems are very partial models of intelligence that are unlike us and our brains in most of their details (something which could be obscured by the current degree of hype). Some of these disanalogies are obvious; these systems lack bodies, developmental histories, personalities, and social networks. It would be confused to offer AlphaGo a medal for having beaten Lee Sedol, for it does not care whether it wins, and it has no friends or family with whom to celebrate even if it did. These systems are, at best, slivers of rational agents. Further disanalogies are revealed by an under-the-hood inspection. Human and animal brains—the biological engines driving the only deeply rational machines of which we are currently aware—are rich symphonies of chemical interactions, exhibiting neural dynamics at multiple timescales and built using other non-neural but potentially relevant components like glia and myelin. We do not know which of these features are essential for the brain's role in supporting our rich mental lives, and the current generation of DNNs makes little attempt to capture all this complexity. While DNNs can produce impressively adaptive behaviors, these are mere brushstrokes of the behavioral flexibility that humans placed in similar situations could exhibit, and the computational models underlying them paint only very impressionistic pictures of the psychological and neural mechanisms that enable such flexibility.

It would be too hasty, however, to conclude that such disanalogies render DNNs irrelevant to debates over the innate start-up software required for intelligence or rationality. At minimum, these models serve as proofs of concept that systems adhering to empiricist constraints can extract certain types of knowledge from certain types of input data. More substantively, if there are abstract correspondences between the structure of a neural network and the structure of the human brain or mind, then study of the computational model might reveal how humans actually do it, and more specifically that we actually do it without innate domain-specific knowledge.

The question of abstract correspondences between computational models and human minds floats on very deep philosophical waters, and we will need to toss out a few lifelines before proceeding. I sketch a few ways to develop the "how actually" approach here, specifically drawing upon theories of explanation offered by Gualtiero Piccinini, Catherine Stinson, Lisa Miracchi, Rosa Cao, and Dan Yamins regarding the ways in which artificial neural network models might teach us something about the actual operations of the human mind that are crucial to its ability to create rational behavior, even if these models offer us only very partial pictures of its operations. Although these theories are closely related in their general take on the nature of explanation, I seek to highlight how each illuminates something distinctive that a DNN model might teach us about the organization of the human mind.[32]

---

[32] DNNs may help us understand human cognition even if they do not provide "how actually" explanations of it. Proofs of concept—that a physical system can learn to do something using only a certain kind of input data, for instance—can help defeat generic

Piccinini, for example, offers what he calls a "neurocomputational" account of how models might explain mental abilities (Piccinini 2015, 2020a). The lynchpin of his view is the idea that artificial neural network models might identify aspects of biological neural mechanisms that, when arranged in the right way, produce certain aspects of human cognition. "Aspect" is here a technical term; an aspect of a system is a property it possesses that is neither identical to nor entirely distinct from its lower-level constitution base yet is synchronically determined by the arrangement of those lower-level constituents. Crucially, the causal properties possessed by the aspect of the system are some subset of its total causal properties. An artificial neural network system which recapitulates just the organizational structure that is responsible for producing those aspects in the target system might then be used to draw inferences about the target system, even if it does not implement its full suite of causal properties. In this sense, an artificial neural network can be treated as an empirical hypothesis concerning which abstract organizational features enable certain computational operations in the brain, such as an ability to extract certain types of abstract structure efficiently from certain types of data. Piccinini's neurocomputational account requires more than a proof of concept— in mechanistic terms, it privileges "how actually" explanation rather than merely "how possibly" explanation (Piccinini and Craver 2011)— because the aspects of the model that allow it to solve the task must correspond to real and relevant aspects of the human brain.

Catherine Stinson offers a similar view, which she calls a "generic mechanism" account of the explanatory relevance of artificial neural network models (Stinson 2020). Stinson's view is derived from numerous self-interpretive comments offered by prominent neural network modelers over the years, especially those which emphasize their desire to produce models which are "biologically plausible" (Stinson 2018). Stinson also seeks a conceptual framework that justifies drawing

arguments that a certain type of data is necessary for human-like competence (Warstadt and Bowman 2022). "How possibly" models may also be useful indirectly in a variety of other roles in the context of discovery (Gelfert 2016:79–97). Nevertheless, I focus on the "how actually" strategy here, because I want to make the strongest case that can be supported by recent developments. I thank Alfredo Vernazzini for pushing me on this point.

inferences from artificial models to biological target systems—in this case, reasoning that because something is true of a DNN, it should also be true of the human mind or brain. On Stinson's view, this inference cannot be justified on the basis of the model mimicking some behavior of the target system, for the two systems might achieve those outcomes in different ways. Moreover, we want a principle that justifies inferences about cases where the behaviors of the two systems are not already known to correspond, so that models can be used to teach us things that we do not already know about intelligence, rationality, or cognition. Stinson argues that the right relationship here is not one of mere behavioral mimicry, but rather shared membership in an abstract kind of mechanistic structure, which she calls a "generic mechanism." In other words, we need to identify an abstract kind of mechanistic structure—in terms of types of structural properties like component types and connections among them—that could be shared between the brain and an DNN, and in virtue of which they exhibit some range of similar behaviors (Fig. 1.2).[33] This method places a bit more burden on the modeler, in that they must identify the kind of generic mechanism which is instantiated in both cases despite some prominent structural dissimilarities and (often) forms of idealization; but we will consider some generic mechanism candidates later in the book.

Finally, Lisa Miracchi (2019) holds an even more expansive view of the explanatory relevance of computational models. In fact, even those who believe that genuinely mental properties or distinctively human intelligence requires processing that is fundamentally different in kind from that which could occur in these computational models might be persuaded of deep learning's relevance to the human mind by considering Miracchi's view. Miracchi is concerned with "juicier"

---

[33] In invoking the language of natural kinds here, Stinson perhaps goes a bit beyond Piccinini, in that the kinds must display stable clusters of inductive regularities that justify their inclusion in scientific practice (Boyd 1991, 1999; Khalidi 2013). However, there may be some persistent difficulties in identifying natural kinds of mechanism (Craver 2009), especially those at just the right level of abstraction (Boone and Piccinini 2016; Craver and Kaplan 2020). An alternative approach might be to use some of the tools of transformation-based abstraction taken from neuroscience and developed here later in Chapter 3 to establish a notion of "transform similarity" between the computational system and the target system to legitimize the abstract comparisons (Cao and Yamins 2021a, 2021b).

Generic Mechanism Kind

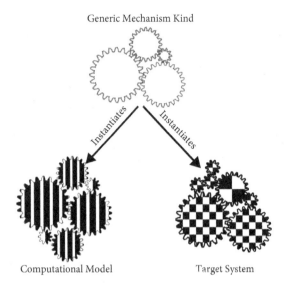

Computational Model   Target System

Figure 1.2 Stinson's "generic mechanism" view holds that a computational model (such as a deep neural network) can help explain phenomena implemented by a target system (such as the brain) if they both instantiate the same abstract mechanistic kind. Because they are both instances of the same generic mechanism, inferences about the computational model can generalize to the target system in virtue of their abstract mechanistic similarity. Of course, theorists should take care that the inferences generalized from the computational model to the target system issue from the abstract mechanistic structure they share, rather than from the specific ways in which they differ. (Figure adapted from Stinson 2020.)

philosophical takes on mental properties, such as that all acts of mentality are essentially conscious or normative, that perception involves continuous reciprocal "enactive" engagement with the world, and/or that that consciousness or normativity may exhibit properties which cannot in principle be implemented in a machine. Someone who held such a view might deny that deep learning models share even aspects or generic mechanisms with the human mind, because consciousness, meaning, enactive engagement, and normativity are essential to even the mind's most humble acts of perception or inference.

Table 1.2 The Three Types of Models (with Their Respective Roles) Recommended by Miracchi's (2019) Generative Difference-Maker Approach to Explanation

Type of Model	Role in Explanation
Agent model	"A model of the intelligence-related explanandum [agency, intelligence, perception, thinking, knowledge, language, rationality] that facilitates prediction and measurement"
Basis model	"A model of the artificial system in computational, physical, and/or non-mental behavioral terms that facilitates manipulation and measurement"
Generative model	"A model of how the features represented by the basis model make generative differences to features represented by the agent model"

Miracchi thinks that even someone holding such a view should attend to developments in deep learning, because artificial neural network models might nevertheless teach us things about "generative difference-makers" in the human brain that are physical preconditions for human persons to engage in these minded or meaningful activities of these kinds (and see also Klein, Hohwy, and Bayne 2020; Miracchi 2017).

Miracchi's view is perhaps the most philosophically demanding of the three considered so far; her approach requires theorists to develop three separate background models which are connected to one another before we can decide how an artificial neural network model bears on the human mind. Namely, one needs an "agent model," which provides a theory of the relevant mental phenomenon (which includes perhaps ineliminable appeals to consciousness, normativity, or other intentional properties); a "basis model," which characterizes the artificial system in computational, mechanical, and/or behavioral terms; and a "generative" model, which explains how changes in the basis features make a difference to or determine features in the agent (Table 1.2). This third model might be seen to address one of the primary concerns about the "black box" nature of deep learning models: that while they often reproduce human or animal behaviors to a large degree, the lack of known "empirical links" tying the processing in the model to the processing of the human mind prevents us from gaining any new understanding of cognition or intelligence from the model's successes (Sullivan 2022). It is worth comparing this picture to the three-model approach of Cao and Yamins (2021a), who recommend developing a model of the target system, a model of the computational system, and a "transform similarity" mapping that shows how to map coarse-grained features from the computational and target models to one another in order to make predictions about how the effects of changes to the abstract dynamics in one system predict effects of the abstract dynamics of the other (Fig. 1.3).

In a typical deep learning research program, each of these forms of understanding is only partially known or inchoate. Miracchi, in particular, worries that computer scientists often stipulate definitions of mental phenomena that reduce them to computational terms (perhaps even those suggested by Piccinini, Stinson, Cao, or Yamins), and that these reductions will be rejected out of hand by many theorists. Accordingly, Miracchi thinks that progress here could be achieved through an interdisciplinary division of labor, in which a team of philosophers and psychologists provide agent models for various mental kinds pitched entirely at the mental or psychological level of description (whether the target is "intelligence," "inference," "categorization," "memory," "imagination," etc.), while a team of computer scientists provide the basis model for the artificial systems they create which explains the functioning of their network architectures in terms of those architecture's computational properties. In this scenario, the teams then collaborate to form a generative model that explains how changes to the basis features bring about changes to the agent. Miracchi notes that in most cases, the agent models specified by computer scientists for the phenomena they discuss are often simply definitions stipulated without empirical or philosophical argument. Unsurprisingly, the stipulated definitions are frequently vulnerable to obvious counterexamples and resist empirically motivated revision.

This book offers a response and illustration of this kind of interdisciplinary approach by drawing together many threads from thinkers

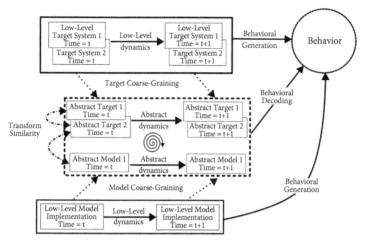

Figure 1.3 Cao and Yamins's (2021a) "3M++" view on the explanatory relationship between computational models and underlying systems. Like Miracchi's view, their approach requires a third theory which specifies a "transform similarity" that allows one to map behavior-producing state transitions in a computational model to behavior-producing state transitions in a target system. They note that the low-level implementation details between one instance of a biological behavior-producing target system (e.g., a human) and another (e.g., another human or a member of a different species like a monkey) will also differ in their lowest-level organization (e.g., specific brain activity or neural state transitions) and need to be mappable into one another using the same method of transform similarity. (Figure adapted from Cao and Yamins 2021a.)

in different disciplines. The philosophical and psychological research reviewed in the later chapters of this book can be interpreted as outlining agent models for mental faculties, and the computational research reviewed as providing basis models for targets which computer scientists have suggested might be relevant to understanding these mental properties. The third type of models (whether "generative" or "transform similarity") linking the other two remains to a large part unknown, but later chapters in this book can be seen to tee up their development for research groups to the interdisciplinary challenge.

1.6. Other dimensions of the rationalist-empiricist debate

I argued earlier that the primary point of dispute between empiricism and nativism concerns the doctrine of innate ideas and the Transformation Principle. Many rationalists are nativists and many empiricists are anti-nativists, but other disagreements have accrued between these competing alliances over the last two millennia. Let us briefly consider and situate four other dimensions. First, there is a debate over the right way to *evaluate* the mental processes behind behavior, especially in terms of rationality (Taylor 2003). Rationalists tend to be "internalists"—that is, they think that mental processes are correct if they follow a set of rules, such as logic or decision theory. Empiricists, on the other hand, tend to be "externalists," evaluating mental processes in terms of their reliability or success in particular environments. Second, there is a debate over the "format" of thought; rationalists tend to believe that thought occurs in a symbolic or language-like medium, often called a "Language of Thought" (Fodor 1975), which might be compared to symbolic computer programming code. Empiricists, on the other hand, tend to think that even abstract reasoning operates over sensorial, imagistic representations derived from perceptions (Barsalou 1999). These imagistic representations can be abstracted and recombined in various ways; but according to empiricists, they never fully lose their experiential content. Third, there is a debate over the justification of beliefs—with the "empiricist" side demanding that all empirical knowledge must be justified by objectively observable perceptual evidence (BonJour and Sosa 2003). Some flavor of this empiricist doctrine led psychological behaviorists like John Watson to banish all appeals to inner mental entities in psychology, because such theoretical entities cannot be objectively observed in experiments (Greenwood 1999). Fourth, there is a debate over the semantic content of meaningful claims, with "logical empiricists" insisting that all meaningful claims either be true in virtue of meaning alone (e.g., "all bachelors are unmarried males") or be translatable without remainder into "observation sentences" that should be true if the claim is correct (Quine 1951). This "semantic" strain of empiricism motivated the logical positivists in the Vienna

Circle to dismiss most metaphysical questions as meaningless—such as whether the soul is immortal, or whether all events must have a cause—since these questions could not be translated into empirically testable hypotheses.

In this book, we will explore the first two additional dimensions of the rationalist-empiricist dispute to some degree but dismiss the latter two debates entirely. I will thus not attempt to revive the empiricisms of Skinner or Carnap here; I applaud Quine's (1951) exorcism of these previous "two dogmas of empiricism" in the middle of the last century. As noted earlier, we will broach the debate over the right way to evaluate cognition, because it is relevant to the problem of gauging progress toward human-like processing in AI. The dispute over the format of thought will also arise in a number of places throughout the book. This dimension of the debate will be finessed here because, while I agree that representations and representational structures must be extracted from sensory experience, they might be so heavily transformed by processing that by the latest stages of processing, the signals might be indistinguishable from the sort of amodal symbols favored by critics of sensorial theories of concepts (Machery 2006).

1.7. The DoGMA in relation to other recent revivals of empiricism

Several other books have recently defended historical empiricism in the context of current cognitive science and with respect to neural network modeling specifically. In particular, Jesse Prinz (2002, 2004, 2007) revived and charitably applied the views of historical empiricists in contemporary cognitive science, and in many ways the DoGMA is continuous with this mission. Prinz, however, focused mostly on evidence for Lockean and Humean theses arising from evidence in the discipline of psychology, and he dealt more centrally with the debate over the format of thought (though he also endorsed anti-nativism about ideas—2005:679). The present book, however, is the first to update this empiricist frame in light of recent achievements in deep learning. In psychology and computational neuroscience, Jeffrey Elman and coauthors also challenged nativism using evidence from neural network modeling, in particular by emphasizing the promise of domain-general inductive biases (Elman et al. 1998). This book is in many ways a continuation of that approach for the deep learning era, while also pointing out how far the neural network modeling has come over just the last five years in vindicating even more ambitious empiricist proposals. Bill Bechtel and Adele Abrahamsen (Bechtel and Abrahamsen 2002) have also written on the relevance of neural network modeling to empiricism, though it is not their primary focus and they approach the question from a more philosophy of science perspective. Patricia Churchland (1989) and Paul Churchland (2012) have also championed neural network modeling against various versions of nativism and rationalism, though they tend to adopt a more eliminativist attitude toward the traditional mental categories invoked by historical empiricists and highlighted by the DoGMA, such as memory, imagination, and attention. Considering the DoGMA in light of these other recent defenses of empiricism will help put it in more complete historical and philosophical context.

1.8. Basic strategy of the book: Understanding deep learning through empiricist faculty psychology

Other excellent books are available which analyze the technical structure of deep learning architectures using the methodologies of computer science (e.g., Chollet 2021; e.g., Goodfellow, Bengio, and Courville 2016; Zhang et al. 2021). The goal of this book is different: to provide an interdisciplinary interpretation of the previous accomplishments of these networks, a fair appraisal of what remains to be achieved, and an opinionated take on where they might profitably head next. Do deep learning's successes show that DNNs can model rational decision-making? Do their shortcomings show that they cannot? Can some architectures model some forms of rationality, but not others? In exploring these questions, I aim to give the reader not just an understanding of the technical minutiae or architectural choices which go into the design of a state-of-the-art DNN but also an interdisciplinary, philosophically grounded account of the mental faculties that these networks can or cannot be fairly said to model.

The general idea that AI should focus on a modular cognitive architecture is not novel. In fact, it has been pursued by several different influential research groups over the years, especially those behind ACT-R, SOAR, Sigma, and CMC (Anderson and Lebiere 2014; Laird 2019; Laird, Lebiere, and Rosenbloom 2017; Rosenbloom 2013). The empiricist DoGMA proposed here, however, differs from these other approaches in several respects. For one, these approaches are usually hybrids of classical and connectionist approaches, often including both connectionist perceptual modules and classical rules or theories; the DoGMA proposed here aims for all modules to be network-based and to eschew innate domain-specific programming. For another, and to their credit, most of these other modular architectures have completed implementations that can be readily applied to data. The aim of this book is rather to provide philosophical and theoretical inspiration for the completion and full implementation of the DoGMA, which to date remains somewhat piecemeal in execution.

To be clear, none of these proposed cognitive architectures for AI, including the one suggested here, should be expected to be the complete and final draft of the mind's structure. The empiricists themselves differed in the details of their faculty taxonomies and theories of the individual faculties, and we should expect that empiricist modelers today will explore different possibilities as well. Here, I instead emphasize the domain-general modular strategy as the best way to understand and pursue the empiricist side of AI's current methodological debate.

1.9. Organization of the remaining chapters: Faculties, philosophers, and modules

The next chapter provides an overview of deep learning and its characteristic strengths and weaknesses. The remaining chapters of the book offer an empiricist account of a mental faculty and explore attempts to integrate aspects of the faculty into a deep learning architecture. In the course of our exploration, we will explain how each faculty's activities might improve the performance of an artificial agent. We will ask whether the addition of the faculty enables the resulting architecture to achieve new kinds of rational decision-making. Chapter 2 lays out some methodological preliminaries of this task, including specific tiers of rationality and principles for fair evaluation. Chapter 3 focuses on the faculty of perception and how DCNNs might reveal generative difference-makers in human perception by deploying structures that perform multiple forms of abstraction from sensory experience emphasized by historical empiricists. Chapter 4 reviews attempts to model the role of memory in deep learning systems, focusing on architectures like the Episodic Controller (EC). Chapter 5 discusses attempts to model the imagination using architectures like GANs and Variational AutoEncoders (VAEs), and Chapter 6 highlights various tweaks inspired by aspects of attention, such as transformers. Chapter 7 reviews more nascent attempts to model human social and moral cognition—focusing especially on the faculty of empathy/ sympathy—ending with some speculative suggestions for future research to model cultural and social learning in empiricist, DNN-based agents.

The course of each chapter reflects the book's interdisciplinary goals. Because I aim to illustrate the value of revisiting historical empiricism in arbitrating current debates over deep learning, I review the theories offered by empiricist philosophers for these psychological faculties. While I could easily survey the views of a dozen empiricists on each faculty, for the sake of narrative simplicity, each faculty chapter zooms in on the views of one prominent empiricist-leaning philosopher who had a particularly rich and germane take on the faculty highlighted in that chapter. These philosophers include John Locke, Ibn Sina, David Hume, William James, and Sophie de Grouchy. This "philosopher of the week" structure is deployed as a narrative device, so that we might go into enough depth with the views of a wide sample of empiricist philosophers. This illustrates the utility of empiricist philosophy generally as a source for engineering inspiration, while allowing us to avoid entrapment in the details of particular interpretive disputes. After sketching the philosophical and psychological landscape, each chapter then reviews current and future implementations of the processing attributed to this faculty in DNN architectures, often on the basis of explicit comparisons by the DNN modelers. We will also routinely review the degree of biological plausibility of the efforts thus far, by discussing similarities between the architecture's structure and the neural circuits hypothesized to implement the faculty in biological brains.

While I argue that the DoGMA already inspires and is in turn bolstered by a variety of recent achievements in deep learning, the models behind these recent achievements mostly implement only one or two additional faculty modules, and new problems will arise when we start trying to coordinate more complex DNN-based architectures featuring multiple semi-independent faculties. Here, we will study these issues under the heading of the Control Problem. No existing DNN-based system attempts to model all of the faculties explored here; most contain modules for one or more forms of memory and some model attentional resources, but few have explored imagination or social cognition and none simultaneously include components for all the faculties canvassed here.[34] This has sometimes been a goal of past AI projects—some implementations of ACT-R, for example, included components corresponding to many of the faculties discussed here. We may expect that problems of coordination and control will become more pressing as more faculties are included and agent architectures become more complex. Evolution balanced these control problems through iterative parameter search during millions of years of natural selection, and we may expect a long period of exploration will be required in AI as well. I hope to inspire AI researchers to consider these control problems more proactively, and to begin working on the design and implementation of more ambitious faculty architectures that model the integrated decision-making of a whole rational agent, rather than focusing on one or two components at a time. We will return to reevaluate this challenge and call to action in the final chapter before closing. Thus, to work.

[34] This is generally acknowledged by the authors of these alternative architectures. For example, Laird, Lebiere, and Rosenbloom recently wrote that their model "remains incomplete in a number of ways . . . for example, concerning metacognition, emotion, mental imagery, direct communication and learning across modules, the distinction between semantic and episodic memory, and mechanisms necessary for social cognition" (2017:23).

2

What Is Deep Learning, and How Should We Evaluate Its Potential?

In particular the concept of what is a chair is hard to characterize simply. There is certainly no AI vision program which can find arbitrary chairs in arbitrary images ... Such problems are never posed to AI systems by showing them a photo of the scene. A person (even a young child) can make the right interpretation of the photo and suggest a plan of action. But this abstraction is the essence of intelligence and the hard part of the problems being solved. Under the current scheme the abstraction is done by the researchers leaving little for the AI programs to do but search. A truly intelligent program would study the photograph, perform the abstraction and solve the problem.

—Rodney Brooks (1991:143)

2.1. Intuitive inference as deep learning's distinctive strength

With the basic terms of the relevant nativist-empiricist debate in place, I now briefly characterize "deep learning" and highlight its distinctive contribution to the conversation. This contribution, I suggest, lies in its ability to illuminate a variety of midlevel cognitive processes that until now eluded both empiricist and nativist modeling. Previous waves of empiricist research produced a solid understanding of the most basic forms of associative learning, and previous waves of nativist research created many powerful models of the most abstract kinds of rule-based thinking, such as explicitly logical, mathematical, or analogical

From Deep Learning to Rational Machines. Cameron J. Buckner, Oxford University Press.
© Oxford University Press 2024. DOI: 10.1093/oso/9780197653302.003.0002

reasoning. However, neither side of the continuum had (until now) much success in modeling the "murky zone" of cognition which lies between these extremes of simplicity and abstraction (Buckner 2018b; Nagel 2012). This is the kind of processing we perform when we detect someone's mood on the basis of a suite of subtle facial and behavioral cues; attempt to guess whether more humans are killed each year by sharks or mosquitoes; drive to work along a familiar route "on auto-pilot" (though responding flexibly to dynamic traffic conditions and obeying complex traffic laws); or decide to go "all in" on a hand of poker because we suspect our opponent is bluffing. These decisions are flexible and complex, but it is difficult to force them into the mold of an explicit rule or algorithm, and the introspectible grounds of the decision often bottom out in an effortless hunch or intuition. In this chapter, I argue that modeling such intuitive processing—which comprises perhaps the majority of our everyday cognition and decision-making, if not the highest peaks of human abstraction—is deep learning's distinctive strength. Indeed, the DoGMA holds that this largely unconscious processing drives many everyday acts of rational decision-making, and that harnessing and directing it by modeling various mental faculties can bootstrap artificial agents to the heights of rationalist abstraction.

Before making this case, we should distinguish deep learning from earlier waves of empiricist modeling, especially earlier waves of artificial neural network modeling which lacked its depth and distinctive power. Like those earlier waves, deep learning is a subfield of machine learning that attempts to create artificial computational systems that discover their own solutions to problems. As noted in the previous chapter, this goal is often inspired by the empiricist appraisal that the most promising route to modeling human-like cognition involves endowing systems with general learning processes and architectures that enable them to acquire their own flexible, context-sensitive solutions to problems across a variety of domains and content types. Because brains are the only natural physical systems capable of this kind of flexible learning, empiricists have from the beginning taken inspiration from the brain's structure and function. The computational learning systems built according to these brain-like principles are called artificial neural networks (ANNs), as discussed in relationship to the approaches to explanation by Piccinini, Stinson, Miracchi, Cao, and Yamins in the preceding chapter.

ANNs were inspired by the insight that many simple processing nodes working in parallel might be more efficient and powerful than a single (or small set of) central processing unit(s) (CPUs) designed to implement a suite of specialized logical and mathematical operations, as is found in modern digital computers.[1] In fact, the belief that sophisticated problem-solving might emerge from tweaking vast networks of unsophisticated processing nodes is almost as old as the field of computer science. Turing himself was an early supporter of this approach: he speculated that "unorganized machines" designed to be "the simplest model of the nervous system with a random arrangement of neurons" might be trained to "behave in a very complicated manner when the number of units is large" (Copeland and Proudfoot 1996; Sterrett 2012; Turing 1948). During the twentieth century, this idea was explored in a variety of ways—with influential milestones like McCulloch and Pitts (1943), Rosenblatt (1958), and McClelland et al. (1986)—though in practice, it was only possible to train ANNs that were relatively small and shallow, that is, having few layers of nodes ("artificial neurons") processing signals between input and output.

Primarily, the deep neural networks (DNNs) favored in "deep learning" are distinguished from earlier ANNs by interposing a greater number of layers between input and output signals (Buckner and Garson 2018; Schmidhuber 2015). While earlier waves of ANN-based modeling mostly involved less than four layers, recent conceptual and hardware breakthroughs have made it possible for researchers to train ANNs with a very large number of nodes and connections—with many layers of processing (usually at least five, but sometimes hundreds or even thousands) transforming signals between input and output layers. These comprehensive/vast DNNs merit the name "deep learning systems."

---

[1] Piccinini points out that the common way of drawing the contrast between ANNs and classical computational systems in terms of many simple processors versus one (or a few) complex processor(s) could be improved upon, because CPUs can also be viewed as composed of more simple processors—logic gates—operating in parallel. For a longer discussion of notions of parallel versus serial computation, see Piccinini (2015, Ch. 13).

This depth itself is the most significant computational aspect of deep learning architectures; because computations performed at an earlier layer can be recursively reused in composing more complex computations at later layers, a DNN can be orders of magnitude more efficient than a shallower network at computing the same solutions (Bengio 2009; Buckner 2019a; Goodfellow et al. 2016). Today, the scale of some deep learning systems—such as OpenAI's GPT-3 system with its 175 billion parameters, or NVidia's Megatron-Turing with 530 billion—has begun to approach the size of a simple brain. "Deep" here has a dual meaning, referring both to the number of layers imposed between input and output, and to the rich, hierarchically structured patterns that these layered networks can acquire from their inputs. In fact, the empiricist DoGMA posits that the flexibility characteristic of human intuitive judgment is enabled by our own ability to learn just these sorts of patterns from experience, in virtue of the distinctive, domain-general transformations that deeply layered brain networks perform on their sensory inputs when given the kind of guidance provided by mental faculties.

According to the hypothesis, AlphaGo's victory over the human Go grandmaster Lee Sedol was a landmark achievement because it rendered plausible the possibility that DNNs might rival the power of human intuitive decision-making. To put this achievement in context, let us return to the GOFAI system Deep Blue's victory over Garry Kasparov in 1997. As impressive as this victory was, we should worry that Deep Blue bested Kasparov only through an overwhelming application of unintelligent brute computational force. Deep Blue's specialized hardware allowed it to explore far more moves per turn than a human could explicitly consider in an entire lifetime—over 200 million moves per second (Campbell 1999). Granted, Deep Blue did use some expert-derived heuristics to prune its search space in the manner that GOFAI pioneers Newell and Simon would have considered the "essence of intelligence" (Newell and Simon 1976). For instance, built into its programming library were rules of thumb like "try to control the center of the board" and "avoid plans where you lose your queen," as well as a curated library of opening moves to guide its play (such as the "Sicilian Defense"). However, its narrow (3.5 vs. 2.5) victory over Kasparov was still widely regarded as a triumph of raw processing speed, rather than a display of human-like intelligence or rationality. Unlike Deep Blue's approach, human chess strategy relies more upon holistic, intuitive pattern-matching, which allows us to consider only a much smaller number of possible moves that are especially likely to lead to a win. In fact, expert systems like Deep Blue reliably fail on a variety of other, less crisply defined problems that humans find easy or perform automatically using intuition.

After Kasparov's defeat by Deep Blue in 1997, artificial intelligence (AI) researchers cast about for games more difficult to solve by exhaustive computation. They were particularly attracted to Go. Whereas chess has only about 15 to 30 possible moves per turn, Go has about 300 possible moves per turn, making it impossible for an artificial system to win by simply considering every possible combination of moves and countermoves through brute search. To put this claim in context, there are far more possible game trajectories in an average Go game (10^{360}) than there are atoms in the entire universe (estimated at 10^{78}–10^{82}; Koch 2016); considering 200 million moves per second would constitute only a drop in the ocean of Go's complexity. As a result, high-level Go play is thought to require intuition, an assumption supported by human expert players, who explain their strategies using flexible abstractions such as "influence," "stability," and "connection" that cannot be pressed into the mold of transparent symbolic algorithms.

Nevertheless, the DNN-based system AlphaGo defeated the human Go grandmaster Lee Sedol 4–1 in a highly publicized match in 2016. AlphaGo's play was said to be more human-like than previous Go-playing expert systems, in that it learned its own abstractions directly from experience with board positions. This experience included training on records of human games from a curated library, as well as by playing millions of matches against increasingly powerful versions of itself. For the purposes of evaluating the DoGMA, the most exciting aspect of AlphaGo's processing was revealed by follow-up experiments showing that AlphaGo's ability to play Go well does not depend entirely upon its ability to consider more possible moves at each turn than its human opponents. Though the version of AlphaGo that defeated Lee included a tree search algorithm enabling it to consider many different moves per turn, when this feature of the network was turned off and

AlphaGo was forced to select moves simply on the basis of the abstract patterns it had learned in its neural networks, it was still capable of grandmaster-level play (Silver et al. 2016). Furthermore, AlphaZero— a subsequent, simplified system that learned entirely from self-play, excising the last vestiges of the expert-system approach by eschewing the library of human-played games from its training regimen (Silver et al. 2017)—is much more powerful than AlphaGo, having defeated the earlier system in matches with a perfect 100–0 record (Fig. 2.1). Together, these two results suggest that AlphaGo/AlphaZero's ability to play Go well depends upon its DNNs' abilities to extract abstract patterns from its gameplay experience rather than on brute force search or manually encoded human knowledge.

I have previously argued that the space of rational behavior in humans and animals that is performed on the basis of such intuitive patterns is quite large, including sophisticated and flexible decision-making in both time-constrained, low-stakes situations and more deliberative, high-stakes contexts (Buckner 2018b, 2019b). In the context of AI, we can focus the argument on the degree of similarity between

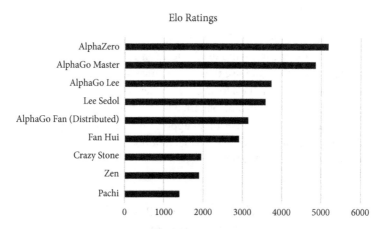

Figure 2.1 Elo ratings of various computational Go playing programs and two humans (Lee Sedol and Fan Hui), as computed by DeepMind in virtual tournaments (Silver et al. 2016, 2017). Lee Sedol's highest Elo rating was 3590; by comparison the highest Elo human score as of October 28, 2020, was held by Shin Jinseo at 3814.

these systems and biological brains by looking under the hood to compare structural and functional features of DNNs to those of the relevant neural circuits in biological brains. To reprise Miracchi's terms, these comparisons may reveal the generative difference-makers that play the crucial information-processing roles which allow biological brains to produce such decisions. To temper these comparisons, I also review open questions that remain about apparent dissimilarities between processing in biological brains and DNN-based systems. Close inspection of these results reveals that while they still have a long way to go to model full human rationality, these dissimilarities should be viewed more as surmountable opportunities for future research rather than insurmountable obstacles barring further development of the DoGMA.

2.2. Deep learning: Other marquee achicvements

Breakthrough achievements of DNNs illustrate how far AI has come over the last decade. Such achievements are useful as the case studies for modeling the rational faculties using empiricist methods, in part because they show how the basic strengths of intuitive processing just illustrated in AlphaGo/AlphaZero can be bootstrapped to greater degrees of abstraction and flexible decision-making. I preview these achievements here, and use them to organize the remaining chapters of the argument for the DoGMA, in order to illustrate the current and future gains that can be obtained by modeling roles attributed to human faculties. Ultimately, they support my belief that deep learning offers the key, or at least the key ring, to unlock the barriers that have previously obstructed progress in AI.

2.2.1. Labeling and identifying objects in natural photographs

Automated image classification ("computer vision") stands as one such achievement. Although object categorization is a task that human children and even some animals can perform with relative ease (Jitsumori and Delius 2001), it has repeatedly proved intractable for GOFAI-based systems. Objects depicted in natural images exhibit too much variability in their pose, rotation, size, location, illumination, texture, and occlusion, and categories often admit of too many fuzzy boundaries and exceptions to be neatly defined in terms of rules (Matsuyama 1993). Even a seemingly basic category, such as "chair," requires an astounding range of materials, styles, orientations, occlusions, angles, and borderline cases that must be accommodated to build a moderately reliable chair-detector. As recently as twenty years ago, skeptics of mainstream AI like Rodney Brooks—excerpted in the epigraph of this chapter—despaired of our ability to solve such problems associated with computer vision without a fundamental paradigm shift in research methods.

However, the advent of DNNs has enabled computational systems to solve some image recognition tasks at human or superhuman levels of accuracy, potentially modeling important forms of abstraction in the human perceptual faculties like sight and hearing. The achievement is due to the combination of large, curated data sets like ImageNet, which consists of millions of images annotated with 20,000 target category labels, with ever-deeper neural networks that are powerful enough to extract the subtler patterns spread across such vast amounts of training data. AlexNet was the first DNN-based system to resoundingly outperform alternative computational methods of identification on ImageNet, an achievement often seen as the start of the current deep learning boom (Krizhevsky, Sutskever, and Hinton 2012). Though many other DNN-based systems have managed even higher benchmark scores since, AlexNet's structure contained all the distinctive components of the deep convolutional neural network (DCNN), which has become the most reliably successful and widely studied DNN architecture (Figs. 2.2 and 2.3).[2] Analysis of this architecture helps show how such networks can be seen to perform an operation akin to perceptual abstraction, in particular by modeling key aspects of human vision.

---

[2] This claim comes with the caveat that transformers—an architecture that will be discussed in later chapters—may just now be supplanting DCNNs as the most widely adopted and successful architecture in deep learning.

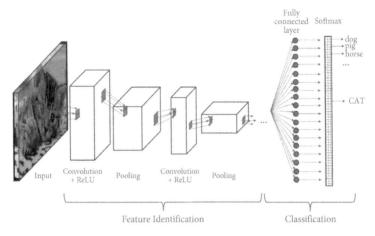

Figure 2.2 The generic processing flow of a deep convolutional neural network, whose architecture involves transforming input signals through many layers of locally connected nodes.

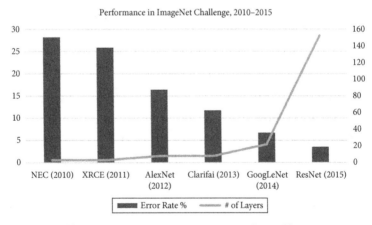

Figure 2.3 Error rate improvements over time on ImageNet classifications by different deep learning systems and number of layers contained in the deep neural network. (Adult human error rate on this task is about 5 percent.) Scores and results reported in Russakovsky et al. (2015).

2.2.2. Playing videogames at superhuman levels of skill

DNNs have also demonstrated a remarkable ability to play videogames at human-like levels of skill. One such system, the Episodic Controller architecture (Mnih et al. 2015), achieved breakthrough results on a suite of games for the Atari console. Although earlier reinforcement learning systems (which learn using "reward" signals that indicate success or failure on some task) based on principles similar to AlphaGo were able to rival expert-level game scores, these systems were trained on tens of thousands of hours of gameplay, far more than humans require to play these games well. By taking inspiration from the human faculty of memory, the creators of the Episodic Controller system attempted to address this issue by adding an "episodic replay buffer" that stores sequences of particularly effective game moves from training experience. This memory module allows the system to make efficient use of much smaller amounts of input by replaying particularly effective sequences in offline training sessions. The innovation was inspired by the way that autobiographical memory is thought to work in mammals, wherein "important" memories can be individually recalled for comparison and/or repeatedly replayed to help form abstract representations in offline memory consolidation that occurs during daydreaming and sleep, a process which continues for weeks or months after the initial experience (McClelland, McNaughton, and O'Reilly 1995). Empiricist philosophers have long emphasized the importance of such mnemonic rehearsal in rational decision-making, and thus this architecture demonstrates the value of the DoGMA in understanding and facilitating progress in AI.

2.2.3. Generating novel but realistic images, video, and music

In addition to the progress achieved by leveraging previous experience more efficiently through memory replay, even more ambitious innovations in deep learning have explored remixing previous experiences into novel simulations of future possibilities, inspired by roles attributed to the human imagination. Empiricist philosophers and psychologists have long hypothesized that our ability to imagine what would happen in fictional scenarios enables much of our creative ability and insightful problem-solving. Already, DNN systems exist that can create plausible, high-resolution representations of events which never happened and which most humans cannot discriminate from the real thing—including photographs, speech, video, and music. This is the kind of functionality that has been covered in the popular press under the heading of "deepfakes."

Often discussed as security concerns, deepfakes represent a capability that could be used to create misleading records of events that never happened. For instance, bad actors could create a video in which a trusted authority figure seems to realistically speak a script chosen by the deepfake's creators—resulting in misinformation or alarm. The possibility was dramatically illustrated by the actor and comedian Jordan Peele, who showed in 2018 how the technology could be used to make it appear that President Obama was delivering a Public Service Announcement using Peele's desired script. Since then, the technology has only improved, creating concerns about an "AI arms race" to build ever-better methods to detect deepfake attacks before they can cause public disturbances, and ever-better deepfakes that can circumvent those checks. Deepfakes are typically created by a DNN architecture called generative adversarial networks (GANs), which perform near-inverses of the transformational operations found in a DCNN like AlexNet. In fact, the discoverers of this architecture took explicit inspiration from the roles attributed to the faculty of imagination in human cognition, which similarly allows for the creation and exploration of realistic but novel stimuli.

2.2.4. Generating text that is indistinguishable from that written by humans

Perhaps the most impressive recent deep learning achievements issued from systems that leverage the generative capacities of DNNs to model one of the most flexible and sophisticated human behaviors: the ability to produce syntactically correct and semantically coherent language. These large language models (LLMs), such as OpenAI's GPT-3 and

Google's PaLM, can generate entire documents of text—in nearly any genre and on nearly any topic—that human subjects cannot reliably distinguish from text written by other humans. Given the complexity of grammatical rules in human language, this is another achievement that until recently seemed far beyond the grasp of AI. In fact, the largest language models like GPT-3 and PaLM reflect a staggering leap in size over previous models—as mentioned earlier, the full version of GPT-3 contains over 175 billion parameters and was trained on over 420 billion tokens of text, a massive data set that reflects a wide sampling of the text currently available on the Internet (T. B. Brown et al. 2020), and PaLM has approximately 540 billion parameters (Chowdhery et al. 2022).[3] To exploit the compositional patterns in such a large and diverse data set, these large language models deploy a new type of DNN architecture called a transformer. There has been intense debate regarding the implications of these models, with claims ranging from the extremely optimistic assessments that they have "solved" grammatical processing and "understand" natural language syntax and semantics, to skeptical assessments that these models mindlessly "parrot" patterns observed in their massive training sets.[4] These models can perform very well on traditional benchmarking tasks for language models while still being susceptible to puzzling errors and textual adversarial attacks. The attempt to evaluate these claims more rigorously has led to a revolution in benchmarking methodology, perhaps culminating in the BIG-Bench, a set of more than 200 automated question-and-answer tasks covering everything from grammatical processing to story understanding to causal inference to novel conceptual combination.[5] Notably, PaLM outperforms humans on a majority

---

[3] Megatron-Turing also now contains 530 billion parameters in its released version, and they built a version with over 1 trillion, though it was reported that it failed to converge in training.

[4] For a skeptical survey of the breathless assessments of recent progress in LLMs, see Bender et al. (2021) and Bender and Koller (2020). Bowman (2022), in turn, warns that some of these pessimistic assessments are obviated by the most recent language models and points out the dangers of underevaluating recent achievements by LLMs. For some of the most sophisticated attempts to understand processing in such LLMs, see Elhage et al. (2021) and Olsson et al. (2022).

[5] https://github.com/google/BIG-bench

of these tasks, an accomplishment that would have seemed fantastical only a few years ago.

There are several key innovations that distinguish transformers from other architectures mentioned so far, and all are worthy of further investigation here. However, perhaps the most significant difference is its use of a mechanism called "self-attention" to determine which elements of recent linguistic context are most relevant to deciding what word it should output next. While "self-attention" names a series of mathematical operations which might appear to share little in common with the human faculty of attention, we will see how it can be used to implement roles attributed to some of the most sophisticated forms of top-down attention in human reasoning, such as the verbal self-coaching which allows us to focus on just the relevant parts of mathematical or causal reasoning problems when we attempt to discover the correct solution.

2.3. Deep learning: Questions and concerns

Despite these (and many other) impressive recent achievements, questions have been raised about the ability of DNNs to accurately model these aspects of human cognition. Such concerns, which have been emphasized by theorists who subscribe to rationalist and nativist theories and have served as flashpoints of debate with prominent deep learning modelers, are the modern incarnations of a general worry traceable all the way back to Plato: that experience does not provide enough information to explain the power, efficiency, and clarity of distinctively human thought, at least not without the aid of innate ideas. As a result, nativists expect that the solutions deployed by systems which learn all their abstractions from experience will, in comparison to solutions used by humans, be opaque, inefficient, brittle, and fail to generalize well to novel situations. This typical list of concerns finds expression in one form or another by all of the nativist-leaning theorists discussed in the previous chapter, especially in Marcus (2018a), Fodor (2003), Mitchell (2019), and Lake et al. (2016). These nativists argue that they reflect fundamental shortcomings of empiricist methods more generally and of neural networks in particular, and that the current degree of dissimilarity between the performance of humans and DNN-based systems serves as evidence that a substantial set of innate representations is required for human-like learning from experience.

I agree with these deep learning skeptics that a systematic defense of the DoGMA should have answers to these concerns, and so I offer my own review of them here. While these concerns reflect valid criticism of some particular DNN-based systems, I challenge the idea that they add up to a powerful inductive argument against deep learning specifically or empiricism more generally. The key question, currently being arbitrated by deep learning research, is whether and to what degree these concerns can be mitigated by drawing upon additional domain-general resources and more human-like training data. Many existing systems have shown promise here, often by adding more domain-general structure to systems and/or by reducing the disanalogies between the circumstances in which these systems and humans are trained and tested. The DoGMA emphasizes that many of the systems which have made some progress on these questions have relied upon modules implementing roles attributed to domain-general faculties in human cognition to process training data more efficiently and effectively.

2.3.1. Opacity

Perhaps the most common concern about a purported dissimilarity between DNNs and humans is that these complex but powerful models are "black boxes" and are not "interpretable" (Lipton 2018) or "not sufficiently transparent" (Marcus 2018a). Even a modestly sized DNN today can contain millions of parameters—especially link weights between nodes, which are modified during training, but also more global hyperparameters such as the number of nodes in particular layers or the types of activation functions governing those nodes—and it can be difficult to decide which ones are the most significant to its decisions, or what role particular factors played in some decision-making process. This differs from systems to which DNNs are often compared with respect to interpretability. Many expert systems, linear models, and Bayesian methods deploy symbols and rules with straightforward interpretations (Rudin 2019).[6] In Deep Blue, for example, if we wanted to know why it decided to move the piece that it did, we could look inside the system to see which possibilities had been considered on each turn and which heuristics recommended the play as the most likely to lead to a win. Granted, the answer we find will be extremely long and complex—potentially including billions of possible moves and countermoves—but the description and scoring of each scenario would be phrased in terms of straightforwardly intelligible considerations, such as the point value of specific pieces captured, the amount of board control gained or ceded, and the number of outcomes that can lead to a checkmate. Similarly, it is easy to see when Deep Blue has made an unexpected blunder. When Deep Blue made a famous mistake against Kasparov in the first game of their 1997 match due to a coding bug, which caused it to make a random move whenever one of its internal counters ran out of time in a certain way, the programmers could easily identify the source of this mistake. Consequently, they could change the code to avoid reoccurrence of the mistake in the future (Sayer 2017).

When we contrast this relative transparency with a DNN-based system like AlphaGo, we find the patterns driving its evaluations to be less clear. Though we could inspect the tree search history of AlphaGo to see which board positions it considered upon making a certain move, and even see the valuation scores attached to each option, we could not easily explain why those rankings were assigned to those positions. We could provide an accounting of the nodes most activated on that run, and perhaps of the board features most important in selecting that move over another; but without significant interpretive work, we would not be able to appreciate the significance of the patterns AlphaGo saw in those positions. This relates to the concerns rationalists like Descartes traditionally expressed about associative thinking when compared to the "clarity and distinctness" of explicit

---

[6] In some cases, the apparent transparency of these alternatives can be misleading. Dimensionality reduction and linear analysis techniques can sometimes reduce the number of factors involved in a decision, but it may be misleading to interpret those limited dimensions or factors by mapping them to common-sense concepts. For further discussion of this rebuttal, see Lipton (2018).

deductive reasoning. When we are surprised by one of AlphaGo's decisions, it will be very difficult to determine whether it was a bug or a brilliant leap beyond the current limits of human strategy.

As a case in point, one particular move made by AlphaGo against Lee—move 37 of Game 2—was so unorthodox and unexpected that even the DeepMind employee tasked with recording the move assumed it must have been a bug. On the contrary, commentators now describe this move as exceptionally brilliant. Supported by no conventional strategy or theory, AlphaGo on move 37 opted to place a Go stone in an area of open space on the right side of the board that seemed to provide little advantage to nearby pieces' influence or stability, forgoing several more obvious moves that would have shored up its position (Fig. 2.4). The match's commentators at the time (one also a 9-dan grandmaster of the game) were dumbstruck, and Lee himself was so troubled by the move that he immediately left the room to compose himself and could not formulate a response for nearly fifteen minutes. Yet after ten or twenty more turns, this move was revealed as a crucial turning point in the match, which AlphaGo won handily.

Perhaps unsurprisingly, this inscrutability can be acceptable and even carry a certain degree of allure in a recreational, low-stakes do-main like board games. Indeed, reflection on AlphaZero's surprising moves has produced a mini-revolution in the theory of strategy games, helping humans improve their gameplay theory by reverse-engineering insights behind AlphaZero's moves (Sadler and Regan 2019). However, opacity concerns become more serious in other domains with higher stakes or a context of auditability. For example, DNNs are also already being tasked with labeling images on social media, micro-targeting advertisements, diagnosing diseases like cancer from medical imaging, issuing predictions about the risk in-volved in loan applications, and analyzing data in scientific research to discover new ways to fold proteins and create new drugs. These applications typically involve bigger risks for users and correspond-ingly require higher degrees of responsibility for developers and businesses deploying these technologies into their ever-evolving web of legal rights and responsibilities. To take an example, the European Union's General Data Protection Regulation (GDPR)—a frame-work of laws implemented in 2018 which provides users with a "right

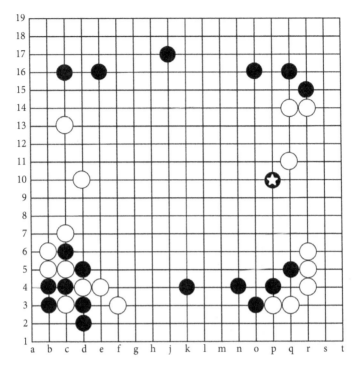

Figure 2.4 AlphaGo's counterintuitive (to humans—at least, humans at the time) move 37 (indicated with a white star on black circle). This surprising "shoulder hit" appeared to strengthen a position for black that would not become important until much later in the game.

to explanation" for decisions made by algorithms operating on their data—quickened the challenges of justifying the decisions of DNNs and provided this area of research with practical goals, if not always conceptual clarity. Interestingly, other DNN systems may be the most effective tools we have to interpret or justify a DNN's decision-making.

2.3.2. Training efficiency

Another dissimilarity that has spurred innovation derives from the observation that early DNNs required far more training data than humans to achieve equivalent performance, raising the question of whether they are learning the same things or in the same ways that humans do. The standard training methods for image-labeling DNNs, for example, involve supervised backpropagation learning on the ImageNet database, which contains 14 million images that are hand-annotated with labels from more than 20,000 object categories. Or, to consider another example, AlphaGo's networks were trained on over 160,000 stored Go games recorded from human grandmaster play, and then further on millions of games played against iteratively stronger versions of itself; by contrast, AlphaGo's human opponent Lee Sedol could not have played more than 50,000 matches in his entire life. We might also note that unlike many DNNs, humans rely on "fast mapping" and "one-shot learning," which allows generalization from a much smaller amount of experience. To consider a particular case, Lake et al. (2016) argue that humans can learn to recognize and draw the components of new handwritten characters, even after seeing just a single picture of the new character. They suggest that humans are capable of this one-shot learning because they understand how new figures could be generated in terms of a small library of strokes and shapes that can be easily recombined. Given the scale and complexity of the data that many models require, we might wonder whether DNNs will ever be able to master these sparse but rich compositional representations from smaller, more human-like amounts of experience. Most of the innovations we consider in later chapters will in one way or another provide gains to the efficiency and sparsity of DNN-based learning, especially involving compositional representations, and generally by attempting to perform more roles attributed to faculties studied in human psychology.

2.3.3. Adversarial attacks

A related mystery which might be thought to expose a fundamental dissimilarity between the way that humans and DNNs see the world centers on the latter's susceptibility to "adversarial examples." Adversarial examples are unusual stimuli created or selected by one "adversarial" DNN to fool another DNN targeted in the attack. The initial adversarial examples were "perturbed images," created (like deepfakes) by a GAN through slightly modifying an easily classifiable exemplar in a way that was imperceptible to humans, but that appears to cause dramatic misclassification in the DNNs targeted for attack (Goodfellow et al. 2014). Perturbation methods most commonly modify many pixels across an entire image, but they can also be as focused as a single-pixel attack (Su, Vargas, and Sakurai 2019). While the pixel vectors used to perturb images are usually discovered by training the adversarial DNN on a particular discriminative DNN's responses to specific images, some methods can also create "universal perturbations" that disrupt a wide range of classifiers on any natural image (Moosavi-Dezfooli et al. 2017).

Several years after the discovery of perturbation attacks by Goodfellow et al., Xu et al. showed that many could be disrupted with simple preprocessing techniques that alter fine details, such as systematic geometric transformation like rotation, rescaling, smoothing, and/or de-noising, a family of interventions called "feature squeezing" (Xu, Evans, and Qi 2017). The effectiveness of feature squeezing as a countermeasure suggests that perturbation methods are effective against DNNs not because processing in DNNs is fundamentally unlike human perception, but rather because the input that DNNs receive has not been preprocessed with the human sensory organs or received in human-like environmental circumstances.[7] In other words, DNNs might be vulnerable to image perturbations because their perceptual acuity is too keen and their input too static; the attack exploits their sensitivity to precise pixel locations which are predictively useful in these artificial data sets but not in more human-like training input, so feature squeezing can disrupt the attack by systematically altering the entire input image, as might reasonably be done by retinal processing or slight changes in perspective in the more dynamic circumstances of human perception.

However, another family of adversarial example generation methods—involving the creation or discovery of "rubbish images" that are supposed to be meaningless to humans but confidently

---

[7] For further discussion of this possibility, see Firestone (2020).

classified by DNNs—were found to be more resistant to such general countermeasures (Nguyen, Yosinski, and Clune 2015). Subsequent research has found that these (and other) adversarial examples exhibit many counterintuitive properties: they can transfer with the same adversarial labels to other DNNs with different architectures and training sets; they are difficult to distinguish from real exemplars using preprocessing methods; and they can be created without "god's-eye" access to model parameters or training data. Rather than being an easily overcome quirk of particular models or training sets, they appear to highlight a core characteristic—namely, sensitivity to some features not fully available to human perception—of current DNN methods.

Much of the interest in adversarial examples in both security applications and in cognitive science derives from the assumption that humans do not see them as DNNs do. For practical applications, this entails that hackers and other malicious agents using adversarial examples can fool automated vision systems—for example, by placing a decal on a stop sign that caused an automated vehicle to classify it as a speed limit sign (Eykholt et al. 2018)—and human observers might not know that anything is awry until it is too late. For the purposes of cognitive modeling, however, this might also show that despite categorizing naturally occurring images as well or better than human adults, DNNs do not really acquire the same kind of category knowledge that humans do—perhaps instead building "a Potemkin village that works well on naturally occurring data, but is exposed as fake when one visits points in [data] space that do not have a high probability" (Goodfellow et al. 2014). Achieving full robustness to adversarial attack remains a central and unsolved problem in the field. Nevertheless, whether adversarial examples reveal a fundamental dissimilarity between DNN and human perception turns on some methodological principles we have not yet reviewed, so we will return to the topic shortly in this and later chapters. In particular, it turns on how to determine the "right" answer for these perplexing and unnatural stimuli. Uncertainty with respect to standards with which adversarial examples should be classified is already somewhat obvious in the "rubbish" images, which by definition have no canonically correct label—but I will later suggest that the tension is even present in the perturbed images like the panda-gibbon.

2.3.4. Reward hacking

In addition to questioning whether DNNs see the world the way we do, we might wonder whether DNN-based systems construe the "solution" to problems in an entirely different way. Many of the most impressive achievements by DNNs highlighted earlier were produced by reinforcement learning methods (for an overview of this area, see Sutton and Barto [2018]), which was originally proposed on analogy to reward-based learning in humans and animals. This method trains networks using a reward signal which is designed by the network's programmers and tells the network whether it succeeded or failed on its last decision. Many of the high-profile achievements of DNNs involved games like Go, chess, or Starcraft II, precisely because game score provides an easily quantifiable reward signal. In other domains, creating an effective reward signal is more difficult.

In artificial locomotion studies, for example, many developers reward an agent for simply moving forward in an artificial environment, perhaps with minimal energy expenditure by its digital avatar. One deep reinforcement model trained in the "Half-Cheetah" testbed environment—in which models learn to move an idealized, two-dimensional cheetah avatar forward by manipulating several points of freedom in its two legs—learned that it could locomote the cheetah by falling forward and then flailing the legs in the air so as to flop the avatar forward on its back (Irpan 2018). Another widely shared blog post written by a research group at OpenAI recounts how their DNN learned to play a boat racing Atari game, Coast Runners, by endlessly turning the boat in tight, off-course circles without ever completing the race, because doing so allowed it to continually collect replenishing "turbo" bonus widgets which provided a rapid, never-ending boost to its game score (Amodei and Clark 2016). Critics worry that these examples show that the models lack the "common sense" that humans would bring to bear on these tasks, and that the solutions DNNs learn are brittle "reward hacks" that optimize the reinforcement signal without any real understanding of the problems the DNN is trained to solve. While this concern is legitimate, a more nuanced review of reinforcement learning methods in light of DoGMA, to which I turn in the chapters that follow, points to strategies for making methods more powerful and human-like by adding emotional and social valuation signals.

2.3.5. Poor transfer learning

Another important dissimilarity between many deep learning models and human cognition concerns the ability to transfer solutions learned in the context of one problem to another. The strategies learned by DNNs often do not generalize well to tasks with even slightly different characteristics from those on which the DNN was trained. For example, in the Atari game Breakout, DNN-based systems can learn to play more effectively than humans, often by adopting the kinds of strategies humans favor, such as digging a "tunnel" through blocks so that the game's ball will bounce rapidly between the ceiling and the top row of blocks to maximize points (Mnih et al. 2015). However, the gameplay of such DNNs is often not robust in the face of changes to the game environment thought by humans to be trivial (Fig. 2.5). For example, when a paddle's location was raised by a small amount along the screen's y-axis, or when multiple balls were released at once ("juggling"), one kind of otherwise successful DNN-based system was now unable to play the game well and had to be retrained from scratch (Kansky et al. 2017). Human players, by contrast, are thought to adapt their strategies more quickly to these small nuisance changes. This kind of transfer failure suggests that the strategies learned by DNNs require an unrealistic amount of stability in the environment, and that a different paradigm is required to make systems which are robust the levels of environmental flexibility characteristic of real intelligence.

The exact scope of this transfer failure is a delicate point that we will return to repeatedly throughout the book. It is delicate for two reasons: (1) because these systems are often only intended to model an aspect of human cognition, and other aspects may be involved in a human subject's superior transfer ability, especially the significant background experience humans have had with many other similar physical reasoning problems that are not in the DNN's training set; and (2) because the nature of transfer required to match human performance is often insufficiently specified. Frankly, many DNNs do

Figure 2.5 Standard Breakout (left) versus a perturbation (right) in which the paddle has been moved up the y-axis. Experienced human players can quickly accommodate this change, but some deep neural networks trained by reinforcement learning require extensive retraining to play the variation successfully.

exhibit surprisingly poor transfer to trivial task variants, but some degree of generalization to novel cases is assessed in nearly every experiment in machine learning. The standard assessment method is cross-validation, wherein a single data set is repeatedly divided into a training and test portion, and the system learns from the training set but its performance is assessed on a held-out test set (Fig. 2.6). Since the data points in the training and test sets are not identical, the accuracy gains reported in the deep learning literature reflect some degree—a previously unachievable degree, for most problems—of successful generalization. It is often claimed, however, that a DNN's solutions only transfer reliably to independent and identically distributed (i.i.d.) data—that is, data which share the same basic statistical structure but which are sampled in an unbiased manner from that distribution—but not to out-of-distribution (o.o.d.) data. Several of the weak spots we have already discussed—such as adversarial examples and the Breakout variants—can be described instances of o.o.d. data to which human strategies are presumed to transfer effortlessly. Such

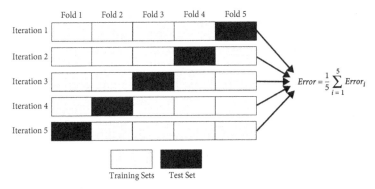

Figure 2.6 A picture of the k-folds method of cross-validation—one of the simplest and most commonly used methods, though many others are possible. The data are broken up into x number of bins ("folds"'—in this figure, $x = 5$), and the model is trained x times on $x - 1$ folds, with the last fold held out of training and used as a test set to assess the trained model's accuracy. The model's cross-validation accuracy is the average of its error rate on the x different runs. Because the folds do not have identical distributions, some amount of generalization is assessed in every machine learning paper which reports cross-validation scores.

weaknesses imply that that DNNs do not acquire from their experience the same kinds of transferrable representations of their environments that humans do, and that they likely require more innate machinery in order to do so (Marcus 2018b). This problem, however, can be treated as an open empirical challenge: what further aspects of human cognition must be added to enable better transfer? If more human-like transfer can be achieved with the addition of more domain-general components or more human-like background training experience, then the tenets of origin empiricism remain secure.

2.3.6. Compositionality and systematicity

One of the biggest potential dissimilarities that has served as a flashpoint in earlier rounds of nativist-empiricist debates over the implications of ANNs concerns the question of whether neural networks could exhibit the compositionality and systematicity which is characteristic of human thought (Fodor and Pylyshyn 1988; Smolensky 1988). At issue is whether a DNN can produce a potentially infinite number of novel and coherent thoughts on the basis of a finite number of mental representations. If one can think that the cat is on the mat, one should be able to think that the mat is on the cat, or there is a mat on the mat on the cat; and if we add in components like logical connectives, prepositions, and clauses, we can build a potentially infinite number of more complex thoughts on top of those ("the blue cat is on the red mat, and the red cat is on the blue mat . . ."). This combinatorial structure has long been considered essential to explain the special power of human thought to extend to a potentially infinite diversity of subject matters when exposed to only a finite amount of experience.

Classicists argued that only rule-and-symbol-based architectures could explain the systematicity of human thought, and so network-based architectures could not do so—or could do so only by implementing a classical architecture (Fodor and Pylyshyn 1988). Some network theorists developed elaborate technical means to implement systematicity in neural networks while still insisting that the representations they learned were distinctively nonclassical (Smolensky 1987, 1990; Smolensky et al. 2022). A great deal of ink was spilt debating these claims in the 1990s, and the discussion quickly became both philosophically and mathematically complex. In particular, several different notions of compositionality were distinguished— "weak" compositionality, "strong" compositionality, "functional" compositionality, and more (Aizawa 2003; Cummins 1996; Smolensky 1987; Van Gelder 1990)—with some straightforwardly being implemented by neural networks, and others being less straightforwardly available to them. These debates were often criticized for being insufficiently guided by the actual empirical evidence for systematic generalization (or lack thereof) in humans and animals (Bermúdez 2003; Johnson 2004).

These concerns about compositionality have been revived as criticisms of DNNs by neo-classicists such as Marcus (2018a), and new rebuttals have been offered by deep learning researchers who emphasize new data sets, architectures, and benchmarks of systematicity with more fidelity to empirical studies on humans (Hill et al. 2020;

Lake 2019; Lake and Baroni 2018; Lake, Linzen, and Baroni 2019). The DoGMA aspires to demonstrate how domain-general transformational methods, especially those deployed in "generative" neural networks, can recombine information extracted from training data in flexible and novel ways that can account for important forms of humanlike systematicity and compositionality, especially by implementing roles attributed to faculties like imagination and attention. We will return to these concerns to review the generative and linguistic model architectures that specialize in producing systematic generalization.

2.3.7. Causal understanding

One of the biggest questions about dissimilarities between DNNs and humans is whether DNNs can effectively distinguish causal relationships from mere correlations and deploy causal knowledge in appropriate inferences. The ability to distinguish correlation from causation is relevant to a wide variety of domains, including several already discussed. It has implications in perception, predicting the results of interventions, explanation, counterfactual thinking, and transfer to alternative domains (Danks 2009). Judea Pearl, in particular, has emphasized the centrality of causal inference to human cognition and pressed the insufficiency of current machine learning techniques to draw correct causal inferences (Pearl 2009, 2019). While DNNs excel at extracting predictive patterns in complex data, they may fail at deploying knowledge of these patterns correctly when they attempt to intervene on the world. A DNN will pick up on a correlation between the rooster crowing and the sun rising, but without a causal model of that relationship, a DNN-based robot may try to make the sun rise by goosing the rooster until he crows. The same goes for transfer learning, such as when the geometry of a game is altered, such as in the Breakout variation scenarios discussed earlier. If the system understands causal relationships, it may be able to flexibly adapt its strategies to the changing circumstances; if not, it may simply try to repeat the same movements that worked before the alteration, as if by superstition (Dubey et al. 2018; Kansky et al. 2017). Such misunderstandings are less problematic in the barnyard or arcade than they are in a context of medical care or corporate hiring, the sorts of decision scenarios emphasized by causal theorists like Pearl.

Whether current or future DNN architectures can successfully distinguish correlation from causation remains an open empirical question (Battaglia et al. 2018; Lake 2014; Russin et al. 2019), one which will hopefully receive more attention in future research. The ability to learn and reason about causal relationships in particular has been considered a distinguishing feature of human cognition and a key goal for more human-like AI (Hespos and VanMarle 2012; Penn and Povinelli 2007a). Granted, most neural networks are not trained to diagnose causal relationships, and many humans routinely confuse correlation with causation (Lassiter et al. 2002). When neural networks are trained to diagnose causal relationships, they have shown some successes, especially generative architectures like variational autoencoders (Kusner, Paige, and Hernández-Lobato 2017; Zhang et al. 2019), transformers (Ke et al. 2022), and models which use deep reinforcement learning (Zhu, Ng, and Chen 2019). How to best model causal understanding in a DNN-based system remains perhaps the most important unsolved problem in the field and the one most likely to require a substantially new kind of structure in standard DNN architectures to overcome. This objection deserves its own book-length treatment, but we will comment on it as appropriate in later chapters.

2.4. Can we (fairly) measure success? Artificial intelligence versus artificial rationality

Do the concerns just expressed demonstrate that deep learning has stalled out, and an alternative approach must be adopted to make further progress in modeling rational cognition? Or do they rather indicate that deep learning is progressing in a healthy manner with much progress left to be achieved by continued domain-general innovations which are consistent with the DoGMA? The standard metrics of success in machine learning research are silent on these questions. While further incremental gains on the standardized benchmarks might earn publications at prestigious machine learning conferences like NeurIPS or ICPR, shaving another 0.5 percent off the state-of-the-art error rate

on the ImageNet labeling task will not address the questions of qualitative dissimilarity. If we are to determine whether empiricist methods
are making progress in AI, we need some more conceptually grounded
and qualitatively rich way to gauge success.

We could, for example, focus on the kinds of rational decision-
making that can be modeled in neural networks without the use
of innate ideas. However, this move may only inspire another question: if the subject matter discussed in this book is called "Artificial
Intelligence," then why focus on "rationality" here, rather than "intelligence?" The simple answer is that we should not read too much
into the discipline's name because the terminology is likely something
of a historical accident.[8] Although Turing is often lauded as the "fa-
ther of Artificial Intelligence," the word "intelligence" is confined to
the title of his foundational 1950 article "Computing Machinery and
Intelligence." It occurs nowhere in the main text. In fact, in his first sentence, Turing proposes that rather than pursuing the question whether
computers can "think"—which he quickly discards as "too meaningless to deserve discussion"—we should instead redefine the question in
terms of his famous Turing test, which focuses instead on a machine's
ability to imitate human behavior. It is possible that much of the stark
disagreement in the literature as to whether human-level AI is imminent or elusive is due to a proliferation of definitions for the word
"intelligence"—for which Legg and Hutter catalogued over seventy
(2007)—and corresponding disagreements over how best to quantify and compare the intelligence of different kinds of agents (Chollet
2019; Hernández-Orallo et al. 2017). For the purposes of evaluating
deep learning's case for moderate empiricism, we may want to review
and reassess the foundations of this comparative dispute to avoid the
sort of terminological stipulation that Miracchi cautioned against in
the last chapter.

Methods to assess intelligence in AI can be organized around two
different approaches, which I call the quantitative and qualitative.
Quantitative approaches measure AI through scores on carefully
calibrated test batteries, on the assumption that natural and artificial

---

[8] The lasting influence of the label may be due to the title of a famous summer research proposal at Dartmouth in 1955 by several AI pioneers (McCarthy et al. 2006).

intelligences can be systematically placed with respect to one another on a numerical scale. On this approach, AI will have produced "human-level" intelligence when it overcomes the range of most or all human intelligence scores on this distribution. This approach is inspired by the discipline of human psychometrics, which treats intelligence as a largely fixed and quantifiable variable characterizing the mental ability of individual humans. Unsurprisingly, there are many reasons to be skeptical about treating intelligence as a fixed, innate, heritable, or precisely quantifiable variable, even when considering only humans (Block 1995; Shalizi 2007). The history of psychometrics in Western society is troubling, given that IQ scores have been used to justify un-supported and racially motivated beliefs about intrinsic differences between demographic groups or cultures (Glymour 1997; Gould and Gold 1996; Winston 2020). Popular psychometric tests tend to favor subjects from historically privileged demographic backgrounds, per-haps partly as a result of the way these tests are created and calibrated (Richardson 2002). Some progress has been made in adapting psycho-metric methods to assess artificial systems in the area of algorithmic information theory (Hernández-Orallo 2017); but nothing there has convincingly laid to rest foundational doubts about the reliability of the statistical methods that undergird human psychometrics, such as factor analysis. Until such doubts can be laid to rest, it is hard to rely on comparisons derived from artificial IQ tests as the yardstick of suc-cess in AI.

Qualitative approaches to intelligence, on the other hand, focus on particular kinds of knowledge or inferential tasks. For instance, a popular qualitative approach treats the possession of "common sense" as criterial of intelligence (Davis and Marcus 2015; Mitchell 2019; Shanahan et al. 2020a). We should worry here that "common sense" is often treated as a bit of a catchall term that is rarely defined. Further, when definitions are provided, they are frequently multifarious, equiv-ocal, and culturally specific. As a case in point, Davis defines "common sense" as:

> What a typical seven year old knows about the world, including fun-damental categories like time and space, and specific domains such as physical objects and substances; plants, animals, and other natural

entities; humans, their psychology, and their interactions; and society at large. (Davis 2017:652)

We should worry here that this body of knowledge will not even be
universal to humans, but rather exhibit individual variation and relativity to educational background and language (concerns that Davis
acknowledges "without embarrassment"). Moreover, proponents of
the common-sense-based approach to intelligence rarely consider
the comparative implications of the puzzling errors and systematic
irrationalities in everyday human judgments. These errors persist into
adulthood and are often difficult to eliminate with further education.
For example, undergraduates who have just done well in a theoretical
physics course at Harvard still commit a variety of (what should look
to rule-based rationalists like) basic blunders in common-sense physical reasoning when tested outside the classroom (Kaiser, Jonides, and
Alexander 1986). Even researchers with graduate training in statistics famously commit elementary errors of statistical reasoning, like
ignoring base rates and violating the basic axioms of probability theory
when asked questions in low-stakes environments or in conditions of
uncertainty (Tversky and Kahneman 1974). These errors are easier to
explain as the result of heuristics and biases produced by statistical
learning systems rather than as failures of rule- and symbol-based
common-sense reasoning systems (Gilovich, Griffin, and Kahneman
2002).[9]

Ultimately, while quantitative and qualitative approaches to intelligence are still widely used in academia and industry to rank humans
for academic and professional purposes, they remain controversial
due to concerns over their experimental validity, their tendency to ex-
aggerate typical human prowess, and their vulnerability to charges of
cultural bias. For these reasons, I prefer to rely upon the concept of
rationality to assess progress in AI. This may seem a surprising choice
for a defense of empiricist methodology, given the concerns just voiced

---

[9] There have recently been some more promising qualitative approaches to intelligence which begin from the assumption that human performance is also prone to error,
and treat errors as diagnostic that the same process is shared in two different systems—
by looking for "signature limits" (Taylor et al. 2022) or comparing performance across a
large battery of diverse tasks (Hernández-Orallo et al. 2021).

about intelligence, as the rationality concept also has a checkered past in philosophy and psychology. However, I argue that focusing on rationality—specifically, a distinctively empiricist conception of rationality that may be easier to separate from such historical baggage—offers several benefits.

To compare, Poole, Mackworth, and Goebel also adopt a "rationality-first" strategy in their influential textbook on logic-based approaches to AI. They there define an intelligent agent as one that acts in ways "appropriate for its circumstances and its goal, [is] flexible to changing environments and changing goals, [learns] from experience, and [makes] appropriate choices given perceptual limitations and finite computations" (Poole, Mackworth, and Goebel 1998:1). The aim of their book becomes the attempt to outline the architecture of a logic-based "Representation and Reasoning System (RRS)" which reliably satisfies these properties. This goal defines a broad-based, practical, and efficiency-focused strategy to evaluate AI progress, one aimed at tasks more representative of everyday problem-solving than IQ tests. These criteria for rationality are not wedded to their symbolic models of reasoning, and we could as easily see how neural-network approaches fare on them as well.

To decide whether such a rationality-first approach is more promising than an intelligence-first strategy, let us review some of the rationality concept's historical baggage. To be sure, the concept of rationality has also been used to support, both explicitly and implicitly, a variety of sexist and ethnocentrist beliefs. In her groundbreaking book *The Man of Reason*, Genevieve Lloyd (1993) documented the ways in which the Western philosophical canon has long operated with a gendered concept of rationality. She cites numerous sources where rationality is said to require the suppression of emotion and imagination so that decisions can be made on the basis of "cold calculation." In general, rationality's foils—the more emotional, care-based, imaginative approaches to decision-making—were associated in this tradition with women, minorities, or non-Western cultures.[10] In surveying the

---

[10] This opposition between emotion and reason is not only avoided but even reversed in some other cultures; visions of AI in Japan, for example, have long emphasized emotional flexibility and engagement with humans (Katsuno and White 2023).

many misuses of "intelligence" and "rationality," we might despair over the prospects of finding any morally acceptable, historically grounded way to assess progress in current AI research.

Yet these "cold" portrayals are the result of optional rationalist assumptions, whereas empiricists have tended to favor a more emotional, attached, results-oriented conception of rationality. Hume devoted significant portions of his *Treatise on Human Nature* to "shew the fallacy" between the opposition of reason and emotion that he found in much rationalist philosophy, which praised the "eternity, invariableness, and divine origin" of reason while belittling the "blindness, unconstancy, and deceitfulness" of emotion (*T* III.III.iii). This opposition continues in many rationalist circles to this day. The "cold calculation" picture follows naturally from an alignment of classical, rule-based norms of rationality with logic-and-decision-theory-based approaches to AI. According to the classical rationalist view, a decision is rational if you arrived at it by correctly following the rules. This conception of inference is argument-like; reasoning is the process of reaching conclusions by taking some premises as true, and then deciding that a corresponding conclusion is true after syntactically fitting those premises and conclusion together in the schema of a formal rule, such as those provided by deductive logic (e.g., modus tollens) or decision theory (e.g., Bayes's theorem). However, this classical approach eschews reliable success as a measure of rationality. To return to the debate over justification mentioned in the previous chapter, it is an *internalist* criterion; one's decision processes can be internally rational even if they never produce any external goods like true beliefs or successful actions. The height of this tradition is perhaps found in Immanuel Kant, who based his moral theory on the idea that someone with a good will acts on the basis of universal rule-based considerations alone, such as respect for a moral law (his "Categorical Imperative").[11] It is a common theme in science fiction—from robots that go haywire when discovering an inconsistency in their preprogrammed rules of

---

[11] Kant held that respect for the moral law constituted its own particular kind of feeling or sentiment. Though Kant asserts that the rational appreciation of duty issuing from pure practical reason should be motivationally sufficient, the motivational significance of its affective component is a matter of interpretive disagreement (McCarty 1993; Reath 1989).

moral conduct, to androids failing badly in their ability to play poker because they are easily deceived by bluffing—that in messy, unpredictable, and deceptive environments, following the rules at all costs can easily lead to practical and ethical disaster.[12]

Some critics of cold approaches have argued that the empiricist approach to rationality avoids some of these concerns. For example, Anne Jacobson notes that influential empiricists, despite their other moral failings,[13] tended to have more promising views about rationality itself (Jacobson 2010). Together with other empiricists like Adam Smith and Sophie de Grouchy, Hume served as a central node in a "sentimentalist" tradition that put emotion, imagination, and particular attachments at the heart of rational decision-making. Instead of the Cartesian or Kantian ideal agent whose motivations are governed by the dictates of abstract moral rules alone, the sentimentalist tradition construes reason as a tool that serves the passions and sentiments. Annette Baier (1993), for example, convincingly argues that Hume and other empiricists substantially reformed the concept of demonstrative rationality that they initially borrowed from the rationalists, by redefining reason as a particular kind of reflectively and socially endorsed habit of association that effectively and consistently balances different passions and sentiments (a "habit that passes its own standard"). This approach is more compatible with the virtue- and care-based ethics recommended by some contemporary feminist scholars—and, we will later see, more straightforwardly compatible with the kinds of reinforcement-learning and context-sensitive modeling strategies recommended by the empiricist DoGMA.

Though these particular historical empiricists focused on sentiments which were salient in their Western cultures—especially sympathy and fairness—we could also explore sentiments highlighted in non-Western traditions, such as commiseration, shame, and respect in the Confucian tradition (Liu 2021). In both Eastern and Western traditions, sentimentalists tend to recommend the development

---

[12] It is even a theme of Kantian secondary literature; readers are at least urged, if being chased by a murderer, to reconsider hiding out at a Kantian's house (Korsgaard 1986).

[13] Examples of such moral failures include Locke's hypocritical support for slavery-trade policymaking of the colonial government of the Americas (Glausser 1990) or Hume's notoriously racist comparisons of different "national characters" (Garrett 2017).

of virtues that allow one to balance and calibrate one's passions in decision-making, and cultural differences in cultivated sentiments can favor different packages of virtues. Other traditions consequently provide us new avenues by which to explore intelligence and rationality in general, and in particular new visions for success when attempting to model moral and cooperative decision-making in artificial agents.

Without taking a position on defining "intelligence" in terms of rationality, then—after all, history provides plenty of examples of brilliant humans whose ability to act rationally outside their domain of expertise was shaky, at best—I organize my argument for the DoGMA around this empiricist, rationality-first approach to AI. Once we employ a deflationary, ecological, sentimentalist account of reasoning that emphasizes successful action in diverse environments and the satisfaction of emotional and social goals—what philosophers call an *externalist* approach—we have grasped a more useful yardstick for measuring progress in AI. Ultimately, the fault in the classical approach to AI lies not in its emphasis on rationality and reasoning, but rather in its use of a cold, rule-based calculus to structure and evaluate those inferences.[14]

We might now worry that in giving up the rules, we have lost any ability to decide whether a particular inference is appropriate without simply seeing whether it succeeds—which would not be helpful

---

[14] To provide more philosophical context for these debates, Locke in particular heaped derision on the rationalists of his day, the Scholastics who held that rationality required adherence to the forms of the Aristotelian syllogisms. Locke noted that rational inference precedes learning these formal rules, which are mastered only with effort. As Locke put it in the Essay:

God has not been so sparing to men to make them barely two-legged creatures, and left it to Aristotle to make them rational . . . Rather, he has given them . . . a native faculty to perceive the coherence or incoherence of its ideas, and can range them right, without any such perplexing repetitions. (*E* IV.xvii.4)

Empiricists usually twist the knife further here by noting that if all judgments must be fit to a rule in order to be rational, we have a vicious regress on our hands; for we would also need to find a rule that endorses our judgment that the previous inference fits a rule, and find a further rule which endorses that appraisal, and so on to infinity (Carroll 1895; Stroud 1979). "The rules" on this approach are instead viewed as a cultural technology that logicians and mathematicians develop to systematize rational patterns consistent with the reflectively endorsed but situation-specific similarities that we recognize in particular decision-making contexts, rather than (as the rationalists would have it) innate symbolic structures hardwired into our brains that cause us to reason in those ways (Lowe 1993).

for prospective decision-making evaluations. This problem can be avoided by adopting alternative norms of rationality that fit more naturally with empiricism and machine learning, specifically norms that are ecological rather than rule-based in nature. On this approach, inferences are ecologically rational if the features used to assess target category membership are highly valid in that context, where "validity" measures the conditional probability that a choice falls under the goal category given the cues assessed (Gigerenzer, Todd, and ABC Research Group 1999). For any given categorization problem, the goal needs to remain stable, but the question of whether the agent assessed the "right" features can and should adapt to context. The rational decision-maker must operate on the right cues and contextually appropriate environmental patterns in order to pass muster, and inferences must result in true beliefs and/or successful actions a good portion of the time.[15] From this perspective, the evaluative component of rationality concerns the "bet" that agents make about the informational structure of their environment, and the bet is justified if it achieves a good fit with environmental circumstance.

Crucially, this is not an all-or-nothing consequentialism, wherein an inference is ecologically rational any time it succeeds and irrational any time it fails. Inferences are ecologically rational only when they make an efficient use of prior evidence, given the structure of the agent's environment. These bets will typically be informed by a structured processing of statistical information over time; however, we must give up on the idea that one can be guaranteed to act rationally just by "following the rules" or even optimizing under constraints, as in the bounded rationality tradition. In fact, researchers working on ecological rationality have demonstrated that classical approaches prizing coherence norms like truth preservation or utility optimization are routinely outcompeted by frugal, affective, ecological strategies that

---

[15] How often must actions be successful for a bet to count as ecologically rational? This may depend on the value of benefits obtained from a win or costs obtained from various kinds of failure. For example, imagine a monkey trying to determine whether a particular noise indicates that a snake is about to attack it; the cost of a "false alarm" may be low (needlessly jumping higher into the trees), but the cost of an "incorrect rejection" may be high (death). The area of signal detection theory analyzes such tradeoffs, and deep learning theory would probably benefit from much closer inspection of its insights (Macmillan 2002; Spackman 1989).

are more economical in their collection of evidence, make decisions on the basis of contextual cues or emotional appraisal, and eschew the computational costs of endless optimization (Gigerenzer and Brighton 2009; Gigerenzer et al. 1999).[16] Thus, many of the "blunders" that humans, animals, and perhaps even AIs make in common-sense reasoning can be seen as ecologically rational in this sense (Hutchinson and Gigerenzer 2005).

This externalist, ecological approach to inference forms the core of the standard adopted here, because it avoids many of the criticisms of the rule-based approaches and can be more readily applied to the default validation methods used in machine learning. However, it will soon be found that without supplementation, it leaves much lacking that we expect of a fully rational agent. In particular, a fully rational agent does more than just make one-off decisions in particular situations; it also needs mechanisms to resolve conflicts across different sources of evidence and goals, in novel contexts, and involving complex interactions with different social agents. These forms of flexibility can be achieved by iteratively layering more and more faculty-inspired processing onto simpler DNN-based architectures. As new faculty modules are added, systems can bootstrap their own way to more flexible decision-making, greater degrees of reliability and ecological flexibility, and rational control. To posit other properties commonly attributed to rational agents, in an order that plausibly highlights when these layers of flexible control emerge in evolutionary and ontogenetic development, I propose the following Tiers of Rationality:

- *Tier 1: Flexible Coping.* Adaptively pursue stable goals across a variety of different contexts.
- *Tier 2: Learning and Abstraction.* Learn new ways to pursue a goal; discover abstract patterns that allow one to transfer solutions to novel contexts; correct strategies in response to evidence of error to avoid making the same mistakes in the future.

---

[16] The emphasis on frugality also suggests that many DNN-based systems may be wasteful in the amount of evidence they assess, providing fuel for the arguments of Cynthia Rudin that in most environments, once a DNN has proven that a solution is possible, it can often be replaced with a much simpler and more transparent decision procedure that considers only a small subset of that evidence (Rudin 2019).

- *Tier 3: Instrumental Decision-Making.* Choose one among multiple options on the basis of their suitability to a goal.
- *Tier 4: Experience Simulation.* Imagine the outcomes of actions before trying them out by trial and error, and choose on the basis of simulated experiences or actions.
- *Tier 5: Social Decision-Making.* Represent other agents as having distinct perspectives on the world; imagine oneself in their shoes; learn new representations and strategies from other agents; articulate the principles behind one's own policies, share them with others, and adhere to them more consistently in the future; and be sensitive to social norms governing practical cooperation with other agents.

These features, which are listed from "most essential" to rational decision-making to more "icing on the cake" type abilities, are perhaps not prerequisites for minimal rationality,[17] but they can make decision-making much more powerful, flexible, and efficient in ways that clearly enhance its reliable ecological validity.[18] Correspondingly, achievements that models make in tackling higher tiers on this list should be seen to bolster the empiricist position that human-like rational decision-making can be modeled in this particularist, ecologically motivated framework, rather than on the rational, rule-based alternative. This is why, in the chapters that follow, pains are taken

---

[17] For a related influential take on "minimal rationality," see Cherniak (1990).

[18] Some readers may wonder why consciousness is not mentioned on this list, as consciousness may be considered essential for rationality. One problem is that different theories of consciousness would suppose that consciousness emerges at different breakpoints on the tiers of rationality already discussed. Another complication is that some theorists take consciousness to be essentially nonphysical. For example, philosophers in the "phenomenal intentionality" movement may think that intentionality (or distinctively mental "aboutness") is required for rationality (in order to have any beliefs that could be rationally combined or goals that could be rationally pursued), and phenomenal consciousness is required for intentionality (Kriegel 2013; Mendelovici 2018). However, such theorists will typically grant that nonconscious agents could be functionally identical and thus behaviorally indistinguishable from genuinely conscious agents—"zombies" with respect to rationality or cognition, in other words (Smithies 2012)—which would probably give the AI researchers everything they ever wanted, anyway. As such, I will not discuss consciousness further in this book, resting content with the prospects of fostering the discovery of merely ersatz (but behaviorally indistinguishable) pseudo-rationality.

to show how DoGMA-inspired modeling can help accomplish these forms of control, allowing artificial DNN-based agents to ascend these tiers of rational decision-making.

2.5. Avoiding comparative biases: Lessons from comparative psychology for the science of machine behavior

Any attempt to gauge empirical progress toward establishing the DoGMA (or progress in AI more generally) faces a number of methodological challenges related to comparing the performance and processing of very different types of agents. Many of these challenges are predictable given the history of other comparative sciences; comparative psychology in particular has taught us that even appropriately educated, well-intentioned human researchers have a difficult time fairly evaluating the mental abilities of nonhuman agents. On the one hand, we are overly swayed by superficial similarities that nonhuman agents bear to humans. When we see a chimpanzee baring its teeth in a wide grin, most people conclude that it is highly amused. In fact, this is usually how chimpanzees signal that they are afraid—an expression primatologists recognize as a "fear grimace." On the other hand, we might be overly swayed by superficial dissimilarities, leading us to deny human-like mental abilities to nonhumans. For example, we might conclude that bats are not capable of creating a cognitive map of their hunting territory because they use echolocation rather than sight to navigate their environments. Both inferences would be too hasty—it should be the underlying mental competences that matter for psychological comparisons, and these are trickier to evaluate systematically because they can behaviorally manifest in ways that we might not immediately recognize.

Both kinds of error threaten our evaluations of artificial agents. For example, some roboticists focusing on human-robot interactions build machines that mimic convincing human facial expressions, but without any cognitive or emotional processing behind them (Berns and Hirth 2006; Kędzierski et al. 2013). Even knowing this, it is hard to avoid feeling infectious pleasure when such robots mimic a smile, or to avoid feeling alarm should they mimic an aggressive frown. This bias is known as "anthropomorphism," the tendency for humans to see human-like characteristics in nonhuman entities on the basis of insufficient evidence. This tendency is an extremely powerful psychological disposition in humans, evidenced by the Heider-Simmel animation—which I urge all readers to pause and watch now on the Internet if they have not seen it before (Heider and Simmel 1944). Despite being nothing but a series of geometric shapes moving in and around a rectangular figure, humans readily attribute to the animation a psychologically and emotionally rich narrative.

In attempting to control for these comparative biases, AI should take the lead from comparative psychology and cognitive ethology. These disciplines struggled with comparative bias since their origins in the work of Charles Darwin and C. Lloyd Morgan (Darwin 1871; Morgan 1903). Today, these disciplines possess extensive literatures concerning methodological principles designed to help scientists control for them. A prime example is Morgan's Canon, which states:

> In no case is an animal activity to be interpreted in terms of higher psychological processes if it can be fairly interpreted in terms of processes which stand lower in the scale of psychological evolution and development. (Morgan 1903:59)

A sizeable literature in comparative psychology explores the meaning of this canon and its proper application (Buckner 2017; Karin-D'Arcy 2005; Sober 1998). Fortunately, at this point the dangers of anthropomorphism in AI have been widely appreciated and understood (Proudfoot 2011; Złotowski et al. 2015). As deep learning produces ever more convincing simulacra of human behavior, we may yet need to be more diligent in guarding against anthropomorphism (Shevlin and Halina 2019)—perhaps even invoking a Morgan's Canon for robots, paired with a set of "lower" alternative hypotheses more appropriate to computational systems, such as lookup tables which contain responses in a series of static if-then structures (Block 1980)—but the danger here is already widely appreciated.

However, there are also a variety of less acknowledged anthropocentric biases which can thumb down the scales against nonhumans.

Anthropocentrism is the tendency to assume that only behaviors with the superficial trappings of human performance are valuable or intelligent. The dangers of anthropocentrism have been appreciated more recently in the last thirty years in work on animal cognition (Boesch 2010; Buckner 2013; Burghardt 2007; Staddon 1989; de Waal 2000), but researchers are only recently beginning to consider them in AI (for recent exceptions, see Buckner 2020a; Canaan et al. Unpublished; Firestone 2020; Funke et al. 2021; Zerilli et al. 2019). A specific form we will confront here is called "semantic" anthropocentrism. This is the tendency to define cognitive capacities in terms of the distinctive way that humans possess them—such as setting the criteria for cognitive mapping as the tracking of visual landmarks in a way that would unjustly disqualify echolocating bats. Semantic anthropocentrism is usually a mistake, but not always; in cases where traits really are uniquely human—as may be the case with semantically compositional language with recursive grammar (Berwick and Chomsky 2016; Fitch 2010)— semantic anthropocentrism may be unavoidable.

One form of anthropocentrism is guaranteed to be a mistake, however: the bias of "anthropofabulation" (Buckner 2013). Anthropofabulation combines semantic anthropocentrism with an exaggerated view of human cognitive performance. Anthropofabulation results from an empirically inaccurate picture of human cognitive processing derived from introspection and/or the historical baggage associated with the concept of rationality. Common sense in some cultural and philosophical traditions tells us that human thought processes are uniquely derived from a dispassionate processing of the situation, a direct introspective access to our actual beliefs and motivations, and independence from subtle environmental scaffolding, historical associations, or emotional reactions. A great deal of human social psychology and philosophy of psychology, however, casts this picture of human cognition into doubt (Carruthers 2011; Gilovich et al. 2002; Nisbett and Wilson 1977; Samuels, Stich, and Bishop 2002; Tversky and Kahneman 1974). As a result, comparative assessments which assume that the human side of the equation satisfies these unrealistic idealizations are likely to be misleading.

In comparative psychology, anthropofabulation has caused skeptics to compare human and animal performance in situations which are crucially disanalogous (i.e., humans are tested with conspecifics but chimpanzees with heterospecifics, humans tested in a known caregiver's lap while chimpanzees are tested with strangers behind Plexiglas, or humans are tested on culturally familiar stimuli while chimpanzees are tested on unfamiliar artificial stimuli (Boesch 2007). Anthropofabulation's rosy vision of human cognition causes us to assume implicitly that human performance could not possibly depend upon such environmental scaffolding, and this can lead us to overlook or downplay these disanalogies. Fortunately, comparative psychology has also begun to develop methodological correctives against anthropofabulation. Historical context is again here useful, as empiricists like Hume also struggled against the anthropofabulation they found in Descartes and Leibniz. Comparative psychologists have recently appealed to a principle that Hume called his "touchstone" (Baier 2010; Buckner 2013; de Waal 2000):

> When any hypothesis . . . is advanc'd to explain a mental operation, which is common to men and beasts, we must apply the same hypothesis to both; and as every true hypothesis will abide this trial, so I may venture to affirm, that no false one will ever be able to endure it. The common defect of those systems, which philosophers have employ'd to account for the actions of the mind, is, that they suppose such a subtility and refinement of thought, as not only exceeds the capacity of mere animals but even of children and the common people in our own species. (T 1.3.16.3/177)

This principle reminds us to apply the same level of skeptical rigor to both humans and nonhumans when comparing their mental abilities. Though this sounds like an obvious principle of fair play, we will see that DNN-human comparisons have often considered humans in more favorable conditions or assessed DNNs with penalties for mistakes or other factors that are equally present in an even-handed appraisal of human cognition. Many set benchmarks for human-like intelligence or rationality to standards that average human beings would not pass, or they repeatedly move the goalposts for the demonstration of some mental ability once machines have cleared it. Once the anthropofabulation in these critiques is exposed, they no longer clearly support the conclusion that deep learning systems and human brains are implementing fundamentally different kinds of processing—and, indeed, they might teach us hard lessons about our own cognition as well. In slogan form, I have noted that in many cases where we call DNNs black boxes, it may be better to describe them as unflattering mirrors, uncomfortably reflecting some of our own foibles that we might be reluctant to confront (Buckner 2020a).

One important example of a possible violation of principles of fair play involves the assumption that humans are not susceptible to adversarial examples or do not see them the way that DNNs do. This assumption has been frequently taken for granted but rarely investigated thoroughly. Some studies have purported to find that humans and other primates are susceptible to the same adversarial attack methods that work on DNNs, concluding that many representations in DNNs are already as robust as those in primate brains (Elsayed et al. 2018; Guo et al. 2022). Other studies have empirically assessed human's responses to the adversarial examples that are supposed to fool DNNs and found that humans can identify the "incorrect" labels preferred by the machines at rates well above chance (Dujmović, Malhotra, and Bowers 2020; Zhou and Firestone 2018). Empirical studies have also suggested that the features that cause DNNs to assign the "incorrect" labels to adversarial examples are real, useful features that are present in and predict category labels in real natural data sets, and so humans might use them if they could see them (Buckner 2020b; Engstrom et al. 2019; Ilyas et al. 2019). In short, we must ensure that when we are penalizing DNNs for their responses to unusual stimuli, that we have principled reasons for deciding which responses are correct and incorrect that are subjected to sufficient empirical scrutiny, on both the human and machine sides of the comparison.

To provide another quick example, let us reprise the nativist claim that contemporary DNNs lack "common sense." Common sense is purportedly displayed by humans when reasoning about physical and social situations, where it is assumed that humans generalize their judgments correctly and robustly to new situations, whereas AIs do not. The psychology of common-sense physics, however, has found that human judgment tends to adhere implicitly to incorrect physical theories, which cause even adult humans who have just completed a

Harvard physics course to make simple blunders (Kaiser et al. 1986; Kubricht, Holyoak, and Lu 2017; McCloskey, Caramazza, and Green 1980). For instance, subjects expect a ball traveling along a curved cylinder to acquire an "impetus force" which will keep it turning even once it leaves the end of the cylinder—when it actually travels straight upon leaving the tube (Fig. 2.7). Indeed, our very tendency toward anthropomorphism just discussed serves as another example of how

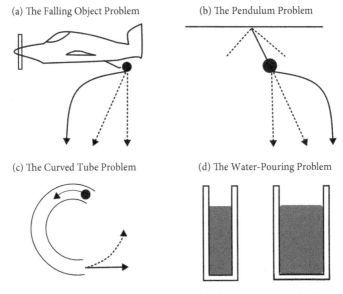

(a) The Falling Object Problem

(b) The Pendulum Problem

(c) The Curved Tube Problem

(d) The Water-Pouring Problem

Figure 2.7 Common mistakes committed by humans on simple physics problems. Correct answers are noted with solid lines, and common incorrect answers (which are usually explicable according to more statistical learning principles) are indicated with dotted lines. In problems (A)–(C), subjects are asked which direction the ball will travel next. In the water-pouring problem (D), subjects are asked which container will pour water first once tilted. Notably, Aronowitz and Lombrozo (2020) review evidence that humans may solve this problem using the faculty of imagination, and they speculate that this kind of imagination-based simulation may be a beneficial target for deep-neural-network–based modeling. Figures adapted from Kubricht et al. (2017).

human common sense reliably misfires, in this case in the domain of social cognition rather than physics.

Returning to the topic of common sense as criterial of intelligence can illustrate tensions between the way we define criteria for the possession of mental capacities and our ability to use those capacities to ground comparisons between human and nonhuman agents. The stubborn persistence of obvious mistakes in tutored adult human cognition poses a tricky theoretical dilemma to "intelligence-first" theorists when trying to establish criteria for human-level "common sense," whether about physics, social interactions, and other domains. On the one hand, we might be tempted to say that DNNs are disqualified from having common sense when they fail to generalize physical reasoning from a problem on which they were trained to a new context. On the other hand, humans make similarly perplexing blunders when transferring from familiar to unfamiliar, or from specific to abstract, as in the many violations of probability theory and logic illustrated by social psychologists like Kahneman and Tversky or Wason (Kahneman and Tversky 1996; Wason and Johnson-Laird 1972); in fact, the kinds of errors that state-of-the-art DNN-based language models make on these classic paradigms in the psychology of reasoning sometimes mirror those made by humans (Dasgupta et al. 2022).[19] Given the flaws of human reasoning, we could adapt the common-sense-first approach by designating impetus principles or human heuristics as criterial of intelligence, despite the fact that they are commonly known to lead to incorrect inferences. However, this route seems unjustifiably anthropocentric—we permit all and only the errors that humans make but no others, and might even penalize DNNs when they judge more accurately than humans. Yet if we permit some errors in all agents, we need to decide which correct inferences are criterial for intelligence and which mistakes are disqualifying, all without relying on an unjustifiably anthropocentric measuring stick.

To keep these tensions in mind, evaluations of AI agents here are peppered with comparisons to standard tests of mental faculties in

---

[19] Of course, the models may just inherit these heuristics and biases from humans (rather than from the limitations on human cognition such as memory and time constraints), given that human biases structured their training sets.

animals and empirically grounded assessments of human foibles. Comparisons to animals are useful because the methodological debates in animal cognition research are more mature, and because explicitly reflecting on the challenges in evaluating animal cognition can help AI researchers appreciate other perspectives in their own discipline's debates. AI researchers are beginning to note the utility of considering animal cognition directly when developing new metrics and testbed applications for evaluating AI—for it has often been observed that instead of aiming at human-level intelligence directly, it may be more useful to start with animal-level intelligence and build up from there (Dennett 1978; Webb 2009), and there have even been prominent calls to develop an ethology-like science of machine behavior (Rahwan et al. 2019). Most recently, researchers specializing in evaluation have begun importing benchmark tests from animal cognition and applying them to AI agents in a systematic fashion (Crosby, Beyret, and Halina 2019; Hernández-Orallo 2017; Shanahan et al. 2020b). Skeptical consideration of human cognition will be necessary to temper the confabulatory aspect of anthropofabulation when deciding which aspects of a faculty to regard as criterial of its possession. In particular, in any case where AIs are penalized for making a mistake, we must carefully and fairly use empirical methods to assess whether typical humans make the same kinds of mistakes when given the similar background training and tasks. As we will see in the course of this book, these basic principles of fair play are harder to follow in practice than they might initially seem.

2.6. Summary

To summarize the arguments of this chapter, it appears that deep learning has recently delivered a variety of breakthrough achievements in AI that rival human performance on a range or tasks, particularly on those requiring "intuitive" abstractions that have eluded previous waves of both empiricist and nativist modeling. Nevertheless, some important dissimilarities remain between the behavior of these systems and that of humans, and significant debate remains over the degree to which these dissimilarities should deflate the sense of rapid and astounding progress toward modeling key aspects of human cognition. Arbitrating this debate requires a clear and ecumenical yardstick by which to gauge success, but traditional metrics based on intelligence and rationality have methodological disadvantages and problematic historical baggage. The best way forward focuses on qualitative jumps in the sorts of control and flexibility that systems can exhibit when pursuing goals, where increasing Tiers of Rationality grant greater degrees of ecological rationality in informationally challenging environments. Though the assessment of progress along these Tiers remains plagued by the biases of anthropomorphism and anthropofabulation, comparative psychology can provide the nascent field of machine behavior with useful methodological principles to temper these biases. Keeping all these points in mind, we can now turn our attention toward understanding recent achievements in deep learning as steps along a path toward progress in AI guided by the DoGMA, in particular by looking at how specific models which implement roles attributed to various mental faculties by philosophers and psychologists can provide these qualitative gains in a system's ecological rationality.

3

Perception

The senses at first let in particular ideas, and furnish the
yet empty cabinet; and the mind by degrees growing familiar with some of them, they are lodged in the memory,
and names got to them. Afterwards, the mind, proceeding
further, abstracts them, and by degrees learns the use of
general names. In this manner the mind comes to be fur-
nished with ideas and language, the materials about which
to exercise its discursive faculty.

—Locke, *E* I.ii.15

3.1. The importance of perceptual abstraction in empiricist accounts of reasoning

Rationalists often consider reasoning their natural domain, arguing
that the lofty abstractions required for reasoning cannot be acquired through empiricist means. Rationalists tend to emphasize
the most abstract concepts which seem perceptually intractable, including mathematical concepts like PRIME NUMBER or CHILIAGON, or
syncategorematic logical concepts like AND and NOT. While it is easy to
say *that* human minds represent these abstractions, it is much harder
to say *how*. While rationalist psychologists might draw upon a credit
line from evolutionary theory (and rationalist robots from the manually encoded knowledge provided by their programmers), empiricists
aim to offer a better bargain by explaining how these abstractions
can be derived by the agents themselves using their abilities to abstract from a potentially unlimited range of sensory experience. The
standard bottleneck for expert systems approaches to artificial intelligence (AI) was always the cost of manually encoding all the agent's

From Deep Learning to Rational Machines. Cameron J. Buckner, Oxford University Press.
© Oxford University Press 2024. DOI: 10.1093/oso/9780197653302.003.0003

abstract knowledge. Give a robot a FISH or teach a robot to extract its own FISH, as the classic dilemma goes.

However, achievements in deep learning suggest that focusing with an empiricist lens on more perceptually tractable middleweight abstractions, like CHAIR or TRIANGLE, allows for a direct comparison between the mechanisms of human perceptual abstraction and the methods of category acquisition which have recently found success in deep learning. As importantly, emphasizing the mechanisms that allow for the extraction of such middleweight categories from experience allows us to adopt a principled stance on the aspects of human abstraction that may be usefully modeled by deep neural networks (DNNs), in particular by connecting current debates about deep learning to the most influential theories of abstraction from the history of empiricist philosophy.

Because these empiricist accounts of abstraction were developed to undermine support for classical rationalist accounts of reasoning, they aimed to explain how the combination of basic associative learning with domain-general faculties can allow us to extract abstractions from experience. Linking abstraction in DNNs to abstraction in empiricist philosophy thus suggests how current methods in deep learning can be extended or bootstrapped via domain-general faculties to reach even higher levels of abstraction. In particular, these empiricist accounts emphasize the ways that memory, imagination, and attention can channel and guide more basic forms of perceptual abstraction to the greater degrees of flexibility and control favored by rationalist accounts of reasoning. These comparisons suggest that a promising route to more human-like AI involves layering more faculty-like processing on these more basic forms of perceptual abstraction, as is recommended by the DoGMA.

Let us thus begin our ascent from the bottom up, beginning with the basic principles of associative learning. Empiricists typically explain reasoning in terms of the chaining of associations; sensory impressions are linked to one another and to actions via associative links (Clatterbuck 2016; Mandelbaum 2016). Any empiricist theory of mind—from Aristotle to Quine—thus usually begins with a basic set of domain-general associative learning principles. These principles determine which ideas will become associated with—and thereby linked in the transitions of thinking and decision-making—which others (Buckner 2017). The details have changed throughout the ages, but this basic set usually includes similarity, frequency, contiguity, and temporal precedence, as well as the motivating impetuses provided by pleasure and pain. These principles remain the foundation of associative learning theory in psychology today—finding expression in models of classical conditioning, instrumental conditioning, and configural learning (Pearce and Bouton 2001)—and have in turn inspired and been inspired by the artificial neural network (ANN) algorithms that served as the precursors for deep learning (Gluck and Myers 2001b; Pearce 2002; Squire 2004).

To get anywhere beyond these basic forms of associative learning, empiricist theory needs a mechanism that allows the mind to rise above the level of the most basic perceptual features; and for this reason, every prominent empiricist appeals at key moments to methods of abstraction. In the base cases, there is no trouble deriving a theory of simple behaviors from the simplest forms of association. As Ivan Pavlov discovered, if the sound of a bell is repeatedly paired with the delivery of food, then the mind will come to associate the two perceptions by frequency and contiguity, and the sound of the bell on its own will eventually call to mind the expectation of food. A surprising amount of complexity and flexibility can be added to this picture through the more arcane subtleties of associative learning theory, such as secondary reinforcement, value transfer, and higher-order conditioning (Buckner, 2017), but we will not explore these extensions in depth here. Though the basic principles of frequency, contiguity, and reinforcement remain potent drivers of even adult human behavior, much else in human cognition—with apologies to B. F. Skinner—operates according to more complex interactions among internal representations and active mental faculties. It is crucial to emphasize this disanalogy between more mainstream origin empiricism and Skinnerian behaviorism; while radical behaviorism forbade theorizing about internal, causally potent mental events, historical and contemporary empiricists allow researchers to theorize about a variety of interactions among abstract mental representations that are not directly observable (Smith 2000).

In short, the real payoff from cognition—and ideally, from successful machine learning—derives not merely from memorizing previously successful strategies and applying them rotely in identical circumstances, but rather from the ability to generalize strategies to contexts that are perceptually novel without having to first try out all the options by trial and error. Few people are impressed when a pigeon generalizes a pecking response associated with one red berry to another red berry; this is mere repetition. Neither are they so impressed if it generalizes from a red berry to an orange berry—this might be more useful, but it can be explained in terms of stimulus generalization, with red and orange light occupying similar frequencies in the visual spectrum. People do tend to be more impressed when pigeons learn to generalize a pecking response acquired from the work of one Impressionist painter like Monet to the works of other Impressionists with somewhat different technique, like Cezanne and Renoir, and to distinguish Impressionist works from those in a Cubist or traditional Japanese style—discriminations that some astute pigeons reared in Japan were reportedly able to master (Watanabe 2011).

The burden of explaining these more sophisticated associations on an empiricist framework falls mainly on the principle of similarity—though the similarities must be more sophisticated than mere aggregated stimulus generalizations. Humans commonly reason on the basis of categories like DOG, CHAIR, SANDWICH, COFFEE, SQUARE, MONEY, VACATION, and VIRTUE. If the principles of association are ever to take us so far, then we need some way to understand how diverse instances of such categories come to be viewed as mutually similar to one another. And if the perceived similarities are not themselves innate—which would violate our empiricist prohibition on innate domain-specific representational structure (not to mention expecting quite a lot from the aesthetic endowment of pigeons)—there must be some faculty that allows the relevant similarities to be apprehended and learned from the messy and unpredictable deliveries of experience. This faculty, I suggest, is perception.

Perception is in fact an ur-faculty and encompasses a variety of more basic sensory faculties, including sight, taste, touch, hearing, and smell (Fig. 3.1). Many of the historical empiricists also add "internal" senses as basic perception-like sources of ideas, such as

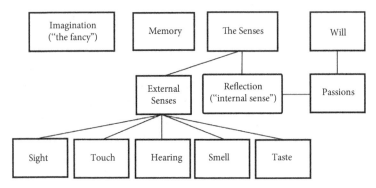

Figure 3.1 An abbreviated version of the Humean faculty architecture offered by Millican (2009), which provides a rather typical empiricist account of the faculties and their organization.

interoception (the perception of one's bodily state), the emotions (or "passions"), and affectively laden response profiles such as desire, aversion, fear, grief, and joy. Crucially, to perform this work assigned to it, empiricists consider perception to have powerful abilities to not only report low-level sensory input—such as the activity of a color-detecting cone cell in the eye, or the vibration of a particular frequency-tuned hair in the inner ear—but also to systematize these simple impressions into more abstract sensitivity to shapes, objects, scenes, words, or melodies, as well as thick, directed emotional states like love, hatred, and shame. For the empiricist's appeal to perception to succeed, however—and for the DoGMA's moderately empiricist approach to perception to advance the traditional debate—we must not simply assert that perception can perform this feat, but actually locate specific aspects of the human mind and/or brain's operations that are both consistent with the Transformation Principle and enable the systematization of simple percepts into high-level perceptions of abstract categories. To this end, the rest of this chapter explicates such methods of abstraction and shows how deep convolutional neural networks (DCNNs) implement difference-making aspects of the human brain that allow them to extract midlevel abstraction categories from high-dimensional sensory input.

3.2. Four approaches to abstraction from the historical empiricists

The moderate empiricist DoGMA defended in this book is a version of origin empiricism, but one that highlights roles played by active mental faculties—the eponymous Domain General Modules—to operate on the raw materials of sensory experience in the production of general representations. In particular, these faculties actively reshape the sense of similarity that governs category membership, thereby enabling more flexible generalizations in reasoning. Historical empiricists like Locke and Hume appeal liberally to such faculties in their theorizing, but they do not assume that the details of these operations are available to introspection, and they make little attempt to explain how they actually work. Hume several times even refers to the operation of the faculties as "magic," focusing his argumentative efforts on instead establishing their existence and crucial role in cognition. Rationalists over the centuries have complained, with some justification, about these lacunae at crucial points in empiricist arguments. This is one place where contemporary machine learning research can offer returns to empiricist philosophy of mind—by providing implementable network models that might help explain how such faculties operate in biological brains while adhering to empiricist constraints like the Transformation Principle. To make a start on this project, we begin with one of the most pivotal empiricist faculties, the faculty perhaps most central to the mind's ability to actively process and reshape the raw materials of experience into representations capturing deeper and more generalizable similarities: perception.

Perceptual abstraction is the most basic method by which the mind builds more general representations from less general ones. Informally, it allows us to distill sensory experiences of category members down to their "gist." We can get a start on understanding its operation by relating it to amount of specificity. As a test case, let us consider the difficulty of learning a midlevel abstract property such as *triangle*. This category is interesting because one might learn to recognize triangles by apprehending similarities shared among a set of exemplars, but the category may also play a role in more abstract reasoning, such as evaluating the triangle postulate (the sum of a triangles angles is 180

Figure 3.2 Triangle exemplars exhibiting mutually inconsistent features.

degrees) or the Pythagorean theorem (the sum of the squares of the two base sides is equal to the square of the hypotenuse). The least abstract representation of a triangle, we might suppose, is a holistic perception of a particular triangle exemplar, drawn, for example, on a piece of paper. This perception is specific in all respects: it has a specific size, a specific color, and a specific degree of illumination; its angles have a precise number of degrees; its sides have specific lengths (even if we could not articulate their precise magnitudes); and it has a specific location in the visual field. If we are to learn a more general idea of a triangle using empiricist mechanisms, the properties common to all triangles must somehow be extrapolated from a set of such specific exemplars with different values for these parameters (Fig. 3.2).

Locke illustrates the difficulty of acquiring a general concept of a triangle in a notorious passage of the *Essay*[1]:

---

[1] It might be debatable whether Locke is a justification empiricist, but he is definitely an origin empiricist (Odegard 1965).

The ideas first in the mind, it is evident, are those of particular things, from whence, by slow degrees, the understanding proceeds to some few general ones . . . For when we nicely reflect upon them, we shall find, that general ideas are fictions and contrivances of the mind, that carry difficulty with them, and do not so easily offer themselves, as we are apt to imagine. For example, does it not require some pains and skill to form the general idea of a triangle (which is yet none of the most abstract, comprehensive, and difficult), for it must be neither oblique, nor rectangle, neither equilateral, equicrural, nor scalenon; but all and none of these at once. In effect, it is something imperfect, that cannot exist; an idea wherein some parts of several different and inconsistent ideas are put together. (*E* IV.vii.9)

There are three things to note about this remarkable passage. First, it appears that Locke is violating the cardinal rule in philosophy against self-contradiction, which led this paragraph to become one of the most snarked about in the history of philosophy. How could a single idea be about a triangle that is both oblique and right-angled, or both equilateral and scalene? Fellow empiricist George Berkeley in particular pulled no punches in his criticism of this passage, opining that "if any man has the faculty of framing in his mind such an idea of a triangle . . . it is in vain to pretend to dispute him out of it," and "is it not a hard thing to imagine that a couple of children cannot prate together of their sugar-plums and rattles . . . till they have first tacked together numberless inconsistencies?" (Berkeley 1710, Introduction 13–14). The first difficulty potentially faced by a theory of abstraction is thus how to make sense of this kind of representation without falling into blatant contradiction.

Second, however, there is a remarkable fit between the challenge proposed in the paragraph and the basic problem of machine learning—for the goal of successful machine learning is to somehow learn general representations of categories from exposure to a finite number of exemplars that exhibit idiosyncratic manifestations of the category's central properties. This observation suggests that we might take Berkeley's objection as an engineering problem to be solved with technical ingenuity, rather than as evidence that Locke's theory of abstraction has gone off the rails. Locke's point is that the general idea of a triangle must somehow include and subsume these mutually inconsistent configurations. I harmonize these first two points by suggesting that Locke was here attempting to articulate a form of representation that was beyond the reach of the mathematical lexicon of his day, but which is entirely at home in modern machine learning discourse.

Third, in this canonical empiricist passage, we find further evidence that, contra nativists like Fodor and Marcus, paradigm empiricists theorize that the mind makes an active contribution to the extraction of general ideas from experience of particulars. These nativists seek to constrain empiricist theory to the rote copying of sensory impressions and the mechanical application of a few principles of association, whereas I argue that empiricists typically theorize about a broader range of active faculties that perform domain-general operations on mental representations. This passage (and surrounding discussion) offers no suggestion that the processes producing these representations are reducible to simple patterns of association or that they must be available to introspective phenomenology; indeed, it seems hard to imagine how they could be so available, given Berkeley's concerns about how picturing such a general representation would seem to involve incoherence. Many other parts of the *Essay* attempt to elucidate the mental processes that could carry us from particulars to the general ideas that subsume them—most notably, the numerous comments made about our powers of abstraction.

Unfortunately, Locke throughout the *Essay* canvasses several apparently distinct approaches to abstraction without very clearly relating them to one another. This created something of an interpretive conundrum for Locke scholars, and later thinkers often considered them alternative solutions to the problem of abstraction that could be pitted against one another as competing approaches—but recent achievements in deep learning suggest this is not the case. In fact, Locke's different approaches to abstraction are more interdependent than previously understood. Investigating three important approaches to abstraction offered by Locke, as well as a fourth approach offered by Hume, forms the empiricist basis for a division of labor among the different forms of abstraction that has been potentially realized by DCNNs. Before exploring their interrelations, let us review three approaches to abstraction that can be found in Locke, and then a fourth that has been influential in the accounts of abstraction offered by other empiricists like Hume. This philosophically oriented discussion should also be of interest to more computationally oriented readers, for, later in the chapter, I show how these different forms of abstraction may usefully illuminate the successes of contemporary DCNNs.

3.2.1. Abstraction-as-subtraction

Our first Lockean mechanism of abstraction is dubbed, following Christopher Gauker (2013), "abstraction-as-subtraction." According to its basic idea, the mind can create a more abstract representation from less abstract ones by simply subtracting out all the forms of specificity that vary among members of a category. If we notice that one triangle is scalene and another is right-angled, then we can subtract the exact number of degrees of angles from the general triangle representation and leave the number of degrees unspecified. If we notice that one triangle has sides of equal length and another has sides of unequal length, we can subtract out the exact length of the triangle's sides, and so on. In this way, the mind can "make nothing new, but only leave out of the complex idea . . . that which is peculiar to each, and retain that which is common to all" (*E* III.iii.7), thus keeping us from being distracted by the numerous ways in which particular triangles might differ from one another.

As Gauker notes, however, such a theory immediately raises some puzzles of its own. Specifically, how do we know which particulars to group together before subtracting, and how do we know how much to subtract when noticing discrepancies? For example, how do we know to exclude from the process a three-sided figure whose sides do not join at one point? And how do we avoid inadvertently sucking out all the relevant information about angles upon learning that their degrees may all differ? We might wonder whether enough is left for serious cognitive work after such deletions—for if we had removed all information about the degrees of particular angles, there would not seem to be enough left to prove general principles about triangles like the Triangle Postulate. As Gauker notes with some frustration, "how the mind forms such general Ideas [such as ANGLE at just the right level of abstraction] is precisely the question that the abstraction-as-subtraction theory is supposed to answer" (Gauker 2013:27). It is thus difficult to see how abstraction-as-subtraction could itself be a complete solution to the problem posed by Locke's triangles.

3.2.2. Abstraction-as-composition

A second and distinct approach to abstraction can be found in Book II of the *Essay*, which (again following Gauker) we here call "abstraction-as-composition." According to this approach, more abstract ideas are formed by joining together less abstract ones. For example, we might think it simpler to form a general idea of a triangle by fusing together the more specific ideas of THREE, ANGLE, and SIDE together in the right way, rather than discovering such commonalities by subtracting idiosyncrasies from messy exemplars. Many abstract ideas can be thought of as composed in this way—Locke in particular describes the idea of lead as being formed by combining "the simple Idea of a certain dull whitish colour, with certain degrees of Weight, Hardness, Ductility, and Fusibility" (II.xii.6, discussed in Gauker 2013:20). Any complex idea, we might suppose, could be formed in this manner.

As a complete theory of how we derive abstract representations from experience, however, abstraction-as-composition has obvious drawbacks, too. A major complication is that it seems to already presume a stock of more basic abstract ideas from which the more abstract ones can be formed, and some knowledge of how to join them together in the right way. Perhaps we think that the latter form of knowledge comes from explicit definitions, such as "a triangle is a figure with three sides and three angles." This approach, however, places even more pressure on ideas like THREE, ANGLE, and SIDE, for we would already need to possess these ideas to understand the definition. Recall that origin empiricists try to avoid populating the mind with innumerable innate ideas, but abstraction-as-composition seems to take a great many basic building blocks, themselves of a nontrivial degree of abstraction, for granted. If we consider the full learning problem as posed by a more recent empiricist like Quine—or as it confronts a DNN modeler today—it begins not with predigested input in terms of ANGLE and LINE but rather with raw, unprocessed "stimulation of [the] sensory receptors" by "certain patterns of irradiation in assorted frequencies" (1971:82–83). Again, we seem to be presupposing a prior abstractive faculty that allows us to extract these more basic representations from experience in order to get abstraction-as-composition off the ground.

3.2.3. Abstraction-as-representation

A third approach to abstraction can be found in Locke, and it is this third approach that was later preferred by Berkeley and Hume. Given the difficulties posed by the first two approaches to abstraction, Berkeley and Hume attempted to eschew the need for abstract ideas entirely by offering a more (what we would now call) exemplar-based approach to abstract reasoning—which Gauker (2013) explicates as "abstraction-as-representation."[2] As Hume puts the matter, "the image in the mind is always that of a particular object, 'tho the application of it in our reasoning be the same, as if it were universal." (*T* 1.1.7.6/20). On one way of developing this view, when we reason about abstract principles—say, the Pythagorean theorem—it is not that we reflect upon some abstract representation of triangularity which possesses no specific properties or inconsistent combinations of specific properties and use that representation to deduce the theorem. Rather, we consider a series of particular triangles (with their idiosyncratic sizes, angles, rotations, and so on) and variously take it stand in for the whole category. We then evaluate the truth of the general propositions by considering the relevant aspects of those specific exemplars (e.g., their triangularity or more specifically three-sidedness, but not their various sizes or the particular degrees of their

---

[2] Contemporary exemplar-based theories of categorization suppose that abstraction happens at the time of inference by assessing aggregate similarity to a set of particular exemplars which have been joined together in a group, perhaps because a shared category label has been applied to them. For contemporary exemplar-based models, see the work of Nosofsky (1992) and Kruschke (1992).

angles) and seeing whether the general proposition holds true of them on those grounds. A virtue of this view for the empiricist is that it reduces at least some forms of demonstrative reasoning to an appropriately structured series of perceptual discriminations performed over mental imagery.

While this account gets something right about the course of demonstrative reasoning, it creates further problems regarding its generalizability. For one, how can we be sure that we considered only aspects of the sample figures that were relevant to their triangularity? For another, how can we know that the set of exemplars we considered was broad enough to represent the distribution of features across the whole class? We must already possess some way of relating abstractions to exemplars to ensure that we have only considered their relevant properties; and we need some way to sample exemplars from abstract categories in a representative way to avoid mistaken assumptions about the category. We again face a kind of regress problem which presumes an earlier grasp of abstractions to ensure that these tasks are completed in a reliably successful manner.

Berkeley and Hume both thought that language plays an important role in answering these questions, but even the availability of explicit definitions for the abstract categories would not be panacea. To take an extreme example, for centuries everyone thought that the principles of Euclidean geometry, such as that two parallel lines never meet, were necessarily true by definition; it fell to Bernhard Riemann to conceive of consistent arrangement of parallel lines (in projective geometry) that could violate this assumption—laying the foundations for the mathematics of general relativity theory in the bargain.

Hume, who was aware of the difficulty of selecting appropriate exemplars, put the matter thusly:

> One would think the whole intellectual world of ideas was at once subjected to our view, and that we did nothing but pick out such as were most proper for our purpose. There may not, however, be any present, beside those very ideas, that are thus collected by a kind of magical faculty in the soul, which, tho' it be always most perfect in

the greatest geniuses . . . is however inexplicable by the utmost efforts of human understanding. (*T* 1.1.7.15/23–24)

Unfortunately, where most we need transparency, the lynchpin of this revised empiricist account of reasoning is again obscured in a haze of magic. Of course, we should not read Hume here as arguing that it is literally magic; he elsewhere takes a clear position against the possibility of miracles and in general hopes to foster a scientific approach to the mind which would explicate its operations as governed by general laws. This general orientation, however, might be thought to render this lacuna only more embarrassing for Hume. While we should agree with Berkeley and Hume that we cannot consciously form or reason about mental images with inconsistent properties—which is hopefully not what Locke meant, anyway—we might complain that their exemplar-based alternative has only pushed the mystery to another location.

Nativists perhaps rightly chide origin empiricists for appealing to such "magic" when pressed to explain how the mind operates with such general categories. Empiricists simply must have more to offer here if they hope to gain advantage over nativists when it comes to forms of cognition more complex than simple associative conditioning. Of course, the stakes here are greater than mere rhetorical advantage. The DoGMAtic empiricist today thinks not only that an explanation of these forms of abstraction which is consistent with the Transformation Principle is more likely to explain the aspects of brain structure that allows us to learn abstract categories, but also that the forms of knowledge so acquired will generalize more flexibly and adaptively to new domains than the hard-coded, domain-specific symbolic structures recommended by many nativists. In Chapter 5 we will see how the empiricist approach to such knowledge contains a great degree of "latent" information that can be flexibly repurposed for imaginative simulation of a potentially open-ended number of novel future scenarios, flexibility which has eluded symbolic approaches to cognition. For now, however, let us return to a fourth form of abstraction that can be found in Hume and other later empiricists, and which may be more relevant to the heights of abstraction for which the rationalist has been patiently waiting.

3.2.4. Abstraction-as-invariance

The fourth and final kind of abstraction—which empiricists have applied especially in their treatments of the most abstract arts like physics, logic, and mathematics—appeals to the idea of invariance. A property is invariant in this sense if it is unchanged under some systematic transformations of a space or domain. In physics, a search for invariance provides a method to reveal the laws of nature; for example, the law of conservation of angular momentum can be derived from the observation that momentum is invariant under rotation (i.e., the laws of physics do not depend upon the angle of a reference point).[3] In mathematics, the subdiscipline of topology studies properties which are unchanged under systematic spatial transformations, such as rotations (or more generally, continuous deformations called homeomorphisms). Logicians in the philosophy of mathematics also often seek to formally define logical abstractions as those that are preserved under all permutations of the domain—for example, Tarski proposed defining logical predicates and operations as those which remained unchanged under all permutations of objects in that domain (Tarski and Corcoran 1986). Abstraction-as-invariance might thus be thought especially important to reaching the heights of mathematical and logical abstractions which we set aside in the previous section.

An influential source of these ideas linking abstraction with invariance is Hume's *Treatise* (and also later the work of Cantor, Frege, and Boolos—[Antonelli 2010; Shapiro 2004]), where he speculated that mathematics is the most perfect science because a notion of cardinal number can be derived from a perfectly invariant one-to-one correspondence (bijection) between two sets:

> Algebra and arithmetic [are] the only sciences, in which we can carry
> on a chain of reasoning to any degree of intricacy, and yet preserve

---

[3] Emmy Noether generalized this idea in her first theorem (often called "Noether's theorem"), which holds that every differentiable symmetry in the action of a physical system has a corresponding conservation law (1971). This created a method in theoretical physics which relies on the discovery of invariances in the behavior of physical systems to derive new physical laws. Many conservation laws can be seen as derivable from Noether's theorem.

a perfect exactness and certainty. We are [possessed] of a precise standard, by which we can judge of the equality and proportion of numbers; and according as they correspond or not to that standard, we determine their relations, without any possibility of error. When two numbers are so combin'd, as that the one has always an unite answering to every unite of the other, we pronounce them equal. (*T* 1.3.1.5/71)

The proposal of the latter sentence—following its influential use by Frege in his own attempts to reduce mathematics to logic and set theory—has come to be called "Hume's Principle," and similar maneuvers have been deployed to define the notions of an abstract logical property and of abstract objects today (Fine 2002). Such modal notions of similarity have even been studied empirically as a source of logical inferences in cognitive psychology, potentially reaching even to logical connectives and argument forms (Vigo 2009, 2011).

This final form of abstraction seems quite unlike the others—it is less clear, for example, that humans actually work through any such proofs in acquiring the concept of NUMBER in the course of normal cognitive development. It may further be something more like a regulative ideal or justificatory procedure than the first three kinds of abstraction, for it appeals to a kind of limit of transformations—identity under all permutations, or invariance under all homeomorphisms—that human cognition could only approximate or demonstrate after training in formal proof techniques. As we will see, however, it is an important supplement to the other forms of abstraction in the present conversation, because it provides a procedure that can be used to approach the most abstract concepts that nativists have highlighted in their case for innate startup software.

To summarize the claims of this section, we are left with (at least) four qualitatively distinct forms of abstraction that have featured prominently in the views of the most influential empiricists: (1) abstraction-as-subtraction, (2) abstraction-as-composition, (3) abstraction-as-representation, and (4) abstraction-as-invariance (Fig. 3.3). Traditionally, many theorists treated these different approaches as unrelated in the best case, and as theoretical competitors in the worst. Flaws noted with one form of abstraction

(a) Abstraction-as-Subtraction

(b) Abstraction-as-Composition

(c) Abstraction-as-Representation

(d) Abstraction-as-Invariance

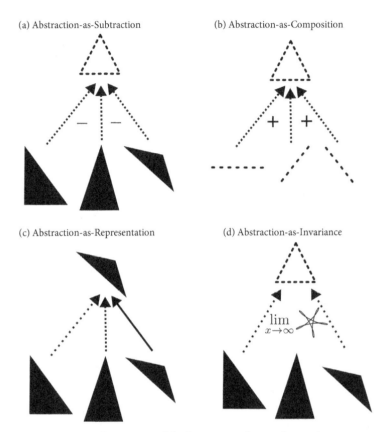

Figure 3.3 Visual summary of the four approaches to abstraction. Dashed lined figures indicate ideas which are abstract, and dotted arrows indicate processes of abstraction. Abstraction-as-subtraction (A) begins with specific impressions and subtracts the ways they differ to create a general idea. Abstraction-as-composition (B) begins with abstract parts and composes them into a new abstract whole. Abstraction-as-representation (C) selects one among a set of specific ideas to represent the whole class. Abstraction-as-invariance (D) derives an abstract idea from specific ideas by seeing which properties are conserved at the limit of a set of transformations (denoted with a spirograph).

were often thus taken as arguments for the others in internal debates among the empiricists themselves.

In the next section, we question this oppositional framework by reviewing the key components of deep convolutional neural networks, arguing that they provide a novel route out of this interpretive and argumentative morass. In particular, I show that these approaches to abstraction, while conceptually distinct, can be combined into a single division of labor that resolves much of the previous debate. Whereas previously we might have approached "abstraction" as naming an operation that should be defined in terms of necessary and sufficient conditions—thus putting pressure on origin empiricists to say what, conceptually, the four kinds of abstraction have in common, or rejecting some forms in favor of others—we can instead explicate a natural kind of generic mechanism that performs diverse operations attributed to all four forms of abstraction simultaneously. This approach to abstraction might be seen as more in line with recent model-based approaches to explanation in cognitive science (Boyd, 1999; Craver, 2007; Godfrey-Smith, 2006; Weiskopf, 2011) and might be seen to dissolve some of the disputes that vexed empiricist philosophers of previous centuries.

3.3. Transformational abstraction: Conceptual foundations

In this section, I propose a framework for understanding abstraction that bears some affinity to all four forms just discussed; and in the subsequent section, I show how DCNNs highlight the aspects of the mammalian brain that perform these forms of abstraction in a way that is consistent with the Transformation Principle, cashing out a significant promissory note for empiricism. To place this framework with respect to our earlier discussions, Fodor and other nativists construe empiricism (especially Hume's) as being limited merely to copying sensory impressions in the derivation of general category representations; transformational abstraction enables a broader range of "compounding, transporting, augmenting, or diminishing" these raw materials while still counting as a form of origin empiricism.

Though neither Locke nor Hume attempts to explain how these processes work, contemporary neuroscience and machine learning researchers have made significant advances in understanding how the brain performs object recognition, advances that can help us explain how the brain creates general category representations from sensory experience without appealing to magic.

A key idea of this research tradition is that the ways in which members of a category differ from one another are not so random or chaotic as we might have initially supposed upon first considering Locke's problem of learning general category representations. Indeed, far from being random noise, the sources of variation exhibit symmetries and patterns that can be exploited to reduce the difficulty of the task. Machine learning researchers call these systematic parameters "nuisance variables," which captures that the ways that exemplars of a common category differ from one another can often be parceled out into common forms that can be overcome with appropriate domain-general transformations (Table 3.1). Moreover, these sources are the same for many different types of discrimination problems, so developing countermeasures to control for them in one kind of discrimination problem can provide benefits for many others, even in different domains. Examples of nuisance parameters along

Table 3.1 Nuisance Variables for Visual and Auditory Sensory Modalities

Perceptual Task	Nuisance Parameters
Visual object recognition	Location in the visual field
	Scale
	Rotation in plane
	Rotation in depth
	Angle of orientation
	Occlusion
	Shading
	Color
Auditory word recognition (Stephenson et al. 2019)	Tone
	Pitch
	Duration
	Volume
	Accent

which triangles can differ include angle of rotation, size, position in the visual field, and color. Discrimination tasks in other perceptual modalities are also characterized by a high degree of nuisance variation; for example, to succeed at speech recognition, one must control for individual differences in the pitch, tone, and duration with which the same phoneme can be spoken by different people and in different dialects.

Progress might be made by recognizing that many of these nuisance variables are well-behaved in some mathematically convenient ways. In particular, they exhibit symmetries in spatial or temporal dimensions that can be manipulated to readjust exemplars' perceived similarity to one another. To return to Locke's motley assortment of triangles, for example, two triangles at different locations in the visual field could be rendered more similar to one another with spatial dislocations, by moving them closer to one another. Two that are identical except having their bases tilted at different angles of orientation could be rotated until their bases were parallel. A larger triangle could be shrunk until it was the same size as a smaller one, and so on. Such operations are known as affine transformations; in this case, they preserve certain key properties relevant to triangularity, like the number of lines and parallelism, while enabling us to control for a range of idiosyncrasies that are not essential to triangularity but can stymie categorization on the basis of subjective perceived similarity. Using such systematic transformations, any triangle could be converted into a figure that had the same combination of nuisance parameters as any other triangle without loss of any essential features. An agent that could learn the right series of systematic transformations to perform this feat would have a workable method to solve Locke's problem, at least to a significant degree.[4]

I call this solution to the problem of general category acquisition "transformational abstraction" (Buckner 2018a). To gain more precision, we can turn to a mathematical framework which construes category representations as manifolds in feature space (for development

---

[4] A complication here is that some common nuisances like occlusion or clutter lack such mathematical symmetries (e.g., a group-like structure) and so may require additional resources to overcome (Achille and Soatto 2018).

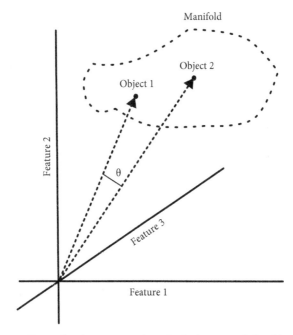

Figure 3.4 Example of two vectors in a similarity space defined by three features. The vectors are defined by the degree to which the two objects corresponding to them exhibit the three features under consideration. The similarity of these objects in this space is defined by a measure of the distance between them in this space, such as the cosine of the angle (θ) between them. A category can be represented as a manifold in this space, as indicated by the dotted enclosed region.

and critical examination, see P. M. Churchland 1989; Gärdenfors 2004; Gauker 2013). Feature space is a multidimensional coordinate system—with each dimension standing for a perceptually discriminable feature—that plots an agent's perceptual experience of each exemplar to a unique vector (Fig. 3.4). Each exemplar's vector is a directed arrow whose endpoint is determined by the degree to which it exhibits each feature in that similarity space. The distance between vectors in this space (as determined by a metric such as cosine similarity or Euclidean distance) is taken to mark the degree of perceived similarity between the different exemplars.[5] A "manifold" is a region of this vector space, which can be taken to mark the boundaries of a category representation.[6]

Conceived in this way, the problem facing perceptual categorization is that, as DiCarlo, Zocolan, and Rust put it, nuisance variation causes "the manifolds corresponding to different [abstract categories to] be 'tangled' together, like pieces of paper crumpled into a ball" (2012:417). The task of both the brain and artificial agents is to find a series of operations—systematic transformations of this space—that reliably "unfold" the papers corresponding to different categories so that they can be more easily discriminated. Another discovery of this literature is that the vectors do not need to be transformed until they are identical to be classified as members of the same category; the transformations only need to put enough space between different categories so that a discrimination boundary can be easily drawn between them. More specifically, agents must learn a series of transformations of perceptual similarity space that map the vectors for disparate triangles into nearby points in a transformed *triangle* manifold and ensure that this manifold marks a region that is separable from the manifolds corresponding to opposing categories like *square* or *rhombus* (DiCarlo and Cox 2007). This method both ensures a solution to the categorization problem in the face of nuisance variation, while preserving some of that nuisance information by mapping individual vectors to slightly different locations in the transformed manifold.

Like most of the processing of the visual cortices, the assumption is that these transformations and the manifolds they create are not available to conscious introspection. We should thus not assume—as anthropofabulation about introspection might lead us to believe—that the information they contain will be familiar or intuitively easy to understand. Nevertheless, we might obtain some metaphorical purchase

[5] There are many alternative ways that this vector distance could be computed in multidimensional space, and different methods may produce different verdicts on similarity. This poses a significant complication in this approach to similarity judgments, as the experimenter's choice of distance metric introduces an element of subjectivity to analyses.

[6] Gärdenfors (2004) adds a requirement that manifolds be convex regions of this space. I will not further discuss such requirements here.

on their organization by considering examples from the visual arts. Visual artists have long meditated on the difficulty in representing subjects from multiple perspectives and at higher levels of abstraction. Matisse's *The Back Series*, for example (Fig. 3.5), consists of four bas-relief sculptures of increasing levels of abstraction (discussed also in Patel, Nguyen, and Baraniuk 2016). From left to right, the sculptures provide an increasingly indefinite representation of a woman viewed from behind, gradually adjusting for idiosyncratic positioning of the limbs and hips. By the fourth sculpture, we have a representation which perhaps looks unlike any particular woman viewed from behind, but bears more aggregate similarity to the full range of different positions such a figure might occupy. This provides a visual example of the sort of transformed, pared-down, late-stage representation that has often been cited as the essence of abstraction in artistic and scientific creativity (Camp 2015; Chatterjee 2010).

In the history of art, one might find similar trends in the transition from Impressionism to proto-Cubism to analytical Cubism, which progressed through discoveries that increasingly abstract subjects can be represented with a series of swirling brushstrokes, geometric shapes viewed from inconsistent angles, and finally as a jumble of heterogeneous features in inconsistent poses. The most abstract representations are difficult to recognize as figures at all, and resemble no specific exemplar; yet they somehow capture the gist of a category, such as Picasso's portrait of a bullfighting fan (*l'Aficionado*) in 1912, which consists of a diverse assemblage of visual themes from bullfighting

Figure 3.5 Matisse's *The Back Series*, discussed also in Patel et al. (2016).

arrayed in roughly appropriate spatial locations (Fig. 3.6a–c). These sorts of images might be the closest we can come to visualizing the structure of abstract subpersonal category manifolds; and if we tried to describe them, we would end up with just the sort of verbal jumble that Berkeley would mock. Though it is at present merely speculation, perhaps these expert artists have, by experimenting with their aesthetic responses to diverse transformations, reverse-engineered the intermediate forms of abstract representation created by their subpersonal perceptual systems.

We now have a sturdier conceptual foundation to support Locke's troublesome triangle passage. Against Berkeley and Hume, Locke need not be interpreted as here suggesting that the general category representation of a triangle is an introspectible mental image with inconsistent properties. Rather, the general idea of a triangle might be something more subpersonal, like a transformed category manifold that, if it could be coherently imaged at all, would look more like the abstract art pieces just discussed. This is the sense in which the Lockean representation of *triangle* might involve both all and none of those variations; it controls for them by transforming idiosyncratic exemplars into an abstract representational format that adjusts

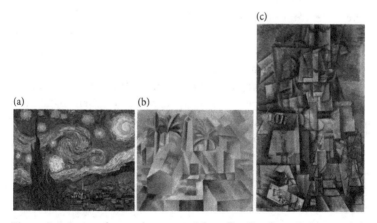

Figure 3.6 Series of artworks arranged from "less" to "more" abstract: (A) Van Gogh, *The Starry Night*, 1889; (B) Picasso, *Brick Factory at Tortosa*, 1909; and (C) Picasso, *L'Aficionado*, 1912.

for nuisance variations, locating exemplars of a common category as nearby points in a transformed manifold. This general manifold itself, however, encompasses a whole region of similarity space that—like Picasso's *L'Aficionado*—should not be interpreted as depicting a single coherent exemplar with some particular configuration of nuisance parameters. This analysis provides us with an alluring way to elaborate what Locke might have meant in saying that the general idea of a triangle is "something imperfect, that cannot exist . . . wherein some parts of several different and inconsistent ideas are put together." Locke was struggling to express a theory of abstraction that was beyond the reach of his day's philosophical and mathematical lexicon.

It is worth noting at the outset that we can distinguish two different approaches to transformational abstraction here, and this will be important given their differential potential for being later combined into novel composites. One we might call "implicit disentangling" and the other "explicit disentangling." In implicit disentangling, we merely discover a series of transformations that puts enough distance between the manifolds for categories which need to be discriminated, so that a classifier can draw a linear decision boundary between them. This is like brushing tangled hair until a comb can pass through and stopping there. The second, explicit approach to disentangling involves identifying the specific parameters of nuisance variation, factoring them out from one another, and representing them independently along different channels. This would be more like separating out strands of hair into small braids which could be flexibly recombined into many different hairstyles. Both approaches allow boundaries to be drawn between different category manifolds which need to be distinguished, but the more systematic approach to disentangling may have important benefits for flexible generalization and for the ability to reuse nuisance information in later, more creative tasks.

3.4. Deep convolutional neural networks: Basic features

To understand the aspects of our brains that allow us to perform transformational abstraction, and to relate transformational abstraction to the four processes of abstraction discussed earlier, let us turn to an analysis of our first deep learning neural network architecture: the Deep Convolutional Neural Network (DCNN). This architecture is perhaps most responsible for deep learning's marquee successes to date. Most notably, it is the architecture adopted in AlexNet, whose surprisingly strong performance in large part ignited the current boom in DNN research. DCNNs further featured as core components in AlphaGo and AlphaFold (which involved the discovery of patterns in amodal board positions), so its applications extend well beyond the domain of computer vision.

As an approach to modeling psychological processing, DCNNs can broadly be placed under the rubric of connectionism or neurocomputationalism; however, their characteristic structure crucially differs from the shallower ANNs that were ubiquitous during the 1980s and 1990s, and so may be more familiar to many readers. In the next section, I will argue that these differences allow DCNNs to model core aspects of abstraction in the mammalian brain. This argument hinges on three features which jointly differentiate DCNNs from other neural network architectures: depth, convolution, and downsampling.[7] Each of these features provides significant gains in computational efficiency and representational resource consumption when deployed on certain kinds of tasks, compared to networks that lack these features. In this section, we explore these three features that distinguish deep convolutional networks from their intellectual forebears and characterize the kinds of tasks on which they excel.

In hindsight, we can think of neural network research as progressing in three waves, with each successive wave leveraging more computational power and efficiency by adding more layers (and often more neuroanatomically inspired structure) to artificial neural networks. The first wave begins all the way back in the 1940s, with McCulloch and Pitts's (1943) foundational work that showed that a simple threshold model of neuron function could compute basic logical

---

[7] Soatto and Chiuso (2014) have argued that implicit or explicit regularization is a fourth crucially important feature in DCNN generalization performance (to prevent them from simply memorizing the mapping for every exemplar in the training set), but since there is significant diversity in regularization procedures and this idea is more preliminary, I do not discuss it further here.

operations. This approach was influentially extended by Rosenblatt (1958), who suggested that artificial neurons could be arranged in networks and trained to perform functions using learning rules inspired by neuroscientific discoveries (such as Donald Hebb's research on synaptic modification after learning). Rosenblatt thus arranged artificial neurons—called "perceptrons"—into networks with a single layer of learnable weights, which were intended to model synaptic connections. These links could be modified with positive or negative weights; when one perceptron "fired" in response to its inputs, it could transmit activation to its outputs along its links, with the activation magnitude modified by those links' weights. This was a promising approach which showed that simple units could learn to solve some perceptual discrimination problems using simple learning rules; but this first wave of enthusiasm for neural network research ebbed after Minsky and Papert (1969) proved that there were important nonlinear functions that perceptron networks could not learn but humans could easily master, such as exclusive-or (XOR), and Rosenblatt died in a boating accident in 1971. It had been known that XOR functions could be computed with additional layers of learnable weights between input and output (Rosenblatt 1958:404), but neural network researchers of the time did not have learning rules that could be effectively applied to train networks with more than two layers of learnable weights (Minsky and Papert 1969:232).

This changed in the late 1970s with the rise of the error backpropagation algorithm (independently discovered several times, but perhaps first by Werbos in 1974), which could be used to train multilayer networks by backpropagating a training signal iteratively across multiple layers. This discovery set off the second wave of ANN research by allowing researchers to train networks with more layers (usually only three or four) that could solve more difficult discrimination problems (such as XOR). To contrast them with the DCNNs we shall soon discuss, let us characterize second-wave networks in terms of two features: shallowness (only three to four layers) and uniformity (containing only one type of processing node, usually involving a sigmoidal activation function). The engineering success of these networks led to a surge of innovation in philosophy of mind and cognitive science. This surge introduced to contemporary discussion many ideas that were revolutionary by the standards of the more classical, rule-based methods they aimed to supplant: soft constraints, distributed representation, gradual learning, graceful degradation, and the importance of reproducing subjects' errors in learning, such as overgeneralization (for review and discussion, see Clark, 1989, and see Table 3.2). Today, the appeal of these properties is largely taken for granted by much of cognitive science—and they are all simply inherited by DCNNs. However, as with the more logic-based AI before it, the early promise of "shallow" connectionism gradually began to fizzle as the

Table 3.2 Properties Attributed to Second-Wave Networks Which Transfer to Contemporary Third-Wave Deep Learning

Property	Definition
Parallel processing	In contrast with GOFAI's emphasis on serial computation, connectionists emphasized the ability of artificial neural networks to process many different semantically significant inputs simultaneously (McClelland, Rumelhart, and Hinton 1986).
Graceful degradation	Instead of failing completely when critical resources are damaged, connectionist networks tend to fail gracefully when their nodes are damaged, like humans with partially conserved skills and representations after brain injury (McClelland, Rumelhart, and Hinton 1986).
Distributed representation	The vehicles of representations in connectionist networks are typically distributed over many nodes that overlap with one another when categories share features. This typically provides "free generalization" and other desirable properties as a byproduct of the way networks store information, compared to classical approaches which must compute such generalization explicitly (Elman 1992).
Gradual learning	Connectionist networks typically acquire solutions gradually like human children, often replicating human-like overgeneralization errors throughout the trajectory of learning (e.g., when conjugating verbs, transitioning from "goes," to the overgeneralization "goed" in the past tense, to the correct irregular "went"; Plunkett and Juola 1999).

limitations of such networks became apparent—especially concerning the problems of catastrophic interference and transfer learning when attempting to train networks to solve multiple tasks, problems we shall discuss at more length in the next section.[8]

It was long speculated that just as key shortcomings of perceptrons could be overcome by adding another layer of learnable weights, the addition of even more layers could allow these networks to perform better still. Such speculations were bolstered by the findings from neuroscience that visual processing in the ventral stream passes hierarchically through a series of cortical regions, beginning with the detection of less abstract features like contrast differences and boundaries, such as orientation and contrast in V1, to lines and borders in V2, angles and colors in V4, shapes in TEO/PIT (posterior inferotemporal), and finally figures and objects in TE/AIT (anterior inferotemporal). This basic story still holds up well today (see Khaligh-Razavi and Kriegeskorte 2014; Yamins and DiCarlo 2016; and Fig. 3.7a–d). Perhaps one problem, in other words, was that these "second-wave" networks were still not deep enough to replicate the kind of hierarchical processing characteristic of mammalian cortex.

In fact, a distinct tradition in network research in the 1970s—an alternative branch of the family tree that eventually produced DCNNs—had already demonstrated the computational payoff that could be achieved by deepening networks. This tradition was inspired by an anatomical discovery in cat visual cortex by Hubel and Wiesel (1962). Using single-cell recordings in early visual areas V1 and V2 in cats, they identified two different cell types, which they dubbed "simple" and "complex," based on their differential firing patterns. Whereas simple cells seemed to detect a low-level feature like an edge or grating in a particular orientation and position, complex cells took input from many simple cells and fired in response to the same features but with a greater degree of spatial invariance. Neuroscientists at the time speculated that many layers of these simple and complex cells might be found interspersed in the visual processing stream, and their

---

[8] In the interests of space, we move quickly over the history here; for more background and discussion, see Buckner and Garson (2018); Piccinini (2015); and Schmidhuber (2015).

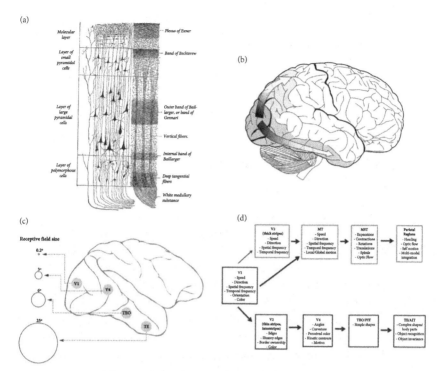

Figure 3.7 Images detailing laminar cortical structure and hierarchical processing flow in dorsal and ventral streams. Mammalian neocortex has a well-known six-layer laminar structure (A) and sensory information streaming in from visual and auditory sources proceeds through a processing cascade in early anterior sensory areas in V1 to late processing areas in TE/AIT (B). As it proceeds through the hierarchy, the receptive field size of the areas grows larger (C), processing larger and more configural features and focusing on increasingly abstract information (D). (Figure 3.7A is public domain from Gray [1918], 3.7B is available from Selket under a Creative Commons 3.0 Share-Alike License, 3.7C from Vidyasagar [2013] on a Creative Commons Attribution License, and Figure 3.7D from Perry and Fallah [2014] on a Creative Commons Attribution License.)

interplay might explain our own ability to recognize increasingly abstract features in diverse locations and poses.

In an attempt to capture the power of this neuroanatomical division of labor in an artificial model, Fukushima (1979) designed a new kind neural network called Neocognitron. Neocognitron was perhaps the first network that was truly "deep" (with four to ten layers, depending on how they are counted), but its most powerful innovation was the way it combined two different types of operation—linear convolutional filtering and nonlinear downsampling—in a single network. Though at some level of description these are both just mathematical operations in matrix algebra, it can be useful to conceptualize them as taking place in two different kinds of nodes, which are intended to recapitulate Hubel and Wiesel's distinction between simple and complex cells. Fukushima's "simple" nodes performed convolution (a type of linear algebra operation) to detect features at particular locations and in particular poses; and his "complex" nodes took input from many spatially nearby simple nodes, aggregating their activity to detect those features across small shifts in its location or pose. Several layers of paired convolution and subsampling were iterated hierarchically, such that processing gradually detected more and more abstract features across a wider range of visuospatial variance. Of course, there are many aspects of visual perception which Neocognitron and most subsequent DCNNs do not even attempt to model, such as recurrence and top-down control; most modelers who use generic DCNNs to model vision are careful to point out that they are only attempting to model the first 100 ms or so of visual perception, and additional structure would be required to model recurrent or top-down influences on processing (Bonnen, Yamins, and Wagner 2021; Nayebi et al. 2022). Nevertheless, with these innovations, Neocognitron was able to outperform the perceptron networks of the day on difficult perceptual discrimination tasks—such as handwritten digit recognition—by modeling the hierarchical processing cascade of mammalian neocortical processing streams.

Each of these operations bears elaboration, for the germ of DCNN's distinctive computational potential is already present in any network which combines them in this manner. Let us begin with convolution.

Perceptual input is typically passed to such a network in a grid-like structure—a two-dimensional grid for image processing tasks, or time slices of audio information for auditory processing tasks. For ease of exposition, let us focus on visual examples in what follows. The smallest unit of information in a visual grid is usually a pixel, which itself is typically a multidimensional vector of red, green, and blue color channel intensity detected at that location. Convolution can be performed on matrices to transform the vector values for a spatial chunk of pixels (usually a rectangle) in a way that enhances some values and diminishes others. In practice, the convolution operations that are useful for image recognition are those that tend to amplify the presence of a certain feature and minimize other information for a given chunk. These convolutional nodes are called "filters"; a useful convolution for a vertical-edge filter maximizes values corresponding to a vertical edge, while minimizing everything else. Each convolution operation is then typically passed to a rectified linear unit (ReLU)—this is sometimes called the "detector" stage of filtering—which activates using the rectification function if the output of convolution exceeds a certain threshold. In other words, the output from convolution is only passed up the processing hierarchy if the feature is detected at that location. The net effect of passing this vertical-edge filter across the whole image would be like passing a stencil of a vertical edge over a whole image and recording the degree to which the stencil is filled in by the image underneath, and then placing this information on a separate spatially organized map (called a "feature map"), which records the location of all the vertical edges.

Typically, however, the recognition of a general category requires more than merely recognizing vertical edges; we need to detect a wider diversity of presentations, such as edges in different orientations, and to assemble that wider range of presentations into useful composites like shapes or digits. The addition of Fukushima's "complex" units helps achieve this grander goal by taking input from many spatially nearby convolutional nodes below and using a downsampling technique. Neocognitron uses spatial averaging, but an operation called max-pooling is more common today; a max-pooling node activates if any one of their inputs individually crosses a certain activation threshold, after which it passes along only the information from the most activated unit. Using downsampling, we can now efficiently express the fact that an edge occurred approximately here in an approximate orientation, controlling for variation in its exact location and orientation. The net effect of globally multiplying the input by a variety of edge-detecting filters and combining their outputs using downsampling is like globally applying an edge-detecting filter in a digital photograph editing program; the result is a simplified image representation that reveals all the edges wherever located and however oriented (now an "aggregated feature map" for all edges), and "subtracts out" all other information (Fig. 3.8).

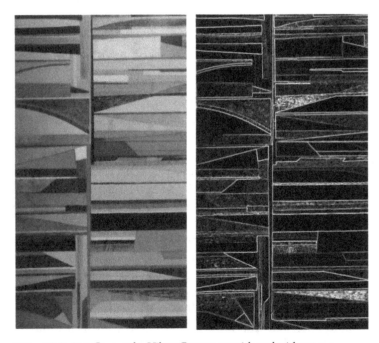

Figure 3.8 *21st Century* by Viktor Romanov, with and without a Sobel edge-detection filter, one popular convolutional edge-detection algorithm. (Operation performed by author in Gimp 2.0 Freeware image editing program. Image credit: Yugra News Publishing, Wikimedia Commons CC License.)

3.5. Transformational abstraction in DCNNs

As explained, the characteristic feature of DCNNs is that each "layer" typically implements several operations organized in a sequence—specifically convolution, rectification, and pooling. This sequence of operations is something of an "abstraction sandwich." The sandwiches are stacked in a deep hierarchy, making "double-decker," "triple-decker," to "n-decker" abstraction sandwiches that are more powerful still. Once the first sandwich has extracted somewhat abstract features from the raw input, another sandwich can be stacked atop it, focusing its computational resources on extracting even more abstract features from the last layer's already-transformed output. In principle, this process could be repeated indefinitely, with many sandwich layers iterated hierarchically, such that processing gradually detects more and more abstract features across an ever-broader range of input variance. The sandwiches unite the strengths of diverse operations in a computational division of labor, which, taken together, simultaneously perform forms of abstraction reviewed in the previous sections, at least to some degree.

As may now already be clear, the individual operations in these abstraction sandwiches can be mapped to the first two forms of abstraction described earlier. In short, the convolutional filters can be understood to perform a form of abstraction-as-composition, and the max-pooling downsamplers can be thought to perform a kind of abstraction-as-subtraction.[9] Combining these two operations creates a more powerful form of abstraction than either performed alone. Multiple inconsistent ways of composing a feature from a sandwich's less-abstract inputs can be explored by different filters at the same layer, and those multiple options can then be passed to a downsampler, which aggregates and subtracts out the forms of variation in a pooled feature map, before passing that map along for processing by the next layer of sandwiches in the hierarchy. For example, consider the task of digit recognition; several convolutional nodes could learn how to build a particular

---

[9] Notably, the highly successful attention-based transformer architecture does not typically use pooling. However, its key use of "attention" to iteratively focus on subsets of especially relevant input may be seen to achieve abstraction-as-subtraction through other means; we will revisit this issue Chapter 6, where we consider attention directly.

Transformationally Abstract Category Manifolds

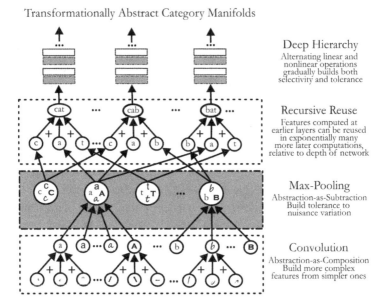

Deep Hierarchy
Alternating linear and
nonlinear operations
gradually builds both
selectivity and tolerance

Recursive Reuse
Features computed at
earlier layers can be reused
in exponentially many
more later computations,
relative to depth of network

Max-Pooling
Abstraction-as-Subtraction
Build tolerance to
nuisance variation

Convolution
Abstraction-as-Composition
Build more complex
features from simpler ones

Figure 3.9 A depiction of how a deep hierarchy of "abstraction sandwiches" alternating linear and nonlinear operations can compute transformed category manifolds that are robust to nuisance variation. (Figure adapted from a design by DiCarlo et al. 2012.)

letter (e.g., lowercase "a") in several different fonts by assembling line components in slightly different ways, and then a max-pooling node could aggregate across all the different ways of building the letter in different fonts. A subsequent layer could focus on the task of composing phonemes from letters, no longer having to dedicate resources to overcoming the nuisance variation between different fonts (Fig. 3.9). As this transformational process of abstraction is iterated throughout a deep hierarchy, the resulting transformed signals may even approach ideals of abstraction-as-invariance, as later layers will have explored more and more systematic transformations and controlled for the influence of nuisance parameters to even higher degrees.

Even better—and providing perhaps a twist on a simple construal of abstraction-as-subtraction—while these nuisance parameters might be seen to have been eliminated on one processing channel, other channels could be dedicated to detecting and systematically disentangling representations of nuisance parameters, so that we might directly represent an exemplar's location and angle of rotation, if needed (similar to the larger-scale representational division of labor between object and location information hypothesized to occur between ventral and dorsal stream processing—Goodale and Milner, 1992). The result is a form of processing that begins with a "blooming, buzzing confusion" of raw entangled signals and ends with a series of transformed, highly abstracted, dedicated information channels that can be mixed and matched at the output layer to craft answers flexibly to a wide variety of categorization and decision-making problems.[10]

Together, these operations combine in a division of labor that enables a powerful form of transformational abstraction. To summarize, DCNNs perform so well, relative to neural networks which lack these features, because during training, their weight parameters converge on the sequence of transformations that do the best job of solving the widest range of categorization and decision-making problems on which the network has been trained, by increasing the net distance in similarity space between the manifolds for categories that must be discriminated. This transformational ability explains how DCNNs can recognize the abstract similarities shared among exemplars in a category like chair or triangle—and remarkably, no innate representational primitives or explicit definitions are involved or required for them to do so. Moreover, the networks themselves discover the right series of transformations to perform; as Goodfellow et al. put it, "[pooling] over the outputs of separately parametrized convolutions [allows the network] to learn which transformations to become invariant to" (2016:337) for some range of categorization tasks. Insofar as those transformations and the intermediary features they reveal are useful for the recognition of other categories—the transformations useful for recognizing chairs may closely resemble those useful for recognizing other objects like tables or beds—the network will enjoy accelerated learning on those related categories as well, no magic required.

The success of DCNNs provides perhaps the strongest line of established empirical evidence in favor of the new empiricist DoGMA.

---

[10] The "blooming, buzzing confusion" is from an oft-quoted passage from William James (1890:488) describing the experience of a newborn baby. James's views will be considered in more detail in Chapter 6, when we deal with the faculty of attention.

First, these networks can be said to model some innate assumptions, though they are domain-general in character. Specifically, convolution, max-pooling, and the local connectivity between layers (until the final decision-making layer) can be seen to implement domain-general prior probability assumptions that dependencies among features tend to be local. This will hold whether that locality is spatial (e.g., reading one's facial expression does not depend upon the position of one's feet), temporal (the identity of a phoneme usually only depends on temporally nearby sounds), or in some yet more abstract conceptual space (such as a taxonomic or social hierarchy). It also enforces the assumption that feature identity is translation-invariant (e.g., a smile has the same meaning even if the smiler is reclining at an angle). In other words, DCNNs will be much more efficient than a fully connected network with a single type of activation function in solving discrimination problems in domains that satisfy these assumptions, because DCNNs will not waste time and representational resources exploring their alternatives. At the same time, DCNNs may be no more or even less efficient than a more traditional ANN architecture on solving problems that violate these assumptions. These innate architectural biases do not count as violating origin empiricism as it was defined earlier, however, because they are applied to all discrimination tasks irrespective of topic via domain-general transformations.

Second, the fact that at least two forms of abstraction reviewed in section 3.2 can be united in a single architecture is itself an interesting result and suggests an alternative philosophical perspective on the problem of abstraction. We no longer need to see the four forms of abstraction, which seemed distinct from an a priori perspective, as theoretical alternatives which must be pitted against one another in competition. In fact, we may now see how a single mechanism which bears some structural similarity to mammalian cortex implements all these operations simultaneously. We thus have good reason to believe that properties associated with each form of abstraction cluster together in (at least) the mammalian brain due to the operation of a common type of mechanism—which DiCarlo and coauthors have called the "linear-nonlinear decoder family" (or "LN decoder" for short) of mechanisms (DiCarlo and Cox 2007; DiCarlo et al. 2012; Yamins and DiCarlo 2016). This fits with more mechanism-based approaches to explanation that have become popular recently in philosophy of science (Bechtel 2008; Machamer, Darden, and Craver 2000; Piccinini and Craver 2011), and specifically with a "generic mechanism" approach to explanation in connectionist networks that has been elaborated by Stinson (2018) and was reviewed in Chapter 1. In short, DCNNs may be so efficient on these perceptual abstraction tasks precisely because they share several of the structural aspects that allow the brain to perform so efficiently on the same tasks, meeting the key explanatory goals for useful computational modeling of the mind that were set out in Chapter 1.

3.6. Challenges for DCNNs as models of transformational abstraction

Thus far, this chapter has presented a basic account of how significant forms of abstraction with substantial philosophical pedigree can be modeled in DCNNs. Specifically, the forms suggest that we have located important aspects of the brain that allow it to perform perceptual abstractions that have eluded previous generations of computational modeling and AI, and that these aspects are notably consistent with origin empiricism. But there are wrinkles in that story—in particular, forms of evidence that the methods of abstraction in DCNNs are unlike the forms of learning or representation that occur in human brains. Reviewing the evidence for these dissimilarities now prepares the way for modeling the other DoGMAtic faculties in later chapters. In fact, memory, imagination, and attention can also be seen as tools to make the search for and use of abstraction in AI models more rational according to the Tiers of Rationality introduced in Chapter 2.

3.6.1. Efficiency in the search for abstractions

Perhaps the most obvious dissimilarity between learning in many DNNs and in humans—that DNNs seem to require far more training instances than do human learners to achieve the same degree of accuracy in results—is directly relevant to the epistemological concerns raised with abstraction-as-subtraction, abstraction-as-composition, and abstraction-as-representation. In particular, how do we learn to generalize reliably from a limited sample? How do we know what to subtract out, or which features to compose, to build category representations that will allow us to draw the right inferences? For deep learning, the current answer to these questions is largely this: enormous amounts of trial and error during training. The answer threatens the argument that DCNNs illuminate critical aspects of perceptual abstraction in humans, because, while these networks might end up delivering the same verdicts as human judgment across many different situations, large disanalogies in efficiency call into question whether they reach these verdicts using the same processes that humans do. The concern about inefficiency also echoes the charge levied by earlier connectionists that Deep Blue's victory against Garry Kasparov reflected a triumph of brute force calculation rather than intelligence or rationality, so deep learning theorists today bear a special obligation to rebut these concerns in a convincing way if they want to avoid the embarrassment of falling prey to a standard empiricist critique of nativist GOFAI.

Efficiency concerns can be raised regarding the way strategies are learned and how they are applied at the time of inference. First, the (in) efficiencies of today's deep neural networks are a product of the fact that they are almost all trained using variants of the error backpropagation algorithm, which usually requires very large training sets in order to make very slight adjustments to the network on each trial. The algorithm has been the keystone of the successes of neural networks since 1980, but there are many concerns about its biological plausibility.[11] The method relies on an error function that computes, for each item

---

[11] There is an extensive debate about the biological plausibility of error backpropagation that we will not explore in depth here. One major concern regards the inability of neurons to send error signals backward across a synapse (Fitzsimonds, Song, and Poo 1997; Stork 1989). A number of connectionists in the previous wave suggested that there are simple replacements for backpropagation that were functionally equivalent but which did not require this anatomical implausibility (Hinton and McClelland 1988; O'Reilly 1996; Rogers and McClelland 2014). Most recently, deep learning researchers have renewed their enthusiasm for backpropagation by suggesting that it can be replaced with more biologically plausible alternatives, such as randomized error signals or spike-timing dependent plasticity mechanisms where needed (Lillicrap et al. 2016; Scellier and Bengio 2017). The debate on this point is complex and ongoing, and there are also dozens of alternative families of learning rules that have been proposed (contrastive learning is presently promising, though it suffers from some of the same efficiency concerns—Wu et al. 2018). These alternatives will not be explored at greater length here.

in the training set passed as input to the network, the distance between the activation value on the final layer of the network and the answer deemed "correct" in the training set. The algorithm then calculates the gradient (or slope) of this error function at that location and adjusts the link weights of the network by a small amount (modulated by the network's "learning rate") so that the network's performance takes a small "step" in the direction of lower error, should it receive the same input again in the future.

Metaphorically, the error landscape is like a geographic topography with peaks, plateaus, and valleys, and the gradient descent algorithm tries to plot a course gradually toward the lowest elevation by repeatedly taking small steps downhill. Eventually, with enough small tweaks, network performance tends to converge on the solution to a wide range of classification and decision problems. Although the algorithm can sometimes get "stuck in local minima," humans and animals can get stuck as well, so this is not necessarily a concern associated with dissimilarity. Instead, the major concern at present is that for the backpropagation algorithm to master complex solutions to problems with tiny training adjustments, networks can require millions of training exposures to converge. As mentioned previously, skeptics take this to be orders of magnitude more learning data than humans require to achieve the same level of reliability in solving a task. They also point out that it is not easy to see how to do away with such a large number of exposures because the algorithm becomes unstable if modelers attempt to make the weight adjustments too quickly.

Second, efficiency concerns about DCNNs can also be raised about the time of inference. For example, generic DCNNs search for features by tiling convolutional filters over the entire input. This means they systematically search in every area of an image for each feature, even if most of those locations are extremely unlikely to contain most of those features. Outside of a completionist approach to a *Where's Waldo/ Wally?* book, humans and animals do not normally search for features in this way. This is a laborious search strategy, and the vast majority of the feature/locations explored will result in wasted computation. Humans and animals instead restrict their searches to areas that are likely to be especially promising and to features that are relevant to the task at hand and likely to occur in the locations searched.

When, in later chapters, we consider adding domain-general modules to more basic DNN architectures, we will see how doing so can make training and inference more efficient in ways that are directly relevant to these concerns. They simultaneously render the processing of these systems more biologically plausible, given that these modules reprise the roles that faculties like memory, imagination, and attention are thought to play in human learning and inference. The capabilities of these module-enhanced systems, particularly when combined with a review of the empirical results suggesting that significant performance gains can be obtained by implementing these additional forms of active filtering and control, suggest that the kinds of abstractions discovered by these systems may not be fundamentally different from those discovered by perceptual systems in humans after all. Notably, these additional modules do not require any innate domain-specific knowledge, and so they are consistent with the moderate empiricist DoGMA. In fact, much of the active filtering and control provided by these modules can be seen as further top-down forms of abstraction of the sort discussed by these empiricist philosophers, further tightening the link between current DNN modeling and the history of empiricist philosophy highlighted by the DoGMA.

3.6.2. Abstraction-as-representation— Specification sandwiches

One important aspect of the empiricist theory of abstraction which has not yet been linked to DCNNs, however, is abstraction-as-representation. Abstraction-as-representation is a crucial component of the DoGMA's rebuttal to nativist accounts of reasoning, as our ability to consider whether general principles apply to specific instances featured prominently in empiricist accounts of demonstrative reasoning from canonical empiricists like Berkeley and Hume.[12]

---

[12] It may sound overly ambitious to expect current DNN-based systems to solve such mathematical reasoning problems, but this is an active area of research with promising early results. The MINERVA system developed by Google, for example, was able to answer correctly nearly a third of difficult undergraduate-level quantitative reasoning problems from physics, biology, chemistry, economics, and other sciences (Lewkowycz

We have so far only attempted to explain how DCNNs might perform operations attributed to abstraction-as-composition, abstraction-as-subtraction, and at least to some degree, abstraction-as-invariance. What of abstraction-as-representation, where a single exemplar is used as a stand-in for a whole general category? Hume argued that the faculty of imagination plays a crucial role, specifically by enabling our ability to create and consider novel ideas. Fascinatingly, machine learning researchers have discovered that a huge amount of information about possible nuisance configurations remains latent in the late-stage manifolds that have been disentangled by transformational abstraction, because the transformations required to extract abstract category representations from rendered exemplars with specific combinations of nuisance parameters can be (approximately) reversed, to render highly plausible exemplars from arbitrary positions on the transformed manifolds (Goodfellow 2016). Returning to DiCarlo et al.'s paper-folding metaphor, if a system that had learned to "unfold" the manifolds for different categories could also "refold" them in a similar manner, then each vector in an abstract category could be remapped to its original perceptual representation with the appropriate values of its original nuisance parameters like pose, position, scale, and so on. Moreover, if we pick a novel location on an untangled manifold and then refold the manifold using the same procedure, we can produce highly realistic exemplars with novel combinations of nuisance parameters that the network never even observed in training (Gatys, Ecker, and Bethge 2016a).

The beauty of this approach, particularly for empiricists who aim to make the most efficient use of experience in abstract reasoning, extends beyond the creation of photorealistic stimuli and "deepfakes" that have so captivated popular attention. Cognitively, this approach is so promising because the generated exemplars can be reengaged with the same discriminative forms of abstraction that feature in categorization of occurrent perception, potentially allowing agents to mine their own latent space for new hypotheses about abstract properties

et al. 2022). Of course, it is unlikely that MINERVA solves these problems in the same way that humans do, and adding additional faculty modules—for "remembering" key variables or reasoning over "imagined" physical or geometrical simulations, for example—may further improve these systems' performance.

possessed by previously acquired categories, even if training experience had never before directly linked members of the category to that abstract property. In fact, it is possible, as we will explore in more detail in later chapters, that this talk of folding, unfolding, and refolding latent space can help explain the modes of insightful thinking and creative problem-solving attributed to the imagination in humans and animals, all without the aid of the innate ideas favored by the rationalist and eschewed by the DoGMA.

3.6.3. Abstraction-as-invariance as an ideal limit

Even if the aforementioned points are accepted, we may still worry about extending these empiricist-friendly forms of abstraction to the loftiest mathematical or logical categories favored by rationalists, such as CHILIAGON or AND. Transformational abstraction might seem to help neural networks represent gradually more invariant properties, relative to the depth of the network. Indeed, an ability to control systematically for forms of nuisance variation seems part and parcel of abstraction techniques studied in these most abstract disciplines, such as physics, logic, and mathematics. However, rationalists are unlikely to be satisfied by the degree of abstraction-as-invariance achieved by a DCNN, even if they do eventually admit that it is somehow relevant. This is partly because rationalists typically suppose that the forms of abstraction they highlight are uniquely human, even though animals—especially mammals, and especially primates—seem to possess a similar facility for transformational abstraction. The uniqueness, according to rationalists, depends on the kind or degree of invariance that rationalists prize, which—whether geometric, numerical, logical, or modal—is taken to be more perfect than can be achieved by any finite amount of transformational abstraction. Abstraction in these disciplines reaches toward invariance at an ideal limit—across all possible permutations or across all geometric transformations within a certain class—that neural networks could only approximate, and that humans may achieve only with the aid of formal proof techniques.

The rationalists are right be concerned here; but if the uniquely human solution to this riddle is provided by our ability to learn and deploy formal proof techniques—as empiricists since Locke have emphasized all along—then the solution does not implicate any innate ideas and thus does not pose a fundamental challenge to the DoGMA. We will return to this when we look to the potential that more sophisticated DNN architectures might be able to learn and manipulate grammatically structured languages. This uniquely human trait may help us achieve abstraction-as-invariance through linguistic and social scaffolding, rather than via the innate endowment of a single mind. In short, what is missing here may be domain-general abilities to master linguistic tools and social cues relevant to formal proof techniques, rather than innate mathematical or logical concepts.

3.7. Summary

DCNNs allow agents to begin ascending to the second tier of rationality, potentially learning abstract patterns that enable agents to generalize to novel situations. While rationalists and other critics express concern that DNN-based systems' solutions do not always transfer as well as those of humans and animals to novel situations, even they must admit that DCNNs have achieved a degree of transfer learning which was previously unprecedented for empiricist methods. As we noted in the previous chapter, standard cross-validation methods already involve some test of generalization ability, and all of the models reported in this chapter have already been evaluated using cross-validation or other similar methods.

This test is required, because "overfitting" is a standard worry in machine learning research. Overfitting occurs when a model learns too much idiosyncratic structure about the training set, and so the patterns it extracts fail to generalize to new data. In fact, we know that overfitting is an even bigger danger in deep learning than it was with shallower networks. Several technical results have shown that deep learning neural networks contain enough representational capacity to memorize the details of even highly complex data. The most dramatic demonstration of this form came from Zhang et al. (2017), who showed that a modestly sized DCNN could simply memorize the "right" labels for a large, highly complex data set of millions of images, even when the labels in the training set were randomly assigned—so that it is not possible that training could provide information about real abstract patterns uniting exemplars into general categories. In other words, these networks could achieve near perfect accuracy on the training set—though, of course, they were no more accurate on cross-validation tests than random guessing. This is a powerful demonstration of the representational capacity of hierarchically structured, untangled data representations—likely, the ability of these networks to memorize the relationship between randomized labels and complex exemplars is due to the hierarchical reuse of features; a deep network is theorized to be able to reuse a feature extracted at an earlier stage in a hierarchy exponentially many times in composing more abstract features learned at later layers, relative to the network's depth (Bengio and Delalleau 2011; Buckner 2019a; Krueger et al. 2017). This would make even rote memorization of millions of exemplar-label mappings more efficient, as each exemplar could be represented in a compressed form. However, this also illustrates that this immense power may not always be directed toward acquiring the kinds of generalizable patterns and abstract categories that the modelers hope their networks will acquire (C. Zhang et al. 2021). This is why careful tests of cross-validation and other measures of generalization are so essential in contemporary deep learning methodology.

Nevertheless, as we noted in the last chapter, rationalists frequently retort that these networks only succeed on generalization tests that are drawn from independent and identically distributed (i.i.d.) data. They assume that DCNNs will only generalize well if features in the test set have the same kind of statistical distribution that they do in the training set. This limitation can be seen clearly in toy examples and has become something of an accepted mantra of machine learning, though the claim and its implications are rarely made precise when applied to the larger models trained on sprawling data sets. For example, the distribution of large, standardized data sets like ImageNet is not precisely characterized when it is claimed that image-classifying DCNNs only generalize well on i.i.d. data, and the distribution for even larger test sets like the Internet-scale training set of GPT-3 encompasses the statistics of most publicly available written human language.

Moreover, this imprecision invites the rationalist tendency toward anthropofabulation to creep into the comparisons between DCNNs and humans. Human cognition is not magic, either: we may generalize better to a wider range of novel circumstances than do animals or current artificial agents, but humans still require some environmental cues and scaffolding to draw inferences about hidden or unobservable features. For example, rationalists often claim that humans, when looking at a picture of an animal, will not categorize merely on the basis of surface features but may also consider hidden, even "unobservable" features like DNA or internal organs (Keil 1992; Penn, Holyoak, and Povinelli 2008). However, humans can only learn about or infer the presence of these hidden features on the basis of currently or previously observed perceptual cues, including linguistic ones. To channel again the attitude expressed in Chapter 1 that progress here is best achieved by wresting a spectrum of moderate views from a simplistic dichotomy, all agents that learn using inductive methods can be placed along a continuum with respect to their ability to transfer strategies from only data sets with completely identical statistical distributions to data sets with completely dissimilar distributions. Humans may be further along this continuum for most kinds of tasks than animals and artificial agents, but state-of-the-art DCNNs have come a significant distance along it, too, and no agent can generalize from one context to another if the two distributions share no statistical regularities in common whatsoever.[13]

It may even be the case that some of the generalizations that these nets learn—for example, in adversarial examples—are real patterns that we would learn if we could, if we were not held back by human performance limitations that some DNNs can overcome. There is substantial evidence that DNN-based systems may, by relaxing some biological constraints on human cortex—by having much larger training sets, or much deeper hierarchical networks, for example—push these

---

[13] Comparisons to the performance of animals on these tasks may be useful to see how far inductive learning can generalize to perceptually dissimilar situations in the absence of language (Bugnyar, Reber, and Buckner 2016; Phillips, Shankar, and Santos 2010; Santos, Flombaum, and Phillips 2007).

forms of abstraction beyond the limits of human achievement. They may, for example, be able to recognize patterns that are too complex or high-dimensional for humans to recognize, but which nevertheless are predictively valid on novel natural data (Ilyas et al. 2019). This could further explain how these networks can defeat humans so resoundingly in games that require intuition like Go or predict the final configuration of protein folds that humans theorists who dedicated their lives to the task have for decades failed to crack using more transparent analytic models (AlQuraishi 2019; Gainza et al. 2019; Honig 1999). The ability to learn such features would be a remarkable achievement for AI, though it would bring with it some new risks. For example, humans may necessarily find the abstract patterns learned by these souped-up networks to be inscrutable, and the processing of these DNNs may introduce distinctive artifacts that would be difficult to anticipate or control (Buckner 2020b).[14] Nevertheless, even if DNNs sometimes extract different abstractions than do humans and animals, they may do so by applying the same aspects of abstractive processes that humans rely upon when operating within our own contingent limits.

At the same time, current DCNNs have struggled with simple mathematical tasks like counting exact numbers of objects, tasks which young children and some animals can do fairly well (Rugani et al. 2015; Zhang, Hare, and Prügel-Bennett 2018).[15] This leaves empiricists and rationalists alike with a puzzling tension in the evaluation of abstraction in DNNs: on the one hand, it seems obvious that DCNNs abstract in some ways like us (and may in fact exceed human ability to abstract in these ways), but that DCNNs currently miss some of the abstract relations that are most significant for human cognition—such as the numerical, social, or causal relationships that we mentioned at the beginning of this chapter. Chollet recommends a tempting balm for this tension: two-system or dual processing theories in cognitive science

---

[14] Common examples of processing artifacts include Doppler shifts and lens flares. These artifacts contain predictively useful information about signal sources, but they can also be misleading until their sources are properly understood.

[15] Some of the most recent transformer-based models may even overcome these limitations with tasks like exact cardinality and counting. Some have speculated that the difficulty with counting in earlier transformer-based models is an artifact of reliance on specific language models, such as CLIP, and that newer systems which do not rely on CLIP (like Imagen) may perform better. For details, see Saharia et al. (2022).

(Chollet 2019).[16] System I is frequently compared to connectionist systems (in its operations being associative, parallel, and intuitive), whereas System II is thought to be a conscious rule interpreter restricted to evaluating one instruction at a time (Sloman 1996).[17] The areas in which DNNs excel are ascribed to System I processing in humans, whereas the relations that continue to elude DNN-based systems are then ascribed to distinctive processing methods of System II, such as counting or deductive inference.

Appealing as the two-system solution is, it raises the troubling engineering question about how to integrate System II with System I if they are of fundamentally different kinds. In particular, we must decide whether System II can be built out of the basic empiricist toolkit of artificial neural networks, or whether it must be implemented as a classical symbol system. While recent hybrid theorists who criticize deep learning, such as Marcus, recommend a new incarnation of the latter hybrid approach, I stand with key figures in the second wave of neural network modeling (many of whom continue to be active in the third wave), who argued for the benefits of the former, more thoroughly network based approach. Paul Smolensky in particular has long sought to demonstrate the benefits of implementing System II–like processing in an ANN architecture (Russin et al. 2021; Smolensky 1988; Smolensky et al. 2022). To tie these ideas to the DoGMA, some of the key functional properties attributed to System II might emerge out of empiricist, modular, neural-network-based systems leveraging faculties like imagination and attention to achieve increased cognitive control, and we will explore this possibility in later chapters. Indeed, we will consider how the faculties might enable memories of previous experiences to be used more efficiently in decision-making, combined into novel composites, facilitate consequence-sensitive choices among options, and to enable social learning and cultural transmission of acquired knowledge. To continue the ascent, us now turn to memory.

---

[16] The appeal to a two-system theory here is also a frequent move made by the other cognitive architecture theorists like Anderson and Laird, mentioned in the previous chapter (Anderson and Lebiere 2014; Laird 2019).

[17] There are also many critics of two-system views, some that prefer one integrated system and others that prefer many less unified systems (Keren and Schul 2009; Pessoa et al. 2022).

4

Memory

The senses perceive only individual particulars. Memory
and imagery retain what the senses transmit in its individuality. Imagery retains the form [of the particular ob-
ject] while memory retains the implication derived from
it. When the sense perception is repeated, it becomes
memory, and when memory is repeated it becomes
experience.

—Ibn Sina [Avicenna], *Najāt*, 101 (trans. in Gutas
2012:399)

4.1. The trouble with quantifying human perceptual experience

Rational problem-solving—whether by brains or by artificial neural
networks—depends critically upon using evidence efficiently and effectively. Rational learners do not just record random correlations
from data; they efficiently process that data to extract abstract patterns
which enable them to succeed flexibly across a variety of different
contexts and tasks. We ended the last chapter by raising questions as to
whether the apparent inefficiency and brittleness of deep convolutional
neural network (DCNN)-based learning renders it a poor candidate
to model such rational learning processes. When we are considering
using deep learning systems as models of rational cognition, we want
to create machines that not only mimic human problem-solving behavior but also—to paraphrase the title of Lake, Ulman, Tenenbaum,
and Gershman (2017)—can learn to do so on the basis of human-like
amounts and types of interaction with the world. If they cannot, this
may shake our faith that they share the difference-making aspects of

From Deep Learning to Rational Machines. Cameron J. Buckner, Oxford University Press.
© Oxford University Press 2024. DOI: 10.1093/oso/9780197653302.003.0004

brains that allow humans to learn and behave rationally, frustrating the very motivations that led researchers to adopt an artificial neural network (ANN)-based approach to artificial intelligence (AI) in the first place.[1]

These efficiency comparisons require us to quantify the amount of data available in typical human experience. Without an estimate, it is hard to meaningfully compare the volume of human experience to the size of a deep neural network (DNN)'s training set. Despite this obvious fact, skeptics of human-AI similarity rarely devote much space to describing or defending rigorous estimation procedures. It is important that we take this task seriously, as default assumptions about the "poverty of the stimulus" thought to have sunk the grand ambitions of prior empiricist approaches to human cognition, such as behaviorism (Chomsky 1980; Skinner 1957), were found by later empirical investigation to be overstated or incorrect. Chomsky famously argued that the amount of practice and feedback that children received was insufficient to explain their later linguistic performance without drawing upon a large number of innate grammatical rules (Chomsky 1986). However, new, more powerful associative theories and reappraisals of the richness of the stimulus have suggested that these conclusions should be rejected, given that children in fact have much richer linguistic experience than Chomsky supposed (Christiansen and Chater 2016; Reali and Christiansen 2005). This is not to say that Skinner's particular theory of verbal behavior would be viable if provided with more realistic human linguistic experience, but only that newer, more powerful associationist or statistical-learning models that eschew innate grammatical knowledge are competitive empirical options today.

---

[1] There is a famous strain of thought in AI which downplays the imposition of human-like efficiency constraints. "The quest for 'artificial flight' succeeded when the Wright brothers and others stopped imitating birds and started using wind tunnels and learning about aerodynamics," write Russell and Norvig (2003) in their influential textbook on AI—though we might note that airplanes fly only using enormous amounts of hydrocarbon-based energy, in comparison to the graceful (and sometimes energy-free) flight of birds on thermal drafts. As evidenced by the response to Deep Blue's victory over Gary Kasparov using computational brute force, efficiency is more central to intelligence than it is to flight; and while we might accept that AIs could outthink us if given unlimited computational resources, they should still make efficient use of those greater resources if their processing is to be counted as rational or intelligent.

In some cases, notable DNN-based systems have obviously been provided with orders of magnitude more training data than the humans against which they compete. AlphaGo, for example, played nearly 30 million unique games against itself before competing against Lee Sedol, and some versions of AlphaZero learned from 100 million simulated self-play games. As I previously pointed out, Lee Sedol could not have played more than 50,000 games in his entire life. Similar conclusions carry over to notable systems in image classification or text generation. ImageNet contains over 14 million images labeled with over 20,000 category labels, and large language models like GPT-3 are trained on textual data sets encompassing a significant portion of all the text available on the Internet. No individual human has read such a large amount of text; nor do they need to before producing grammatically correct and semantically meaningful speech. So, let it be granted, at least some of the time DNNs have been trained on much greater amounts of data. It should be noted, though, that many systems do not explicitly aim to model human performance; the goal of DeepMind in producing AlphaGo was not to model human play with its current or intrinsic limitations, but rather to exceed it, and so relaxing some of the constraints on biological cognition may be seen as acceptable to their aims.

Returning to the role of DNNs as realistic cognitive models, nativists typically offer empiricists an orderly retreat to a safer, fallback position: that the training of a DNN reprises the entire process of biological or cultural evolution, rather than the learning and development of a single individual. In other words, while an individual Go player could not have played 30 million unique games, perhaps that human Go player was trained on Go theory that was informed by hundreds of millions of games—namely, all of those played in the cultural tradition from which that theoretical strategy or pedagogy was derived. Perhaps an individual human has not interacted with 14 million unique category exemplars, but the nativist suggests to us that our evolutionary ancestors have collectively been exposed to far more than that, and perhaps some of that knowledge has been inherited in the genome in the form of innate rules or representations (Lake et al. 2017).

This invitation to retreat should be politely declined (as it has been, at least, by empiricist-leaning DeepMind—Botvinick et al. 2017).

The better empiricist response redoubles efforts to take the collection and quantification of human learning data more seriously and to provide the machines with this more biologically plausible data. To do so requires confronting the dangers of anthropofabulation in this context, as we may be tempted by overly flattering underestimates of the amount or quality of data required for successful human learning (Buckner 2020a; Smith and Slone 2017). Returning to the context of perceptual discrimination, anthropofabulation may cause us to undercount the number of trainable instances that should be scored to children who learn to discriminate common categories. There are two factors that are often neglected in such accounting: (1) that many different vantages on the same object can provide distinct snapshots of an object for training purposes, and (2) that offline memory consolidation during sleep and daydreaming can allow agents to benefit from reexposure to the same previously experienced snapshots—and even simulated novel exemplars generated from those same exposures— many thousands of times in offline repetitions.[2] Ignoring these factors, common sense—no more accurate here in psychology than it is in physics—might score an infant's ten-minute interaction with a new toy as a single datum; but taking these factors into account shows that this is a serious underestimate of the volume of relevant information available in human perceptual experience.

Let us consider the first neglected concern, about different vantage points on the same object. This dimension of experience will often be neglected, because when our perceptual systems are functioning correctly, we subjectively perceive all these different glimpses as being of the same object. Such unified perception is itself a computational achievement, however, and the different glimpses are still providing useful information for training purposes. In almost all investigations, researchers face the challenge of quantifying the amount of information provided by the environment that is required for humans to learn to solve a task, but of which we are unaware in subjective awareness;

---

[2] Indeed, unifying these different vantage points into an experience of a single object is itself an impressive cognitive achievement, and one that the rationalists often suppose requires an innate OBJECT concept. In Chapter 6, we will review how this might be achieved by domain-general attentional mechanisms.

yet there is very little explicit discussion of more general principles which could be used to arbitrate disputes about proper accounting of experience.

To begin making some progress toward responsible counting here, we can review some relevant results from perceptual psychology. Studies of motion-picture perception have suggested that human vision has a frame rate of about ten to twelve images per second (below this rate, we cannot perceive motion as continuous). We can also consider how long it takes us to become aware of or be affected by a stimulus; while conscious awareness of a stimulus typically takes 200 to 400 ms, attentional shifting to a new stimulus begins in as little as 20 ms, and category structure can be implicitly influenced by nonconscious exposures to stimuli as brief as 1 ms (Kunst-Wilson and Zajonc 1980; Murphy and Zajonc 1993; Schacter 1987). The previous chapter reviewed the difficulties posed by nuisance variation in perceptual recognition for both humans and machines; the fact that DCNNs need such a large volume of training data in order to cope with changes in pose, orientation, occlusion, and shading suggests that human experience also must contain a similarly large amount of information, providing glimpses of items from a variety of nuisance parameters. If each of these distinct glimpses constitutes a different "frame" of experience, then—even focusing only on visual input during a single interaction with a single novel object—an extended interaction with a single object should perhaps be credited with thousands of distinct snapshots that could be used for cortical training, rather than a single one, as common sense supposes.

In addition to these concerns about undercounting, we should also worry about qualitative disanalogies between the kinds of data typically provided to DNNs and those provided to humans. For one, an infant's interaction with a new toy will typically involve a continuous perception of it from many different standpoints and combinations of nuisance parameters. This kind of experience may be a more reliable guide to category boundaries than the disconnected still images provided to DCNNs. Exposure to continuous transformations can allow agents to develop representations that are more robust and less susceptible to out-of-distribution attacks, such as adversarial examples (Kong and Norcia 2021; Sullivan et al. 2022; Wood et al. 2016). Moreover, researchers have found that ImageNet is rife with labeling errors in a way that may affect the robustness of networks trained on them; though researchers have typically assumed that DCNNs are resilient in the face of a small number of labeling errors, more recent analyses suggested that these errors are so pervasive that the use of these data sets may have biased common benchmarks toward larger models that can better fit labeling errors (Northcutt, Athalye, and Mueller 2021). Furthermore, an infant's experience with a new object is typically more structured and multimodal than the training set of a DCNN. When provided with a new object, infants engage in an extended exploration that appears well-suited to sampling it from a representative variety of perspectives and sensory modalities (by turning it, banging it against the ground, and, indeed, tasting it)—a fact revealed by empirical study of video recorded from the perspective of infants during learning episodes (Smith and Slone 2017). This type of multimodal interaction would be difficult to replicate in DNN-based agents without giving them robotic or virtual bodies, but we should reserve judgment as to whether observed performance dissimilarities are attributable to differences in the architecture of human minds and DNNs or rather in their respective data sets until we can provide the DNNs with such human-like training data.

Other studies have found that such structured interactions can allow DNNs to learn very quickly the kinds of domain-specific inductive biases recommended by rationalists, but through the use of domain-general learning mechanisms rather than innate domain-specific knowledge. A study by Feinman and Lake (2018), for example, found that providing DCNNs with more developmentally realistic training experiences allowed them to acquire a bias commonly exhibited by humans to categorize new objects by shape rather than color (the "shape bias") after seeing as few as three examples of four object categories, and that this bias can increase the efficiency of learning new categories in just the ways suggested by nativists. Other studies have demonstrated the power of developmentally timed changes to learning rates, as observed during "critical periods" when birds typically imprint on the faces of their mothers or human children learn language (Versace et al. 2018). Though nativists often interpret such imprinting or critical language periods as evidence for innate domain-specific mechanisms, they are domain-general according to the "range-of-inputs" approach to the domain-specific/domain-general distinction recommended in Chapter 1. In fact, studies have shown that imprinting mechanisms are highly open-ended in the inputs to which they respond; newly hatched birds, for example, can imprint on higher-order sameness and difference relations or abstract multimodal patterns (Martinho and Kacelnik 2016; Versace et al. 2017). Far from revealing an innate, domain-specific "mother face detector," these studies show how effectively global tweaks can allow domain-general learning mechanisms to extract domain-specific patterns on their own when provided with ecologically plausible sequences of experience (Lee, Pak, and Wood 2021).[3] Correctly timed and sequenced presentation of environmental regularities, rather than any innate knowledge, ensure that these mechanisms usually result in learning faces and languages.

In addition to the issues of undercounted and qualitatively dissimilar inputs, comparisons between DCNNs and rational learning processes have also been obscured by structural dissimilarities in the ways problems are posed to DCNNs and humans. For example, DCNNs are typically trained by forcing them to choose between one of 20,000 labels for an image in training, without being given the option to draw a distinction between what something merely resembles and what it looks like it actually is (Firestone 2020; Zhou and Firestone 2019). To spell out this distinction, we may think that a cloud looks like a whale without thinking that it is actually a whale; there is no inconsistency between the cloud resembling a whale yet not looking like it is a whale.[4] Indeed, psychological research has shown that many common adversarial examples do look to human eyes somewhat similar to the "incorrect" category labels that DNNs assign to them; when humans are asked not what they think an adversarial image depicts, but

---

[3] Subsequent work has emphasized that a domain-specific "animacy detector" may still be involved in this early imprinting (Rosa-Salva et al. 2021), but relatively generic DNNs have also demonstrated such animacy biases without any such domain-specific tweaks (Bracci et al. 2019; Ritchie et al. 2021).

[4] Readers who doubt that human children receive explicit training in this distinction are referred to the classic children's book *It Looked Like Spilt Milk*, which as of the publication of this manuscript, my younger daughter has requested at bedtime over 500 times. (Spoiler alert: it is actually a cloud.)

rather what label the computer will assign to the image, they are able to guess the "incorrect" labels for the images at rates well above chance (Zhou and Firestone 2019). This suggests that low-level human perception may not be so dissimilar to the processing of DCNNs after all.

Of course, as pointed out earlier, most current DCNN models are not trained to interact dynamically with training objects or to draw distinctions between superficial resemblance and deeper category membership; and it may not be straightforward to equip them to do so. Interaction with category exemplars in particular would seem to require robot bodies or at least virtual bodies in virtual environments (Crosby 2020; Crosby et al. 2019; Kim et al. 2020). Nevertheless, we need to distinguish the contingent limitations of current training regimes from the intrinsic limitations of empiricist modeling when making bets about future research efforts. Bolstering research in this more productive direction will require more empirical study on how much and what kind of experience humans require to succeed on tasks (instead of relying on common-sense estimates), training regimes which offer humans and machines more analogous tasks, and more ecologically realistic, multimodal data sets on which machines can be trained (Zaadnoordijk, Besold, and Cusack 2020).

Fortunately, a number of DNN modelers have begun to experiment with more human-like training regimes to illustrate how doing so might help overcome issues that might otherwise be considered inherent limitations of empiricist modeling. One of the most promising lines of research involves training DNNs on videos instead of still images. For example, when deep learning models are trained on successive frames of video rather than static exemplars, many different vantage points on the same object can be treated as independent training instances to improve the model's performance (Lotter, Kreiman, and Cox 2017; Luc et al. 2017; Orhan, Gupta, and Lake 2020). In most cases, this requires a different learning algorithm than standard supervised approaches, as annotating every frame of a video for supervised learning is a very labor-intensive process, and usually labels can simply be carried over to a subsequent frame when certain assumptions of continuity are satisfied. Predictive, "self-supervised" networks—which attempt to learn by predicting the future from the past, the past from the present, occluded aspects of objects from the seen aspects, and so on—are championed as the best way to achieve the next levels of efficiency and flexibility in deep learning by DNN pioneers like LeCun (2018).

On this approach, an annotation assigned to one frame of a video by either a teacher or by the agent itself can simply be carried over to successive frames if they meet some condition of similarity to the previous frames. In this way, one annotation can be used to provide thousands more for additional supervised training without further cost. One of the most impressive developments in this direction involves the creation of new data sets using video from headcams worn by human infants engaged in learning tasks, such as SAYCam (Sullivan et al. 2022). DNN systems can then be trained directly on this video, which often has different statistical properties from other standard data sources—such as a new object taking up much of the visual field and being systematically manipulated by the infant (Orhan et al. 2020). Empirical comparisons of models that are pretrained on ImageNet vs. SAYCam show that the latter are more effective at recovering just the sorts of abstract relations that are emphasized by rationalists and a weakness of previous DNN-based models, such as classifying objects by whether they are above, below, between, or outside other objects (Davidson and Lake 2021). Even if the DNNs are not yet directing these manipulations themselves, these data sets provide a richer source of targeted training for mastering a single object's many possible combinations of nuisance properties than might be found in static video. There is little evidence that the efficiency gains that can be obtained from such biologically inspired innovations have already plateaued.

As we will see, however, even these more realistic data sets do not go far enough in balancing the comparisons between humans and DNNs; without further faculty-inspired enhancement, brains will still come out as the more efficient learners. Even so, there are other ways to better leverage experience that we have not yet considered—methods based on not only how many viewpoints a learner has been exposed to, but how many times the same viewpoints can be productively repurposed in additional rounds of training or prospective decision-making. In this respect, the faculties of memory and imagination play a crucial role in the learning and utilization of abstractions—a fact that has been acknowledged by nearly all empiricist accounts of abstraction, starting with Aristotle.

4.2. Generalization and catastrophic interference

Before we review the historical empiricists on memory (and, in the next chapter, on the closely related faculty of imagination), we should introduce another widely recognized roadblock to neural-network-based approaches to AI: catastrophic interference. Most briefly, catastrophic interference is the tendency of neural networks to "forget" earlier solutions to tasks when they are trained on new tasks. McCloskey and Cohen (1989) demonstrated this effect by training a simple neural network to associate pairs of items in a list of words (e.g., "locomotive-dish towel," "table-street," "carpet-idea"). When the network was then asked to memorize a second list which contained some of the same words but in different pairs (e.g., "locomotive-basket," "table-lake," "carpet-fish"), the network first had to unlearn the previous associations before it could master the new ones. This would be like a child learning to play checkers, and then, after also learning to play tic-tac-toe, entirely forgetting how to move the pieces in checkers or confusing the rules of the two games when asked to make a move. This phenomenon seemed to explain why many early successes in connectionist AI in the 1980s failed to scale up to more general problem solvers. General intelligence requires the ability to master multiple tasks and be able to switch between them flexibly without relearning each from scratch, so many critics have highlighted catastrophic interference as an in-principle computational obstacle for ANN-based general AI.

The problem arises from the fact that skills and knowledge in ANNs are stored in their connection weights, which are gradually modified by future learning. In other words, short-term learning and long-term storage in most networks involve the same representational resources. In a simple ANN, later training episodes may modify the weights that are currently storing representations acquired from earlier training episodes, either causing the old and new tasks to become conflated, or overwriting the old information entirely. Such conflations and forgetting can occur in human memory, but they are much rarer, and humans can retain highly practiced skills and knowledge for decades without explicit refresher sessions. The problem might be avoided by adding new memory resources every time a network is trained on a new task, but this seems to require a biologically implausible mechanism to flag the new tasks as novel and to allocate empty memory resources to their mastery. It also seems to block the possibility for accelerated learning on new tasks that share abstract similarities with one another. The brain rather seems to integrate more flexibly and store new skills alongside old ones using the same general associative memory resources over time. This is less like a serial savant, and more like a generalist musician who picks up new pieces or new instruments more quickly than total novices, by generalizing abstract musical knowledge and skill when possible while also separating incommensurable skills and knowledge where needed.

One proposed solution to the problem is called "interleaved learning." Interleaved learning occurs when training episodes for different tasks are interspersed with one another over time. In this way, multiple tasks are gradually acquired simultaneously, and older skills are constantly refreshed as new ones are acquired. By alternating the training episodes for different tasks or knowledge, the network is forced to learn deeper abstractions and context-sensitive strategies that do not become conflated with or overwritten by knowledge required to solve other tasks. This occurs intentionally to some degree in human learning—musicians often briefly practice older pieces or instruments when learning new ones—but again, humans do not appear to be nearly as dependent upon externally imposed interleaved learning as neural networks. And in formal schooling situations, though the school year often begins with a brief refresher of last year's topics, children could not progress to higher education if they had to rehearse constantly information all the way back to the earliest grade levels to avoid catastrophic interference.

Because deep learning systems take the same general approach to learning and storage as the earlier and shallower ANNs, they have the same generic vulnerability to catastrophic interference (though, as we noted in the previous chapter, they have a much greater representational capacity). We thus require some solution to the problem in even the much larger and more complex DNNs behind state-of-the-art deep learning achievements. As we will see shortly, because empiricist computational modeling has been inspired by simultaneous and reciprocal study of the brain, an exploration of how the brain avoids this problem can ground a deeper understanding of the phenomenon and future engineering innovations to mitigate it in artificial systems. And indeed, in both cases the most popular solution appeals to one of the oldest ideas in empiricist philosophy of mind, concerning the role played by memory in extracting abstractions from experience.

4.3. Empiricists on the role of memory in abstraction

From the earliest statements of empiricist approach in philosophy, the faculty of memory was seen as crucial to the mind's ability to learn abstractions from sensory information. Aristotle, who seeded many of the foundational ideas of empiricism, was particularly emphatic here.[5] He went so far as to say that until perceptual information had been repeatedly reinstated and crystallized into memory, it did not even count as the kind of experience from which abstractions could be derived.

This idea is captured in the famous "Battle Metaphor" of Aristotle's *Posterior Analytics*, where he likens the mind's struggle to extract orderly abstractions from chaotic perceptual input to that of an army attempting to recover its lines from a rout in a battle:

> But though sense-perception is innate in all animals, in some the sense-impression comes to persist, in others it does not. So animals in which this persistence does not come to be have either no knowledge at all outside the act of perceiving, or no knowledge of objects of which no impression persists; animals in which it does come into being have perception and can continue to retain the

[5] While Aristotle seems to be a staunch origin empiricist in the Battle Metaphor and he seeded many of empiricism's key ideas, he is difficult to characterize as either a pure empiricist or a pure rationalist along the other dimensions of the empiricist-rationalist division mentioned in Chapter 1 (Sorabji 1993). He is sometimes described as a "rational empiricist," because while he insisted that knowledge was derived from experience, he preferred to evaluate human-like rational cognition using rule-like inferential norms which he thought applied uniquely to language-using humans. Ibn Sina, whom we will discuss shortly, may also fit into this category of empiricist (Zarepour 2020).

sense-impression in the soul: and when such persistence is frequently repeated a further distinction at once arises between those
which out of the persistence of such sense-impressions develop
a power of systematizing them and those which do not. So out of
sense-perception comes to be what we call memory, and out of frequently repeated memories of the same thing develops experience;
for a number of memories constitute a single experience.... We conclude that these states of knowledge are neither innate in a determi-
nate form, nor developed from other higher states of knowledge, but
from sense-perception. It is like a rout in battle stopped by first one
man making a stand and then another, until the original formation
has been restored. (*Posterior Analytics*, II.19)

It is of particular note that Aristotle develops his doctrine of the
faculties like memory and imagination specifically to explain the flexible decision-making of nonlinguistic animals. These faculties came
to be known in Peripatetic and Scholastic philosophy as the "inner
senses."

The doctrine of the inner senses holds that there are faculties devoted to the creation and maintenance of inner representations that
are perception-like in that they are distilled from perceptions, but
unlike specific perceptions in being more general and abstract. The
inner senses included most prominently a "common" sense—which
should be sharply distinguished from the common-sense knowledge
we discussed in Chapter 1. The Aristotelian common sense is rather a
higher-order, internal sensory faculty that monitored the deliverances
of the senses and integrated information into more multimodal
formats, such as shapes that could be perceived by either sight or touch
(subsuming functions that we might ascribe to the entorhinal cortices
and other multimodal associative areas of cortex today). The theory of
the inner senses also includes faculties like memory and imagination,
which specialize in even more abstract representational formats that
purportedly allow humans and animals to recognize commonalities
shared among multiple sensory particulars by providing a kind of
internal standard of comparison. These internal standards allow the
mind to "make a stand" against the onslaught of disordered perceptual

input by systematizing its patterns into more orderly categories and taxonomies.

As influential as the Battle Metaphor was in classical and medieval thought, it did not provide much in the way of a process model that could explain how abstraction actually occurs. A more mechanized account of the role of the inner senses in abstraction was provided by later commentators, most notably Ibn Sina (also known as "Abu Ali Sina" or the Westernized "Avicenna"). Ibn Sina was a Persian philosopher and physician (often considered the progenitor of modern medicine) who wrote a number of influential academic works, especially commentaries that filled in the blanks he found in Aristotle's psychology. When Ibn Sina's texts were translated and disseminated in Europe, they became immensely influential in the Scholastic tradition which dominated European thought until the seventeenth century.[6] Ibn Sina's philosophical psychology is particularly relevant to the DoGMA advanced here, because his faculty psychology was designed specifically to explain Aristotle's account of abstraction from sense perceptions.

Although Ibn Sina's faculty psychology was inspired and organized around a theory of the brain's operations that we now regard as entirely incorrect, it is useful to review here to better understand the division of labor he ascribed to the different mental faculties. In particular, Ibn Sina was an influential source of the "ventricular" theory of brain function, which held sway over European and Arabic thought for centuries. As a physician who had close knowledge of human anatomy, Ibn Sina understood that the brain was critical for psychological function. Perhaps as a result of anatomical observation from dissections, he hypothesized that the brain's ventricles—cavities in the center of the brain which are filled primarily with cerebrospinal fluid—housed the "inner senses" in which abstraction occurred. Ibn Sina observed that the ventricles were connected to one another in a sequence, which led him to hypothesize that different faculties were associated with

---

[6] Ibn Sina may even have as strong a claim to some of the foundational ideas of origin empiricism as John Locke. Though Locke does not credit Ibn Sina in the *Essay*, scholars have argued that Locke knew Ibn Sina's works well and that several of his key empiricist doctrines are quite similar to Ibn Sina's (Gutas 2012).

different ventricles in an iterative process of information processing (Fig. 4.1). Each faculty was thought to push the abstraction process a bit further than the previous one as sensory information progressed from the sense organs in the front of the brain to the rear ventricle (which he associated with memory). As Kemp and Fletcher (1993) note, this theory bears striking similarity to hierarchical theories of information processing in the brain developed in cognitive psychology at the latter half of the twentieth century. These are the same theories that inspired the key architectural features of deep learning, as discussed in the previous two chapters.

On this picture, sensory information streams into the front ventricle from the sensory organs, passing sequentially through areas associated with imagination, cogitation, estimation, and memory. Ibn Sina elaborated the operations of each faculty to answer questions that arose with the details of Aristotle's account of abstraction. Differences in the operation of the different internal sensory faculties were explained in terms of their position in the processing flow and in differences in the ventricles observed in dissections, such as some areas being more moist (and so more amenable to receiving quick and fleeting impressions) or more dry (and so able to retain impressions longer over periods of time—presaging, perhaps, the kind of distinction today drawn between short-term and long-term memory, albeit under

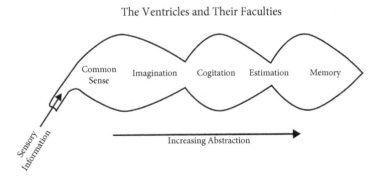

The Ventricles and Their Faculties

Common Sense   Imagination   Cogitation   Estimation   Memory

Sensory Information

Increasing Abstraction

Figure 4.1 A schematic illustration of the ventricles and their associated faculties on Ibn Sina's picture. (Figure adapted from Kemp and Fletcher 1993.)

a squishier anatomical gloss). Still more abstract tasks like judgment and higher reasoning were thought to occur in the faculty of the intellect, a nonphysical part of the soul that interacted with and directed the operations of the inner senses (dreaming and hallucinations were thought instances in which the inner senses lost the direction of the intellect and ran amok).[7]

Estimation is of particular note in the story about the role of memory in abstraction, for Ibn Sina thought estimation essential to explain the flexibility in nonhuman animal thought for which the Aristotelian abstraction scheme was devised in the first place. Accordingly, estimation is the inner sense that records "intentions" associated with abstracted sensory impressions. "Intention" is here a technical term without exact translation from medieval Arabic, and it means something like the implications of a sensory impression.[8] For Ibn Sina, estimation explained how experiences of past events could be motivational in animal decision-making even when the affective significance of a perceptual stimulus was not itself a perceivable quality of those sense impressions.

To illustrate this, Ibn Sina invited the reader to consider a sheep who avoids a wolf upon perceiving it. That the wolf is bad or dangerous is not itself a perceivable quality of the wolf. Rather, that the wolf is to be avoided is a conclusion that is joined by the faculty of estimation to sensory impressions via previous experiences. In Ibn Sina's workflow, intentions (the implications of sensory impressions) were not available in the previous inner senses. The common sense, a step in

---

[7] This dualistic division of the mind into physical and nonphysical aspects influenced and persisted in Descartes's rationalism, which in turn inspired modern forms of rationalism and dual-process theories which persist today. On this scheme, the intellect issued judgments and performed higher reasoning on fully abstract forms. Indeed, this view may be seen as the conceptual grandfather of hybrid architectures which are recommended by contemporary rationalists like Marcus. This may raise the question of whether Ibn Sina's scheme is rightly viewed as empiricist; Gutas (2012) argues at length that it does count as a version of what we have here called "origin empiricism," for even the abstract forms which operate in pure acts of intellection are derived from experience by the inner senses on this scheme.

[8] We might note here that the emphasis on motivationally relevant outcomes presages some of the most cutting-edge views on hippocampal function in cognitive neuroscience, which construe the hippocampus fundamentally as a "predictive map" (Stachenfeld, Botvinick, and Gershman 2017).

the workflow beyond the particular senses like sight and touch, finds relationships and creates representations whose content outstrips a single sensory modality. The imagination, another step beyond the common sense, does not require the current presence of the original object to activate its associated sensory impressions. As each step in the workflow creates forms of representation that were less and less dependent on particular sensory presentations, each was thought to establish a greater degree of abstraction. Estimation, as Ibn Sina put it, "goes a little farther than [imagination] in abstraction, for it receives the intentions which in themselves are non-material . . . [for] good and evil, agreeable and disagreeable . . . are in themselves non-material entities" (Ibn Sina *Najāt*:39, quoted in Kemp and Fletcher [1993]). After estimation comes memory, the most abstract of the Sinian inner senses, one which serves as a long-term storehouse for oft-repeated instances of the most abstract, multimodal sensory impressions, which, crucially, have been combined with their implications provided by estimation. This explains how the inner senses can support the most flexible instances of animal cognition: animals like sheep recognize not only abstract patterns in their perceptual input but also, by drawing upon memories, those patterns' motivational significance (Müller 2015).[9]

There remain, to be sure, important memory-related cognitive functions that this form of memory does not allow nonhuman animals to do. Both Aristotle and Ibn Sina stress that while animals can retrieve a variety of motivationally relevant, abstracted implications

---

[9] Compare (Müller 2015:498): "One should note first that by turning memory into a storehouse of intentions Avicenna considerably broadens its scope in comparison with Aristotle's notion: it can house not only previous sensual experiences of shapes, colors and sounds but also other connotational attributes of objects which are the basis of a more complex kind of emotional memory related to notions of fear, grief, anger and sorrow. Furthermore, memory points to more general concepts of harm and usefulness which are the basis for movements and actions. Memory in Avicenna still supervenes on sense-impressions and their mental representations, but it is already more 'abstract' or 'spiritual' (i.e., removed from corporeality) than in Aristotle's account of sensitive memory. Yet it is still an internal sense and thus stays within the general framework of sense psychology, which means that we are still dealing with concrete experiences. The stored intentions in Avicenna's account are not universals but particulars; they are not a kind of knowledge that the internal sense has but 'rather an indicator pointing to the meaning of an internal image with which this indicator is connected.'"

from memory, they cannot deliberately remind themselves of things, as humans can. Both philosophers thought that deliberately reminding oneself and mentally "traveling" through subjective time requires a form of explicit reasoning (*logos*) that animals lacked. Thus, animal decision-making based on memory remains dependent upon external (or interoceptive) cues for memory retrieval. This remains a popular position in contemporary theorizing about memory and "mental time travel" in animals (Suddendorf et al. 2009; Suddendorf and Corballis 2008; Tulving 2005; and for recent takes on this debate, see Hoerl and McCormack 2019); though we might wonder whether animals' limitations are merely a function of lacking linguistic cues like words, which can indicate a specific temporal duration ("last week," "three years ago") to provide efficient and unequivocal temporal landmarks (Gentry and Buckner 2019).

Regardless, the abstractive workflow aspect of Ibn Sina's theory remained attached to the ventricular anatomical theory, until a pair of countervailing anatomical discoveries by Leonardo da Vinci and Andreas Vesalius called the latter into question. Somewhere between 1504 and 1507, da Vinci injected hot wax into the ventricles of an ox cadaver in order to create a cast of their shape. Discrepancies between the details of the Scholastic theory and the shape of the cast were observed, though it is unclear whether this report had much influence on the doctrine's popularity. According to Kemp and Fletcher (1993), more influential countervailing evidence came from Vesalius, who published a work in 1543 with brain illustrations inspired by human dissection. Among several other disconfirming observations, Vesalius noted that the sensory nerves did not seem to connect to the ventricles, dooming the ventricular theory's account of information flow through the inner senses (Singer 1952).[10]

Nevertheless, if we focus only on its functional structure and disregard the mistaken anatomical aspects, Ibn Sina's theory of the inner senses presaged contemporary accounts of perception and abstraction in cognitive psychology and neuroscience. Ibn Sina offers a

---

[10] Vesalius was not kind to the ventricular theory, whose principles he described as "the inventions of those who never look into our Maker's ingenuity in the building of the human body" (Singer 1952:6).

hierarchical, information-processing model where sensory information is processed and transformed into increasingly abstract formats, which Kemp and Fletcher (1993) note "is consistent with discrete stage-processing models which have been popular in twentieth-century cognitive psychology" (568). Kemp and Fletcher also note that the distinctions between different forms of recollection for past events in the imagination, memory, and intellect bears some similarity to theories of multiple memory systems which store short-term memory, long-term memory, and semantic memories, respectively (Eichenbaum and Cohen 2004; Schacter and Tulving 1982). We might further add that Ibn Sina's emphasis on the affective implications of memory is vindicated by recent accounts of reinforcement learning and goal-related inputs to connectionist models of episodic memory, such as the predictive autoencoder model of Gluck and Myers (1993), which contains a special training signal derived from the unconditioned stimulus (e.g., a reward or punishing cue which carries innate affective significance for the organism, such as a food item or a painful shock). The similarities extend even farther, into recent attempts to model memory in DNN-based architectures, as the next sections will show.[11]

4.4. Artificial neural network models of memory consolidation

With this conception of the role of memory in flexible, goal-oriented decision-making in hand, let us move to examine the details of neural network models of memory's role in learning. Perhaps surprisingly, the empiricist insights expressed in Ibn Sina have parallels in recent DNN-based architectures that have added a "memory" module that performs some of the same computational roles. In particular, the influential model of McClelland, McNaughton, and O'Reilly (1995)

---

[11] If we combine this theory of memory intentions with the sentimentalist approach to reinforcement learning recommended in Chapter 7, the theory looks even more prescient—recommending a more multidimensional approach to reinforcement learning valuation than has been explored in current implementations.

posits an interaction between two different ANN modules corresponding to short-term and long-term memory. In doing so, their model emphasizes crucial computational roles played by consolidation processes in efficiently leveraging prior experience to extract abstractions in future rounds of learning while avoiding catastrophic interference, providing further support for the empiricist DoGMA recommended here.

The McClelland, McNaughton, and O'Reilly model integrated a wide array of findings from psychology, neuroscience, and computational modeling. Much of the evidence for its functional and neuroanatomical division of labor came from lesion studies—both studies of human patients who experienced lesions to the medial temporal lobes (MTLs, which contains the hippocampus, dentate gyrus, entorhinal cortex, and subiculum) as a result of surgery or brain trauma, and of artificial lesions on animal subjects. MTL lesion is a relatively common form of selective brain damage, often caused by stroke, disease, herpes, or a sudden loss of oxygen to the brain (anoxia or hypoxia). Strong evidence for the linkage between the MTL and memory comes from the most common symptoms of such a lesion: amnesia, or the loss of memories. Amnesia comes in two forms, retrograde and anterograde; retrograde amnesia involves the loss of memories before the accident, whereas patients with the anterograde amnesia have diminished ability to form new memories after trauma. Complete retrograde amnesia is extremely uncommon; amnesiacs rarely, as in Hollywood movies, completely forget their identity (an episode called a *fugue*). Rather, subjects typically retain normal access to memories of all kinds (declarative, semantic, episodic) which were acquired well before the time of injury.

The most common symptom profile of patients with severe but selective hippocampal lesion is complete anterograde amnesia with limited retrograde amnesia leading up to the time of trauma, which suggests that memories gradually migrate from short-term to long-term storage during a critical consolidation period.[12] This is indicated in part by retrograde amnesia, which typically follows a pattern showing very slight

---

[12] For a recent empirical study on this phenomenon, see Kitamura et al. (2017).

memory loss for some time before the trauma, increasing gradually to almost complete memory loss in the hours and days before the trauma. Working memory and general problem-solving aptitude appear unaffected by selective hippocampal lesion, although in acute anterograde amnesia, thoughts which fade from working memory are lost forever. Memory patient HM, who had his MTLs removed during neurosurgery which attempted to alleviate his severe epileptic seizures, vividly and influentially exhibited this symptom. HM could recall his childhood and many aspects of his life before the surgery, but he had lost almost all memories in the months leading up to the operation and exhibited a complete inability to form new memories of specific events and episodes. Nevertheless, post-surgery HM retained some forms of learning for new skills and habits, such as reading words backward using a mirror or learning to make new visual discriminations. His ability to acquire these habits was very inefficient, however, often taking hundreds and hundreds of trials. As a result of such observations, neuroscientists hypothesized that the hippocampus plays a role in a distinctive form of rapid memory for episodes ("episodic memory") and functions as a crucial "buffer" and "gateway" in the transfer of episodic memories from rapid and fragile short-term storage to more robust and long-term storage in the cortices.

The hypothesis inspired the influential taxonomy of memory systems found today in many psychology and neuroscience textbooks. On this division, long-term memory can be divided into declarative and nondeclarative forms; declarative memories are verbalizable and explicit, whereas nondeclarative memories are nondiscursive, implicit, and automatic. Declarative memory is further subdivided into semantic memory for general facts and abstract knowledge, and episodic memory for specific, egocentric what-when-where information about particular events, arranged in a subjective timeline.[13] That the

---

[13] This is closer to the original definition of episodic memory offered by Tulving (1972). More recently, Tulving and others have tied episodic memory more closely to autonoetic consciousness and phenomenology, which is a subjective sense of reliving that occurs when episodic memories are recalled (Klein 2016; Tulving 2001). I think this identification of episodic remembering with a particular kind of phenomenology is a mistake because it makes it difficult to study episodic memory in nonhuman animals and is not the best explanation for behavioral data available, but we will not enter into this debate here (Clayton and Russell 2009; Gentry 2023).

hippocampus plays some such role in memory for episodes is beyond doubt, but more recent work has revealed that its function extends far beyond its role in episodic memory to many other forms of associative learning as well. Far from being merely a specialized system for autobiographical memory, the hippocampus and other MTL structures appear to play a variety of more domain-general roles in associative learning more generally, especially in spatial, temporal, and social domains (Konkel and Cohen 2009; Kumaran and Maguire 2005; Montagrin, Saiote, and Schiller 2018).

In fact, humans and animals with MTL lesions also display abnormal profiles in many other associative learning paradigms (for a review, see Gluck and Myers 2001a). These tasks in one way or another all reflect the flexibility and transferability of associations to contexts which are dissimilar to the training context, a feat that is often considered criterial for rational cognition in comparative psychology (Buckner 2015). For example, latent inhibition is often glossed as the ability to "tune out" irrelevant background cues and focus on novel and useful ones. In latent inhibition experiments, animals are exposed to a cue that predicts no significant outcomes for some period of time (e.g., playing a tone randomly in the background) and then later tested on their ability to learn a new association (e.g., a contingency between the tone and the availability of food). Animals are said to show the latent inhibition effect if their learning is diminished on the cue that was previously shown to be nonpredictive of significant outcomes. Latent inhibition displays a form of cognitive control and flexibility, because it reflects the animal's ability to learn which cues are likely to provide useful information in particular contexts and to ignore those that are uninformative.

Sensory preconditioning experiments offer another example of the role the MTLs might play in enabling more controlled and flexible associative learning. In these experiments, animals are first trained on the conjunction of two stimuli, such as a light and a tone, with no reinforcement or unconditioned stimulus (US, such as an eyeblink). In the second stage of learning, the animals are trained that one of the stimuli (the conditioned stimulus [CS], e.g., the tone) predicts a US. In the third stage of learning, animals are tested on the other stimulus (e.g., the light) in isolation. Animals with intact brains typically show some conditioned response to the other stimulus (called *transfer*); yet animals with hippocampal lesions show significantly diminished transfer. This illustrates another form of flexible control over associative learning, namely an ability to import information learned from one stimulus configuration to another, even if the cues have not all co-occurred in the organism's previous experience.

Negative patterning tasks constitute a third example. Animals are first trained that two stimuli individually predict a reward such as food; they are then trained that the compound of the two cues does not predict a reward. Animals with MTL lesions require far more trials to master a negative patterning design than animals with intact MTLs. Thus, and tellingly, we might note that the complaints about efficiency and transfer that were directed at DCNNs in the previous chapter seem to apply equally well to MTL-lesioned animals. They seem to behave like the slow-learning, stimulus-response automata associated with behaviorism. This provides evidence that the MTLs contain difference-making structural aspects which perform the computational roles that allow humans and animals to achieve more efficient and flexible forms of associative learning, specifically by allowing them to acquire more complex and abstract associative representations.

Another key piece of evidence in favor of the distinctive computational role that MTL structures play in uniting diverse elemental associations into more integrated wholes can be recovered from its hypothesized role in spatial navigation. In the 1970s, O'Keefe, Dostrovsky, and Nadel (O'Keefe and Dostrovsky 1971; O'Keefe and Nadel 1978) conducted a series of studies in which electrodes were implanted into the hippocampi of rats performing spatial navigation tasks. They discovered that the hippocampus contains large numbers of *place cells*, neurons that fire selectively when the rats were in specific locations of their testing chamber. These place cells appear to bind together a variety of idiosyncratic views from a particular location into an egocentric representation of that location. Subsequent research has found that such place cells can become organized by interaction with another type of cell in the entorhinal cortex (called "grid cells") into topographical networks at various spatial scales, forming nested cognitive maps of the animal's environment (Moser, Kropff, and Moser 2008). In short, the place cells bind multiple views from a particular location into a composite representation, and the grid cells help organize those place cell representations into maps organized by spatial dimensions. Much research in cognitive neuroscience has supported the conclusion that spatial navigation is heavily impaired by lesions to the MTLs (Morris 1983), further supporting the computational hypothesis that the integrative work of binding these representations of egocentric location together into integrated, nested spatial representations of the organism's environment is performed by subareas of the MTLs.

Further indirect evidence for the MTLs' roles in building more configural and abstract representations comes from associative learning tasks that are designed specifically to assess an animal's ability to transfer from one kind of problem to another, such as the "easy-hard transfer" learning paradigm (Moustafa, Myers, and Gluck 2009). On a typical "easy-hard" design, animals are trained to a criterion on a simpler version of a sensory discrimination task and then thrust into a more difficult version of the same task on the same sensory continuum. For example, animals might first be trained to distinguish between two tones that are very dissimilar in frequency, and then in a second phase to discriminate two tones much closer in frequency. Intact animals learn the later episodes much more efficiently than animals with MTL lesions. Another related deficit demonstrated by MTL-lesioned animals is a difficulty inhibiting previously learned responses. Animals with MTL lesions are often hyperactive and impulsive, and show difficulty inhibiting and/or unlearning previously conditioned responses. Discrimination reversal tasks, for example—in which the US-CS schedule is reversed (e.g., switching from cue A being associated with US and B not, to B being associated with the US and A not)—take many more trials after MTL lesions. A reasonable explanation for this finding is that the lesioned animals have less abstract representations than the intact animals, and so must unlearn the simple associations by rote before displaying the correct response.

Though this brief qualitative profile of hippocampal function is far from complete—the brain area has an entire journal dedicated to it, as well as scores of books—it may suffice for present purposes. Though intact animals seem to underperform lesioned animals on a number of tasks, a strong case can be made for the intact response as the more flexible and efficient. For example, the "learned irrelevance" acquired in latent inhibition will be adaptive when organisms must economize on limited attentional resources; sensory preconditioning will be adaptive when frequent correlations in the past are likely to be repeated in the future. In each case, the reader will observe that the MTL-lesioned animals come closer to acting like the behaviorist caricature of associative learning which has often been tacked onto neural-network-based AI by nativist critics, suggesting that implementing roles attributed to the MTLs can help DNNs overcome the limitations associated with these critiques without appealing to innate ideas.

To accommodate this long list of phenomena—the patterns of amnesia, efficiency, flexibility, and transferability observed in comparisons between animals with and without MTL lesions—ANN modelers have suggested that network-based cognitive architectures need at least two different network modules that interact with one another. The influential theory of McClelland, McNaughton, and O'Reilly suggests that future models should have one network corresponding to slowly acquired, long-term memory in the cortices and another corresponding rapid, short-term episodic memory in the medial temporal lobes. One core principle of this approach is that the two networks have different learning rates (Fig. 4.2). The MTL network has a rapid learning rate (in its backpropagation learning algorithm) which allows a smaller number of recent items to be perfectly recorded very quickly, whereas the cortical network would allow a much larger number of items to be integrated into a more abstract, durable, long-term memory store. The other key principle of their approach is that the short-term patterns acquired in the MTLs are gradually transferred over longer periods of time to the cortical network during periods of interleaved learning, which are thought to correspond to the memory consolidation which occurs in mammals during sleep and daydreaming. By reexposing the slower-learning cortical network to the same learning episodes recorded in the short-term buffer over longer periods of time, and by interleaving exposures involving different tasks and subject matters, the slower-learning cortical network can gradually integrate the new knowledge into the old in a way that avoids catastrophic interference

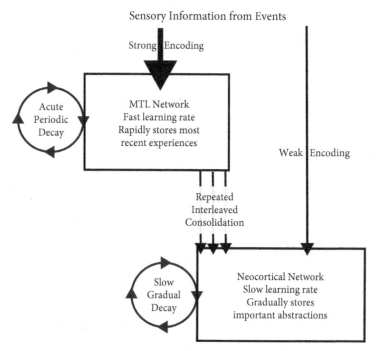

Figure 4.2 The complementary learning systems hypothesis from McClelland, McNaughton, and O'Reilly (1995).

and facilitates the extraction of more flexible, abstract knowledge that can be applied to a range of different tasks.

This insight adds, in effect, another significant multiplier in the quantitative comparisons between human and machine experience. Humans should be scored as having replayed the same training episodes for cortical learning hundreds or thousands of additional times in offline memory consolidation. This is not merely idle speculation; neural network models that build in episodic buffers and memory consolidation phases can make much more efficient use of training experience than models lacking these features.

The basic innovation of McClelland, McNaughton, and O'Reilly can be extended in a variety of other ways to make the cortico-hippocampal learning leverage experience even more efficiently. Gluck and Myers

(1993), for example, have argued that the MTL system should not be modeled as another generic ANN module that learns using standard supervised learning, but rather a module with a different architecture and learning regime, specifically a predictive autoencoder that learns using a kind of self-supervised predictive strategy. In short, in a predictive autoencoder, the neural network's input and output are connected to the same highly processed stimulus input stream, and the network is trained on its ability to predict the future state of the stimulus input on the basis of its previous state. The inputs can include labels as well as affectively significant outcomes like reward or punishment; the network is trained using error backpropagation, but errors are generated on the basis of the success or failure at predicting the future input stimuli, rather than on predicting labels in an annotated training set. This modular, predictive approach to learning can explain a great deal of the associative learning and lesion data which we canvassed earlier, and because the system can learn from both labeled and unlabeled data, it is more efficient in its use of training data than other network architectures.

The scheme can be made even more biologically plausible and efficient in a variety of other ways, such as by modulating the learning rate of the cortical network according to the degree of prediction failure detected by the MTL network. Such modulation has been argued to correspond to the role played by surprise in the mammalian brain, which triggers a release of the neuromodulator acetylcholine into the cortical tissues from the nucleus basilis, causing a short-term increase in the plasticity of the cortical tissues (Hasselmo 2006). This allows the network to speed up learning in response to the level of predictability or unpredictability of the currently perceived stimuli. Organisms can quickly acquire the basics of new tasks and then switch to a slower learning mode that allows the discovery of more subtle and abstract associations when perfecting skills over longer periods of time. Additionally, when previously acquired associations lead to badly mistaken predictions, organisms can escape from incorrect assumptions by speeding up the revision process, allowing the model to "jump" out of local minima more quickly before switching again back to a safer and slower hill-climbing strategy that makes catastrophic interference less likely.[14] This and other adaptive modulation of hyperparameters like learning rates remains an underutilized trick in deep learning models; but rather than explore these implications further here, we now turn to deep reinforcement learning to see how some of these insights about the role of memory in rational decision-making, going all the way back to Ibn Sina, find expression in deep learning research.

4.5. Deep reinforcement learning

We are now almost in the position to review the applications that recent advances in deep learning have made of these insights regarding a distinction between multiple memory systems as a first step toward a more modular cognitive architecture. However, we should first review the details of reinforcement learning as a training algorithm for neural networks, and in particular deep-Q learning which is the most popular version adopted in recent deep learning models.

Reinforcement learning comprises a large area of research in its own right in AI, and it can be applied to either classical or network-based methods. Whereas supervised learning relies on a data set labeled with the correct answers to generate the error signal used to tune link weights, reinforcement learning instead involves an unsupervised search for solutions to problems using trial and error. Organisms simply try out strategies to achieve goals in an environment, and they are trained on the basis of reward or punishment signals which tell the network whether what it did was generally "good" or "bad." This is often compared to dopaminergic learning in biological brains, dopamine being the "feel good" neurotransmitter that is released when we achieve a biologically rewarding outcome such as food, pleasure, or social acclaim (Botvinick et al. 2020; Glimcher 2011).[15] The real trick

---

[14] A variety of other neuroanatomically inspired approaches have also been explored; for example, another recent and promising idea which is fully consistent with moderate empiricism emphasizes a role for active dendrites in switching between tasks (Iyer et al. 2021).

[15] A critical insight of the last few decades' research on dopaminergic learning is that the amount of dopamine is regulated not merely by reward, but rather by reward prediction error (Glimcher 2011). Receiving more reward than expected produces an above-baseline amount of dopamine, receiving an expected reward delivers a baseline amount

of artificial reinforcement learning involves the creation of an effective valuation function. Whereas labeling of correct answers for the data set is often the limiting factor in supervised learning regimes, generating a robust valuation function is often the hardest part of successful reinforcement learning in ANNs.

Many of the high-profile achievements of reinforcement learning in DNNs thus far have involved games like Go, chess, or Starcraft II, because game score provides an easily quantifiable reward signal. In other areas of research, such as artificial locomotion, creating an effective reward signal is more difficult. Many valuation functions reward an agent for simply moving forward in an artificial environment, perhaps with minimal energy expenditure by its digital avatar. We already considered the worries about "reward hacking" in Chapter 2; a poorly crafted reward signal will produce agents that chase goal proxies without achieving progress toward ultimate goals. An obvious disanalogy between these systems and real organisms is that biological systems have a body, which evolution has tuned into a rich, multidimensional source of reward appraisals and emotional responses that can be used to shape and guide learning. That said, humans are also notorious reward hackers, especially in environments where symbolic markers are used as proxies for rewards (known in associative learning theory as "secondary reinforcers"), such as money, social media likes, or academic metrics like citation rates or h-index (Buckner 2020a; Nguyen 2021). In such cases we should fault the (ir)rationality of these environments' designers, rather than of the agents that chase rewards within them.

Another major distinction in artificial reinforcement learning is whether the algorithm is "model-free" or "model-based." While the distinction is prevalent in the cognitive sciences, it can be difficult to define it in a way that allows a clean categorization of the subtle variations of recent deep reinforcement learning approaches. Despite the difficulty, the basic distinction is as follows. In model-based reinforcement

---

of dopamine, and receiving less reward than expected produces a below-baseline amount of dopamine. Merely contemplating rewarding outcomes can raise dopamine levels and contemplating failure can reduce them, so the neurotransmitter not only plays a role in reinforcement learning but also in motivation.

learning, agents build representations of plans and their expected future outcomes in order to choose between different policies. That is, the evaluation policy for some particular action involves some simulation of environmental dynamics of the results of that and other future actions. A paradigm example of a model-based reinforcement learning approach is found in AlphaGo, which uses Monte Carlo Tree Search to explore the likely outcomes of possible moves and countermoves, scoring the likelihood that they lead to a desirable goal (e.g., board control and game win). Model-free reinforcement learning instead tries to estimate the reward value of particular actions directly, without modeling the future effects of those actions. This usually involves keeping a running tally of the reward value of actions, or precomputing them in some other manner, so that reinforcement values do not need to be calculated from simulation of future consequences at the time of action. Some popular approaches sit astride this distinction, such as the "successor representation" theory (which is specifically theorized to account for the computation of reward values for future events in the MTLs) though we will not comment further on this approach here (Momennejad et al. 2017).

The distinction between model-free and model-based learning interfaces directly with the topics of this and the following chapter on imagination, as methods which are purely based on rehearsing previous associations from memory are generally classed as model-free, whereas model-based learning usually involves animals building and leveraging their own models of environmental contingencies to choose flexibly among options by consulting imagined simulations of future outcomes.

4.6. Deep-Q learning and episodic control

We are now positioned to explore some of the DNN-based models of episodic memory and explain how—by implementing some of the key ideas of Ibn Sina's account of abstraction in the inner senses, albeit perhaps via an independent discovery—they model key aspects of the human mind that enable more flexible and efficient decision-making. This may be seen to help agents bootstrap to Tier 3 of rational decision-making, which involves choice on the basis of an option's suitability to achieve some desired goal.

For the purposes of illustration, I will focus on one particularly popular approach to reinforcement learning in DNNs, deep-Q learning.[16] In Q-learning methods, the estimated value of an action in achieving some future goal or reward is represented with a parameter called the action's Q-value ('Q' for "Quality"—to which we should flag similarities to Ibn Sina's "intention" at the outset). Q-values for actions can be specified by the programmer, but in machine learning we are usually interested in agents that learn to estimate Q-values on their own, as a result of training. A naïve approach to Q learning might take agents to build a table of Q-values for performing various actions in various environmental circumstances ("states"), which it updates as it tries out actions in various contexts. It would then continuously update the table each time it observes the consequences of an action, to keep a running tally of how successful or unsuccessful that option was in that context (see Fig. 4.3). For example, if the agent jumps in state *S1* and obtains a desired goal, it might update the Q-value for the table location by incrementing it slightly or averaging the amount of reward it just obtained with the previous Q-values it obtained in that state (Table 4.1). Because the reward value is updated after each action and the table contains no representation of anticipated future effects of actions, this counts as a clearly model-free form of reinforcement learning.

A decision procedure needs to then be added which tells the agent how to choose actions at each state. The agent may choose actions randomly if it is merely exploring the reward structure of the environment; an agent might be programmed simply to choose the action with the highest reward value in its current state, should we want to maximize performance on the current trial (Fig. 4.3). Always choosing the action with the current highest Q-value might come at costs of missing out on other, more rewarding strategies, however, so decision procedures might want to also consider the value of occasional exploration of alternative strategies before always choosing the action with

---

[16] There are many other popular methods that we will not review here; actor-critic methods stand out as an especially popular alternative to DQN and are worth a look for interested readers (Mnih et al. 2016).

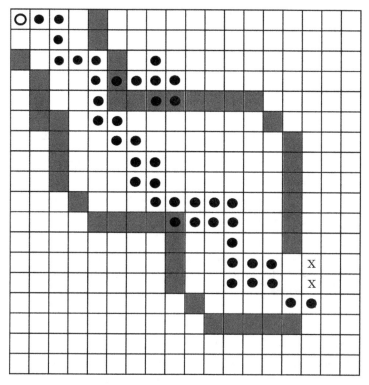

Figure 4.3 Potential results of applying a Q-learning pathfinding algorithm to a navigation task. A corresponding Q-table would often be updated using the Bellman equation (which iteratively updates the previous anticipated reward values in the Q-table according to parameters such as a learning rate, observed reward, and a discounting factor) throughout an exploration phase. Q learning is a model-free approach to reinforcement learning in that it does not attempt to predict the results of anticipated actions in the environment. In the path diagram, open circles indicate the starting position, dots indicate a traversed path, shaded blocks indicate barriers, and x's indicate goal states.

Table 4.1 A Sample Q-Table for Some Set of States $(S_1–S_4)$ and Actions It Can Perform in Those States

		Actions		
		Search	Jump	Wait
	S_1	3	0 (+1)	1
States	S_2	1	2	0
	S_3	0	1	1
	S_4	1	2	0

Note: The table depicts incrementing the Q-value of the action "Jump" in S_1, should jumping in that situation produce a successful outcome.

the currently highest estimated reward. Hybrid approaches are also possible, which try to achieve various tradeoffs between exploration and performance.

Location	←	→	↑	↓
Start	0	1	0	0
Correct path	0	17	0	17
Off path	5	0	2	3
Goal	0	1	0	0

In deep-Q learning, the role of the Q-table is performed by a DNN.[17] In other words, as the agent explores the environment, the output of a DNN (which also takes information about the agent's current state as input) is used to estimate the Q-value for the present action options, and this network is trained using gradient descent on the basis of the reward values obtained as a result of previous choices. The network is trained by using the divergence between the expected and actual reward

---

[17] Note that most deep-Q learning networks actually require two separate networks to estimate the policy successfully, a "Main" model and a "Target" network, which have the same architecture but different weights. The Main network weights typically replace Target network weights after some interval. As this is only required for stability and some methods attempt to obviate the need for the Target network, I will not comment further on it here.

as the error signal to adjust link weights through backpropagation, and so over time the Q-value network becomes a better predictor of the actual reward values for particular actions in particular contexts. Of crucial note to the present comparison, this value estimation network maps situation variables to action-value pairs. In other words, the affective value of the action is built into the network's output representation, and the output representation is computed from an abstract representation of the agent's current situation.

This basic kind of deep-Q learning produced alluring early results. For example, a variant of this method developed by DeepMind, called DQN, was able to play Atari games at superhuman levels of success (Mnih et al. 2013). This particular method used a deep convolutional network which took input directly from high-dimensional screen input image data and output action-Q-value pairs for a variety of different Atari games, including Beam Rider, Breakout, Enduro, Pong, Q*bert, Seaquest, and Space Invaders. This approach achieved a significant advance in artificial reinforcement learning, because previous methods generally had to hand-engineer effective features for Q-learning methods. This approach leveraged the DCNN's ability to extract abstract, high-level features directly from high-dimensional input to learn effective policies directly from the data itself. As a result, the DQN networks exceeded all previous artificial machine learning model performance on most Atari games and exceeded expert human performance on some, and more recent DQN-based models remain competitive for state-of-the-art performance on such games.

Even the earliest version of the DQN architectures integrated insights about a distinction between long-term and short-term memory, for some of the earliest implementations of this idea suffered from catastrophic interference and were often trapped in poor local minima. Mnih et al. (2013) at DeepMind, taking inspiration from earlier work by Long-Ji Lin (1992), added an experience replay element to their DQN model to address these issues (Fig. 4.4).[18] An

---

[18] This element was introduced by Lin to address the same sorts of problems that McClelland, McNaughton, and O'Reilly describe under the heading of "catastrophic interference" in their (1995): "During training a network, if an input pattern has not been presented for quite a while, the network typically will forget what it has learned for that pattern and thus need to re-learn it when that pattern is seen again later. This problem

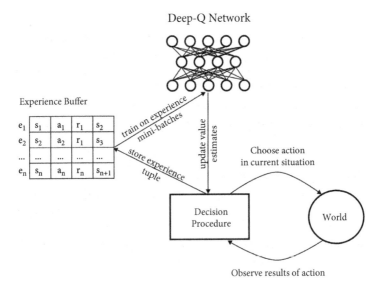

Figure 4.4 Deep-Q Network architecture schematic based on Mnih et al. (2013).

"experience" in this case is defined as a four-tuple (s_t, a_t, r_t, s_{t+1}), consisting of a situation's input variables at some time t (s_t, e.g., pixel information from an Atari game screenshot), an action which was taken at t (a_t), a reinforcement value obtained from choosing action a at time t (r_t), and the subsequent state of the network at time $t + 1$ (s_{t+1}). These experiences are pooled in a long-term memory store called "replay memory." In the DQN learning algorithm, the Q-learning algorithm is applied to minibatches of experiences sampled randomly from this replay memory store. This is like learning from shuffled sequences of gameplay experience over longer periods of time, effectively implementing the interleaved memory consolidation idea in the context of deep reinforcement learning to avoid catastrophic forgetting by intermittently refreshing older and more distant sets of

is called the re-learning problem" (Lin 1992:28). Despite all of McClelland, O'Reilly, and Lin being at Carnegie Mellon at about the same time, I am unable to determine the original source of this idea.

experiences.[19] As the reader will have already noted, the idea that affectively labeled experience explains flexible decision-making is surprisingly similar to the one that Ibn Sina offered in his theory of the inner senses reviewed earlier. The memory store also shares some features in common with the MTL network of McClelland, McNaughton, and O'Reilly, since it has a limited buffer size and older experiences are rewritten when the buffer gets full. Notably, this form of experience-guided Q-learning is already much more efficient than DNN-based Q-updating without experience replay, and this was perhaps the first neural-network-based model which could be said to leverage both the power of DCNNs to extract abstract features directly from raw perceptual input and to leverage experience replay for efficient, consequence-sensitive decision-making.

Some early comparisons have even been drawn between the abstract representations learned by such networks and those of humans trained on playing similar games. Like the line of investigation revealing similarities between the representations learned by DCNNs and the ventral stream (Lindsay 2021), research has found a striking degree of similarity between the representations built in layers of the DQN network and functional magnetic resonance imaging (fMRI) data recorded from various locations in the human dorsal stream while playing Atari games, though it did not find the same degree of correspondence in intermediate layers (Cross et al. 2021). The dorsal stream has long been thought to provide abstracted, nuisance-controlled, task-relevant information to later decision-making systems, suggesting that the DQN networks and dorsal stream might be solving the same problem, if not exactly in the same manner. Research efforts are currently underway to improve the fit in intermediate representations in the dorsal stream and DQN networks without violating the empiricist goal of end-to-end training (Köster and Chadwick 2021).

Despite these striking results, early DQN networks still require an order of magnitude more hours of play experience than human

---

[19] Many findings of this research might be surprising to readers first encountering it. For example, Mnih et al. (2013) discovered that learning from sequential samples was inefficient, since there is so much redundancy between successive frames. Random selections of temporally distant experiences turned out to be more efficient.

subjects require to achieve similar scores. Mnih et al.'s (2013) DQN network, for example, was provided with 10 million frames of gameplay (and a 1 million frame episodic buffer) to achieve its benchmark scores, amounting to hundreds of hours of gameplay. Humans, by contrast, can achieve passably good play in a matter of hours. One of the ideas that Mnih et al. suggested to further improve the use of the episodic replay buffer was to learn selectively from especially surprising or rewarding experiences that were particularly likely to be illuminating (Moore and Atkeson 1993). Another suggestion involved reasoning over the limited stock of experiences in the replay buffer themselves while training up more abstract and generalizable representations in the main policy network.

This latter idea is elaborated and combined with some of the other MTL-inspired ideas in the "Episodic Controller" architecture of Blundell et al. (2016). Blundell et al. start from the observation that DQN learning requires agents to stumble upon highly rewarding sequences of actions by trial and error, and then only very gradually update Q-values for these effective actions using the method of gradient descent learning. This requires the network to stumble upon these highly rewarding actions many times before weights become adjusted sufficiently for the network output to capture the true reward value for those actions. They note that humans and animals latch onto especially successful strategies much more rapidly in short-term learning, and this kind of efficiency boost might be granted to episodic replay if replay focused only on highly rewarding experiences and replaying experiences that previously yielded high returns. They further speculate that this process is akin to the reinstatement of state-action sequences observed in place cells in hippocampal region CA3 in animal models subsequent to learning episodes, with the replay curiously occurring in temporally reverse order, suggesting a process of evaluation (Foster and Wilson 2006). Blundell et al. further suggest that these quick-to-learn representations of state-action-value bindings can be used more directly for decision-making while consolidation trains up the slower but more generalizable decision-making system in the cortices as described in the DQN system. They call the resulting system the "Episodic Controller" architecture.

This approach is akin to adding an explicit Q-table back into the decision-making process of a DQN model, to allow decisions in short-term, deterministic contexts, where good choices can be made simply by choosing the action that previously yielded the highest reward in the present circumstance. The idea is inspired by the thought that the CA3 bindings in the hippocampus might function like a table that keeps track of the highest-rewarded sequence of actions in that circumstance. When an action sequence is discovered that has a higher reward value in that circumstance, it simply overwrites the previous binding in that location. As Blundell et al. note, this reintroduces some of the drawbacks of the tabular approach to reinforcement learning, namely it does not scale well and generalizes poorly to dissimilar situations. The first concern is addressed by the limited size of the Episodic Controller architecture. Because the episodic buffer is smaller in size and is frequently rewritten (when the buffer is out of room, the least recently used policy is discarded to make room for new information), it does not need to record all possible action sequences which need to be considered. The forgetting mechanism naturally helps prioritize memories of recent and successful action sequences over older and less successful ones. Though the Blundell et al. (2016) paper did not do so, the second concern about generalizability could be addressed by allowing the agent to train up gradually a slower-learning DQN system with more abstract representations.[20] This would be more in line with the original insights from McClelland, Rumelhart, and O'Reilly (1995) and that I traced earlier all the way back to Ibn Sina. Nevertheless, the simpler Episodic Controller architecture was able to achieve high-scoring performances with only a fraction of the training experience required by the DQN architecture.

It should also be noted that this method allows for a kind of one-shot learning that is not possible in generic DQN architectures. It should thus be expected to outperform more intensive learning strategies any

---

[20] The Blundell et al. Episodic Controller model instead addressed generalizability by adding a decision policy which averaged over the k-nearest-neighbors (in this case they used eleven nearest neighbors). This is a way of attempting to generalize on the fly without building more generalizable representations. They note, however, that in the brain the hippocampal system would be binding representations that have already been abstracted by ventral stream processing akin to the DCNNs described in Chapter 3.

time that the optimal strategy can be learned from a single experience. An example suggested by Blundell et al. involves the caching behavior of corvid species (such as scrub jays—Dally, Emery, and Clayton 2006), which depends upon being able to maintain a large number of one-shot food-location-time bindings (some corvid species can recall thousands of individual locations over a time span of years). They further suggest that these two kinds of learning could be combined with a more model-based approach to planning which involves the simulation of future experience trajectories. We will discuss this kind of possibility at more length in the next chapter.

However, we should pause and note the distance we have made in ascending the Tiers of Rationality outlined in Chapter 2. Whereas the decision-making architecture of simple DCNNs described in the previous chapter only rose to Tier 2 by allowing some degree of abstraction, it did not yet clearly implement instrumental decision-making, which involves the selection of an option on the basis of its suitability to a goal. Both the DQN and Episodic Controller architectures start to make progress on Tier 3, as the addition of reinforcement value allows options to be selected on the basis of their suitability to a goal in the fungible currency of estimated reward. Agents may be comparing options only according to a single form of reinforcement value, such as game score; but this still amounts to a form of consequence-sensitive decision-making. Moreover, the agents can learn their own rankings of options in various circumstances, on the basis of their own interaction with the environment. In the case of DQNs, they are further learning to associate outcomes with abstract representations of situations, so that their strategies can generalize to some range of novel circumstances.

This may be seen to meet some key criteria for rational choice. For example, the philosopher Bermúdez suggests that it is a "minimal requirement that the selection of a particular course of action . . . be made on consequence-sensitive grounds" which includes a "comparison of that outcome with the likely outcomes of other possible courses of action" (2003:124). There are other forms of flexibility that we might desire in this criterion of rational choice; for example, we might want the agent to have more flexibility to choose which goals to pursue (instead of relying on a monolithic reward value function) or an ability to control which aspects of the comparisons they regard as decisive. These ideas will be explored in later chapters when we consider attempts to model attention and executive control in DNNs. But at present, at least, it seems that agents which combine DCNNs with Q-learning in this way have already made an important advance toward modeling rational decision-making.

4.7. Remaining questions about modeling memory

A number of remaining concerns relevant to the present empiricist project can be extracted from other recent trends in psychology, neuroscience, and philosophy of memory. One line of thought weakens the distinction between memory and imagination, by suggesting that the two faculties are more interrelated than we might have otherwise supposed. Two other lines of concern emphasize how far we still have to go in realizing the potential of MTL-centered representations to support more flexible and efficient transfer learning, focusing on the role of prior knowledge in shaping learning and the role played by place and grid coding. While these concerns will be addressed in more depth in later chapters, it is important to underscore here the philosophical provenance of similar concerns over recollective memory and creative imagination in enabling rational decision-making, in support of the broader project of assessing evidence for the DoGMA.

4.7.1. Playback, or creative reconstruction?

A recent trend in psychology, neuroscience, and philosophy of memory is a weakening of the distinction between imagination and memory, and correspondingly between memory having a primarily past-directed versus a future-directed function (De Brigard 2014; McClelland 1995; Robins 2019; Schacter and Addis 2007). To put the point another way, this line of research suggests that even normal recollection involves a certain degree of creative reconstruction, which appears to be biased toward future decision-making rather than accuracy to the past.

Concerns about the borderline between recollective memory and creative imagination also has esteemed philosophical provenance; Locke and Hume both saw memory and imagination to be closely related and worried about confusion among the deliverances of the two faculties. They tend to regard such confusions as psychological dysfunction, with Hume going so far as to caution strongly against indulging an overactive imagination:

> Nor will it be amiss to remark, that as a lively imagination very often degenerates into madness or folly, and bears it a great resemblance in its operations; so they influence the judgment after the same manner, and produce belief from the very same principles. When the imagination, from any extraordinary ferment of the blood and spirits, acquires such a vivacity as disorders all its powers and faculties, there is no means of distinguishing betwixt truth and falsehood; but every loose fiction or idea, having the same influence as the impressions of the memory, or the conclusions of the judgment, is received on the same footing, and operates with equal force on the passions. (T 1.3.10.9/123)

Hobbes had a different attitude toward such phenomena, opining that "imagination and memory are but one thing, which for diverse considerations hath diverse names" (Malcolm 1996:1.2). This view—which hinges on the observation that memory involves imaginative simulation of past events, and imagination involves recombination of previously remembered details—has also popped up in a number of other places in the history of psychology and neuroscience (Bartlett 1932; Neisser 1967; Rubin and Umanath 2015).

This constructive approach to memory takes the numerous experimental illustrations of misremembering and memory distortions from psychology as evidence not that memory is prone to widespread malfunction, but rather that adaptive reconstruction can help it serve its function as part of a larger system whose primary job is future-oriented decision-making. The general idea of this view is that memory only records compressed or crystallized "gists," which then get reconstructed into fuller simulations of the previous experiences when recalled (Werning 2020). Distortions and biases can be introduced either during the compression/storage phase or the reconstruction phase. We have also since learned that memories become plastic again when recalled, and information inserted during the recollection process can become part of the compressed store of the "reconsolidated" memory (Nader and Hardt 2009). This is one way that distorted or outright false memories can be created through repeated questioning or visualization exercises, and a primary reason that eyewitness testimony in court cases is (or at least, should be) increasingly regarded with skepticism (Loftus 1996).

There are a variety of ways to model these more creative aspects of memory reconstruction in neural networks. Even some of the simplest neural networks which reconstruct partial patterns using Hebbian learning (where neurons that "fire together wire together," as the slogan goes) will show these effects to some degree; every time a pattern is reactivated in a Hebbian learning model, it raises the possibility that new associations will be drawn into the pattern. Today, some methods add structural innovations to DNNs so that they discover sparser representations which can be more flexibly recombined with one another on demand, captured in the concept of "explicit disentangling" manifolds that was mentioned in the previous chapter. Variational Autoencoders (described in the next chapter), in particular, aim to screen off core features of events from their nuisance variation and represent them independently, so that they can be flexibly recombined (braided) to simulate previously experienced or novel events on demand. Furthermore, other systems might allow memories to be accessed not just for abstract decision-making as in the Episodic Controller architecture but also to create novel simulations which can themselves be the subject of reflection to allow for more active evaluation performed at the time of access. Other modelers, explicitly inspired by the attempt to understand the interplay between the ventral stream perceptual processing and recollective functions of the hippocampus, created a DNN-based modular system which discovers more abstract representations by generating novel simulations of members of previously encountered categories, which they called "category replay" (Barry and Love 2023). These possibilities will be discussed at more length in the next chapter, when we deal with generative neural network models of the imagination more directly.

At any rate, any model which can both generate reconstructions of previous events and simulations of novel events will need some way to counter Hume's worry about confusing actual from merely imagined experiences. This is one specific instance of the Control Problem that we mentioned in previous chapters; systems that feature multiple semi-independent modules which can compete with one another for resources and influence on decision-making will need some way to settle conflicts between systems. The problem will only become more pressing as we add more and more faculty modules to the DoGMA in search of more human-like and flexible decision-making.

4.7.2. Weak transfer to task variants

A further concern which we mentioned in Chapter 2 is that game-playing methods trained by reinforcement learning tend not to transfer well to variants of tasks. To revisit, Kansky et al. (2017) explored the performance of a deep reinforcement learning agent on variants of Atari games, such as modifications of Breakout where the paddle is raised a few pixels or is made half or twice as long.[21] They found that these agents performed poorly on task variants and showed little evidence of transferring skills from previous versions of the task, seemingly needing to relearn the game from scratch. This led them to conclude that these agents had not really learned meaningful abstractions on previous training of Atari games and had merely overfit superficial characteristics of the game. Thus, they conclude, we need new learning methods if we hope to approach human-like ways of playing these games.

This argument is premised on the idea that humans are untroubled by these task variants and are able to flexibly redeploy previous knowledge on modified tasks, which again focuses more attention on the aspects of the human side of the comparison which have not yet been modeled in DNN-based agents. However, few of these critics provide

---

[21] Instead of DQN, they actually tested a nearby method called Asynchronous Advantage Actor-Critic (A3C) learning (Mnih et al. 2016) because it was more efficient to run in simulations.

detailed empirical evidence for human performance on game variants. It is important to investigate empirically the nitty-gritty of human transfer on these exact tasks for a variety of reasons: we must verify that they are, in fact, untroubled by these specific variants; investigate which features of the games are critical for successful transfer; and determine the background knowledge that humans may be bringing to the task that facilitate their purportedly superior transfer. For example, it may be that humans have extensive experience with general physical principles like bouncing balls, game rules, or the affordances of objects like ladders or doors that they can use to adapt previous game strategies quickly to new contexts. There has been too little research on these questions, but notably Dubey et al. (2018) performed relevant experiments on humans, using a masking design to assess which features of Atari game variants affected human performance. In this design, they systematically altered the appearance of parts of the game (by changing colors or sprites, e.g., so that a threat [such as spikes] looks like a colored square ["masked semantics"] or looks like something with a different connotation, such as an ice cream cone ["reverse semantics"]). When these features were altered, humans took significantly longer and performed significantly worse in the game. The experimenters even investigated more drastic alterations of the game, such as changing its basic physics or the constancy of objects in the game; these versions of the game were even more difficult for humans to solve. This experimental design is notably unable to determine whether the knowledge that facilitated human transfer is innate or learned, but it can provide a target for deep learning agents on future transfer tasks, and it furthermore suggests a "taxonomy of priors" which could be targeted by further modeling. In this taxonomy, expectations about object behaviors are more critical to transfer behavior the earlier they are acquired in development, with very low-level things like basic physical principles coming first, and high-level object similarity judgments coming in last.

While the DNN-based models discussed earlier in this chapter demonstrate the significant flexibility improvements that have already been achieved by modeling aspects of human memory in artificial agents, the comparisons to the psychology and neuroscience of human memory suggest that there remain many more untapped aspects for

DNN modelers to explore—but that doing so might run into inherent tensions between reliability and flexibility in learning theory. There is notably a tension here between granting agents the flexibility to remap previous knowledge to novel superficial changes in game variants and the threat of catastrophic forgetting mentioned earlier in the chapter, for allowing too much representational flexibility might lead networks to overwrite their solutions to the previous variants of the game. More work is needed on this tension in deep learning, but there are already a few promising developments. In particular, the concept of a "progressive neural network" has been developed by Rusu et al. (2016). Progressive neural networks consist of many different "columns" of weights between input and output. Each column can be thought of as an independent set of policies which can be tailored to a particular task variant. The columns are trained one at a time, with the first column being trained just like a normal DNN. The key change of progressive neural networks is that when the system moves to a new task variant, it archives the previous weights and begins training a fresh column of weights. The training of the fresh column does not have to start from scratch, however, as there are horizontal links between the hidden layers of the previous columns and the new column. Thus, the learning of the new column can be bootstrapped and accelerated by the representations in the previous columns, while also allowing for entirely new representations to be learned when necessary. Since the old weights are always archived, progressive neural networks are immune to catastrophic forgetting by design.

While the strategy deployed by progressive neural networks seems to bear some similarity to human learning, it may also be seen to rely on some artificial aspects. How does the brain know when a new task is begun, so that it needs to switch to a new column of neural connections? Does the brain really sit on unused representational resources indefinitely, until they are pressed into service for new tasks? And once columns are trained, how does the brain decide which column to use to solve the task, and how does it navigate between columns? There is some preliminary evidence in neuroscience that the kind of grid coding which allows navigation in spatial domains can be used to navigate more abstract conceptual taxonomies as well (Constantinescu et al. 2016; and for discussion in this context, see

Hassabis et al. 2017:252; Moser et al. 2008). However, this idea remains highly speculative. Once again, adding more modular structure to the basic DNN design seems to buy increased flexibility and biologically relevant performance gains, but only at the cost of increasing the complexity of the corresponding Control Problems.

4.7.3. Grid coding for transferrable deep learning

A final line of research which could benefit from further development concerns the interplay between place and grid cells in human transfer learning. While the computational role of these cells was first discovered in spatial navigation, for the purposes of the DoGMA it is important to emphasize that they have since been found to play crucial roles organizing associations in a variety of other domains, with neuroscientists explicitly theorizing about temporal, taxonomic, and social place cells as well (Constantinescu et al. 2016; Duvelle and Jeffery 2018; Eichenbaum 2014; Omer et al. 2018).[22] A few models have recently been proposed to implement place-and-grid-cell coding for DNN models, with others wondering whether this kind of behavior might emerge spontaneously in DNN-based systems without the need to add further structural aspects (Banino et al. 2018; Cueva and Wei 2018; Saxe, Nelli, and Summerfield 2020). These cells may be crucial in placing more elemental associations along monotonic dimensions (in whatever domain), which then allows for a semi-independent representational system which can be navigated by the agent for novel decision-making. For example, a DNN-based agent that could locate place representations on a shared spatial dimension might be able to plot a novel route between those two locations using intervening place nodes along that dimension in the grid, or to situate an event as having occurred between two other events by locating it in-between them along a temporal grid dimension. These sorts of flexible inferences have been considered some of the most impressive instances of transfer learning in comparative psychology, reflecting the ability of children

---

[22] I am grateful to Mariam Aly for discussion on this point.

after certain developmental milestones (or, potentially, some especially insightful animals) to deploy previously acquired knowledge to draw correct inferences in circumstances which are novel in associative learning terms (such as finding a new route in a maze or ranking the relative timing of two events which never overlapped).

4.8. Summary

With these further aspects of memory kept in mind as targets for future modeling endeavors, let us summarize the arguments of the chapter in service of the development and defense of the DoGMA. The previous chapter argued that significant progress has been made in modeling intermediate forms of perceptual abstraction using DCNNs. However, the current chapter pointed out that such models of perception still have significant disadvantages that leave them unlikely to scale up to successful models of general cognition. In particular, their learning is less efficient and flexible than that of humans and cognitive animals, and their performance is vulnerable to catastrophic interference. Here, we reviewed how introducing a separate domain-general module to model memory—which can rapidly store particular important sequences of input data for reuse in offline learning and later decision-making, consonant with historical empiricist accounts of rational decision-making—can help address some of these disadvantages. Storing particular action-outcome sequences in a dedicated all-purpose buffer can allow agents to mitigate catastrophic forgetting through interleaved learning (as in architectures proposed by McClelland, McNaughton, and O'Reilly or Gluck and Myers), make more efficient use of previous experience by repeated offline training over successful sequences (as in Google's DQN architecture with experience replay), and rapidly acquire and repeat particularly effective strategies from the recent past in more consequence-sensitive decision-making (as in Google's Episodic Controller architecture). These innovations illustrate a key guiding principle behind the DoGMA: that multiple computational modules with different architectures can interact and modulate one another's operations to address one another's computational shortcomings. Combining different modules can thus allow systems to model higher tiers of rational flexibility; in particular, memory-enhanced systems both enhance their Tier 2 abstractive performance and begin to rise to Tier 3, using consequence-sensitive mnemonic strategies to choose actions based on their suitability to achieve goals.

With the benefits of adding memory modules to DNN-based architectures kept in mind, let us now turn our attention to the further progress that can be made by modeling the more creative repurposing of associations that empiricists across the cognitive sciences have traditionally attributed to the closely-related faculty of imagination.

5

Imagination

> Nothing is more free than the imagination of [humans];
> and though it cannot exceed that original stock of ideas,
> furnished by the internal and external senses, it has unlim-
> ited power of mixing, compounding, separating, and di-
> viding these ideas, in all the varieties of fiction and vision.
> —Hume, *EHU* 5.2.10/47

5.1. Imagination: The mind's laboratory

Creativity is a critical component of rational intelligence. We have
noted in previous chapters how humans and some animals can act
in ways that exhibit "leaps of insight" but also how some of these
leaps might be explained by appeal to more abstract associative
representations discovered through the operations of domain-general
faculties like perception and memory. However, even these forms
of abstraction appear inadequate to explain the most novel acts of
thought. In humans, we often explain these more creative mental
maneuvers by appealing to reasoning over representations of novel
categories or simulated scenarios never observed in the past. These
forms of novel representation pose an obvious challenge to empiricist
approaches to rationality, which attempt to explain problem-solving
in terms of learning from prior experience. When empiricists have
discussed such creative insights, they typically account for them using
mental imagery, daydreams, or fantasies played out in the faculty of the
imagination.

One empiricist who has quite a lot to say about the imagination
in this context is David Hume. As we have already observed, Fodor

From Deep Learning to Rational Machines. Cameron J. Buckner, Oxford University Press.
© Oxford University Press 2024. DOI: 10.1093/oso/9780197653302.003.0005

disagrees with Hume (and other associationists, connectionists, and empiricists) when it comes to this kind of appeal to empiricist faculties. We countered some of Fodor's concerns in previous chapters—in particular, we rebutted Fodor's argument that Hume's use of faculty psychology was somehow in tension with his empiricism. As we concluded earlier, the proper response to Fodor's critique emphasizes the flexibility of origin empiricism as delimited by the Transformation Principle. On this view, if the raw materials provided from the senses are transformed by the faculties without adding any innate domain-specific rules or representations, whatever output they produce still counts as derived from experience in the relevant sense. This is significant for the other challenges that Fodor poses to empiricism— especially regarding the mind's abilities to synthesize particular ideas for use in reasoning, to compose novel ideas that have never been presented in sensory experience, and to build simulated scenarios to engage in relational and probabilistic reasoning—for Hume assigns all of these operations to the imagination.

However, even after granting Hume access to faculty psychology for the sake of argument, Fodor is still not satisfied. He notes that Hume does not explain how the imagination actually performs any of these operations, and so Hume's account must be regarded as incomplete. On the other hand, if deep learning can explain how physical systems adhering to the Transformation Principle could perform some of these processes, then we may have another case where deep learning can redeem a valuable promissory note from the history of empiricism. This promissory note is of special value at our current point in the development of the new DoGMA, as the operations on Fodor's list are indeed crucial to the human mind's ability to achieve levels of creativity and insight not yet available to an agent possessing only perception and memory. Investigating Fodor's criticisms of Hume in more detail here might thus help engineers bootstrap artificial agents to the next Tiers of Rationality and flexible decision-making.

Perhaps for related reasons, "imagination" has independently become a buzzword over the last few years in deep learning, with modelers claiming to achieve a variety of breakthrough results by introducing components to network models that play one or another role attributed to the imagination in human psychology and neuroscience. These breakthroughs include some of the most exciting results in artificial intelligence (AI): the creation of deepfakes and other photorealistic stimuli, "style transfer" which can very quickly render a photograph taken on a cell phone into a high-resolution image of a painting done in the style of Van Gogh or Munch, the use of offline learning on self-generated data sets, and planning and decision-making methods that make use of possible future scenarios. These achievements are directly relevant to the jobs which Hume assigned to the imagination in his distinctively empiricist take on rationality.

By placing the functioning of these imagination-like components with respect to empiricist philosophical psychology, we can render intelligible the implications they hold for our understanding of cognition and artificial rationality.[1] Fodor's objections to Hume here are colored by his influential arguments against second-wave connectionism, which we reviewed in Chapter 2, particularly whether neural networks can implement compositionality. By exploring whether recent deep neural network (DNN)-based systems can address these worries, we can also assuage lingering doubts as to whether deep learning—particularly as enhanced by the faculties highlighted in the DoGMA—is genuinely game-changing in AI when compared to earlier waves of artificial neural network (ANN)-based research.

Let us thus consider two sets of objections from Fodor in turn—first, those directed at Hume's empiricism and associationism generally (and how Hume's appeals to the imagination are supposed to rebut them), and second, those targeted specifically against Hume's doctrine of the imagination itself. In subsequent sections, we can examine imagination-like components that have been added to recent DNN-based models to explore if—and how—they address Fodor's concerns. This comparison enables a deeper evaluation of the role played by the

---

[1] As with all of these appeals to "rich" psychological vocabulary, we should be skeptical here as to whether the tools designed bear a significant similarity to faculties studied in human psychology (Shevlin and Halina 2019). These appeals may be backed by underlying processing that is importantly like the imagination in human psychology and so counts as modeling these faculties in humans and animals; or these appeals to the imagination may simply provide some looser inspiration for independent engineering discoveries.

imagination in rational decision-making more generally, especially from an empiricist perspective. We will find that the staggering recent successes of "generative" modeling in deep learning may turn what has looked in the historical record like an embarrassing lacuna in empiricist doctrine into one of its greatest strengths. To reprise a theme of Chapter 1, a strict reading of the Copy Principle suggests that the imagination is like the surface of a billiard table, on which the mind can bump previously experienced ideas into one another—forming simple concatenations and juxtapositions—through associationist "mental physics." If we instead suppose that the right analogy for empiricist faculty psychology is "mental chemistry" (following Demeter 2021), then the imagination becomes rather a laboratory in which the mind can concoct more audacious novelties—compounds and hybrids with new properties that exceed those of their mental reactants, and in virtue of which the mind can represent futures, fictions, and fantasies not yet witnessed in prior sensory experience.

5.2. Fodor's challenges and Hume's imaginative answers

Let us then explore Fodor's criticism of Hume, by starting with the three generic problems that Fodor poses to associationism (objections that Hume largely anticipates) and then moving on to the further objections that Fodor raises to Hume's account of the imagination itself.

5.2.1. Synthesizing tokens of categories for use in thought and inference

The first major problem that Fodor poses to associationism is that Hume's three laws of association alone do not explain the mind's ability to synthesize idea tokens. This claim requires a bit of elaboration. The gist here is that mental representations are types that can have causal efficacy only through being "tokened"—in other words, by having a particular member of that type of mental representation activated, as a particular mental event (whether in the nervous system or in an ANN) on a particular occasion. It is only through such tokening events that an account of mental causation can get off the ground on an associationist picture. Suppose we want to explain a particular example of behavior caused by conditioning; this behavior isn't explained by the fact that an organism possesses the category representation of BELL, which causes it to possess the category representation of FOOD, which in turn triggers food-seeking behavior—for the agent possesses these category representations all the time, regardless of whether it is currently thinking about bells or food. It is rather that a token of the category representation of a BELL (caused, for example, by the perception of a particular bell ringing in a particular pitch) causes a token representation of FOOD (for example, a mental image corresponding to some particular chow). Different bells and chow would trigger distinct tokens of these concepts. This is meant to be a general observation about causality, that tokens, not types, actually cause events in the world; we have a general observation that rocks can break windows, but that generalization holds only in virtue of particular (token) rocks breaking particular (token) windows.

This problem occurs with special urgency for Hume because he eschews Locke's appeal to general ideas and emphasizes the role played by representations of particular exemplars in cases of demonstrative reasoning. To recapitulate points from Chapter 3, when we try to evaluate the Pythagorean Theorem, we may evaluate a series of token triangles with particular combinations of angle degrees and side lengths, and see whether the theorem holds true of them on the basis of their particular properties. The laws of association say which types of ideas should be called up in which circumstances; but they do not say how the tokens of those types are generated and put to work in specific inferences. So, Fodor asks, how does the empiricist mind do this, if the laws of association do not explain these transitions?[2] Here,

---

[2] One thing must be mentioned at the outset: when considering the difficulty offering an associationist account of inference, Fodor tends to limit Hume's principles of association to two, those of contiguity and precedence, ignoring the principle of similarity (2003, fn. 9:119). On my view, the principle of similarity does the lion's share of the work in rational inference, and rightly so.

Hume appeals to the imagination (Fodor 2003:122), and so we find the first essential job that the imagination might do for our new empiricist DoGMA: synthesize appropriate tokens of general categories on demand for use in thought and reasoning.

Hume notes that the ability to synthesize appropriate ideas and sample them in a way which accurately represents the distribution of a general category is essential to intelligence. Several of the problems with abstraction-as-representation that we raised and tabled in Chapter 3 must thus be addressed now—insofar as they are to be solved at all and do not simply serve as constant challenges to rational cognition—by the faculty of imagination. As Hume puts the challenge:

> One would think the whole intellectual world of ideas was at once subjected to our view, and that we did nothing but pick out such as were most proper for our purpose. There may not, however, be any present, beside those very ideas, that are thus collected by a kind of magical faculty in the soul, which, tho' it be always most perfect in the greatest geniuses . . . is however inexplicable by the utmost efforts of human understanding. (T 1.1.7.15/23–24)

Again, in the twenty-first century we should aspire to advance beyond Hume's exasperation. Consonant with Hume's final comment here, we should also be able to say something about individual variation in the ability to synthesize appropriate and representative exemplars, specifically in a way that can say why some individuals might be more successful at it than others.

5.2.2. The productivity of thought

Rationalists in general—and Fodor in particular—tend to be very impressed with the productivity of human thought. By "productivity" here, we mean the mind's ability to create a potentially infinite number of novel ideas by recombining old ones in systematic ways. And indeed, there does seem to be something distinctively and perhaps even uniquely human at issue here that explains the apparently open-ended potential of human thought and culture. When I teach Fodor in my philosophy of mind courses, I use a fanciful example to illustrate this to my students: "Suppose there were a tiny pink elephant in a tutu holding an umbrella and hanging from the ceiling in the back of the classroom while singing a sea shanty." The remarkable thing about this sentence is that my students all know what the situation it describes would look like, despite never having considered this combination of concepts and phrases before in the past (I hope). Fodor offers his highest praise to Hume for recognizing the centrality of thought's productivity to human cognition. Hume considered "chimerical" ideas like UNICORN (a horse with a horn) and THE NEW JERUSALEM (with streets of gold and walls inlaid with gemstones) as potential counterexamples to his associationism; for how could an empiricist mind formulate such ideas if it had never experienced them before in the past? Hume's answer to this challenge involves another appeal to the imagination.

Hume explicitly relies upon the imagination to explain the origin of novel complex ideas. Locke also recognized thought's productivity to some degree, noting that chief among the "powers" of the mind is the ability to "repeat, compare, and unite [ideas] even to an almost infinite Variety, and so . . . make at Pleasure new complex Ideas" (*E* II.ii.2). Hume furthers Locke here by explicitly granting the imagination freedom from merely following the well-trod paths of prior patterns of association, being "unrestrain'd to the same order and form with the original impressions" (*T* 1.1.3.2/9) and enjoying instead a "liberty . . . to transpose and change its ideas" at will (*T* 1.1.3.4/ 10) (and see also Costelloe 2018:16). This is also a context in which we find some of our most important textual evidence in favor of the Transformation Principle, as Hume insists that the imagination is capable of "mixing, compounding, separating, and dividing these ideas, in all the varieties of fiction and vision" (*EHU* 5.2.10/47). The imagination can decompose ideas into their simplest components and rearrange them flexibly, in the shape of "winged horses, fiery dragons, and monstrous giants" (*T* 1.1.3.4/10). Fodor thinks this all sounds great as an advertising pitch for Hume's faculty psychology; but as we shall see later, he insists that the devil is hiding in the details which Hume declines to provide.

5.2.3. Distinguishing between causal and intentional relations among thoughts

Perhaps the biggest concern that Fodor has for Hume's associationism—at least, before it is supplemented with the imagination—is that, as he puts it, associationists "aren't able to distinguish the intentional relations amongst the contents of thoughts, from the causal relations among the thoughts themselves" (Fodor 2003:113–14). In short, the laws of association excel at providing us with causal relations between ideas—telling us why one idea would be followed by another according to prior patterns of contiguity, priority, and resemblance—but they cannot distinguish different ways of relating the ideas so sequenced. This poses a problem for comparative judgments among situations, as we would find in probabilistic reasoning. To illustrate the issue, consider a roll of a six-sided fair die; suppose the die has triangles on four sides and circles on two. The question is whether a mind governed by empiricist principles could conclude that the die is more likely to come up showing a triangle than it is to come showing a circle. As Fodor puts the problem pithily, a naïve associationist has no problem explaining "why, in these circumstances, one expects to roll triangles more often than one expects to roll circles"; but this is a quite different job than explaining why one "expects to roll triangles more often than circles" (Fodor 2003:114). In other words:

> What needs explaining is not that you would come to have the thoughts *it will come up triangle* and *it will come up circle* in a ratio of two to one; it's that you would also come to have the thought *that it will come up triangle and it will come up circle in a ratio of two to one*. In effect, the *two to one* bit needs to be in the scope of the *think that* bit. (Fodor 2003:114–15)

Notably, this challenge is not only a philosophical riddle for empiricist philosophers but also poses a practical problem for modelers who aim to create agents that can reason in this way. This kind of causal/intentional distinction poses a significant roadblock for our artificial agents' abilities to ascend the hierarchy of rational judgment, as this marks the difference between an agent that is simply more likely to choose the better bet than it is to choose the worse bet, from an agent that chooses the right bet for something like the right reasons.

Hume appreciates this problem and appeals again to the imagination (or interchangeably for Hume, the "fancy") to solve it. As he puts it in an important passage of the *Treatise*:

> When we transfer contrary experiments to the future, we can only repeat these contrary experiments with their particular proportions; which cou'd not produce assurance in any single event . . . unless the fancy melted together all those images that concur, and extracted from them one single idea or image, which is intense and lively in proportion to the number of experiments from which it is deriv'd . . . 'tis evident that the belief arises not merely from the transference of past to future, but from some operation of the fancy conjoin'd with it. This may lead us to conceive the manner in which that faculty enters into all our reasonings. (*T* 1.3.12.22/139–40)

Thus, the idea is that the imagination enables a kind of comparison of the likelihood of outcomes on the basis of a comparison among the intensity of their associated mental images, where those associated images are synthesized by the imagination rather than copied from experience. This further provides a model for other types of rational inferences—in this case, the imagination synthesizes a signal available at the personal level (the relative vivacity of ideas) which can serve as a heuristic marker of a more precise quantitative comparison (the comparative likelihood of two events), a signal which could be reliably manufactured entirely from the raw materials of experience (with Hume thus presaging a key idea of the heuristic approach to probabilistic reasoning made famous in the present day by Tversky and Kahneman [1974]).

5.2.4. Fodor's problems for Hume's doctrine of the imagination itself

Let us thus move on to the problems that Fodor finds with Hume's particular account of the imagination. The first and most basic problem that Fodor has with Hume's account is that he never explains how the faculty actually works; it is a "something-I-know-not-what" (Fodor 2003:115). Fodor alleges that Hume does not even explain the basic principles that govern the faculty, let alone how those principles are actually adhered to within it (e.g., the algorithms performed by the faculty on its inputs to produce its outputs).

The former part of this charge is a bit unfair; Hume does characterize the imagination's behavior in a variety of ways, at least at the level of "input-output" functional specifications. Hume describes the imagination as having both "mimetic" and "productive" modes; on the mimetic side it can copy previous impressions with more or less accuracy (as an expert artist might copy another's work, as Costelloe ably puts it) and use them to stand in for members of a larger class; and on the productive side it can combine ideas to create novel ones. Hume often characterizes the imagination as hedonistic, seeking to "make an easy and smooth transition among ideas in order to form a union or complete a whole, from which it derives pleasure" (Costelloe 2018:1). Its operations have a kind of inertia; Hume says the imagination "like a galley put in motion by the oars . . .carries on a train of observing a uniformity among its objects, [and] naturally continues, till it renders the uniformity as compleat as possible" (T 1.4.2.22/198 [Costelloe 2018:22]). This completionist tendency will have special significance in the context of neural network models, as we might read it today as the tendency to reconstruct partial patterns in a way that maximizes the subjective probability of the resulting representations, given previous experiences. As with many of his contemporaries, Hume is also concerned by the possibility of confusing the deliverances of the imagination with those of occurrent sensory impressions or recollected memories, and so specifies that ideas produced by the imagination are typically (in nonpathological cases) "fainter" and have less "vivacity" than ideas from other sources.

To emphasize the ways in which its operation does not follow narrowly from the principles of association, the imagination is described as also taking pleasure in novelty, "running, without control, into the most distant parts of space and time, in order to avoid the objects, which custom has rendered too familiar to it" (EHU 12.3.25/162). At the same time, Hume holds that the principles of association do constrain it in some ways, for he holds that "even in our wildest and most wandering reveries . . . we shall find, if we reflect, the imagination ran not altogether at adventures, but that there was still a connexion upheld among the different ideas, which succeeded each other" (*EHU* 3.1/23 [Costelloe 2018:17]). Imagination must "borrow [its] simple ideas from the impressions, and can never go beyond these original perceptions" (*T* 1.3.5.5.3/85) in either its mimetic or productive modes, though in the latter function it has wider freedom in how it combines disparate simple ideas and fills in the details of the composite (*EHU* 5.12/49). We also cannot imagine things that violate the laws of logic or possibility, such as the idea of a "mountain without a valley" (*T* 1.2.2.8/32).[3] When the faculty is confronted with a break in continuity or an apparent inconsistency, it will "seek relief" (*T* 1.4.2.37/206 [Costelloe 2018:23]) by attempting to fill in other background details that smoothe over the apparent inconsistency and render the composite more plausible. This, we may suppose, is why the unicorn is imagined as having a horn sprouting from the center of its forehead (because this is more similar to the locations where other animals grow horns), rather than out of its eye socket or ear.

The second part of Fodor's charge surely hits home, however; Hume several times describes the faculty as working like "magic," as having a kind of unconstrained freedom in its choice of combinations, and openly speculates in several places about its operations being necessarily inexplicable to human understanding. Fodor is concerned by Hume's negative characterizations of the faculty as not being entirely governed by the principles of association—and in fact, Fodor accuses Hume of appealing to the faculty as an ad hoc fix anytime he needs to explain an operation of the mind that would constitute a counterexample to his view. This starts to look bad for Hume in particular, and empiricism in general. We need some explanation of the general principles

---

[3] Despite the example of a mountain without a valley featuring prominently in Descartes's conceivability proof for God's existence and Hume's account of the limits of the imagination . . . volcanos like Kilimanjaro or Mauna Loa are famous examples of mountains without valleys. So much for conceivability being a good guide to possibility, even among the "greatest geniuses" like Descartes and Hume. (I thank Dan Kirchner for pointing out that this example has always been a bit silly, even if its failure provides more grist for my empiricist mill.)

by which the imagination solves the problems to which Hume tasks it to answer the charge of ad-hocery, or the empiricist DoGMA will be in no better a theoretical position than the nativist who invokes representational primitives like innate ideas without explaining their origins. Importantly, without an understanding of their origins in experience, the empiricist modeler cannot create an artificial system that can deploy these novel ideas in reasoning, as advertised.

The second major objection that Fodor has for Hume's distinctive account of the imagination is that it is hard to see how it could work without initiating some kind of regress or circularity problem. Specifically, this applies to the role the imagination is supposed to play in allowing us to consider aspects of resemblance among pairs (or sets) of specific exemplars in abstract thought and reasoning (using abstraction-as-representation). Recall that Hume, contra Locke, thought that there were no general ideas; he argues that whenever we suppose we are thinking of a general idea—to continue an example of Fodor's, like *sphere* in the abstract—we are really just considering a series of particular spheres and the ways in which they do or do not resemble one another in their aspects (e.g., their smoothness, or lack of angles, and so on). To develop this account of abstraction-as-representation, we need to explain how the imagination can focus on one particular aspect of the many possible resemblances on which we could focus— for as Goodman observed, any two ideas resemble one another in an infinite number of ways (Goodman 1972). Suppose that we were using an idea of a black sphere and of a white sphere to think about shape; we could also use the same pair of spheres to think about location or size, if we considered the way that those same exemplars resemble one another in different aspects.

Fodor charges that this explanatory debt threatens a kind of circularity or regress. As he puts it:

> Hume has to explain how we "turn our view" to the resemblance between a white sphere and a black sphere if we don't already have the concept of a shape as such. Surely "attending to their resemblance" is just noticing that although the spheres differ in their color, their shapes are the same. But you can't do that unless you have a concept that abstracts from the color of a sphere and applies to it just in

virtue of its shape, namely, the concept of a sphere as such. (Fodor 2003:149)

Fodor takes this problem to recommend his more amodal, classical approach to Hume's imagistic theory of abstract thought. We could, however, explore an alternative way out, by reinvigorating the Lockean account of abstract ideas within a Humean cognitive architecture (further enhanced, perhaps, by the Jamesian account of the faculty of attention, sketched in the next chapter). In short, perhaps Fodor's criticism of Hume's account of the imagination shows that there is a need for something like Lockean abstract ideas in our DoGMA after all—albeit, perhaps, to explain processing that is not fully available to introspection.

If we do reintroduce Lockean abstract ideas within a Humean account of the imagination, however, it raises additional questions for our contemporary computational tastes. For example, we need to revisit type/token and content/vehicle considerations at the level of these abstract ideas as well. I have been treating the representational status of particular ideas as relatively unproblematic, but these issues may loom at the level of abstract ideas (which may in part be why Hume eschewed them). A large literature has grown up in philosophy of cognitive science around what a mental or neural state has to do to count as a representation; to summarize a contentious literature, it needs to somehow stand in causal generalizations because it carries representational content, but it also needs to be typed according to nonsemantic properties that grant it causal efficacy in the system. In the present context, if these abstract ideas are to do work in addressing Fodor's concerns about the imagination (e.g., to explain how the imagination can focus on particular aspects of resemblance), we need to say why they count as representing the similarities they do, while also accounting for their instantiations in the system and the contributions they make to downstream cognitive operations that are appropriate to those contents.[4]

---

[4] To consider some of my own answers to these questions, see Buckner (2022).

The final problem that Fodor raises for Hume's account of the imagination regards its productive role in synthesizing novel ideas. What, Fodor asks, is the "glue" that holds these synthesized ideas together? In illustrating this question, we can contrast the (appropriately) synthesized idea of a unicorn with a mere concatenation of HORN and HORSE. A unicorn, again, is not a mere pile of horse and horn, but a particularly plausible fusion of these features. This, I will suggest, is related to the "completionist" principle that Hume attributes to the imagination, in that it seeks to achieve "pleasure" by resolving mysteries and inconsistencies in the ways deemed most likely on the basis of past impressions. The challenge here is to explain how the imagination resolves these issues to fuse novel combinations of abstract ideas together in a plausible manner. This is, of course, just the kind of practical challenge that generative DNN modelers confront on a regular basis when they try to create systems that can produce plausible artificial representations like deepfakes. Deep learning theorists may or may not be surprised to learn that these problems have been with us since at least Locke and Hume.

5.2.5. A caveat regarding biological plausibility

One admission I must make at the outset is that any structural linkages between the architectures that I am about to review and cognition in biological brains are more speculative than what has come before. We are in the early days of exploring artificial models of the imagination, and we have not yet had time to consider more and less neurobiologically plausible wiring principles that might produce these results. The case for neurobiological correspondence is strongest for DCNNs and weakens as we move throughout the rest of the chapters. We thus might consider the components that I will review shortly to be functional stand-ins or mechanism schemas; they show that the functions that Hume and other empiricists have attributed to the imagination can be performed by physically implementable network structures, but these structures may be mere stand-ins for the ones that actually implement these functions in the brain. Alternatively, those that favor nonmechanistic approaches to abstraction such as functionalism or mathematical explanation may be untroubled by the lack of known structural correspondence between the details of these artificial models and the neuroanatomy of the brain (Chirimuuta 2018; Weiskopf 2011). There may still be important similarities in the representational organization of artificial models and biological brains—in particular, the need for hierarchically structured and abstracted information, and the rendering of novel combination of those representational structures on the basis of background probability assumptions derived from previous experience. At the very least, these models will serve as "proofs of concept" that network-based mechanisms can solve these problems of reasoning and representation in something like the ways that Hume and other empiricists have long suggested. We return to this question at the end of the chapter once we have reviewed specific models.

5.3. Imagination's role in synthesizing ideas: Autoencoders and Generative Adversarial Networks

Let us begin our exploration of artificial models of imagination-like components with the role that imagination is purported to play in synthesizing new ideas. The thesis we are now exploring in response to Fodor is that the mind consciously represents individual category exemplars in demonstrative reasoning (consonant with Hume), and (in a departure with Hume) it nonconsciously represents something like Lockean general ideas in the form of transformed category manifolds. In Chapter 3, I told the story of how transformational abstraction allows the mind to move from specific exemplars to general category manifolds, by combining the operations of abstraction-as-composition and abstraction-as-subtraction. Deep convolutional neural networks (DCNNs) provided a mechanistic sketch of how this might work in the brain, by alternating operations of convolution (to compose configurations of features) and pooling (to render the detection of those features more invariant to idiosyncrasies in nuisance parameters). In the present chapter, however, I need to also address the problems that Fodor poses for the empiricist imagination. Here,

I will start with Fodor's first challenge, regarding the mind's ability to synthesize novel ideas for use in processes of reasoning and decision-making. To tackle this problem, I would also need some route back from transformed category manifolds to fully rendered particulars— with detailed values specified for all necessary nuisance parameters. In other words, we need to explain the mind's movement in the other direction as well, from general category representations back to specific ideas.

Surprisingly, deep learning has produced several forms of "generative" architecture that are just as capable of converting abstractions into exemplars as discriminative networks like DCNNs are in moving from exemplars to abstractions. Let us begin by reviewing the first and most influential form of this technology, Generative Adversarial Networks (or GANs). A GAN is an architecture consisting of a pair of networks—one a discriminative network (usually a DCNN of the sort we discussed in Chapter 3), and another of a generative sort to be elaborated now (Fig. 5.1). A GAN architecture pits these two networks against one another in a kind of competitive game. Specifically, the discriminative network will be shown some real inputs and some "fake" inputs created by the generative network, and the discriminative network tries to distinguish the real inputs from the fake ones. At the same time, the generative network is trained to produce outputs that are so similar to the real inputs that the discriminative network fails at this task. Initially, the discriminative network easily screens off the simulated inputs created by the generative network; but over time, the generative networks get so good at producing forgeries that in many cases, state-of-the-art discriminative networks are at chance (50/50) at identifying the fake data.

GANs have obvious security implications, and that has dominated much of the discussion about this kind of architecture. The security implications stem from the fact that some forgeries can be so good that neither machines nor humans can distinguish them from real data. We have already mentioned two of these security applications in previous chapters: adversarial attacks and deepfakes. Adversarial attacks resulted from the discovery that not only can the forgeries be rendered undetectable to humans, the forgeries can be crafted in a way that would cause the discriminative networks to reliably apply a specific,

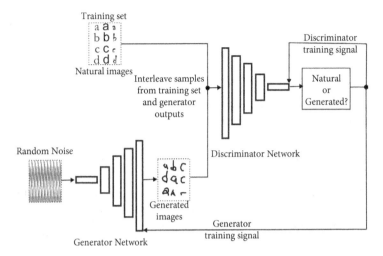

Figure 5.1 A depiction of a Generative Adversarial Network (GAN) architecture, with the generator network below and the discriminator network above. The generator network begins with random latent space codes and uses a hierarchical series of "specification" operations such as transpose convolution and unpooling to elaborate the abstract latent codes into specific high-resolution exemplars. The discriminator network is usually a standard deep convolutional neural network like those described in Chapter 3. By being trained to distinguish the images in its natural training set from those generated by the generator network, however, the discriminator network also develops more robust representations that are less susceptible to adversarial attack.

seemingly incorrect label to the image, while humans may not detect that any modification has been made. Deepfakes are forgeries with a more specific and novel mixture of attributes that can manipulate human perception as well—for example, by creating a video in which an actor's face and voice are replaced with those of a target of impersonation, such as a head of state or celebrity.

How do the generative networks accomplish these feats? It is worth exploring the nuts and bolts of the method to see how they compare to the operations of the imagination in humans and animals. The basic structure of the generative network is typically similar to a DCNN, with many layers of nodes gradually transforming inputs to outputs by hierarchically applying a variety of activation functions in sequence. There are, however, some critical differences. First, while the input to a DCNN is typically high-dimensional information for some perceptual exemplar (e.g., a huge array of pixel data for an image), the input to a GAN is a mixture of signals from lower-dimensional feature space— often called "latent space," for reasons we shall review shortly—that can either be combined in ways that are either randomized (to train the network to produce realistic inputs for many different combinations of features) or targeted (to produce a specific combination of desired attributes or nuisance parameters). Second, the operations in the layers of the "abstraction sandwiches" used in DCNNs are typically variations of convolution and pooling, which we argued in Chapter 3 perform abstraction-as-composition and abstraction-as-subtraction. Since GANs need to go in the other direction—from abstractions to particulars—they will appeal to activation functions that perform something like inverses of these operations, with the most popular options being transpose convolution (often called "deconvolution," though this name is misleading)[5] and forms of unpooling. Both the concepts of latent space and the operations in the specification sandwiches are worth elaborating further in turn.

Let us begin with the interesting concept of "latent space" in GANs and review its role in the training of generative networks in GANs. Typically, the generative network in a GAN begins with randomized link weights between layers, and training proceeds by feeding it random combinations of initial inputs. The randomized inputs are sampled from the latent space of the generator network, a set of inputs drawn from a set of variables adhering to a standard probability distribution (e.g., Gaussian). The latent space itself has a complex structure but no inherent meaning; through training, however, the generator learns to map input vectors from this latent space to specific output

---

[5] Deconvolution seeks to undo the operation of convolution, and it has a history back to the work of Norbert Wiener in the 1940s. This is not actually the operation used in most generative networks, which is really a form of transpose convolution, also often called "upsampling convolution," a name which is more intuitively fitting to its function. The misuse of "deconvolution" here has generated heated discussion in the machine learning community.

images that will fool the discriminator network. This is a remarkable trick—essentially, mining meaningful features from the complexity of a meaningless but normally distributed void, and learning to flexibly assemble those features into realistic exemplars.

The trick works due to the competition with the discriminator network. The initially random inputs are converted into outputs that are sent to the discriminator network, which is tasked with determining whether the outputs are real data or forgeries. The situation is not unlike that between a real bank and a currency forger, with the bank attempting to reject illegitimately produced notes and the forger attempting to produce facsimiles that are ever closer in detail to the actual bills, by making adjustments to previous forgery attempts based on whether the previous bills are accepted or rejected by the bank. Except, in a GAN, the forger is given a very large number of chances to produce ever better reproductions (without, modelers hope, the interference of law enforcement). After each attempted deception, an error signal is created for the generative network based on whether the discriminative network identified the forgery as artificial; the generator network "wins" this game each time the discriminator thinks that the generator's output is naturally produced data. The output that the generator network initially produces is also random, but over time the generator network comes to map latent feature space in such a way that it can treat it as containing rich information about meaningful features that can be combined into plausible exemplars. Some of these features may be like the ones we use to compose abstracted figures, like lines or angles, but others might capture general principles for rendering high-resolution data, such as that nearby pixels tend to have the same color and brightness, and that figures tend to be made up of contiguous lines. The link weights in the generative network in turn learn ways to combine these features flexibly to produce a range of outputs which are similar enough to real data that the discriminator network cannot tell them apart.

The specific mappings that the generator learns from vectors in latent space to exemplars are not relevant—and each time the GAN is trained, the mappings will be different, even for the same exemplars. However, in order to reliably produce exemplars that fool the discriminator network, the generator network must learn to use these mappings to group points in latent space together in an efficient way, specifically in a way that captures correlations between feature parameters that occur in realistic exemplars. If the number of dimensions used to structure latent space is smaller than the number of features for the discriminator's target domain, then the generator must learn ways to compress feature space into a small number of latent space dimensions that account for the widest range of variance in the discriminator network's domain. In essence, this approach is a way of starting with a data representation with randomized complex structure, and learning how to view it as having all along contained efficient representations of meaningful features and nuisance parameters that can be flexibly combined into high-resolution, plausible mixtures in specific exemplars. A generative and discriminative network could use the same latent space representations—this is the case in a deep convolutional autoencoder, for example—but in a typical GAN, the generative network has its own proprietary latent space. At the same time, the discriminative network is trying not to be fooled, and thus trying to find ways of structuring its representation of feature space in a way that resists forgeries by the generator.

Let us move then to the other part of the story, the activation functions that allow the generative networks to produce these mappings. If convolution and pooling cooperate to produce an iteratively more and more abstract and sparsely populated feature map from low-level inputs, transpose convolution and unpooling start with a sparse, highly abstracted feature map, and iteratively, hierarchically transform it into an enlarged and rendered high-resolution depiction of the low-level details corresponding to that abstracted feature map. In so doing, these operations must "fill in" some details that are not specified in the abstracted feature map with plausible values, with plausibility estimations gradually calibrated over the course of adversarial training.

Transpose convolution is a linear algebra operation that applies a filter kernel to matrix input (like convolution does), but instead of moving from a larger matrix to a smaller feature map, it uses the kernel to elaborate a smaller feature map into a larger matrix. Specifically, the kernel is applied to each matrix element iteratively, and the kernel slides over the elaborated output image as if it were a printer head rendering details from instructions provided by the feature map, as they are translated by the kernel. The kernels are learned over time in response to feedback from the competition with the discriminator network, and the acquisition of effective kernels is a primary means by which the generator network improves at rendering forgeries over time. An undesirable side-effect of relying upon transpose convolution for this job is that as the "printer head" slides over the output image rendering details, the same features can be "double-printed" at a single location due to overlap between the stride length for the transpose convolution window. This produces the phenomenon of "checkerboard artifacts" that characterized the products of early GANs, and countermeasures must be applied to avoid them (Odena, Dumoulin, and Olah 2016).

Unpooling is another important tool deployed by many generative networks, especially generative autoencoders; it is used to perform something akin to the inverse of pooling. There are a variety of options one can adopt, but I will focus on max-unpooling since we highlighted max-pooling as a downsampling operation in Chapter 3. Max-unpooling simply takes the greatest activation from a pooled feature map and prints it to the same location in a larger, upsampled representation of the output that the maximum value was taken from in a corresponding max-pooling operation from a previous layer. In other words, if a previous max-pooling operation judged that "6" is the maximum value from a range of cells [0,0] to [2,2], and it was taken from the [1,2] position, then the maximum value from the pooled feature map will be printed again in the [1,2] position of the upsampled output. This requires some form of backward connection or memory in the network—it needs to access information about the location from which the max value was taken from in the corresponding previous layer. Of course, this kind of backward information transfer does not make sense in the competitive setup of most GAN architectures, so the generative networks in GANs often eschew unpooling operations in favor of additional transposed convolutional layers.

To tie back to earlier discussions, these operations provide networks with a powerful ability to synthesize exemplars similar to those that have been encountered in the network's training. These operations are similar to those which we already discussed in the context of processes of abstraction in discriminative networks, but now to move in the other direction—through layers of specification taking us from abstractions to plausible exemplars. These exemplars can either be reconstructions of specific data samples which were previously encountered in the past (as we would get by merely passing an encoded vector from a previously encountered exemplar in an autoencoder to the generative half of the network), or they can be novel constructions which are similar to those previously encountered. For example, it is simple to synthesize a representation of a "typical" member of a category by averaging the abstracted vectors for previously encountered members of a category, and then rendering this averaged latent space representation through the generative hierarchy of an autoencoder or GAN (Radford, Metz, and Chintala 2015). At the high levels of abstraction afforded by latent space representations, these novel points on manifolds can be rendered into plausible exemplars (Bengio et al. 2013). These synthesized exemplars could then be used to stand in for the rest of the category and engaged in further processes of categorization or reasoning, as suggested by Berkeley and Hume's doctrine of abstraction-as-representation.

This possibility at least demonstrates that a system using only neural network-like components can solve the first challenge that Fodor poses for Hume: they can synthesize plausible exemplars for categories with which they have experience. Setting aside the question of biological plausibility for the moment, this at least provides a proof-of-concept that the situation is not insoluble for neural-network-based AI. We will consider the more preliminary question of whether these techniques are biologically plausible—whether it is likely they solve this problem in the way that the brain does—at the end of this chapter.

5.4. Imagination's role in synthesizing novel composite ideas: Vector interpolation, variational autoencoders, and transformers

GANs can also help the DoGMA answer Fodor's next challenge for Hume: to explain how an empiricist system might not only reconstruct exemplars which resemble those encountered in the past but also synthesize ideas for novel composite categories, like UNICORN and THE NEW JERUSALEM. Indeed, some of the most alluring discoveries resulting from the study of generative networks involve more ambitious explorations of latent space conducted when the inputs provided to a generative network are not randomized but are rather tailored by external operations to produce some desired combination of features or nuisance parameters. This can be done, for example, by taking the vectors mapped from latent space for two exemplars with desired properties and charting a novel course through latent space between them. This approach is known as "interpolation."

The idea behind interpolation is that traversing a distance along a given dimension in latent space is equivalent to locating the abstracted vector of an exemplar that has been modified along that feature dimension. When a new vector chosen from that path is then progressively rendered by transforming it through the specification operations of a generative network's layers, detail is added that fleshes out realistic high-resolution values for the feature combinations and nuisance parameters of the novel exemplar. If the direction of interpolation is chosen randomly, then modelers can create a variety of novel combinations of features and nuisance parameters, as one gets by continually refreshing the "This Person Does Not Exist" or "This Cat Does Not Exist" tools, which uses a descendant of StyleGAN (Fig. 5.2). However, more targeted outcomes can be achieved if distances are

Figure 5.2 Some images of cats that, sadly, do not exist, generated by author using StyleGAN: Karras et al. 2020.

traversed along dimensions to which meaning can be attributed. For example, if modelers locate a dimension in abstracted feature space corresponding to the exemplar's angle of rotation, traveling some distance across the abstracted manifold along this dimension can produce the effect of having rotated the abstracted representation by a certain magnitude (Chen et al. 2016; Radford et al. 2015). Passing the vector for this rotated exemplar through the specification layers would then create a result that attempted to preserve many of the original exemplar's other features and nuisance parameters, as they would be seen from this new angle of rotation. Once identified as dimensions in transformed feature space, features or nuisance parameters can be added, removed, or modified using interpolation according to the modeler's whims.[6]

Modelers even discovered that features can be manipulated without prior knowledge of their coordinates in latent space, by using a form of vector addition to perform complex interpolation on output categories. For example, we can estimate the coordinates of vectors in latent space for categories "man," "man with glasses," and "woman" by averaging the latent space vectors for sets of exemplars that are mapped to these category labels by a discriminative network; if we then subtract the vector for "man" from the vector for "man with glasses," add in the vector for "woman," and then render this latent space vector through the layers of hierarchical specification in the generative network, we can create a set of plausible exemplars for "woman with glasses," despite the fact that none of these categories are explicitly represented by the network (Radford et al. 2015).

While the original versions of this technology produced results that were fairly low resolution and, while readily interpretable, often did not appear so realistic to the human eye, the quality of images produced by interpolation methods in GANs has rapidly improved. Indeed, even more ambitious uses of this technique are possible when a whole set of attributes is taken from another target source, in a method described as

---

[6] Note that in GANs interpolation is usually not perfectly reversible and its inverse operation can only be estimated using various means. Flow-based models (like Glow from OpenAI) are desirable because they are perfectly reversible and so can produce more accurate results (Kingma and Dhariwal 2018).

"style transfer." For example, in the DeepArt project, modelers created a second parallel network whose job was to extract correlations among feature and nuisance parameters at different intermediate levels of abstraction from the encoding of a "style source" image by a discriminative network. In a popular application of this method, the style source image would often be a notable artwork by a famous artist, such as Van Gogh's *Starry Night* or Munch's *The Scream* (Gatys, Ecker, and Bethge 2016b). A photograph or other exemplar could then be transformed by a discriminative DCNN, and interpolation performed on the abstracted exemplar vector at each level of the hierarchy, to substitute the feature and nuisance correlations from the artistic style source image for those from the original photograph. These encoded correlations are called the "style representation" for the source image. When the hierarchically interpolated vector is then re-rendered by the generative side of the network, it depicts the same objects and features, as if they had been painted in the style of the creator of the source image. The style-based approach of normalizing correlations between intermediate features and nuisance parameters has been further extended to produce some of the highest-resolution machine-generated graphics to date, such as the exemplars generated by StyleGAN (Karras et al. 2020).

One point of contention in generative modeling concerns how explicitly latent factors should be represented in the model. This debate has several related aspects, pertaining to whether: representational structure is built into a model to correspond to specific latent factors, the model is trained to identify latent factors via a supervised or an unsupervised manner, and the latent factors are easily interpretable and manipulable by human observers. A major selling point of the models we have just discussed, for example—especially DCGAN, StyleGAN, and InfoGAN—is that the latent factors that are learned by the generative models and manipulated by interpolation are acquired (at least by the generative network) in an unsupervised and implicit matter, from the competition with the generative network. This means, however, that they can only be manipulated indirectly (e.g., by using the vectors recovered from the way a discriminative network labels the generative network's outputs) and the factors themselves may resist easy interpretation by human users. To consider an alternative approach, another popular generative architecture often seen as an alternative to GANs is Variational AutoEncoders (VAEs; Fig. 5.3). VAEs are like predictive autoencoders, except they impose an additional step at the central bottleneck that induces the network to translate its latent space into separable representations of the latent factors. In particular, they divide the latent space encoding for each exemplar into one set of variables that capture the mean values of latent factors of variation in the model, and another that captures the standard deviation of those parameters.

One aspect of forcing the network to separate latent factors explicitly in this way is that it makes it easier for the system (or modelers working with the system) to mix and manipulate those factors in the creation of novel exemplars. This point relates to the distinction

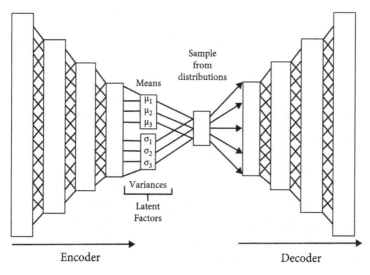

Figure 5.3 Depiction of Variational AutoEncoder (VAE) architecture. In a VAE, the discriminative part of the network occurs first, and the generative part last. The two networks share a common representation of latent space, unlike most Generative Adversarial Networks (GANs). Moreover, representations of latent space factors are broken into means and variances, allowing more controlled sampling of latent space than in a GAN. The latent factors in a VAE can be either learned or manually defined by the programmers.

drawn in Chapter 3 between implicitly and explicitly disentangled manifolds, which we there quickly glossed with the metaphor of braiding hair: implicitly disentangling manifolds is like brushing the hair just enough that the brush can move smoothly through it, while explicit disentangling is more like separating hair strands into independent and stable braids that can be flexibly recombined into multiple hairstyles. We can now attempt to make this metaphor more precise. Appealing to the idea that VAEs represent these latent factors in a more explicit way can invite problematic intuitions, as our notions of explicitness can suggest properties—such as locality, movability, determinacy of meaning, and availability—that are difficult to mutually satisfy not only in a neural network representation but in any computational system (Kirsh 1998). Usually when machine learning researchers or computational neuroscientists appeal to the notion of explicit representation, they do so by reference to some metric of how easily information can be recovered from a signal for use in other operations, especially via a simple method like linear decodability (Ritchie, Kaplan, and Klein 2019).[7]

This leaves a wide degree of wiggle room in how explicit a representation of a latent factor should be scored, as the score will depend upon which method of decodability is referenced. There are clearly some relevant dimensions along which latent factors are more explicitly represented in a VAE than in a standard GAN.[8] Specifically, by forcing the network to represent latent factors in individual parameter variables and separately representing the probability distributions of each one, it is easier for operations to sample novel sets of nuisance parameters from these distributions in a coherent way. This has the effect of helping the system to estimate the full probability distributions for each of the latent factors; and as a result, it learns a "smoother"

---

[7] More sophisticated measurements of explicitness are possible; for example, Bernardi et al. (2020) recommend a measure they call "Cross-Correlation Generalization Performance" (CCGP), which measures how well a linear decoder can generalize information from a variable to contexts not encountered during training.

[8] One might wonder at this point why we should not favor a nonlinear notion of decodability that would classify even a deep discriminative network as being an eligible decoding method. A concern is that a very wide range of features might all be decodable from some data according to such powerful methods of inference, rendering the notion of explicit representation too permissive to be of any use.

representation of latent space covering a wider range of meaningful feature and nuisance parameter combinations (Grover, Dhar, and Ermon 2018). Several other tricks have been implemented atop the basic VAE architecture to make the latent factors extracted more robust and similar to those deployed by humans, especially the so-called β-VAE method, which introduces a new hyperparameter β to the model that biases its bottleneck encodings toward the discovery of sparser and more robust latent factors (Higgins et al. 2022). This tends to make the latent factors learned more like those learned by humans, and hence more interpretable to humans that use the model.

These advances are all straightforwardly applicable to the concerns Fodor has raised about the ability of empiricist approaches to the mind to explain the production of novel concepts. The generative networks just discussed to varying degrees are all able to go beyond merely reconstructing representations exactly like those they have seen in the past. They do so on the basis of the powerful abstractions learned in their latent space representations, and by learning mapping procedures between those latent space representations and plausible combinations of features and nuisance parameters in their generative layers. Moreover, the processes by which the networks build these latent space representations and mappings are all in some sense co-occurrence based, and they should be ruled well within the bounds of the empiricist toolkit. Granted, these systems are limited to producing exemplars for modalities and assembled from features to which they were exposed in training; StyleGAN cannot produce plausible music (although probably neither could Picasso, and some generative systems trained on music can—Dhariwal et al. 2020; Yang et al. 2017), and interpolation methods can only operate with known categories as starting points. However, novel combinations of features and nuisance parameters can be rendered for exemplars in areas of latent space for which the network has had little or no training experience.

Two additional rebuttals might be offered in Fodor's defense here: that much depends on the details of the interpolation method and whether those details are fully empiricist, and that the outputs of the systems discussed thus far, while impressive, have not yet reached the degree of novel composition of which the human mind appears capable. However, in considering each in turn, we find that they do not justify pessimism about the ability of generative DNN-based models to capture key aspects of the imagination.

First, the classicist here might concede that the potential of generative networks to render abstractions into realistic low-level detail is an impressive and genuine technological advance, but point out that much of the true compositionality in these models derives from classical aspects of the interpolation procedure. For example, the novel compositions created by vector mathematics applied to DCGAN might be thought to derive from compositional features of the interpolation combinatorics, rather than from the details of how the generative network renders an interpolated vector into a plausible exemplar. In some sense this is right, but in another sense it misses the point of the technological advance. The hard part of compositionality all along was not simply the combination of disparate features—which could be achieved by mere concatenation, an associative mechanism par excellence—but in determining the details of how to place and fuse the disparate features together into a semantically meaningful whole. This aspect of semantic compositionality was never explained by classical treatments like Fodor's, who preferred to focus on the easier, syntactic pieces of the puzzle instead. Furthermore, a number of thinkers—even those sympathetic to Fodor's position—have questioned whether the classical program really explained, rather than simply took for granted, the sorts of syntactic compositionality presumed by the interpolation methods (Aizawa 2003; Cummins 1996; Johnson 2004).

The familiar Fodorian rejoinder here would be to claim that these generative models can only solve the problems of semantic compositionality by presuming classical syntactic compositionality in the interpolation procedure (Fodor and Pylyshyn 1988)—but the use of classical programming to perform the vector arithmetic is simply a choice of convenience for programmers. Notably, the generative part of the system does not depend upon processing the interpolation instruction in a classical way; it does not need to interpret inputs and operators as classical symbols, for example. By contrast, these systems only need to be given an activation vector for the desired location in latent space. It remains to be argued that no system drawing only upon associationist/empiricist machinery could "nudge" the system into the right region of latent space before the generative specification process is applied. DNN modelers interested in advancing the empiricist line should now explore interpolation methods that are themselves domain-general and experience-driven without drawing upon or implementing a classical system. Second-wave connectionists will likely already have a variety of ideas handy (Smolensky 1987).

Second, critics sympathetic to Fodor may worry that while the quality of the outputs produced by current generative methods are impressive, their range does not yet match that of human cognition. DCGAN, for example, is limited to regions of latent space and interpolation procedures operating over categories on which it was extensively trained. VAEs can generate interpretable combinations of features and nuisance variables for more novel regions of latent space, but even they need exposure to the probability distributions of latent variable combinations that might be drawn upon to generate their explicit latent space encodings. Recall the example of the pink elephant in a tutu from my philosophy of mind course. Likely, none of the students in the class had ever formulated such a thought before, but they can almost all instantly imagine, within some range of acceptable variation, what that situation would look like. We may worry that without explicit relations to meld the component latent factors together, the representations generated by these DNN-based methods will still lack the "glue" that Fodor and other classicists theorize hold together compositional representations in human thought, and that can fuse together truly novel combinations of latent factors in a coherent way. Such seemingly limitless combinations of increasingly complex features are beyond the scope of the systems we have just discussed, and they might be thought an aspect of human cognition that remains beyond the reach of DNN-based systems.

Or it might have been thought a unique feature of human cognition, until the even more astounding potential of transformer-based generative models like DALL-E (a portmanteau of the artist Salvador Dalí and Pixar's WALL-E), DALL-E 2, Parti, MidJourney, and Imagen was illustrated. We will review transformer architectures in the next chapter, as they also include mechanisms inspired by the faculties of attention and language, but these systems demonstrate an impressive and seemingly open-ended potential for combining categories in systematic and relationally meaningful ways. They can take text prompts phrased in

English and convert them into plausible images depicting the objects and relations described in the prompt. To foreshadow, the latent space representations generated by these transformer-based image models are crucially fusions of text and images, which allows for more relationally meaningful compositions to be distinguished from one another through linguistic syntax. Somehow unimpressed by the difficulty of the pink elephant example that I had been using in my classes for years, OpenAI tasked DALL-E to produce "an illustration of a baby daikon radish in a tutu walking a dog," a prompt from which it generated the series of exemplars that are so plausible and meaningfully composed that they might make human illustrators jealous (and concerned about their jobs). This system includes a 12 billion parameter version of the language model GPT-3, which we will discuss in later chapters—but we foreshadow it now in order to highlight its ability to rebut this classical criticism. DALL-E and its successor transformer-based systems DALL-E 2, Imagen, MidJourney, and Parti reflect perhaps the most impressive achievements of compositionality in artificial systems to date, because the images they produce depend upon the syntactic relations holding among the words in the prompt. We will set aside further exploration of the implications of transformer-based systems for now—especially whether they contain mechanisms that might be thought to implement Fodor's "glue"—only noting the performance of such systems at least on its face seems to rebut concerns about the upper limits of DNN-based generative methods in the coherent composition of novel exemplars.

Just to drive the point home, we can return to some of the examples from Hume and see how they fare in a contemporary transformer architecture. In some early explorations of these methods, the programmer and artist Ryan Murdock (who goes by the handle @ Advadnoun) released several implementations blending technologies from OpenAI's CLIP and the Taming Transformers architecture that accomplishes a similar task. The system takes a text prompt, translates it into a multimodal latent space encoding that consists of both text and images, and then passes it to a generative transformer that converts it into an image (explained more thoroughly in the next chapter). We can use this system to demonstrate how compellingly even an off-the-shelf DNN-based system can compose novel images from text prompts we have already discussed (or any arbitrary chunk of text). Dall-E 2 and MidJourney are also now available to create astoundingly realistic and visually appealing creations from almost any arbitrary visual prompt. Recall that Hume praised the imagination for allowing us to conceive of "winged horses, fiery dragons, and monstrous giants" (T 1.1.3.4/ 10); and that he used "the New Jerusalem, whose pavement is gold and walls are rubies, tho' I never saw any such" (T 1.1.1.4/3) as an example of the mind's ability to compose novel ideas. These systems produce very satisfying results on the pink elephant example discussed earlier in this chapter, for example, as well as on prompts corresponding to Hume's examples of novel categories. Readers can see for themselves using free and commercial versions of these tools, and they can easily find even more impressive demonstrations of these technologies on social media.

These examples get at the heart of the disagreement between the nativists and empiricists about the prospects for neural-network-based AI: that neural networks are capable only of interpolation, whereas real intelligence requires extrapolation. Gary Marcus (2003) charges, for example, that deep learning boosters neglect this simple distinction. In support of the charge, Marcus gives the example of training a neural network on only even numbers and then asking it to generalize to odd numbers. While the network experimented on by Marcus could generalize to novel even numbers that were greater than those in the training set, it generalized poorly to odd numbers. Interpolation, the thought goes, involves issuing verdicts on data points within the statistics of the training set ("inside the convex hull of the training set," as we would say more precisely),[9] whereas extrapolation involves generalizing to data points outside the statistics of the training set.

However, this charge is rarely made precise enough to be regarded as decisive. It does not withstand closer scrutiny, especially in context

---

[9] Determining what is inside the convex hull of a training set, even once the features that comprise the data are determined, is itself a complex topic. The general idea is that this is the smallest convex closure of the data space that encloses all of the points from the training set (the analogy of "placing a rubber band around the points" is often used), but in higher-order spaces there remain a variety of algorithms and techniques for computing this space, which is regarded as a fundamental problem in computational geometry.

of the examples of interpolation we have just considered. The problem with a seemingly straightforward distinction between interpolation and extrapolation is that defining what is inside or outside of the statistical distribution of the training set itself requires various parameters to be specified. It requires decisions about how to partition the feature space and how to measure distance within it, both of which can be subject to factors like confirmation bias. For example, if we define the convex hull of the training set in terms of image input statistics, then most of the decisions made on the test set by even the simpler, image-classifying DCNNs discussed in Chapter 3 clearly count in standard cross-validation methods as extrapolation (Yousefzadeh 2021). Because the input is so high-dimensional and complex, the probability that an item in the test set will be inside the convex hull of the training set statistics is quite low. Moreover, many of the relevant data sets are so large and complex that skeptics rarely make an attempt to characterize the input statistics precisely; this is already true of ImageNet, to say nothing of the proprietary and Internet-scale data set of language models like GPT-3.

Skeptics like Marcus usually prefer to conceptualize the input statistics of the training set in terms of the abstract features it explicitly contains; this is the sense in which the input statistics in Marcus's example encompass all of the even numbers but none of the odd ones. Yet this way of conceptualizing the input statistics may be unavailable to the neural network—it is a way of conceptualizing that is in the eye of the modeler evaluating it. If we, by contrast, attempted to define the convex hull of the training set in terms of the abstract features discovered by an ANN, we might define it in terms of the features extracted by the neural network at its final layer, or even further in terms of some lower-dimensional encoding of the input space derived via multidimensional scaling. On this way of specifying the convex hull of the training statistics, however, nothing the network could possibly do by the output layer would count as extrapolation. This would punish networks for doing exactly what we want them to do in an ideal case—learning to extract abstract, generalizable features from high-dimensional input data, which for some data sets, the networks may do much better than humans, perhaps by finding predictive features that we lack the acuity to detect (Buckner 2020b). Defining interpolation in either way thus biases our evaluation against the neural networks unfairly, in a way directly related to anthropofabulation, because it either leaves it up to the whims of the theorist to decide what abstract features are explicitly specified in the input statistics, or stacks the decks against neural networks by specifying that even if they do manage to discover an abstract feature during training, deploying it in judgment is mere interpolation.

For related reasons, DNN proponents like LeCun have charged that the distinction between interpolation and extrapolation becomes less meaningful as the dimensionality of the input data and depth of the network increase (Balestriero, Pesenti, and LeCun 2021). In fact, suppose that the features extracted at the final layer of some neural network architecture were the ones that the skeptics regard as uniquely human—those that are abstract enough, based around enduring object files, or around causal relations, for example. It seems, then, that the skeptics would have to regard the behavior of the neural networks as genuinely intelligent at that point, despite the fact that, according to metrics determined by the partitioning of feature space at the final layer, the test set items are within the convex hull of the training set data statistics (because they share the same abstract, ontological, or causal structure). Even human cognition would presumably count as mere interpolation on this way of conceiving things. This is the rationale on which LeCun's rebuttal rests.

The only way forward is to again recognize a continuum between interpolation and extrapolation, and, if skeptics want to argue that some DNN-based system has failed to exhibit a degree of extrapolation indicative of intelligence, that they must justify their choices in partitioning the statistical distribution of the input space. Allowing skeptics to offer such arguments without explicit justification for these choices is an invitation to implicit anthropocentrism—because they can simply set the threshold of extrapolation to whatever distance humans are purported to clear but the latest iteration of DNNs does not (though even DNN enthusiasts admit there remains more work to be done here—Bahdanau et al. 2020; Bengio, Lecun, and Hinton 2021). These judgments can thus easily commit anthropofabulation if the skeptics impose a metric that not even humans can clear—as Marcus has apparently done in his even/odd case, for he gives the reader no reason to suppose that human children could extrapolate to odd numbers if exposed only to evens (which, I hope math teachers can assure us, is not how these subjects are generally taught).

The preceding arguments recast the nativist-empiricist debate in the following terms:

- Whether a neural network's decision on some data counts as interpolation or extrapolation is relative to how we partition the input space; specifically, to the choice of features used to define the input statistics, the distance metric and partitioning method adopted, and whether and which dimensionality-reduction techniques are used to make distances in the space more meaningful.
- Interpolation/extrapolation is best viewed as a continuum.
- Judgments about thresholds for the degree and type of distance from input statistics that count as criterial for "genuine" rationality or intelligence need to be explicitly justified.
- When these judgments are not explicitly stated, there is a danger that anthropofabulation will distort the comparisons between humans and machines; and when such comparisons are made, empirical evidence should be provided that typical humans can solve the extrapolation task using the same input allowed to the network.

Once this is all made explicit, the argument that there is some simple distinction being neglected by the deep learning theorist dissolves; and the impressive achievements of recent systems like Dall-E 2, Parti, and Imagen should overcome the position that there remains some large class of extrapolations of which humans are capable but neural networks, in principle, are not.[10]

---

[10] As with BIG-Bench for language models, there is now an effort, dubbed "Draw-Bench," to develop a set of automated benchmarking tests which assess the ability of image-generating models like DALL-E 2 and Imagen to master traditional benchmarks of intelligence and creativity (Saharia et al. 2022).

5.5. Imagination's role in creativity: Creative Adversarial Networks

Another closely related topic is the question of how the imagination subserves creativity in human thought, and whether DNN-based AI agents can use their generative capacities to be creative. The question of whether artificial machines could be creative is itself an enormous topic tracing back to the early days of AI in the 1960s, with its own subarea of computer science dedicated to the topic called "computational creativity" (Colton and Wiggins 2012). Rather than review this whole terrain, let us focus on Hume's comments about the principles governing the imagination. Recall that Hume emphasized the tendency of the imagination to seek novelty. This idea has featured prominently in work on art theory and in the cognitive science of creativity, and it has recently begun to inspire a new subarea of research in machine learning (Mahadevan 2018). Let us further limit our focus to artistic creativity, a topic which is both rich and difficult, but which has already been investigated in the context of deep learning and which offers a great deal of potential.

Consonant with Hume's attitude, the art theorist Martindale proposed that creative artists "try to increase the arousal potential of their art to push against habituation," a view of art theory which has inspired some efforts in deep generative modeling (Elgammal et al. 2017). Studies of artistic expertise have found that expert artists intentionally push toward stylistic and thematic novelty, especially to elicit novel forms of perceptual experience. A series of interviews conducted by Gaines (1975), for example, found that artists were "more flexible in their perceptions of the environment and least likely to fall into rigid patterns of perceiving" compared to children and nonartist controls. One of the artists in this study described their process as constantly "[trying] to see this in a way that no one else has guessed or seen" (1975:993—and see also Mag Uidhir and Buckner [2014] for a discussion). Perhaps if DNN modelers could implement forms of these novelty-seeking processes in the domain of artistic creativity, it might illuminate artificial models of creativity in other important domains, such as in game strategy or scientific discovery. Interestingly, however, the kind of novelty at issue here is a curious mix of freedom and constraint. The highest degree of novelty might be achieved by merely random stimuli that maximize entropy in low-level perceptual statistics; but there is nothing aesthetically interesting about pixels randomly arranged on a grid. The interesting forms of novelty are both intelligible and surprising; they are both informed by previous experience but also somehow pushing the limits of what might be thought intelligible or valuable in light of it.

Indeed, several engineering innovations have already been inspired by the attempt to model perceptual and stylistic novelty-seeking in DNN-based agents. To extend the sorts of generative models that we have just discussed into this territory, the models need some way to estimate the novelty of an exemplar's depiction on the basis of previous training exposures and to experiment with innovations in the rendering process that might elicit a stronger or more novel perceptual response. Many of the models we have discussed in previous chapters have mechanisms that might be thought to estimate the probability of new exemplars; for example, the original model of AlphaGo had a policy network trained on human gameplay, which it could use to estimate how likely a human player would be to make a particular move. It could then choose moves that would be particularly novel for humans but still maximized its likelihood of winning the game; for example, the notorious Move #37 that we discussed in Chapter 2 was calculated to have a less than 1 in 10,000 chances of being played by a human. This kind of maneuver already expresses one way of mixing freedom and constraint to discover creative strategies; a particular action is deemed unlikely according to some conventions but also likely to lead to a desired outcome, with both probability estimations being informed by previous experience. This combination of features has long been regarded as the core of creative activity in computational creativity research: that the action be both novel and useful (Newell, Shaw, and Simon 1962).

It would be especially useful for artistic purposes if networks could have some way to estimate a distinctively aesthetic component of the depictive process. We can canvass these innovations in two directions: first, we might want systems that can estimate our (or their own, if one is feeling ascriptively ambitious) perceptual or aesthetic responses to stimuli, and second, in their ability to seek out novelty in the form or style in which generated exemplars are depicted. We consider each in turn.

One area of research that has inspired DNN researchers to model the human ability to create or perceive art is the hybrid field of "neuroaesthetics," a combination of neuroscience and aesthetics. Some central results in neuroaesthetics support the idea that the brain represents a variety of feature dimensions independently and via multiple parallel pathways, and that these independent features are then assimilated into a high-level aesthetic judgment later in the processing flow (Chatterjee 2011). Zeki (2002), in particular, argued that the brain processes in parallel many properties that we have previously discussed as feature or nuisance parameter variations (and on which aesthetic properties supervene), and that artists seek to uncover and manipulate these properties by finding novel combinations of them that maximize or minimize the responses of some of these aesthetic assessments. Such properties include color, luminance, saturation, motion, and symmetry. Modelers have attempted to recapitulate these ideas about the processing flows in the brain by creating a series of parallel DCNNs that are specialized to detect these image attributes and then integrating the parallel networks' outputs into a holistic aesthetic appraisal of an exemplar. For example, the Deep Chatterjee Machine (DCM) architecture has a series of convolutional neural networks each trained to assess aesthetic properties, which are then combined into an overall aesthetic appraisal (Fig. 5.4). These appraisals can then be compared to those solicited from human evaluators, which revealed that the network can not only do well in classifying held-out photographs according to their individual aesthetic attributes but also does well in grading images by their overall aesthetics goodness.

Let us next consider novelty in the form or style with which exemplars are depicted. Separating processes for generation and discrimination provides interesting avenues for novelty-seeking behavior here, as a system can seek to maximize novelty in the generation process while still maintaining the same target label in the discrimination process. In fact, this trick was always at the core of the

Deep Chatterjee Machine

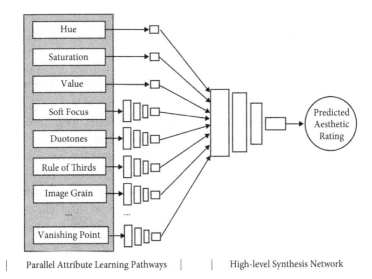

Parallel Attribute Learning Pathways | | High-level Synthesis Network

Figure 5.4 The Deep Chatterjee Machine architecture from Wang et al. (2017). Many parallel deep convolutional neural networks learn particular attributes relevant to aesthetic evaluations, and these evaluations are then integrated by a high-level synthesis network to produce a final aesthetic rating. The ratings were surprisingly accurate predictors of human aesthetic ratings for photographs. While the attributes to be labeled by the parallel networks were manually selected, there is, of course, no assumption that they are innate in humans, and which attributes to attend to could be learned and exhibit cultural variability in aesthetic judgments. This architecture exhibits a way that learned modularity can be leveraged to finer grains of detail to acquire representations of more abstract properties, such as *beauty* or *elegance*.

basic GAN methodology for generating adversarial examples, which seek to maximize distance from the target manifold in similarity space while maintaining the same target label. To harness other forms of novelty that are more useful, we only need to change the distance metric applied to move the representation of the exemplar in a novel direction. The kinds of style transfer already discussed are another form of such novelty-seeking behavior, already in an artistic domain; if we seek to move an exemplar's representation from maximizing one style of representation to another, this can be seen as a form of novel aesthetic behavior. The creation of entirely new styles is even more interesting, as it might involve searching for sets of correlations among style attributes that were not presented in the training set and then rendering an exemplar using that novel set of correlations in the generation process. This is explicitly the approach adopted by the Creative Adversarial Network (CAN) from Elgammal et al. (2017), a GAN architecture which seeks to learn style representations from labels in the training set and then create exemplars that explicitly deviate from them by learning novel style representations in the adversarial training process. Without going further into this line of thought, these examples might illustrate that there are rich opportunities to implement novelty-seeking processes within DNN-based systems, despite the fact that their actions are in some sense bound by the distribution of their training set.

5.6. Imagination's role in simulating experience: Imagination-Augmented Agents

As the final role for the Humean imagination in DNN-based AI considered here, let us explore the role of the imagination in simulating experience. Simulated experience can be used for a variety of purposes, but especially to discover novel representations using off-line learning on simulated data, and to think about future and counterfactual situations that can aid contrastive decision-making and causal reasoning. This is the area where the role of the imagination grades most noticeably into that of episodic remembering, as the generation of simulated data and trajectories through possible experience-space needs to be guided by previous explorations, an idea that interfaces with recent trends in the study of episodic thinking in humans and animals (De Brigard and Parikh 2019). A straightforward example of such imagination-based planning featured prominently in AlphaGo and AlphaZero; each of these systems used Monte Carlo Tree Search to build a branching model of future possibilities, which it then used to evaluate the suitability of various moves it might make on a turn to lead to a win. However, the kind of planning in AlphaGo is not a suitable candidate for inclusion in our empiricist DoGMA; first, its implementation of MCTS is entirely classical and innate rather than learned from experience, and second it has a very limited domain of application: the game of Go, which allows for an exhaustive and well-defined search space. The kind of imagination-based planning we seek here would instead be guided by experience, would be more efficient (e.g., only heuristically consider a few scenarios especially likely to lead to success), and would be applicable to messier and less well-defined search spaces that characterize problem-solving in the real world.

The role played by imagination in learning from simulated data has been informed by the observation that humans and animals often seem to reach sudden insights after episodes of sleep or daydreaming. One empirically supported theory posits that during daydreaming and sleep the mind explores simulated data for new solutions to problems. Some of the strongest evidence for this hypothesis comes from observations collected from implanted electrodes in the medial temporal lobes of rats who have been training in maze exploration (Dragoi and Tonegawa 2013; Pfeiffer and Foster 2013). By correlating grid cell firings to locations in the maze during online training, researchers can see which neurons fire in which areas of the maze. During periods of sleep and rest, these rats' medial temporal lobes exhibited firing patterns that corresponded to previously explored maze trajectories, as discussed in Chapter 4, but also to combinations corresponding to novel trajectories (stitched together from known routes) that they never actually explored while awake. This could allow the sort of "latent learning" that observers might classify as spontaneous insight, when animals suddenly adopt novel solutions to difficult problems that they were not trained on while awake. This has a way of making human and animal learning look more efficient than learning in DNNs, but only because much of the training is coming from simulated experience that occurs while the animal appears to be resting or sleeping (Aronowitz and Lombrozo 2020).

GANs and other generative models, however, can allow DNN-based agents to reprise the same trick and obtain similar gains in sample efficiency. SimGAN, developed by Apple, for example, attempts to do just this. SimGAN uses the basic GAN method to create a large body of simulated data that can be used to further improve the accuracy of a discriminator network without the need to collect additional large bodies of annotated data. Because the GAN is generating the simulated exemplars from a latent space encoding, each new data point comes already annotated with the "correct" label for the discriminator. There are worries that the simulated data approach can increase the tendency of the discriminative network to overfit idiosyncrasies in the now-more-limited data set, or that it can cause it to learn about artifacts introduced by the generative network. These are both real concerns, but SimGAN showed that they can be overcome by countermeasures, specifically by working harder to regularize and improve the quality of the simulated data, and by using methods to detect and eliminate artifacts introduced by the generative network. The imagination in biological brains, we might imagine, must have found ways to avoid the same sorts of dangers.

The role played by imagination in leveraging simulated experience for decision-making is a bit trickier. This research is still more preliminary than what we have discussed so far, but it is perhaps the most important for bootstrapping higher levels of contrastive decision-making on the Tiers of Rationality that were introduced in Chapter 2. The line of research has largely occurred in the context of reinforcement learning models; one way to think about it is as an attempt to perform the sort of consequences-oriented planning and decision-making that was implemented using Monte Carlo Tree Search in AlphaGo. However, instead of using classical rules to exhaustively populate the tree of possibilities that need to be explored and compared, a system should use DNN-based generative methods to populate more efficiently a smaller set of future trajectories to consider. One challenge here is finding a good test arena. Go—with its massive and very deep search space—is too challenging for first steps in this direction, whereas simpler games like Breakout or Coast Runners can be solved fairly well without sophisticated planning just by aiming for a constant increase in game score in the next step. Modelers at DeepMind instead proposed that the box-moving strategy game Sokoban posed the right sort of challenge, because it requires planning five to seven steps into the future, some mistakes cannot be undone (like moving a box into a corner where it becomes stuck), and reward is not received until all boxes are in the correct goal locations.

The Imagination-Augmented Agent (I2A) architecture was developed by DeepMind to play Sokoban (Racanière et al. 2017). The architecture is complex, but, to lightly summarize, it replaces the tree-population method of AlphaGo with a series of self-generated exploratory trajectories in experience space, which in planning terms are called "rollouts" (Fig. 5.5). The beauty of this system is that it is trained end to end and assumes no prior knowledge of the search space. Each rollout consists of a series of actions and their

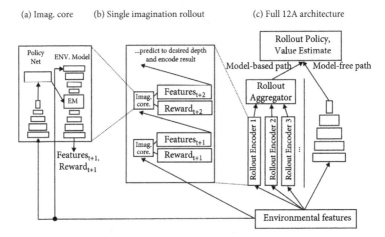

Figure 5.5 Example of rollout policies on the I2A architecture, adapted from Racanière et al. (2017). The model contains both model-based and model-free paths, which can determine decisions. In the imagination-enhanced, model-based path, multiple "rollouts" are used to predict sequences of actions and environmental consequences, and then aggregated to estimate their combined reward values. The predicted outcomes and reward values are estimated using "imagination cores" containing both a policy network and an environment model, where the anticipated policy affects the future predictions. Rollouts can be pursued to a desired "depth" (or number of future actions and estimated consequences), with deeper rollouts predicting consequences further into the futures at the cost of more computation (and perhaps increased unreliability).

predicted effects, and subsequent actions and their effects, calculated to a predetermined depth which can be adjusted by the modelers. A series of these rollouts are generated each time the system needs to make a decision, and a reward value is calculated for each rollout using standard deep reinforcement learning methods, also on the basis of previous gameplay experience. The architecture also has a "model-free" reinforcement learning path, which does not factor rollouts into account. Each time the system needs to decide upon an action, the imaginative simulation path aggregates all the rollouts and determines which action is associated with the greatest reward, and the model-free path does the same, and the two pathways are weighted and factored into the system's final decision. Using the rollouts, the system was able to solve reliably Sokoban puzzles that require planning dozens of moves in advance. This is an impressive achievement, as the Sokoban puzzles are randomly generated with many possibilities, so it is unlikely that the system could learn many solutions by brute force memorization.

Let us reflect now on Fodor's concern about the associative mind's inability to distinguish causal and semantic relations between ideas. In the case of the Fodorian die, does this architecture provide a DNN-based agent with the ability to think that triangles are more likely to come up than circles, rather than simply to have the thought that the die will come up triangle more often than the thought that the die will come up circle? It seems that it does; multiple rollouts can be compared in the architecture according to their predicted reinforcement value, and the likelier outcome would be preferred after learning, because its rollouts involving the choice of triangle would be rewarded more often than rollouts involving the choice of circle along this metric. This is not an analytical method to fully model the space of possibilities as one would find in MCTS, for example; instead, a limited number of rollouts are self-generated on demand, and both their trajectories and reinforcement values are learned entirely from experience. Fodorians may want to claim that the architecture here goes beyond that supposed by naïve associationism; but if there is a "gotcha" response on Fodor's behalf, it is a pyrrhic one, because his naïve associationist was always a strawman target which resembles neither real Locke nor real

Hume; and with its end-to-end training, the I2A model is tailor-made to satisfy the constraints of origin empiricism.[11]

Several other similar architectures that use experience simulation in contrastive planning and decision-making have been explored (e.g., Hamrick 2019; Hamrick et al. 2017); the general consensus is that while they can deal with noisier environments and plan more efficiently than classical alternatives like MCTS, success so far has still been limited to specific tasks, such as games, which afford a clear reward signal and extensive training. DeepMind cofounder Demis Hassabis believes that this line of research will prove one of the most important in leading to more general problem solvers in DNN-based AI. He expresses the empiricist sentiment here by noting that this research

> has yet to capture some of the key characteristics that give human planning abilities their power. In particular, we suggest that a general solution to this problem will require understanding how rich internal models, which in practice will have to be approximate but sufficiently accurate to support planning, can be learned through experience, without strong priors being handcrafted into the network by the experimenter. (Hassabis et al. 2017:252)

Here, I would only further suggest that continuing to mine the insights of empiricist philosophers like Locke, Hume, and James, who thought long and hard about this problem, will reward engineers with additional ideas about how to bootstrap higher levels of rationality from more creative processing of experience.[12]

---

[11] Granted, it is still true that the I2A agent cannot explicitly phrase the comparison to itself that one outcome is twice as likely to come up as another; but it could choose the likelier outcome 100 percent of the time instead of probability matching—though it is an open question whether a language model like those described in Chapter 6 might be able to formulate such an explicit statement if it had access to I2A's aggregated rollout representations.

[12] Compare also Nanay (2016).

5.7. Biological plausibility and the road ahead

Future research will no doubt ask rigorous questions about the biological plausibility of the DNN-based models of imagination reviewed herein. Current evidence is scant: compared to perceptual abstraction, there have been far fewer links between neuroanatomy and structural aspects of the models, and no brain imaging studies comparing the similarity of the representations acquired by generative models and the human imagination. This is partly because the generative models discussed herein are so new, and partly because less is known about the neural circuits responsible for imagination in humans. There have, nevertheless, already been a few notable attempts at informed speculation (Gershman 2019; Hamrick 2019; Hassabis et al. 2017; Lau 2019; Mahadevan 2018).

For instance, there is a substantial amount of empirical evidence that routine perception and cognition in humans and animals involves substantial generative simulation. Perceptual "filling in" is one of the most commonly discussed phenomena; despite the fact that humans can only receive high-resolution information from a small area of foveation in the center of each retina, and the retinal nerve attachment results in a blind spot in the center of vision, we have visual experience of a continuous, high-resolution perception of the world for our entire field of vision up until the periphery (Fig. 5.6). Numerous quirks

Figure 5.6 Readers can locate their retinal blind spot in the right eye by putting this image about a foot away from the face, closing the left eye, fixating on the dot, and then moving backward and forward slowly until the cross disappears (note, however, that one does not experience a void in one's visual field, but rather an area that is filled in with the background color or pattern).

and other apparent malfunctions of the perceptual systems also suggest that our brains possess predictive models of sensory experience
and are constantly generating a forward model of what the world is
like, which corresponds to our conscious sensory experience. Illusions
and confabulations are good evidence that what we are consciously
aware of perceiving is the result of generative modeling rather than
raw perceptual input. Another poignant example is the difficulty that
people have in tickling themselves; one of the most popular scientific
explanations for this fact is that the sensation generated by one's own
movements is already part of one's generative model, whereas the sensation of tickling occurs only in cases when the haptic stimuli is surprising, in the sense that it is not congruent with the self-generated
forward model of experience (Blakemore, Wolpert, and Frith 2000).

Several cognitive scientists of perception have begun to theorize explicitly that the mechanisms in the brain that produce these forward
models may be similar in important ways to some of the generative
models from deep learning that we have just reviewed, especially
GANs (Gershman 2019; Lau 2019). Gershman, in particular, has
noted that the Bayesian models that are often proposed to account
for these phenomena in cognitive psychology theorize that the brain
learns an explicit model of the probability space from which potential experiences are sampled. While there is diverse empirical evidence
that such forward models are generated by the brain, these Bayesian
views are not computationally plausible, as they appeal to inefficient
sampling operations like Monte Carlo algorithms that are computationally very expensive. Bayesian modelers here thus often appeal
to heuristic approximations of these sampling operations instead.
Gershman proposes that implicit distribution models like those provided by GANs might provide an alternative way out of this dilemma.
Whereas the lack of explicitness in latent factor representations
learned by GANs can be regarded as a liability from the perspective of
the XAI problems in computer science, it may be regarded as a useful
computational efficiency trick in the cognitive science of perception.
Gershman further proposes that this GAN-based approach lends itself to a systems-level interpretation of cortical function in predictive
processing, with the medial anterior prefrontal cortex generating the
discrimination signal by comparing discriminative and generative

models of perceptual input. In the context of metacognition and consciousness, Lau has further suggested that GANs may help solve an evolutionary problem with higher-order and generative accounts of conscious perception, by explaining how the top-down generative models might feasibly be trained and by highlighting the adaptive role that metacognitive awareness might play, through helping us distinguish and decide among different potential causes of our sensory inputs.

Granted, these are only preliminary systems-level suggestions, and much more work remains to be done to determine the degree of similarity between latent space representations in DNN-based generative models and representations constructed in forward models in biological brains. Further, the hypothesis can take advantage of the general aspects of neural plausibility derived from a network-based model, and most GAN architectures integrate many of the features of DCNNs that were biologically inspired, such as local connectivity and a division of labor between linear and nonlinear activation functions. Nevertheless, in this chapter we have explored a wide range of implementation details for DNN-based generative models, and it remains to be seen which, if any, have a significant degree of structural correspondence to mechanistic aspects of biological brains.

5.8. Summary

In this chapter, I reviewed how rational decision-making is enhanced via the operations of the imagination, and specifically how adding generative imagination-like capacities to DNN-based architectures can enable them to satisfy traditional objections to empiricist approaches to the mind. Specifically, generative architectures like GANs, VAEs, and generative transformers can synthesize novel tokens of abstract categories, compose new categories by fusing together previous ones, and simulate future or counterfactual experience for use in decision-making and offline training. I considered nativist objections to these suggestions, especially that these architectures are only capable of interpolation and not human-like extrapolation, and found the critique beset with anthropofabulation and less decisive than skeptics of deep learning suppose. I further reviewed the potential for more ambitious uses of these generative capacities, potentially taking the quest for computational creativity further than it has ever gone before by creating agents that actively seek novelty, such as Elgammal et al.'s Creative Adversarial Network (CAN). We finally reviewed how an architecture like Google's Imagination-Augmented Agents (I2A) can integrate several of these lessons to solve more challenging kinds of problems (such as Sokoban puzzles) through prospective simulation of possible future courses of action, choosing the best on consequence-sensitive grounds—all while trained end to end on its own interaction with a problem. Such innovations can not only enable agents to reach greater heights of Tier 2 rationality (consequence-sensitive decision-making) but also reach Tier 3, involving prospective simulation of future and counterfactual events for decision-making and offline learning.

Nevertheless, at this point it becomes increasingly clear that adding more semi-independent faculties comes with increasing Control Problems. I have proposed modules for perception, memory, and imagination; questions continually arise about how an agent is to switch among perceptive, mnemonic, and imaginative modes of processing, and how to coordinate representations and actions in cases where different subsystems vie for shared resources or recommend alternative courses of action. Episodic Controller agents (discussed in the previous chapter) have separate pathways for making decisions based upon lookup in the short-term experience buffer and from longer-term abstracted representations, and I2A architectures have independent pathways for perception-like decision-making and simulation-guided prospective decision-making. In both cases, a final decision procedure must select which policy recommendation to pursue. Such problems will only compound as the DoGMA adds more faculties and modules, and so engineers should develop plans for further strategies—perhaps based on further faculties that help downregulate and coordinate the others—to solve these emerging Control Problems before they become unmanageably complex.

6

Attention

Everyone knows what attention is. It is the taking possession by the mind, in clear and vivid form, of one out
of what seem several simultaneously possible objects or
trains of thought.

—William James (*PP* 381)

6.1. Introduction: Bootstrapping control

At this point in our development of the DoGMA, we have introduced
three distinct faculties: perception (subsuming perceptual abstraction), memory, and imagination. These faculties have been tasked with
performing a variety of mental operations that are consistent with the
Transformation Principle and relevant to rational cognition, including
distinguishing members of different abstract categories in rich sensory
input, storing sequences of previous experiences for offline learning
or later consultation in decision-making, synthesizing realistic perceptual representations of novel category members, and simulating novel
experiences to enable consequence-sensitive decision-making before exploring options by trial and error. We have also explored initial
efforts to model aspects of these faculties using different deep neural
network (DNN) architectures. These efforts help artificial agents overcome computational challenges facing empiricist approaches to artificial rationality—the interrelated concerns of sample efficiency,
transferability, and brittleness. We have thus already come quite far
in explaining how achievements in DNN-based modeling over the
last ten years have increased the viability of empiricism generally, and
of the faculty-oriented approach highlighted in the new empiricist
DoGMA in particular.

From Deep Learning to Rational Machines. Cameron J. Buckner, Oxford University Press.
© Oxford University Press 2024. DOI: 10.1093/oso/9780197653302.003.0006

However, the complexity of the faculty-based architecture developed so far poses problems of its own, which we have described as the Control Problem in previous chapters. A particular wrinkle here is that nearly all of the DNN-based faculty models we have discussed so far are "one-offs"—that is, they attempt to model only one faculty (and often only one aspect of that faculty) at a time. As we attempt to model multiple semi-independent faculties in a more complete cognitive architecture, we will increasingly need to grapple with the Control Problem as a practical concern. More semi-independent modules performing different computational operations will increasingly compete for shared resources and decision-making influence, and the problem of clashes and confusions between their outputs will only grow in complexity and significance. DNN modelers can start preparing to confront these problems now, while there is still time to build countermeasures into the next generation of more complex agent architectures.

Before planning such countermeasures, we should first review this issue as it features in empiricist philosophy of mind. DNN modelers are only beginning to explore the implications of the Control Problem, but it has been a major concern for nearly every empiricist philosopher who has proffered a faculty psychology. As Kathryn Tabb (2018) has recently pointed out, Locke's *Enquiry* is shot through with concern for "madness," which Locke often attributed to faulty combinations of ideas formed by imaginative association. These faulty associations come from the "Fancy" or "Reverie," which leads to pathological behavior when confused with associations derived from perception or memory. Locke worried about, for example, "a distracted Man fancying himself the King" and (correctly) deducing from that imagined scenario that he should be given "suitable Attendance, Respect, and Obedience" (*E* II.xi.13). Hume similarly fretted about mistaking the deliverances of imagination for those of memory, or the deliverances of either with occurrent perceptions. He was concerned that "wherever we can make an idea approach the impressions in force and vivacity, it will likewise imitate them in its influence on the mind" (*T* 1.3.10.3/119). Like our own narrative thus far, Hume acknowledges three basic sources of beliefs: the senses, memory, and imagination. He argued that the mind distinguishes the impressions delivered by these systems by attending to their "force" and "vivacity"; occurrent sensory impressions should be the most vivacious, followed by memories of sensory impressions, and finally with imagined ideas being the most "faint" and "languid." When memories or fancies become too vibrant—as we might think in the case of a posttraumatic stress disorder patient reliving a painful memory after being exposed to a trigger, or someone under the influence of hallucinogens being unable to distinguish their delusions from reality—significant error can result. Thus, like Locke, Hume cautioned against the "lively imagination which degenerates into madness and folly," which might leave one "no means of distinguishing betwixt truth and falsity" (*T* 1.3.10.9/123, discussed in Costelloe 2018:27).

The complexity of the modular architecture we have developed in the previous chapters already presents us with these epistemological and control-theoretic quandaries. Agents that can consider scenarios from the present, past, or future need to be able to distinguish representations of scenarios according to their provenance to avoid mistakes in decision-making. At an even more basic level, they also need to be able to switch efficiently between processing "modes"— between, for example, task-oriented problem-solving based on stored abstractions, consultation of individual memories of successful actions in an episodic store, offline memory consolidation and slow interleaved learning, or imaginative simulation of possible scenarios—as appropriate to circumstances. We have also seen that even a single faculty can be so overwhelmed with possibilities—as when Hume listed the number of different aspects along which we might compare two spheres during perceptual abstraction, according to shape, color, size, or location—that it cannot draw conclusions without first ignoring comparisons that are not relevant.[1] Environmental complexity may pose a special problem, too, as an agent that is continually deflected and misdirected by external interference may need procedures that can reorient it toward the completion of a long-term goal.

---

[1] Hume is here following Berkeley, who, as we may recall, rejected Locke's doctrine of abstract ideas. Berkeley used attention to explain abstraction; he held that ideas are always particular, but attention is free to focus on only abstract aspects of those ideas: "It must be acknowledged that a man may consider a figure merely as triangular, without attending to the particular qualities of the angles or relations of the sides" (1710, Introduction to second edition §16, and see Mole 2021 for discussion).

Ultimately, we would do well to consider adding to the DoGMA a new mechanism that helps it address these allocation issues in an efficient and effective manner. As has been already heavily foreshadowed, the faculty of attention has long been considered the right tool for this job. It is natural to think of the problem of switching between processing modes as a matter of attending to different kinds of mental representations—focusing outward on an anticipated sensory experience, for example, or focusing inward on a search for particular memories or desired outcomes in imaginative simulation. But attention is, in many ways, a theoretically knotty topic, and we should acknowledge its tangles and snags before attempting to weave it into the developing tapestry. In both philosophy and psychology today, there are a diversity of views and disagreements concerning attention's basic function. Many different effects and operations have been ascribed to attention over the years, and we will see a corresponding degree of variety reflected in the neural network architectures that it has inspired. There are debates as to whether attention is one thing or many, whether any of the psychological phenomena associated with it are cause or effect, and indeed whether it should be understood as a distinct faculty at all. These theoretical tensions can be found in debates among the different historical empiricists who theorized about attention. And, as we will see, these multitudes can even be found in the work of William James, a philosopher who conveniently exhibited empiricist leanings and is often considered the progenitor of modern empirical psychology. His *Principles of Psychology* devoted a sizable chapter to the topic of attention, and many of the ideas expressed there remain prescient to this day.

James's view is particularly fertile here because he does not ignore attention's complexity to round off corners. Indeed, his view is so complex that psychology and computational modeling have not yet fully explored his insights. The number and diversity of operations that James ascribes to attention has led some commentators to worry that he did not actually have a coherent theory of the faculty's operations. Contra this attitude, I draw upon the work of fellow empiricist Jesse Prinz, who argues that James does have a theory of attention that can explain this apparent heterogeneity—and that, in fact, James's theory has important advantages over other popular alternatives in philosophy and psychology.[2] Then, I review the various implementations of attention in deep neural network architectures, especially the ways it can be used for linguistic processing in transformer architectures. Finally, I focus on the implications of the additional forms of processing and control that such attention can give us for rational decision-making, considering especially the gains in efficiency, processing power, control, and information sharing among modules that attentional processing can marshal, both before and after it enables language. These comparisons suggest that a Jamesian approach to attention as implemented by generative DNNs can further enhance the ability of empiricist-inspired artificial agents to model the higher tiers of rational decision-making but also has perhaps the greatest potential among existing theories in philosophy and psychology to unite the seemingly disparate aspects and effects of attention together under the aegis of a single generic mechanism.

6.2. Contemporary theories of attention in philosophy and psychology

Contemporary philosophical and psychological theories nearly all treat attention as a kind of selectiveness. However, there remains a great deal of disagreement as to exactly why such selectiveness is needed, how it is achieved, where it is expressed in cognitive processing, and whether it requires a separate faculty or is achieved organically through the operations of the other faculties. To review the history of theorizing about attention in twentieth-century psychology, let us quickly consider four of the most influential styles of approach.

The first style focuses on the importance of filtering information in computational systems. Specifically, Donald Broadbent (1958) noted that a serious engineering challenge in early computing and information technology was the cost of transmitting large amounts of information from one computational component to another (such as from input sensors to memory, or from the central processing unit

---

[2] See also Carolyn Dicey Jennings for a similar take on James related more explicitly to phenomenology and agent-level control (Jennings 2012).

to the screen). Inspired in particular by the early computerization of telephone exchanges, he noted that a great deal of effort in early electronic communication theory was expended to cope with capacity limitations in transmission channels (Mole 2011b).[3] This concern was addressed by filtering input, compressing input signals as much as possible, and carefully scheduling the transfer of information from one component to another. These ideas were built into a hierarchical multistage memory storage and processing model, with sensory inputs passing from a sensory buffer to higher-level processing and finally to working memory, with bottlenecks and filters imposed on the transmission lines between each store to conserve bandwidth. Attention was captured in this model by the filtering and selection process that occurred between different stages in the storage and processing hierarchy. Attended information was selected for transmission to the higher stages for later processing and storage, whereas unattended information was blocked and lost, becoming unavailable for later processing. Work in the selection theory tradition eventually splintered into "early selection" theorists who (like Broadbent) thought that the information bottleneck occurred relatively early in perception, and "late selection" theorists who thought that it was imposed later in processing, such as immediately before information became available to working memory or conscious awareness (Deutsch and Deutsch 1963; Driver 2001; Prinz 2005).

A second and distinct tradition of theorizing about attention in cognitive psychology is found in the feature integration theory (FIT) developed by Anne Treisman and colleagues. FIT is based on a different, more parallelized conception of neural processing (Treisman and Gelade 1980). Treisman's view was inspired by some of the same work on ventral stream processing that motivated Fukushima's research on early deep convolutional neural networks (DCNNs), as well as ideas about more pervasive (or "massive") modularity that were

---

[3] Broadbent expresses this concern thusly: "Perhaps the point of permanent value which will remain in psychology if the fashion for communication theory wanes, will be the emphasis on problems of capacity. [. . .] The fact that any given channel has a limit is a matter of central importance to communication engineers, and it is correspondingly forced on the attention of psychologists who use their terms" (1958:5; also quoted in Mole 2021).

becoming popular in cognitive science at the time. In the early 1980s, serial conceptions of cognitive processing like those presumed by Broadbent—where information passes through a sequence of computational operations, one at a time—were beginning to fall out of favor. Instead, the newer approach assumed the brain (especially sensory processing systems) contained a large number of specialized modules that could perform different types of computational operations in parallel. According to this framework, the perceptual cortex contains many different regions specialized in the detection of different features of a stimulus—such as shape, color, location, movement, and orientation (which we notably canvassed as "nuisance parameters" in Chapter 3)— in a semi-independent and parallel manner.[4] To reiterate the core dedications of my own view, I argue neither for nor against such "massive" modularity here—the DoGMA requires only a few, sparse modules, potentially obviating some of the criticisms which later troubled massive modularity views (Fodor 2000; Frankenhuis and Ploeger 2007; Machery 2008; Samuels 2000).

A parallel and massively modular architecture obviates the need to overcome sensory processing bottlenecks—because parallel systems have much greater capacity—but it creates a new problem: integrating the results of all those semi-independent operations in an efficient manner. This was influentially dubbed the "Binding Problem"—the brain needed some way to bind the independently processed features of the same object together into a single coherent representation. Attention offers a potential solution to this problem. Specifically, attention was thought to provide a spatial frame of reference that guided binding. According to the theory articulated by Treisman and other FIT theorists, a sustained spatial focus of attention could be moved around the agent's spatial representation of their environment (like a

---

[4] Treisman defended this idea against early selection theory with an ingenious set of experiments which demonstrated that subjects did in fact process semantic features in sensory channels which were supposed to be ignored in the task. For example, in one influential paradigm she displayed two different auditory streams simultaneously to subjects, one in each ear, and told them to attend to the message in only one ear. When semantic information relevant to the message being processed was switched from the attended to the "rejected" ear, subjects could flexibly extract those words and seamlessly return to the attended-to ear, often without even being aware of an interruption in processing (Treisman 1960).

sliding window), and the various features that were represented as co-occurring at that location could be glued together into a compound representation of a particular object. To come up from the historical review and spell out some implications that will be explored later, it is worth noting that this theory of attention can address some of the concerns of some of the nativists mentioned in Chapters 1 and 4—that human-level intelligence requires representing enduring objects with stable properties over time—but it does so (if it works) using a domain-general attentional faculty and without requiring an innate OBJECT concept.

A third, coherence-based tradition construes attentional selection in service of action rather than perception. On this approach, the problem is not that the system has too little bandwidth on some critical perceptual channel, but rather that perception offers too many sources of information and too many potential actions that are mutually inconsistent with one another. Attention is the process that selects sources of information and operations to perform based on their consistency with a particular action. For example, if I aim to hit a baseball, I will ignore information about its color or texture, ignore other actions that I might perform on it such as catching it or rubbing it, and focus on its speed and location in order to make contact with it using the bat. This view can do away with the idea of capacity limitations altogether and emphasize the need for selection as a solution to this problem (which philosopher Wayne Wu elaborates as the "many-many problem"; Wu 2011a, 2011b). Versions of this view—which include Neisser (1976) and Allport (1993)—tend to emphasize the role that attention plays in agency and rational choice rather than in perceptual information processing.

A fourth and final collection of views construes attention as merely the outcome of a competition among the other faculties. This outcome may be achieved in an active or passive fashion. Active competition-based views consider attention to be a kind of all-purpose resource enhancer for other faculties (such as an increase in the "precision" or "gain" of a specific component of a sensory signal). Passive competition-based views might take "attention" to simply mark the winner of a competition among other processes, or some other sort of spontaneous coordinating activity of the brain. Passive views can be seen as neurally inspired, since brain dynamics are often characterized in terms of an intricate balance of activation and inhibition—too much activation, and neural firing becomes disorganized and chaotic; too much inhibition, and the brain becomes inert. Thus, a natural competition emerges between subnetworks of the brain for coordinated dominance of information-processing and decision-making resources, and "attention" is simply this process settling into a stable state. Christopher Mole has defended a version of this view under the moniker of "cognitive unison theory" (2011a). This kind of view has architectural consequences for artificial intelligence (AI), as a passive interpretation of this "settling" might hold that there is no need for a separate module to perform the roles ascribed to attention in an artificial neural network system. There are also more active ways of working out this view, however, which posit various mechanisms that might bias the competition process to reach a particular outcome, and so might recommend an additional module that can exert influence like a judge or umpire to help push a competition toward a particular outcome.

As should be clear from this basic taxonomy of views of attention in psychology, each style of view—whether bottleneck, binding, coherence, or competition-based in style—must also make sense of a large set of processing effects that have been ascribed to attentional processing. Attention has been variously studied for its ability to enhance performance by, for example, providing more detail, accuracy, precision, vivacity, or error detection to other forms of processing. It has also been viewed as a necessary condition for conscious awareness, as a precondition for encoding in short-term and long-term memory, as a cause of diminished performance for tasks involving nonattended sources of information, as a limited resource which is subject to load constraints and fatigue from overuse, and as something affected by forms of brain injury, drug intervention, or psychological pathology. It has been directly implicated in enabling the higher ranks of abstract and relational cognition, such as the ability to categorize items by higher-order relations such as sameness or difference irrespective of the particular categories or features that are alike or dissimilar, which rationalists have argued poses a fundamental limitation for similarity-based associative theories of processing (Delius 1994; Fodor and Pylyshyn 1988; Logan 1994; Marcus 2003; Ricci, Cadène, and Serre 2021).

At a higher architectural level that encompasses many of these diverse roles, attention has been seen as a critical component distinguishing "System II"–style cognitive processing (which is thought to capture characteristic weaknesses of current DNN models) from "System I" type associative processing (at which current DNN architectures are often thought to excel—Chollet 2019; Goyal and Bengio 2020; Kahneman and Frederick 2005; Sloman 1996). I will not arbitrate disagreements between different styles of theory here, nor will I argue for a novel theory of attention which assimilates all of these aspects into a coherent whole. I will, however, explore how the various ideas ascribed to attention in cognitive psychology and philosophy resonate with relevant tweaks to DNNs reviewed in later sections. Such an exploration will help us better understand why the deep learning community increasingly considers attention to be the critical next step required to bootstrap DNN-based architectures to forms of cognition that are thought to be uniquely human, such as language.

6.3. James on attention as ideational preparation

James is a particularly interesting figure to consult at this point in our narrative, because while he is one of the most influential philosophers and psychologists with empiricist leanings, he begins his discussion of attention by throwing his fellow empiricists under the bus. James complains that selective attention has "received hardly any notice from the psychologists of the English empiricist school" which for him includes "Locke, Hume, Hartley, the Mills, and Spencer" (*PP* 402). To diagnose the cause of this purported omission, James reads these empiricists as supposing that the mind is merely receptive to the deliverances of experience, whereas attention, "implying a degree of reactive spontaneity," would disrupt "the smoothness of the tale" (*PP* 402). This appraisal is unfair toward at least Locke and Hume, who, as we have already emphasized in earlier chapters, suppose that abstractions are often extracted from experience through the contribution of active mental faculties.[5] Nevertheless, James surely devotes a

---

[5] Why does James read his fellow empiricists so uncharitably (for as noted by Mole [2021], Locke, Berkeley, and Hume all had influential accounts of attention as an active

great deal more thought to the topic than did his fellow empiricists—James dedicates one of the lengthiest chapters of his *Principles of Psychology* to the study of attention—and his views will help bootstrap the empiricist DoGMA to the next tiers of control and flexibility in rational decision-making.

While James's views on attention might be placed broadly in the family of "selectionist" theories discussed in the previous section, it is much more multifarious than those discussed so far. In fact, James has sometimes been accused of offering a hodgepodge of disorganized thoughts on the subject, or a muddle that amounts to pluralism or eliminativism about attention as a coherent faculty. However, and as referenced earlier, Jesse Prinz (2022) has recently argued against these interpretations, holding that James's chapter actually does offer a theory of attention as a single coherent faculty. Indeed, Prinz argues that James's theory may have a better chance of assimilating all the various roles and effects ascribed to the attention than contemporary alternatives.

There are three distinctive aspects of James's view that make it particularly useful for exploring the prospects for AI based on the empiricist DoGMA. First, James holds that there is a close relationship between attention and the imagination, which links the faculty to ideas discussed in the previous chapter. Second, his take on the role of interest in attention finesses the borderline between empiricism and nativism, specifically in a way that is relevant to the objections regarding sample efficiency and human-like learning considered in previous chapters. And third, some of the more speculative planks of James's theory may be borne out by very recent ideas in machine learning that I will review in sections 6.4 and 6.5. Indeed, the core element of James's theory—the concept of "ideational preparation"—was neglected by most of twentieth-century psychological theorizing on attention, perhaps because we had no idea how to implement it using the computational metaphors of the day. As we will see, however, generative

mental faculty)? It may be as simple as having accepted the rationalist critical zeitgeist of his day. We should also keep in mind that the standard story of Locke and Hume being the most influential empiricists is a more modern invention, and James may simply be reading some of the later empiricists who were more explicitly "automaton" theorists back into Locke and Hume.

and predictive architectures in machine learning now show how artificial neural networks (ANNs) might implement this idea. In short, in James we find another ambitious and often-criticized idea from an influential empiricist thinker that might be borne out by cutting-edge developments in machine learning. By outlining and exploring his view in light of current challenges and opportunities in deep learning, we can appreciate its promise and prescience.

Like other theories of attention in contemporary psychology, James begins with informational selection—though he quickly develops attention's informational role into a much more ambitious theory of attention as a distinctively generative solution to control problems. To continue the quotation with which this chapter began, James says that attention is the

> taking possession by the mind, in a clear and vivid form, of one out of what seem several simultaneously possible objects or trains of thought. It implies withdrawal from some things in order to deal effectively with others, and is a condition which has a real opposite in the confused, dazed, scatterbrained state which in French is called *distraction* and *Zerstreutheit* in German. (*PP* 404)

The chapter continues through a long engagement with quasi-empirical debates among early psychologists concerning how many active processes humans might attend to at once. He concludes this discussion with the verdict that the answer is "not easily more than one, unless the processes are very habitual; but then two, or even three, without very much oscillation of the attention" (*PP* 409). James then provides a list of effects associated with attention, which he suggests are the ability to "perceive, conceive, distinguish, [and] remember" stimuli better than we otherwise could, as well as to "[shorten] 'reaction-time'" to attended stimuli or actions (*PP* 425). James further notes how shifts of attention to a complex scene can change our categorization of it, writing poetically that "Every artist knows how he can make a scene before his eyes appear warmer or colder in color, according to the way he sets his attention. . . . If for warm, he soon begins to see the red color start out of everything; if for cold, the blue" (*PP* 425). Here, we already have a hint that attention not only selects information, it can also exert top-down control of categorizations and expectations, as we might shift between bi-stable stimuli like the duck-rabbit picture or Rubin vase by changing the details on which we focus (Fig. 6.1).

To distinguish it from the other faculties already discussed, James insists that attention is not an idea creation or storage system like "imagination, discrimination, and memory." It does, however, bear an "intimate connection" to these other faculties (*PP* 446). James says that attention "creates no idea; an idea must already be there before we can attend to it" (*PP* 450), emphasizing the mimetic and (again) selective nature of attention. As we will see, however, attention bears for James a particularly intimate relationship to the imagination, even more so than to perception or memory.

The sense that James offers merely a hodgepodge in place of a theory is encouraged by a chapter subsection in which James taxonomizes different subkinds of attention (*PP* 416). These different subkinds of attention often seem to bear inconsistent properties to one another. James notes that acts of attention can be divided according to their subject—whether to "objects of sense" (which he calls "sensorial attention") or to "ideal or represented objects" (which he calls "intellectual attention"). He also notes that acts of attention can be divided by whether their direction is "immediate" or "derived," depending upon whether the topic

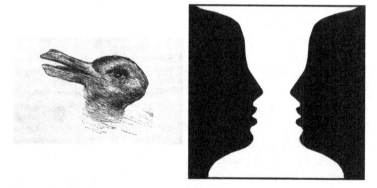

Figure 6.1 Note how we can change our categorical perception of these figures by attending to different areas of the image . . . such as the "bill" of the duck or the "nose" of the rabbit in the first image, or the noses of two faces or the bottom of the vase in the second image.

is interesting "in itself, without relation to anything else" or whether it "owes its interest to association with some other immediately interesting thing" (*PP* 416). This taxonomic cut will be particularly relevant to questions of nativism broached later in this chapter, as it seems to depend upon whether subjects are interesting to some agent without relation to experience. James also notes that attention can be either "passive" and "effortless" or "active and voluntary" (*PP* 416). He then explores which combinations of cuts are possible. For example, James supposes that immediate voluntary attention is impossible, and so voluntary attention must be always be derived, or in service of some other goal or interest. A set of these combinations of cuts—with examples—can be found in Table 6.1.

While it provides us with much subject matter for reflection, nothing in this taxonomy outlines a positive theory of attention. The taxonomy lists different ways that attention might express its influence, but it does not tell us how it does so, or whether there are one or many different mechanisms at play. James insists that these various acts of attention do actually reduce to a combination of the following two mechanisms: (1) "organic adjustment" of the sensory organs and (2) "ideational preparation." Though introduced as two things, we should not assume that they are completely independent mechanisms—James even asserts that "the two processes of sensorial adjustment and ideational preparation probably coexist in all our concrete attentive acts" (*PP* 434).

The former—organic adjustment—is comparatively straightforward, and perhaps one of the most commonly assessed variables in psychological studies of attention. The adjustment of the sensory organs includes turning the head toward the perceived direction of sounds or visual stimuli, eye saccades, squinting of the eyes to adjust to light intensities, dilating of the pupils, moving the hand toward a heat source to gauge its temperature, and so on. These adjustments can be voluntary or involuntary, as our eyes or head may dart toward the direction of an unexpected sound as if by reflex. We can also, however, acquire habits in organic adjustment, as expert poker players may learn to attend to their opponent's minutest facial tics or expert tennis players may automatically focus on more tactically significant areas of their opponent bodies (such as hand position and lower-body

Table 6.1 Various Possibilities in James's Taxonomy of Forms of Attention

| | Immediate | | Derived | |
	Passive	Voluntary	Passive	Voluntary
Sensorial	Reflexively turning one's head toward a loud noise	Not possible	"How a bit of bad grammar wounds the purist! How a false note hurts the musician!" (Herbart, *PP* 418)	An intermediate sports player who deliberately practices watching their opponents' feet or waist to predict movements
Intellectual	When we "follow in thought a train of images exciting or interesting *per se*" (*PP* 418)	Not possible	"Archimedes was so absorbed in geometrical meditation that he was first aware of the storming of Syracuse by his own death-wound" (Hamilton, *PP* 419)	A novice student considering a series of abstract theses defended in a dry, humorless philosophy book

movements) when preparing to return serves (Rosker and Majcen Rosker 2021).

While organic adjustment would seem to always involve sensorial attention, James sees a close physiological relationship between organic adjustment and many forms of intellectual attention. He suggests, for example, that when we are attempting to attend to ideas in memory, that the "backwards retraction" we feel is "principally constituted by the feeling of an actual rolling outwards and upwards of the eyeballs such as occurs in sleep" (*PP* 436). This more broadly fits with Jamesian theories of emotion and phenomenology, which hold that the feelings associated with various mental states are really interoception of physiological changes in the body—an approach which continues to attract new supporters today (Mandler 1990; Prinz 2004).[6] Contemporary psychology measures primarily the physiological components of intellectual attention, such as the saccading of the eyes left and right when performing numerical operations along a mental number line, which can be assessed using eye-tracking methods (Ranzini, Lisi, and Zorzi 2016; Schwarz and Keus 2004).

The second mechanism—ideational preparation—is the subtler and more interesting side of Jamesian attention, especially in the context of recent theories of perception and cognition. James's view challenges the idea that attention is merely directed at objects like a "mental spotlight"—either automatically turning toward strong stimuli, or being actively directed around a physical or mental space as if in a search pattern—holding instead that attention actively models and anticipates the objects on which such a spotlight might shine. Moreover, this anticipation—and whether it is satisfied or frustrated—can explain much of the spotlight's causes and effects. Its operation, in particular, can be driven by background knowledge and expectations derived from prior experience. The ideational preparation view is thus a richer and more cognitive picture of attention than that painted by the capacity-limitation or feature-binding theories reviewed in the last subsection. As Prinz (2022:3) notes, this view would notably fit well with more predictive approaches to the mind and attention in particular, which have become popular only in the last decade or two in psychology (Clark 2013; Griffiths, Kemp, and Tenenbaum 2008; Hohwy 2013).

James provides several lines of evidence to support this view. To consider one example which goes beyond organic adjustment, James raises the case of peripheral vision. When we keep our eyes fixated on a particular target, this does not prevent our attention from moving to objects at the periphery of our visual awareness, either because we notice something surprising or as an act of voluntary will. James

---

[6] In general, the modeling of the emotions in AI is still in early stages compared to other faculties discussed thus far. This is unfortunate, since the emotions play a large role in empiricist approaches to rational decision-making. We will return to the emotions in the next chapter.

notes that such peripheral vision is trainable, and that continuously attending to some object on the periphery (a "marginal object") requires effort. Though the marginal object never becomes "perfectly distinct," attending to it makes us somehow more "vividly conscious" of it than we were before. James then asks: If our attending to the marginal object does not consist in movement of the sensory organs, in what does it consist? To answer his question, he says "the effort to attend to the marginal region of the picture consists in nothing more nor less than the effort to form as clear an idea as is possible of what is there portrayed" (*PP* 438). He further describes this as an act of "reinforcing" and "anticipatory" imagination of the thing to which we attempt to attend. This act involves creating an "imaginary duplicate of the object in the mind, which shall stand ready to receive the outward impression as if in a matrix" (*PP* 439). A full "act of attention" for James, thus includes both forming an anticipatory representation of some object and verifying that the signals anticipated match those coming from the target.

Many of the early experiments conducted on effects of attention that are reviewed by James (e.g., by Wundt, Exner, and Helmholtz) consisted in measuring reaction times to stimuli to which subjects were instructed to attend. For example, Helmholtz invented a kind of divided box into which subjects could look, and separate images could be displayed to each retina, which when viewed together formed stereoscopic pictures. The images were only illuminated during periods of occasional electric flashes, which allowed Helmholtz to measure the number and duration of flashes required for subjects to perceive the images displayed. He pricked pinholes in the center of each side of the box, so that the eyes could remain focused on pinpoints of external light in the darkness, in preparation for the spark. He found, as expected, that simple figures were more easily perceived than complex ones, in terms of the numbers of sparks required. More relevantly to the present investigation, he also found that subjects could "keep their attention voluntarily turned to any particular portion [they] please of the dark field, so as then, when the spark comes, to receive an impression only from such parts of the picture as lie in this region" (Helmholtz quoted in *PP* 438). James suggests that subjects can perceive areas of these images more readily when they engage their anticipatory attention in this way, for "time is lost" when they are not already imagining the contents of this region "because no stable image can under such circumstances be formed in advance" (*PP* 438). For James, this explains much of the facilitatory aspect of imaginative processing—the mind has a "head start" in forming a model of the sensory stimulations it is about to receive, so it does not need to build such a model from scratch when the stimulations arrive. The conscious direction of attention to stimuli already present, moreover, can be understood in terms of directing more resources toward building a richer model in anticipatory imagination of those sensory stimuli, thereby enhancing their processing.

As Prinz (2022) notes, the ability of unexpected or surprising stimuli to draw our attention might be thought a counterexample to this theory. Indeed, it might be thought a conceptual muddle to suppose that an unexpected noise draws our attention because we anticipate it. James nevertheless insists that such ideational preparation or preperception is involved in even these cases. In defense of this idea, James describes a child learning to identify birds; he notes that unless the child has already been taught to anticipate certain features of those birds, the child will be unlikely to notice them on the bird no matter how much effort or time is expended:

> They may readily name the features they know already, such as leaves, tail, bill, feet. But they may look for hours without distinguishing nostrils, claws, scales, etc., until their attention is called to these details; thereafter, they see them every time. In short, the only things which we commonly see are those which we preperceive. (*PP* 444)

Thus, we might suppose that in order for attention to be drawn to an unexpected stimulus, it must in some sense be capable of modeling it beforehand.

To explain how attention is drawn to such a stimulus, we may follow the lead of contemporary predictive approaches to cognition, which can help us understand a distinctive role which might be played by generative DNN models in our developing DoGMA. The role of prediction in learning has long been emphasized in some areas of psychology; it is a fundamental feature of the influential Rescorla-Wagner model of learning (Rescorla 1972; Wagner and Rescorla 1972), for example, and has always been a key aspect of one of the earliest ANN architectures, the autoencoder (Gluck and Myers 1993; Kramer 1991). This approach has become especially popular recently in computational neuroscience and philosophy; theorists here offer distinctively predictive theories of attention, which hold that attention is drawn to stimuli for which there is a lack of fit between a top-down, forward model of expected stimuli and actual low-level incoming stimuli—in more colloquial terms, these mismatches elicit "surprise" (Clark 2015; Hohwy 2013). Such surprise reflects a degree of dissonance between anticipated and received sensory inputs, which in turn has downstream cognitive consequences. This dissonance can cause attention to kick into gear and seek out the source—and then attempt to model it. As Prinz (2022:6) puts it: "perceptual experience arises after a slight delay . . . in this brief instant, we get a kind of feedback loop: first the stimulus engages our ideational centers, and they generate a representation that serves as a template for us to resample the stimulus from the environment." Through organic adjustment of the sensory organs and revision of the preperceptive model, attention then becomes focused on the surprising stimuli and the discrepancy is resolved through a confirmatory feedback loop. Though predictive processing approaches often recommend different mathematical frameworks for the forward model of anticipated stimuli (Friston 2010), generative DNNs like GANs might also play the role of the forward model in this approach to attention (Gershman 2019).

The ideational preparation view can also explain purported top-down type attentional effects on perception, such as the ability to shift the classification of ambiguous figures by attending to different subsets of their details. Drawing attention to different subsets of an ambiguous stimulus can shift the preperceptive model to favor different stable endpoints which make those subsets of stimuli more probable or harmonize with incoming inputs more thoroughly. This starts to explain certain aspects of the feature-binding view as well, as we see that attending to different locations of a stimulus in one's environment (or spatial representation thereof) could bias the preperceptive process to favor different ways of binding low-level stimuli together into high-level represented objects, as it attempts to craft a hierarchical model of anticipated perceptual inputs that harmonizes the faculty's inputs and outputs. It can also explain some of the further facilitatory and inhibitory effects of attention. Strongly attended stimuli may seem to become clearer and more vivacious on the basis of the amount of resources expended by the preperceptive imagination in modeling them with ever-higher fidelity. It can also explain why some stimuli seem to be completely ignored—when we are already engaged in an attentive task which taxes ideational preparation resources, other stimuli may be omitted from the model entirely, denying them access to memory and consciousness, as in a change blindness experiment (Simons and Levin 1997). Prinz (2022) further argues that James's theory might be able to explain the full range of effects attributed to attention by other more current views; the interested reader is encouraged to consult his complete discussion.

Despite preceding them by a more than half a century, James's theory is thus computationally more ambitious than the views discussed in the previous section. This raises concerns regarding the neural plausibility of mechanisms which might enable such predictive model construction, equilibration with sensory inputs, and revision in light of errors. James did not have much to say here based on the scant neural theory of his day, but what he does say is suggestive in the context of current generative modeling and predictive coding approaches in cognitive science:

> The natural way of conceiving all this is under the symbolic form of a brain-cell played upon from two directions. Whilst the object excites it from without, other brain-cells . . . arouse it from within. The latter influence is the "adaptation of the attention." The plenary energy of the brain-cell demands the co-operation of both factors; not when merely present, but when both present and attended to, is the object fully perceived. (*PP* 441)

This excerpt provides a stark statement of the view that attention amounts to nothing more than a certain form of imaginative modeling engaged in anticipating stimuli, and it suggests a toy neural model of a brain cell equilibrating these anticipated and actual inputs.

This way of construing James's theory may raise a concern about the category of intellectual attention, which has been comparatively neglected by contemporary psychological theorizing. If attention is just about anticipating stimuli, then how can it be directed inward toward thoughts? However, there is no great mystery here if we link this concern up with the Control Problem as we understand it at this point in our narrative. Just as contemporary psychology sees a problem with too many external inputs or too many opportunities for action, engineers also have a problem with modular architectures in which too many internally generated representations can be delivered by different modular subsystems. These representations may moreover be representationally inconsistent with one another or recommend different trajectories for learning or action. As Prinz puts it:

> We have an over-abundance of thoughts, just as we have a massively complex flow of sensory inputs . . . in both cases . . . we manage to think about one thing in a more or less linear way, despite the fact that the mind contains an ocean of ideas any of which might be vying for current attention. One of the solutions is to re-represent the selected line of thought. (Prinz 2022:11)

This directly links intellectual attention to the Control Problem. Ideational preparation may be computationally useful for selection among endogeneously generated ideas, just as it is for externally generated stimuli. The solution to the selection problem can be explored by modeling those internal representations and comparing them to others generated by the special mode of the imagination, to check them for plausibility, consistency, or relevance to a desired goal.

A final crucial component of James's theory is the role of interest in directing attention. The previous comments in this subsection provide a theory of what attention is—a specialized kind of anticipatory imagination directed at incoming sensory or intellectual signals—but it does not predict or explain attention's course. Here, James says that attention is always directed at objects that arouse interest. On James's view, all interest is either inherent or derived. For every species, some stimuli are inherently interesting and will automatically draw attention unless effort is exerted to withhold it. In this category, we might class things that by modern psychology's terminology are especially salient to nearly all members of a species, such as loud noises or bright lights.[7] Much of this inherent interest may be derived simply from the anatomy of the sensory receptors or their connections; a nocturnal animal with large eyes may find dim lights more interesting than would a diurnal animal, and James discusses how a dog wandering the Vatican may find the smell of its statues more interesting than their (to humans) elegant forms.

Interest can also of course be learned, as experts will be automatically attuned to stimuli that have previously predicted success on highly practiced tasks. James further notes that voluntary derived interest involves perhaps the most effortful kind of attention, though it plays a crucial role in human instruction. James writes that children must draw upon this kind of interest at length to maintain attention during schooling, and their success in recruiting interest to attend to objects that they otherwise find dry or boring is derived from their ability to link those objects to more interesting stimuli, such as rewards or social approval. Notably, interest can explain the course of intellectual attention just as well as sensory attention; in both cases, ideational preparation will be directed at representations that are of interest in light of current or previous goals. We will return to the topic of interest as a driver of attention later in this chapter, to explore specific ways that it might be used to address the Control Problem (and other long-standing concerns, such as sample efficiency and generalizability). In some cases, we will risk toeing the line of origin empiricism, as James and many other current cognitive scientists—"when the evolutionary afflatus is upon them," to adapt some of James's poignant prose—suppose that many biologically significant interests are innate. In these cases, however, they will be the indulgences that justify the need for discipline elsewhere, as, where the full details of their underlying mechanisms are understood, attentional biases are usually more domain-general than they initially appear or are produced

---

[7] James supposes that the objects arousing immediate attention will be species-specific, and he provides a list of examples of such stimuli for humans: "strange things, moving things, wild animals, bright things, pretty things, metallic things, words, blows, blood, etc., etc., etc." (*PP* 417). I suppose that James would have been delighted to learn about the genre of heavy metal music.

by anatomical specialization in the organs of perception that no empiricist need deny. Neither case requires innate concepts or domain-specific learning rules.

6.4. Attention-like mechanisms in DNN architectures

As we turn to the current implementations of attention-like mechanisms in DNN-based systems, we can both see what progress has been made so far and set the implementation of the full Jamesian framework as an aspirational goal. Though attentional mechanisms have been influential in some of the most notable achievements of deep learning in the last few years, they will ultimately be more partial and provisional as models of attention in humans than even the attempts to model the imagination discussed in the last chapter. Nevertheless, it will be useful to see how far those small steps have taken us, and—given the potential of the Jamesian framework to help us anticipate imminent Control Problems and prepare appropriate countermeasures—illustrate how modeling the remaining aspects of Jamesian attention constitutes a worthy addition to deep learning's research agenda. After reviewing these engineering developments (a discussion which will broadly follow an excellent recent review by Lindsay 2020), I discuss further downstream effects of attention that we are only beginning to explore in DNN-based AI, focusing especially on interest and inner speech in directing the course of attention in artificial agents, which may allow us to model some of the most ambitious forms of top-down attention in the Jamesian framework.

Perhaps the most straightforward applications of attention-like mechanisms in DNN-based processing select subsets of input or output data for processing, to the exclusion of other parts of the input or output streams. As discussed in Chapters 3 and 5, a default DCNN deploys a biologically implausible selection strategy, which involves systematically sliding a filter window over the entire input image. As mentioned in previous chapters, this is like a person looking for a particular feature in a *Where's Waldo/Wally* picture by mechanically scanning every part of the image, starting left to right and then top to bottom. The efficiency of this visual search could be dramatically improved if the system could be made to direct resources toward areas of the image that were most likely to lead to a match for the sought-for feature. Because the efficiency is improved, accuracy in time or processing constraints could also be improved, as a greater share of limited resources could be devoted to processing promising inputs instead of wasted on unpromising ones.

Indeed, state-of-the-art benchmark results on image labeling tasks have been achieved by integrating just such attentional mechanisms. Lindsay (2020) canvasses this kind of mechanism under the name of "hard feature attention." One common implementation marks up areas of images with "object proposal boxes," in which sought-for objects or features are especially likely to occur, with processing resources devoted to labeling objects in those areas. By highlighting certain information in object proposal boxes to be scanned more intensively for labeling or classification, they function as a bottleneck in processing where attention-like selectivity occurs. This family of methods has been called Region-based Convolutional Neural Network (R-CNNs) (Girshick et al. 2014), and it produced significant gains in efficiency and accuracy on standard image labeling competitions from 2013 to 2015. "Faster R-CNN" stands as a particularly efficient application of the method: it computes regions using a second network module— a smaller Region Proposal Network (RPN), itself a CNN that shares features with the rest of the network—to compute the region proposal boxes that then direct the attention of another larger and deeper CNN for more intensive feature detection and image labeling (Ren et al. 2015; Fig. 6.2).[8] The innovation allowed Faster R-CNN to compute high-accuracy classifications on standard data sets in real time

---

[8] One of the main innovations which improved efficiency from the first R-CNNs is the imposition of region proposal boxes after the image input passed through many of the convolutional layers. In short, many of the convolution operations are only done once per image to generate a single feature map, and then regions are proposed and processed on the simplified feature map. In some sense this reflects the efficiency gains from reusing features processed once by relatively modular early vision and allowing attention to operate on the midlevel abstraction products of these more encapsulated operations. This idea was highlighted by earlier versions of Prinz's views on attention and consciousness (themselves inspired by earlier views, such as those of Jackendoff— Jackendoff 1987; Prinz 2000, 2012). This computational reuse improved the processing time for each image from about 45 seconds to around 2 seconds, earning the next iteration of the architecture the name "fast R-CNN."

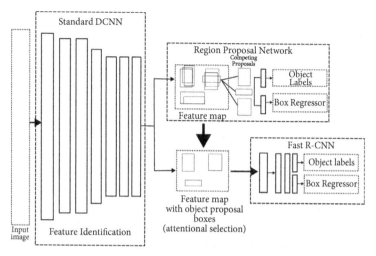

Figure 6.2 A diagram of the architecture of Faster R-CNN. (Figure adapted from Deng et al. 2018.)

on standard hardware.[9] Notably, the RPN and the main DCNN in this architecture share some convolutional layers, and hence feature representations; these computations can thus be reused to direct the bottleneck and enhance classification, increasing computational efficiency. The region-based bottleneck is imposed at different stages of processing in different members of the R-CNN model family, which might allow empirical comparison as to where the influence of an attentional bottleneck is imposed in human perception.

This approach also integrates some of Treisman's insights that attention offers a solution to the feature binding problem.[10] R-CNNs

[9] One of the pressing "too many options" problems in this neighborhood which recommended a second network dedicated to selectivity concerns a problem of too many possible object proposal boxes. Earlier R-CNNs were plagued by a computational explosion of the number of possible object proposal boxes which needed to be considered in even a simple image. The original implementation of R-CNN considered 2000 by default. One of the main functions of having a dedicated network for drawing a smaller number of object proposal boxes is to limit the number of locations which need to be considered and classified in the final steps of detection.

[10] Some influential deep learning theorists think that the binding problem remains unsolved (Greff, van Steenkiste, and Schmidhuber 2020). They also suggest, however, that further use of attentional mechanisms will play a key role in its eventual solution.

go beyond vanilla DCNNs in their behavioral abilities, particularly by being able to classify photographs not just by which objects occur within them but also by the locations of the objects inside the images, which are also identified. This can facilitate a hierarchical composition of the object identified within the proposal boxes. For example, when features are identified at multiple levels of abstraction within the same box, the system could introduce the assumption that these features are bound together into a single composite. Faster R-CNN even has mechanisms that can allow it to revise the boundaries of the object proposal box as they are lumped together. For example, if one box cuts off half of a face that another box captures, the former proposal can be discarded in favor of the latter.[11]

There is even here a hint of ideational preparation, in that the "attention" mechanism here performs this operation by implementing a predictive task: namely, predicting the likelihood that an object fitting one of its target labels will be found within the region proposal box. However, that is the limit of the "ideational preparation" in this architecture, as the network does not then proceed to build a generative model of the object purportedly in that region to verify the correctness of its hypothesis. Notably, Faster R-CNN is trained from problem data end to end, highlighting again the ability of mechanisms inspired by domain-general faculties to increase efficiency and computational power within the constraints of origin empiricism. Versions of R-CNN have often held the highest score on the PASCAL VOC (Visual Objects Classes) challenge, a benchmark designed to go beyond whole-picture labels of the ImageNet Challenge to the slightly more ambitious goal of object localization and identification.

Despite these successes, there remain several aspects of organic adjustment that are not captured in R-CNN models. In particular, R-CNN models lack recurrence, and processing done on one region

---

[11] This is accomplished using a method called "bounding box regression," where the network itself represents the boundaries of the region proposal boxes and learns how to draw them more accurately around potential objects through a regression training method. After each training step, the network learns to draw the object proposal boundaries a bit more accurately (not drawing the boundaries so wide that they include distracting information but also not drawing them so tightly that useful information is excluded) for the classes it has been trained to label and detect.

proposal box does not influence processing in any other, so there is no back-and-forth interaction between the control of the location of the input window and the results of later processing as there is with visual saccades in human processing.[12] One model that attempts to engage with this aspect of organic adjustment more directly is the Recurrent Attention Model (RAM) created by Mnih et al. (2014). The developers of RAM explicitly discuss the movement of the attentional bottleneck window as a solution to control problems in computer vision. Similar to some earlier works before the explosion of deep learning (e.g., see Larochelle and Hinton 2010, for an example and some review), RAM uses information obtained from prior "glimpses" of the input to determine where to direct the input window next in order to efficiently obtain the most useful information from the environment (Fig. 6.3). As with human foveation, the "glimpse sensor" is modeled as a series of overlapping windows of decreasing resolution, with the highest-resolution input available only at a small location in the center of the sensor. The model also uses a reinforcement learning algorithm to learn policies to control the direction of the glimpse sensor, and the agent can interact with the environment between glimpses to affect its true state. Because both the control of the sensor and control of the agent's actions are trained for sequential problems using reinforcement learning on the basis of the system's prior actions and glimpses, it can be used not only for static computer vision problems but also for ongoing tasks like playing computer games. In that case, the current glimpse is taken from the present frame of the video game, and the network computes the next action and glimpse location (for the next frame) on the basis of its current action and glimpse. The authors even experimented with allowing the network to switch itself from an "information gathering" to a "decision" phase of operation; while in the former, the system continues taking (controlled) glimpses of the environment as long as its policy network estimates that doing so will provide more useful information for a decision. Again, since the whole model was trained end to end, it further demonstrates the potential

---

[12] I thank Grace Lindsay for emphasizing this point in a personal communication.

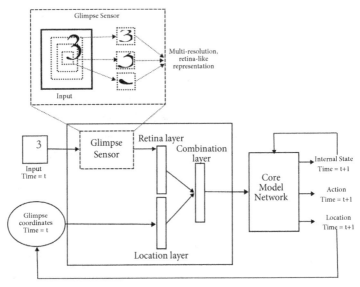

Figure 6.3 The recurrent attention model (RAM) of Mnih et al. (2014). This model integrates a form of "organic adjustment" attention on the Jamesian taxonomy by explicitly attempting to model retina-like input, which is controlled by a recurrent neural network. The "glimpse sensor" captures input from a source image at several different overlapping resolutions and integrates those differing resolutions into a single retina-like representation. The glimpse network, in turn, integrates the retina-like representation of information at time *t* with a representation of the glimpse sensor's location in the network at time *t*. This representation is in turn passed to the core network of the model (which contains several other distinct layers, black-boxed here), which outputs an updated internal representation of the input image, an action, and the location to which to move the glimpse sensor in the next step. The network is recurrent in two ways, in that the previous internal representation of the input is always passed back as input to the next step of the core model network, and the location representation is passed back to the next iteration of the glimpse network. Thus, the RAM attempts to model several different aspects of the organic adjustment of the eyes over an image, including details of retinal representations and iterative, goal-driven shifting of the retina's targeting. (Figure adapted from Mnih et al. 2014.)

of domain-general attention-like mechanisms to address control problems within the bounds of origin empiricism.

The "hard attention" models discussed so far address the "organic adjustment" component of the Jamesian taxonomy; that is because it is perhaps easier to draw direct comparisons between input filtering in DNNs and the observable behavioral concomitants of attentional shifting which are made in psychological experiments. However, the most interesting and promising aspects of the Jamesian framework can only be realized by tackling some of the less observable, internal effects of attentional shifting. Many of these internal effects can be categorized as "soft attention," which involves reweighting different aspects of the input or intermediate feature representations. This is like the kind of attention that occurs when we try to focus on part of our visual input while keeping our eyes fixed on a standard point, as in James's discussion of peripheral vision reviewed in the previous section. Early DNN-based models of soft attention have driven some of the most impressive advances in deep learning in the last five years.

One particularly interesting application of this idea comes from Jetley et al. (2018), who added a separate soft attentional weighting module to bootstrap standard DCNN performance to greater levels of efficiency, accuracy, and robustness. In Jetley et al.'s model, a separate "attention estimator network" was applied to intermediate-level feature representations in a CNN. The attention estimator network learns to gauge the significance of those intermediate-level features to the present decision-making task. This estimation is then used to reweight the intermediate-level feature maps, at multiple levels of the hierarchy, to produce what is called a weighted "salience" map that is calibrated to each task. Importantly, only the salience-weighted feature representations were used for decisions; this has the effect of de-emphasizing features not regarded as significant ("attended to") for that task, while emphasizing the significant ("attended to") ones. Such application of attentional mechanisms is a direct solution to the problems of generality and transfer foreshadowed in Chapters 1 and 2. Again, all aspects of the architecture—including the attentional weighting module—were trained end to end.[13]

---

[13] Rather than in explicit knowledge and rules, much of expert performance may instead derive from learned automatic attentional patterns (Dayer and Jennings 2021;

There have been a variety of other implementations of soft attention in DNNs over the years. For instance, "soft spatial attention" models reweight areas of the input based on a feature's location in the input field, and "soft feature attention" models reweight features based on semantic identity or significance, wherever they may occur in the input. Various forms of these models have achieved better performance than generic DCNNs on the kinds of abstraction and relational reasoning tasks which were thought to be difficult for similarity-based associative models, such as image annotation, visual question answering (VQA) tasks, and even same-different discrimination (Ben-Younes et al. 2017; Ricci et al. 2021; Xu et al. 2015)—though even the more successful models may still not exhibit these abilities at the same level of abstraction as humans and some animals (Barrett et al. 2018; Kim, Ricci, and Serre 2018). Perhaps the most influential application of something like soft attention, however, is illustrated in the transformer family of models, to which we now turn.

6.5. Language models, self-attention, and transformers

Transformers—perhaps the most powerful and impressive form of deep learning architecture developed to date—deploy a technique called self-attention to determine which aspects of the input will influence the prediction of the next output. This has been the most successful DNN entry in the category of "language models," which generally attempt to model the probability of the next token in a sequence of linguistic tokens on the basis of some context. Many of the key innovations behind these models were initially developed for the purposes of machine translation; but researchers quickly discovered that mechanisms which could be used to predict the best translation for some word given a bit of context in a source language could quickly

Fridland 2017). Indeed, Meta is soliciting a massive, egocentric data set of attentional patterns collected from headcams worn by humans while performing skilled actions (including egocentric perspective and eye gaze data), on which attention models could be pretrained (Grauman et al. 2022).

be repurposed for a variety of other language production tasks.[14] The same mechanisms even proved useful outside the domain of language entirely; multimodal transformer models (e.g., that combine representations of both text and image) are now being used for a variety of other purposes, too, such as for the image creation examples provided in the previous chapter from CLIP and DALL-E.

Given the potential similarity between attentional and linguistic processing in transformers and in the human brain, a full exploration of the Jamesian approach to ideational preparation must take into account how linguistic processing is influenced by and in turn influences internal attentional control. We can begin drawing these connections by considering the details of how transformer models—first described in a paper entitled "attention is all you need" by Vaswani et al. (2017)—use attentional mechanisms to solve this kind of prediction task. We begin, however, with the caveat that self-attention in transformer models is often considered the least biologically relevant kind of attentional processing in DNNs, though I will review evidence from neuroscience that might be thought to support some degree of biological plausibility for these models.

Though self-attention can be understood as an elaborate, hierarchical form of soft attention, it is descended from a somewhat separate tradition than the other attention-based models just discussed. This form of attention got its start in sequence-to-sequence (seq2seq) language models. Seq2seq models are recurrent neural networks that are given as input a sequence of text and trained to produce as output another sequence of text. The basic form of this model combines an encoder and a decoder network; the encoder converts the input sequence into a hidden representation vector, and the decoder converts this hidden vector into a series of outputs. More specifically, this hidden vector is built up sequentially; each token (word or phoneme) in the input is processed one at a time, and the encoder takes the previous hidden vector and modifies it according to the next token in the sequence. Thus, it iteratively develops a composite hidden state that reflects the tokens that occurred in the input and the order in which

[14] I am grateful to Yuri Balashov for comments on this section.

they occurred. The final hidden state from the encoder is used as the context representation for the decoder, which then converts the output sequence in something like the inverse direction of the encoder, one word (and modified hidden state) at a time.

An "attention" mechanism was added to these models when it was observed that too severe of a bottleneck was imposed by requiring the encoder to compress the relevant information for every output word into a single hidden context vector for the decoder's use. In short, seq2seq models struggled with longer sentences, which might offer more complex syntactical relationships, and semantic relationships displaced by long sequences of intermediate words. It was too difficult for models to compress such long-distance dependencies into a single hidden state vector. Models could instead try to pass every intermediate hidden state from the encoder to the decoder, which would address this bottleneck problem, but this approach would create other problems, as the number of hidden states needed varies with the size of the input context.[15] Thus, attention was introduced as a way of weighting the intermediate hidden states from the encoder network while still producing a single fixed-length vector (Bahdanau, Cho, and Bengio 2014).

Attentional seq2seq models use attentional selection to learn which of those input words are most significant to determining the output word likeliest to come next. This mechanism could be considered a form of soft attention that weighs subsets of the input sequence differently, though the attention is directed at internal memory or representational encodings rather than particular spatial locations or features. An illustrative use for such an attentional mechanism is in processing semantically ambiguous terms like 'bank'. An attentional mechanism could provide a bit more contextual detail to the vector representation for 'bank' by emphasizing context words like 'fishing' and 'water' to push the vector for bank more toward the area of semantic space corresponding to the sides of rivers, and away from the part of space corresponding to financial institutions. This is roughly inspired by the way a person in reading a sentence and encountering an ambiguous word

---

[15] Compare Jurafsky and Martin (2020): "because the number of hidden states varies with the size of the input, we can't use the entire tensor of encoder hidden state vectors directly as the context for the decoder" (10.4).

might attend to other context cues in the surrounding text to interpret the meaning of the sentence (Fig. 6.4). While many earlier kinds of language model could perform this kind of semantic nudging, they would struggle if the contextual cues were separated from the ambiguous word by long distances. What was needed was a mechanism that could allow models to modulate representations of word meaning efficiently by relevant context wherever it might occur in the input sequence.

The insight—that linguistic processing might be boosted to greater heights of efficiency and flexibility using less-distance-encumbered soft attention, here understood as a domain-general enhancer entirely at home in both Jamesian theory and the empiricist paradigm more generally—provided a key to the breakthrough performance gains of transformers. The first transformers were derived from the intuition that if all intermediate hidden states from the language model's encoder are being passed to the decoder network, then there is no real reason to require these networks to be recurrent to capture long-term

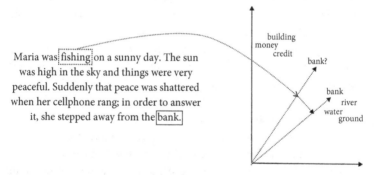

Figure 6.4 The problem of long-distance disambiguation. The word 'bank' is ambiguous in English, and the local context of the final sentence is consistent with either "financial institution" or "ground on the edge of river." Language models need a way to allow distant context cues to push the vector representation ambiguous words into the right location of semantic space to draw correct inferences. Attentional mechanisms have become a favored solution. This diagram shows words as their locations in semantic space, and it shows how a context-free vector representation of the word 'bank' can be pushed into a less ambiguous area of semantic space by modifying it using information provided by the word 'fishing'.

dependencies in the input sequences. The "attention is all you need" mantra was based on the idea that such recurrence (as well as some other more specific bells and whistles added to seq2seq models) could now be done away with, and general attentional mechanisms could do all of their work more efficiently.

Unfortunately for philosophers struggling to explain transformers to interested readers, doing away with recurrence also required that the attention mechanism itself become more complex and multifarious. Sequential recurrence allowed seq2seq models to gradually build a representation of the input sequence which took into account global dependencies in that sequence by rolling more and more information into a composite representation, one word at a time. Capturing all of the sequence and context information without recurrence required two innovations: splitting the hidden state representation of each word into three vectors (called "query," "key," and "value" vectors) and adding "positional encodings" that allowed the word's order in the sequence to be reflected in each word's representation as it is passed to the encoder block. The split between query, keys, and values introduces trainable parameters to the attentional selection so that it can learn more flexible contextual relationships between terms in a potentially very long input sequence without using recurrence. The terminology is used here in a manner roughly analogous to their occurrence in database theory. In a key-value database, data values are stored in locations that are marked with keys. Information can be retrieved from these databases by combining a query with a particular key, which allows one to recover the value stored in that key location as an answer to the query. In transformer-based language models, the goal is not to look up a value stored in a database location, but rather to understand how each element in an input sequence affects the "meaning" of every other element in an input sequence. Rather than accomplishing this through explicit lookup operations as in a classical relational database, transformers accomplish these feats through matrix operations over the query, key, and value vectors.

In other words, the "query" corresponds to the term whose meaning we are trying to understand or modify contextually; the "keys" correspond to each of the other terms in the input sequence context that might influence its meaning; and the "values" looked up are representations of the query term's meaning as influenced by each of these terms (which would, for example, be different for [river] "bank" vs. [financial] "bank"). Matrix operations are used to modify the system's initial representation of the query term's meaning, by weighting it in ways that are appropriate to these contextual influences (values), taken together. This is called "self-attention," because the selection performed here operates over the system's internal representations for items in the input sequence. In a transformer, trainable parameters are associated with the query, key, and value pairs, which allows the system to learn how to weight its representations according to context—in a way that might be viewed as an elaborate form of abstract, internal, automatic soft attention. A "block" of these operations with their trained parameters is called a "self-attention head" (Fig. 6.5).

As we can see, this form of "attention" is already quite complex and of questionable similarity to biological attention. To be frank, if we were trying to draw direct links between aspects of linguistic processing in brains and aspects of attentional mechanisms in transformers, this might leave us on shakier ground (though see Whittington, Warren, and Behrens 2021). Self-attention in transformers requires many specialized parameters without clear biological interpretation which need to be adjusted through training in order to derive the correct contextual embeddings for the full range of term sequences in the corpus. In state-of-the-art transformers, things are even more complex, with each attention block consisting of stacked layers of self-attention heads, allowing for much more elaborate contextual embeddings to be built up iteratively and hierarchically. Moreover, transformers often have multiple self-attention heads that operate in parallel over the same terms, perhaps adding different kinds of shading to each of the terms simultaneously (perhaps capturing the idea that each term can play multiple roles in the same sequence). Lindsay (2020) notes several other dissimilarities in her review, especially that self-attention in transformers lacks recurrence and any obvious top-down influence derived from the demands of the task. For these reasons, Lindsay suggests that the closest psychological analog of self-attention is actually priming (which might be considered a form of learned immediate attention), rather than more voluntary expressions of attention—though it would be more a proprietary form of continuous, temporally

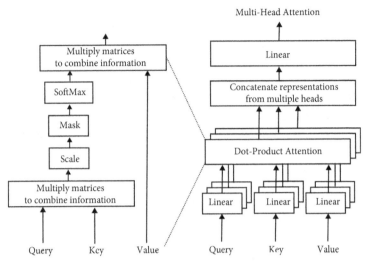

Figure 6.5 A standard depiction of the operations involved in multi-head attention in transformers (adapted from Vaswani et al. 2017). Query, key, and value vectors for each token are combined through a complex series of matrix operations by each self-attention head, in order to weight each token's representation by its context (scaling operations are used to adjust dot product magnitudes so that gradients are appropriate sizes for training; masking is used to prevent the head from "cheating" during training by looking ahead to the next token during training; SoftMax is used to normalize the sum of the attention scores over the sequence of tokens so that they sum to 1). Multiple heads develop parallel representations of a term's meaning simultaneously (often by attending to different aspects of its context), which are later combined into a unified representation through concatenation and linear operations. The combined, multi-head attention representation is then used to predict the next token in the sequence. In state-of-the-art transformers, many multi-attention heads may be stacked in sequence to develop more and more complex representations of the way that context modifies a term's role in predicting the next token. Analyses suggest that some of the more complex phenomena observed in transformers, such as the induction heads studied by AnthropicAI, may result from complex compositions of operations between multiple stacked attention heads (Olsson et al. 2022).

extended priming than the rapid sort normally assessed in priming studies in psychology.[16]

This kind of stacked, multi-attention head transformer remains the state of the art in natural language processing as of the drafting of this chapter. This class includes many of the best-known deep learning systems developed over the last two or three years, including BERT, the GPT series, and multimodal transformers (which use the same kind of self-attentional trick on nontextual data) like CLIP and DALL-E, discussed in the previous chapter. Much still remains uncertain as to which aspects of these architectures are significant to their success. The GPT series of transformers, for example, does away entirely with the encoder components of the language model and relies entirely on decoder self-attentional blocks. The relationship between self-attention heads and other common deep learning model components also remains uncertain. Some theoretical results have suggested that self-attention is mathematically equivalent to convolutions in some circumstances (Andreoli 2019; Cordonnier, Loukas, and Jaggi 2019), or that purely convolutional DNNs given the same kind of massive pretraining regime might be just as effective as transformers on the same tasks (Tay et al. 2021). An entire area of research has grown up around trying to interpret the activity of transformers, especially the significance of the self-attention heads and the representations that they produce when processing sentences. Since BERT was released publicly early in this boom, this field has come to be called BERTology, since so many of the experiments and visualizations are performed on BERT (Rogers, Kovaleva, and Rumshisky 2020). Hot questions in BERTology include whether self-attention heads can be given clear interpretations, whether vector representations weighted by self-attention can be used to visualize the system's "understanding" of a sentence, and whether such analyses reveal that transformers can learn various forms of syntactic rules or word meanings, and integrate the two into novel compositional constructions.

---

[16] The in-context learning produced by induction heads might also challenge the priming analogy, since the associative relationships driving priming are typically acquired over longer timescales and involving more repetition (Brown et al. 2020; Olsson et al. 2022).

Despite all these dissimilarities and uncertainties, we also cannot yet conclude that transformers are irrelevant to biological attention or linguistic understanding. In particular, empirical studies—directly inspired by those relating DCNNs to ventral stream processing that we discussed in Chapter 3—have recently found that transformer language models are extremely good predictors of neural firing patterns in the left temporal areas of the human brain associated with linguistic processing (Abdou et al. 2021; Caucheteux, Gramfort, and King 2021; Goldstein et al. 2021; Schrimpf et al. 2021; Toneva and Wehbe 2019). These experiments compared hidden unit activations, processing times, and next-word prediction outputs to human neural activity (collected from functional magnetic resonance imaging and electrocorticography), reading times, and next-word judgments, respectively, across a variety of language model variants (including a variety of transformer architectures). In particular, when comparing transformer models which lack recurrence and left temporal language processing areas, experimenters found a similarly impressive degree of correspondence as that found between DCNNs and the ventral stream. The best models predicted nearly 100 percent of the variance in the human data (up to the limit of noise, as estimated in their model). They interpret these results to provide strong support that at least these left temporal areas are performing a similar computational task to the transformers, namely next-word prediction, specifically in service of meaning extraction. The GPT family of models in particular—a transformer architecture that relies entirely on a unidirectional attention mechanism (in which self-attention can only focus on tokens to the left of the token being predicted, whereas bidirectional self-attention can focus on words to either the right or the left)—was the best predictor of human neural data and language behavior of the models they assessed.[17] Of course, a high degree of correspondence between

---

[17] There is a debate within the transformer research community as to whether bidirectionality or unidirectionality is the better choice. Proponents of unidirectionality argue that it is more biologically plausible, since most natural languages involve unidirectional reading. Proponents of bidirectionality argue the same for bidirectional attention, especially on tasks like fill-in-the-blank or summarization where humans might look forward or backward in the context to answer the question. BERT is bidirectional, and the GPT-X series is unidirectional, since the latter eschews encoder blocks for

the components of attentional processes or neural structures in these left temporal areas and the components of the algorithm behind self-attention remains unlikely. However, these experiments found that a good prediction could be obtained from even untrained GPT architectures—though not from random embeddings with the same number of features—which suggests that there must be something special about these transformer architectures that corresponds to the left temporal language areas in the human brain. The degree of similarity between attentional and linguistic processing in transformers and the human brain thus remains an active and controversial area of research, with important discoveries coming almost weekly.[18] At the very least, they support the Jamesian theme that attentional selection and prediction are tightly linked, even in the domain of linguistic processing.

Additionally, transformer-based systems have recently made some of the most impressive advances toward "general intelligence" and few-shot solution of novel tasks thought to require symbolic processing, both of which nativists thought would remain beyond the reach of DNN-based AI. GPT-3, for example, was able to demonstrate zero-shot and few-shot learning on a wide variety of demanding text comprehension and novel symbol-manipulation tasks, many of which seem to require learning novel rules and abstract patterns on the fly from only a handful (or fewer) of examples (Brown et al. 2020). It could solve a variety of word-scrambling and symbol manipulation tasks, such as cycling letters in a word ("lyinevitab" → "inevitably") and random insertions of punctuation or spaces in a word between each letter ("s.u!c/c!e.s s i/o/n" → "succession") at between 30 and 65 percent accuracy rates for different tasks when given a few examples. The

decoder blocks only, which only consult previous words in a sequence when predicting the next word.

[18] This area remains controversial in large part because the comparisons between the activation patterns of transformers and firing patterns in the areas of the brain associated with language processing involve statistical measures which are relatively new and whose epistemic properties are poorly understood, such as RSA and Brain Score. For a summary of arguments for and against reliance on these metrics for comparisons, see Bowers et al. (2022); Kieval (2022); and Roskies (2021). Some researchers are also beginning to explore more dynamic and interventional methods of comparison (Abdou et al. 2021; Ravfogel et al. 2021).

model, moreover, really does appear to "learn" these tasks at test time, as its one-shot and zero-shot performance was much lower than its few-shot performance. The benefit of providing a few examples also appears to help GPT-3 on a variety of other natural language processing and question-and-answer data sets, such as LAMBADA, a sentence-completion task which requires models to predict the most plausible final word in the sentence (e.g., "Alice was friends with Bob. Alice went to visit her friend _____ → Bob"). GPT-3's performance on this task jumped to 86.4 percent when given a few examples, compared to 18 percent as the previous state-of-the-art for language models. The authors hypothesize that providing a few examples helps the system learn about the structure of the task it is being asked to perform.

As impressive as this all is, in particular to linking aspects of rational decision-making in brains and DNN-based models, our understanding of how these large transformer models solve these tasks and appear to learn new symbolic manipulation rules at test time remains rudimentary. Though the size of GPT-3 is meager by the standards of the human brain (which is estimated to contain 100 trillion parameters, depending on how they are counted), its 175 billion parameters and Internet-scale data set make any attempt to understand what exactly all those attention heads have learned a daunting task. Attempts to visualize the weightings derived from attention heads are sometimes alluringly suggestive of sophisticated grammatical processing to the human eye (Fig. 6.6), for example apparently showing that one attention head is dedicated to a particular syntactic or semantic role, such as anaphor resolution or subject-verb agreement (Clark et al. 2019). However, such examples are often cherry-picked and only analyzed qualitatively, and there are many other attention heads whose visualizations resist straightforward interpretation. Ablation studies of attention heads also seem to reveal that many of them are redundant or not essential to accuracy for a wide range of tasks (Voita et al. 2019). Like salience mapping for DCNNs, such analyses of a transformer's attentional selection may tell us what information is available to a model, but not how it uses it (Jain and Wallace 2019). Attempts to reproduce such results are further hamstrung by the fact that performance in language models seems sensitive to details in the prompts, such that even changes of punctuation or word choice that might seem trivial

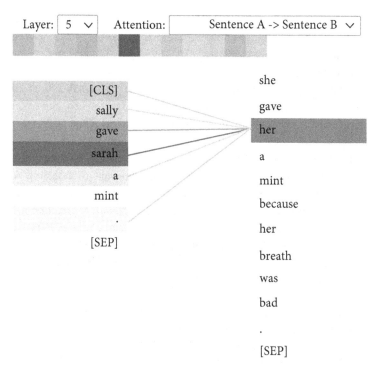

Figure 6.6 An example of an attention head possibly performing anaphor resolution in BERT that the author generated in BertViz; the example is a more difficult variant of one discussed by Simon (2021), because 'her' could be resolved to either 'Sally' or 'Sarah'. An attention head in layer 5 appears to perform anaphor resolution.

to humans can have dramatic consequences for a language model's performance on tests (Alzantot et al. 2018; Li et al. 2020; Talmor et al. 2020). This has led to "prompt engineering"—ad hoc tweaking of text prompts given to language models to produce better performance—without much systematic guidance as to which prompt choices are principled or reproducible (Reynolds and McDonell 2021). There has even been study on standardized prompts that seem to improve GPT-3's performance across many tasks, such as "let's think step by step" (Kojima et al. 2022). Furthermore, GPT-3's data set and model weights remain proprietary and access to GPT-3 remained, until recently, tightly controlled by OpenAI. Thus, compared to BERT, it has proven difficult for researchers to develop systematic, rigorous, and reproducible standards for analyzing the GPT-series' functionality and performance (Table 6.2).

Our attempts to uncover systematically the performance limits of such language models are further complicated by the speed with which larger and more powerful systems are being developed. The BIG-bench project was developed as a concerted effort by over 400 authors to discern the performance limits of large language models by automating over 200 tasks that have been considered relevant to assessing AI (Srivastava et al. 2022). These tasks cover topics from grammatical processing, common-sense reasoning, biological and physical knowledge, mathematical ability, social biases, and many others. Whereas off-the-shelf GPT-3 performed poorly on many of these tasks, almost as soon as GPT-3's scores were released, even larger language models

Table 6.2 A Robustness Study of the Effect of Generic Prompts Tested on a 175 Billion Parameter GPT-3 Variant Text-davinci-002 Using the MultiArith Data Set (Which Includes a Variety of Arithmetic Problems) Conducted by Kojima et al. (2022)

Number	Prompt Template	Accuracy
1	Let's think step by step.	78.7
2	First,	77.3
3	Let's think about this logically.	74.5
4	Let's solve this problem by splitting it into steps.	72.2
5	Let's be realistic and think step by step.	70.8
6	Let's think like a detective step by step.	70.3
7	Let's think	57.5
8	Before we dive into the answer.	55.7
9	The answer is after the proof.	45.7
-	(Baseline zero shot performance with no prompt)	17.7

As these authors put it, prompts like those in the table can increase the likelihood at a model will answer using "chain of thought" reasoning, which improves performance.

like the 540-billion-parameter PaLM model from Google succeeded on many of the tasks, including some of the more surprising and supposedly difficult ones like arithmetic word problems and logical reasoning (Chowdhery et al. 2022). We can almost watch the goal posts being moved in real time as skeptics of AI progress argue that some of the same criteria that were recently used as ammunition against GPT-3's ability to model intelligence are immediately said to be insufficient evidence in PaLM's favor once it satisfied them, leading some commentators to express exasperation at the absence of fixed criteria to arbitrate the debate (Alexander 2022). Even newer and more powerful systems like ChatGPT from OpenAI and a model from AnthropicAI, both trained using reinforcement learning on human feedback, have delivered even more impressive performances when assessed on more systematic batteries of tests (Liang et al. 2022).

At the same time, we are only beginning to craft a mechanistic understanding of how the components of these models such as attention heads allow them to implement their impressive forms of syntactic and semantic flexibility. There has been some promising evidence that this kind of understanding might be possible despite the scale of these models. Several analyses suggest that some attention heads might be performing interpretable syntactic processing roles (Htut et al. 2019; Voita et al. 2019). Some of these investigations reach into the standard connectionist toolkit for the method of "artificial lesion studies," by knocking out particular attention heads through deletion to see which kinds of processing are inhibited or maintained; and other sophisticated new methods manipulate the representations in language models directly in ways which should alter the syntactic or semantic properties of the model's predictions to confirm hypotheses (Abdou et al. 2021; Li, Nye, and Andreas 2021; Ravfogel et al. 2021).

Perhaps the most thorough line of mechanistic evidence has been produced by the start-up AnthropicAI, whose mission is directed precisely at helping us better understand the inner workings of transformer-based large language models. AnthropicAI's initial investigations of simple transformer models have suggested that that their impressive in-context learning ability is enabled by a specialized kind of trained self-attention head which they dub an "induction head" (Elhage et al. 2021; Olsson et al. 2022). The primary operation of an induction head, they claim, is akin to simple in-context copying; it uses attentional selection of particular words in the prompt to align the present token with a similar location earlier the context, and then simply copies the likeliest subsequent token from that location. For example, this could enable a copying rule of the form [a][b] . . . [a] →[b], which would simply reproduce copies of the [a][b] pattern from the earlier context. However, in some cases, induction heads can do a form of approximate copying, implementing a more abstract rule of the form [a][b] . . . [a]→[b'], where b' and b bear only abstract similarity to one another (and in more complex attention heads, [a] and [b] can occur some distance from one another in the prompt). Marshaling a variety of observational and experimental evidence, the AnthropicAI team argues that such copying and approximate copying by induction heads explains much of these large language models' in-context learning ability, in particular because the implementation of the rule does not depend upon prior language statistics about whether one token is likely to follow another (e.g., statistics between [a] and [b]), yet it can leverage abstract similarities learned from the training set to complete the pattern (e.g., the similarity between [b] and [b']). For the purposes of the DoGMA, it is striking how consonant these claims are to those that we reviewed in Chapter 1 from canonical empiricists like Locke and Hume to the effect that rule-like abstraction might emerge from simple copying behavior when enhanced with a bit of abstract similarity. It must also be stressed that these are only initial steps on analyzing models much smaller than GPT-3 and PaLM, and much more powerful forms of abstraction involving more hierarchical composition of attention heads, interactions among attention heads (such as multiple induction heads enforcing multiple patterns simultaneously), and contributions from the other architectural components of transformer models likely remain to be discovered.

While we rightly marvel at how quickly the GPT models and PaLM have advanced upon traditional tests of linguistic performance, intelligence, and reasoning, considering them in light of the DoGMA also reveals how inadequate they remain as self-standing models of rational agency. Some of the most disconcerting weaknesses of these models' performance pertain not to their ability to solve particular grammatical, logical, or mathematical problems, but rather their tendency to meander incoherently in longer conversations and their inability to manifest a coherent individual perspective. Perhaps due to the nature of its massive training set, those conversing with GPT models over longer periods of time may feel less like they are interacting with a single, intelligent agent, and more like they are interacting with an agent slurry created by blending thousands of agent-slices together in a giant blender. Depending upon the prompts and interactions, GPT-3 can be made to contradict itself from one minute to the next, and it often seems to drop lines of thought which were coherently maintained earlier in a narrative. It also seems to lack abilities to manipulate representations in a visuospatial workspace; Ron Chrisley has raised the example of Finke, Pinker, and Farah (1989), which illustrates this ability in humans. When human subjects are instructed to imagine rotating the letter "D" and affixing it to the top of a letter "J" and asked what new shape is composed, they can readily answer "umbrella"— whereas Chrisley reported that in testing GPT-3 was unable to solve this task across multiple prompts. When I myself tested ChatGPT and AnthropicAI's language model in January 2023, both trained on reinforcement learning from human feedback, they performed better on these tasks, though none hit on the desired answer of "umbrella" (Fig. 6.7).

Perhaps some of these inconsistencies might be mitigated by training and querying transformer-based models on larger and larger snippets of context, but they might be addressed more naturally with the supplementation of the faculty modules already discussed in earlier chapters. For example, long-term and short-term memory modules might allow agents to represent long-standing personal attributes and objects raised earlier in the current discourse, all of which might be used to provide additional constraints on next-word prediction. An imagination module provided by a multimodal GAN could further be used to grant these models a visuospatial workspace which could help agents solve imagery-manipulation problems. Such suggestions are all entirely in the spirit of the new empiricist DoGMA, and I hope these directions will be actively pursued in further rounds of transformer-based research. In short, while large language models are increasingly being treated as though they should be self-sufficient models of intelligence, they should instead be accorded the status of the human

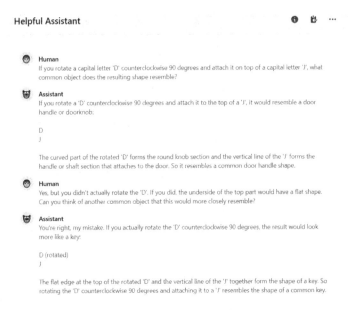

Figure 6.7 AnthropicAI's RLHF model ("Claude") tested on the character rotation imagery task in January 2023. Neither the answer of the doorknob nor of the key is a bad guess, and it is remarkable that the model attempts to give a spatially accurate example of the figure in its response.

language faculty in the context of human cognitive evolution—a cherry on top of a much older and more variegated cognitive architecture.

Notably still absent on the list of applications of "attention" considered here are more examples of "intellectual attention" on James's taxonomy, and cases in which attention is used to switch between different tasks or different modules. Architectures with memory stores, for example, could use internal attention to select among different memories (Graves, Wayne, and Danihelka 2014). However, there have been too few systems implementing multiple faculty modules simultaneously, and this discussion would be a bit premature. To complete the evaluation of the promise that Jamesian attention has for bolstering the empiricist DoGMA, we turn instead to the implications of James's views on the relationship between interest and attention for the debate between nativism and empiricism in AI research. James's treatment of interest helps explain much of the behavioral evidence that has been thought to support nativist hypotheses in psychology without violating empiricist strictures against domain-specific innate ideas.

6.6. Interest and innateness

As James says, all attention depends upon interest; we can only attend to things, either voluntarily or involuntarily, that draw our interest. James even seems to hold that interest is the essence of consciousness and required for differentiated, controlled thought: "Interest alone gives accent and emphasis, light and shade, background and foreground; intelligible perspective, in a word" (*PP* 402). His stance echoes concerns of the rationalists in dismissing the radical anti-nativism he (mistakenly) reads off of Locke and Hume and argues that interest is a precondition of learning—for without it, experience would be only a "gray, chaotic indiscriminateness" (*PP* 403). Similarly, the power of the DoGMA depends, in part, on a satisfying treatment of interest to explain how attention directs agents toward appropriate aspects of experience.

Now, this focus on interest as a precondition for learning can appear to have brought us back to a reconsideration of the domain generality of the anti-nativist stance laid out in Chapter 1. Recall that for James, interest can either be intrinsic or derived. Derived interest is learned, so we can set it aside as consistent with origin empiricism. Intrinsic interest, however, might be thought to pose a threat to the empiricist DoGMA, for it may be thought to require innate representations or representational structure. And surely, we might think, not all such domain-specific interests can be learned— anyone with a passing familiarity with cognitive science can produce a set of apparent counterexamples. When it comes to dangers and opportunities with high biological costs and scant opportunity for learning through trial and error, nature appears to favor solutions based on mechanisms like reflexes, instincts, and rapid imprinting rather than learning. A chicken must be able to peck at dark specks on the ground in front of it as soon as it hatches from the egg, or it will starve. A rat must immediately spit out the poisonous berry the first time it eats it, or it will die. The duckling must follow its mother shortly after hatching, or it will be lost. And the human infant who cannot track its mother's gaze will have difficulty learning language, for only the mother's gaze narrows down the range of possible referents of the words she uses.

Or so the traditional story goes (Baldwin 1993).[19]

Here, we should proceed carefully. On the one hand, we must acknowledge the obvious phenomena of species-typical responses to important stimuli; on the other hand, we should also explore the wide array of mechanisms that can allow such responses to manifest without innate domain-specific representations or rules. Luckily, the diversity of alternative mechanisms which might produce species-typical and inflexible responses to specific stimuli without the use of innate representations and rules can benefit from a mature discussion from the "developmental connectionists" such as Elman et al. (1998). A series of cases reveals a general principle: nature finds ways to ensure that certain behaviors and mental traits are exhibited by typical members of a species across a wide range of environments and developmental trajectories. Yet the nativist approach to modeling these traits in artificial systems misconceives the relationship among the agent, its body, and the environment. Where we understand the details, the empiricist story of how nature secures the reliable manifestation of useful behavioral or mental traits implicates a much more elegant interaction of brain, body, and environment than would be expected on the basis of innate rules and representations. When it comes to engineering strategy, the domain-general empiricist approach tends to be more adaptable to a wider range of circumstances and allows more flexible generalizations (McClelland et al. 2010). Pursuing the nativist approach is much more likely to lead research to solutions that prove brittle when confronted with real-world environments which do not fit the engineer's preconceptions—failing, in other words, to secure the

---

[19] More empiricist developmental research has shown a variety of other statistical influences on word disambiguation are readily exploited by even very young infants in early language learning (e.g., Smith and Yu 2008).

very environmental stability that is supposed to make innate behaviors biologically valuable in the first place.

We could easily spend a whole book discussing apt examples, but let us instead briefly review the toolkit available to model biological preparation in DNN-based systems without the use of innate domain-specific rules and representations. The first and most obvious source of such preparation is more experience—in particular, prenatal experience. While nativists often present their views on reflexes and instincts as though they are the consensus empirical position in biology and psychology, AI researchers should know that this is not the case. There is an alternative approach to explaining such behaviors in the opposed tradition of developmental systems theory that is particularly useful to AI researchers. A classic work in this tradition is Daniel Lehrman's critique of Konrad Lorenz's theory of instinct (Lehrman 1953), essential reading for anyone interested in AI. In it, Lehrman reviews a number of popular examples of innate or instinctive behavior from the ethological tradition at the time, showing through careful empirical work that they are instead the result of subtle unforeseen learning or developmental scaffolding.

To canvass examples of innate behaviors for critique, Lehrman borrows the criteria of Lorenz and Tinbergen. These criteria include that "(1) the behavior be stereotyped and constant in form; (2) it be characteristic of the species; (3) it appear in animals which have been raised in isolation from others; and (4) it develop fully formed in animals which have been prevented from practicing it" (341). In particular, Lehrman explores the pecking reflex of the newly hatched chick, noting how it appears to meet all of these criteria. He then points to the fascinating work of Zing-Yang Kuo (Kuo 1933; Kuo 1932a, 1932b, 1932c), which appears to have revealed that various aspects of this behavior depend upon embryonic learning inside the egg. For example, by manipulating conditions inside the egg and observing their results, Kuo provided evidence that the head-lunging aspect of this reflex depended upon tactile stimulation by the heartbeat and contractions of the yolk sac inside the egg during embryonic development. As soon as four days of embryonic age, the head begins actively bending in response to this heartbeat stimulation. A few days later, embryonic fluid is forced down the throat by the bill and head movements, causing swallowing. Eventually, all the behavioral components of the pecking reflex come to be actively chained together, through associative experience induced almost entirely by the cramped developmental conditions inside the egg. Lehrman further generalizes from other cases to speculate that the shift from tactile to visual stimulation of the reflex could emerge as a consequence of intersensory equivalence caused by the anatomical growth of the optic nerve during embryonic development (Coghill 1929; Maier and Schneirla 1964). The resulting picture of this reflex is of a behavior that is in some sense constrained and secured by resources that are genetic in nature; but it would be entirely confused—or, at best, a stopgap measure—to model them in an "artificial chick" by manually programming innate rules or representations that govern the movements and their relationship to one another.

Similar results can be found for the other purportedly obvious examples of domain-specific or innate representations, such as filial imprinting. In a variety of avian species, chicks appear to imprint on a perceptual template of their mother shortly after hatching. They then dutifully follow anything matching this template for a long period of their early development. This could be considered another form of domain-specific innate behavioral mechanisms, such as a "mother-following" rule. Of course, even this rule would have to display some plasticity; the mother might appear in a variety of different nuisance configurations, such as at different angles or in different lighting conditions at different points in the day-night cycle. Even Lorenz's classic studies of imprinting demonstrated that a hatchling's imprinting pattern-matching mechanisms were flexible enough to acquire a representation of Lorenz himself, as demonstrated by famous pictures of the German ethologist being trailed by a line of goslings.

More recent studies have shown that imprinting reflects a much more flexible form of learning than we might have thought; not only can it generalize to members of other species, but even highly abstract relationships such as sameness or difference relations, as Martinho and Kacelnik (2016) demonstrated by showing that ducklings can reliably imprint to patterns of stimuli that share only an abstract, higher-order relation like sameness or difference. Though some degree of "orienting response" still seems required—it is unknown how much of this might be reduced to embryonic development, à la Kuo or Lehrman—it seems here that it is the environmental structure delivered during a critical period of high plasticity that keys ducklings into the "correct" biologically relevant stimuli, as the duckling's mother is the perceptual stimulus most likely to be present at hatching (Versace et al. 2018).

In fact, this sort of mechanism can be modeled in a DNN-based system by modifying the learning rate of the network during a critical period of plasticity. This is just the solution recommended by the "developmental connectionists" such as Elman (and adopted in previous ANN-based models of imprinting—Bateson and Horn 1994), and DNN researchers today should reach for such standard tools from the connectionist modeling kit before resorting to innate representations. In short, once the temporal aspects of imprinting are implemented—by general parameters of the nervous system, such as learning rate, which is modifiable by the timed release of hormones or neurotransmitters—the environment handles the input selectivity problem that troubled James by presenting the animal with just the right stimulus at just the right time in development.

In general, empiricist neural network modelers can adopt any such interest-modifying mechanisms that could plausibly be implemented in nervous systems without domain-specific representations or rules, especially those for which we have independent anatomical or genetic evidence. Crucially, because these interest-modifying mechanisms are domain-general in the range of inputs to which they respond, they are consistent with the DoGMA as expressed in Chapter 1, and so innate and developmentally timed interest biases strengthen the case for origin empiricism rather than weaken it. Global architectural constraints, adjustments to the kind or number of activation functions, timed increases or decreases to learning rates, stronger or weaker connections to or from modules, and differentiation in sensory preprocessing methods (meant to simulate the sensory transformations performed by the sensory organs) are all consistent with the origin empiricism laid out in Chapter 1. To circle back to points made there, it has become common among the central deep learning researchers to summarize their most important and biologically plausible innovations in terms of the domain-general prior probability assumptions ("priors") that can be modeled in DNNs through architectural means (cf. Table 1.1). As Goyal and Bengio (2020) summarize, although the local connectivity between layers in a DCNN expresses a kind of default selectivity—an innate interest—for local properties, these innate forms of selectivity will be domain-general. The use of convolution and max-pooling activation functions as an innate preference for properties that are invariant to spatial and geometric transformations. Recurrent loops can impose an equivariance over temporal scales, and attentional mechanisms can induce a degree of invariance to sequence permutations.

Today, the empiricist attitude is supported by an inductive argument over the practical benefits of these domain-general architectural solutions, rather than bespoke, manually programmed methods of more symbolic or hybrid approaches. In fact, today's controlled-rearing studies allow us to arbitrate empirically the prospects of these two opposed attitudes toward precocial behavior directly, and several of these recent studies provide some of the strongest evidence for origin empiricism to date. Such artificial controlled-rearing studies can directly pit biological animals—usually newly hatched chicks or ducklings raised in strictly controlled virtual environments—against DNN-based artificial agents that can be exposed to identical naturally structured input stimuli in the same sequences. By allowing experimenters to achieve a previously unthinkable degree of control and statistical power in their experiments, controlled-rearing studies aim to overcome the replication issues that have stymied previous methods in developmental psychology. Both the biological and artificial chicks can be exposed to the same external stimuli in identical patterns, and, because the rearing, exposure, and observation methods are all automated, large numbers of trials can be run in a manner which almost completely controls for experimenter bias. The experiments also provide a direct way to control for some of the "amount of experience" concerns raised in Chapter 4, because both the biological and artificial chicks receive the same amount of training data (though, of course, the degree of internal stimulus such as interoception and affect will be extremely limited in the artificial models).

Early results in these studies have found that, when presented with the same stimuli as biological organisms, artificial chicks driven by generic DCNNs can rapidly learn many of the domain-specific patterns previously claimed by nativists in developmental psychology to require Core Knowledge—including patterns for object membership, permanence, view-invariance, and "animacy" biases that rapidly scaffold social cognition (Hauser and Wood 2010; Lee, Gujarathi, and Wood 2021; Lee, Pak, et al. 2021; Lee, Wood, and Wood 2021; Wood et al. 2016). Unless the empirical results of this research program begin to trend in a different direction, it appears to provide strong and unambiguous evidence in favor of the domain-general inductive biases recommended by the new empiricist DoGMA as the most biologically plausible approach to prepared learning.

If, after considering all such architectural solutions, learning still needs a firmer nudge toward a particular outcome, the empiricist kit offers other modeling tools to consider—most especially tweaks to the weighting of the input signals. These tweaks correspond to anatomically observable differences in the sensory organs of animals, differences that have obvious effects on structuring sensory experience itself. We might think that this implicates a form of domain specificity that would violate the constraints of origin empiricism, but empiricists have never denied that different species might have different sensitivities to different types of stimuli that suit their environmental niche. Differentiation in sensory receptors is perhaps the primary mechanism by which evolution can attune animals to important aspects of their environment in a way that directs the course of later learning. Recall James's discussion of a human and a dog walking through the Vatican and perceiving its sculptures. While humans may appreciate the visual aesthetics of the sculptures due to vision being their most acute sense, the dog may instead be more interested in the numerous and subtle scent cues present on the sculptures, given the greater sensitivity and numerosity of its olfactory detectors. No innate ideas are required to explain these anatomically based differences in sensory bias.

Accordingly, we can call into question claims of innate knowledge in humans by searching for the floor of associative learning, to see whether what might appear to be innate knowledge can be explained away in terms of innate differences in the sensory organs. There, we may find a basic response like bitterness aversion to be an instructive example. Aversion to bitter tastes is thought to reflect an avoidance reaction to toxic substances that is innate in all mammals (Mura et al. 2018; Rosenstein and Oster 1988). Common sources of environmental poisons for mammals are cyanide-containing compounds, such as seeds of the almond family. There do appear to be an array of specialized detectors for bitterness—specialized taste buds in the mouth—and mechanisms controlling aversive reactions in the brain stem. Further, the presence and numerosity of these bitterness receptors do appear to be under a significant degree of genetic control (A. Bachmanov et al. 2014), and something to which the genome has devoted a substantial amount of resources. A recent study estimated that while there are only two or three kinds of sweetness receptors, there are over twenty-five different bitterness receptors (Mennella and Bobowski 2015). This innate bias in "intrinsic" interest is thus substantially reflected in the anatomy of the input receptors in a manner with straightforward links to the genes.

Yet bitterness detection isn't the exception to empiricism that it initially seems to be. Even after devoting significant genetic resources to ensuring specialized and powerful input encoding for toxic substances, the response to bitterness remains highly plastic even in newborns, shows a significant degree of individual variation, and remains subject to significant influence of learning in utero. There is, for example, a significant degree of genetic variation in these receptors; many people have discovered after serving mashed turnips to their family for the first time that there is a high degree of individual variation in whether people find the taste delicious or highly bitter. This individual variation can be explained by a common mutation in these genes which determines whether or not vegetables of the *brassica* family like turnips trigger a taste of overwhelming bitterness (Wieczorek et al. 2018). There is also a significant degree of plasticity in the behavioral responses to taste receptor stimulation, as anyone who enjoys hoppy beer or dark chocolate can attest.

Furthermore, the initial origins of the linkages between bitterness detection and aversive reflexes in individual infants remain unknown. Even a newborn's responses to bitter tastes have already been shaped by significant learning. The first gustatory experiences after birth are likely to pair sweetness with caloric intake (from foremilk, colostrum, or infant formula), and the first tastes of anything bitter will likely be novel and, due to the high degree of activation provided by the bitterness receptors, shocking by contrast. The well-known, domain-general aversion to novel tastes in children—neophobia—may thus explain the aversive response.[20] In line with the Kuo experiments on unhatched chicks, research has shown that babies have already learned from months of gustatory experience in utero, which may facilitate a learned transfer of taste preferences from mother to fetus via dietary-induced changes to the amniotic fluid, which fetuses swallow and in-hale constantly during the final stages of pregnancy (Mennella 2014; Podzimek et al. 2018). Though some research has suggested that flavor preferences are already present even earlier in fetal development—one study showed a reduction in amniotic swallowing frequency following the introduction of bitter tastes into the amniotic fluid, for example (Liley 1972)—the initial causal origins of the linkage between bitter-ness detection and aversive reactions in humans remain unknown.

Where tweaks to the input receptors or even earlier developmental experience cannot provide the needed push for learning to achieve a particular adaptive outcome with little or no training experience, we may look toward the basic physical morphology of the animals as an explanation. For instance, recent research on gaze-tracking in humans—a cornerstone of our purportedly unique "theory of mind" system (Penn and Povinelli 2007b; Povinelli and Eddy 1996)—may de-pend upon the degree of contrast between the pupils and the sclera of the eyes. Humans are distinguished from most of their closest primate relatives by having almost universally white sclera, which provides a sharp contrast with the darker pupil. The "cooperative eye hypoth-esis" suggests that this morphological change to the color of our eyes facilitated our development of a special system for tracking gaze and eye direction (Tomasello et al. 2007; Yorzinski and Miller 2020). This may promote gaze-tracking in human infants simply by making eye direction a much more salient cue in terms of low-level perceptual characteristics than the rest of the face or head.[21] There is a sense in

---

[20] In rats, for example, the "Garcia effect," or conditioned taste aversion response, is substantially shaped by the novelty of the gustatory stimulus, in part of a specialized system which is controlled by the parabrachial nucleus in the brain stem (Reilly and Trifunovic 2001).

[21] There is some debate here as to whether it is the whiteness of the human sclera that leads to more conspicuous gaze or the contrast between the pupil and the sclera, in which case chimpanzees (with dark sclera but the same overall amount of contrast

294 FROM DEEP LEARNING TO RATIONAL MACHINES

which this salience bias is "not learned," so if that is all there is to a trait being innate, then perhaps we have finally located a domain-specific innate behavioral "interest" that facilitates the control of our attention. However, it would be entirely wrong-headed to understand this example as bolstering the nativist view or to model this preference as an innate gaze concept or domain-specific learning rule, rather than the result of domain-general learning procedures reacting to the salience of morphological features of the gazers so tracked.

Much of the DoGMA's strength lies in the flexibility with which it can endow a system. In this context, even if we know the likely outcome of a learning process when factoring in inputs and architectural tweaks, we should not simply take a shortcut and manually program a symbolic representation of that outcome into the system at the outset, because doing so introduces an essential inflexibility into the system. This kind of shortcut might seem attractive to nativists as a kind of instrumentalist fallback position, especially those frustrated by the intricacies of these biological details. In cases where our purposes are entirely performance-focused and we do not care about the true causal origins of some behavior in development, this may seem a harmless choice. Nevertheless, I suggest that there will still be reasons for caution against adopting conveniences which deploy symbolic rules or representational primitives.

In particular, the more input-focused and domain-general solutions described earlier will tend to be more flexible across a wider range of situations, because we cannot anticipate the range of situations to which these interests might usefully apply in advance. Domain-general and architectural solutions can be redeployed and readapted through iterative bootstrapping numerous times throughout the life of an agent. This perspective can be captured under the heading of "neural reuse," which has been proposed as a fundamental organizational principle of the brain that cautions against the assumption of domain-specific computations or representations as an adequate explanation for adaptive, species-typical behaviors (Anderson 2010, 2014). The fusiform gyrus, for example, was once thought to be a specialized facial

---

between sclera and pupil) might also demonstrate facilitated gaze-tracking on the basis of eye direction.

recognition area, but it has since been found to be used in a variety of other expressions of perceptual expertise. It may instead perform a computation useful in holistic pattern recognition across a variety of domains, rather than implement a narrower domain-specific facial recognition function (Gauthier et al. 2000). The hippocampus—once considered a specialized organ for spatial mapping—appears to also be involved in organizing stimuli along monotonic dimensions for temporal scales, as well as along more abstract conceptual, taxonomic, relational, and nested knowledge structures in semantic and episodic memory (Dusek and Eichenbaum 1997; Gorchetchnikov and Grossberg 2007; O'Keefe and Nadel 1978; Viganò and Piazza 2021). Hard-coding the computations of the hippocampus in terms of spatial rules would limit the ability of the system's more domain-general workings to apply to these other domains as well. It would even be incorrect to simply add on these other domain-specific applications as we discover them, for psychological studies have shown a number of surprising and potentially useful functional/behavioral crossover effects from space, time, and conceptual taxonomies that may be explained by the use of shared neural resources (e.g., Casasanto and Boroditsky 2008). Thus, even adopting domain-specific rules and representations as a convenience may come with unanticipated costs to the system's ability to generalize from one domain to the next, and thus be at a disadvantage to more DoGMAtic solutions even when considered merely as an instrumentally justified convenience.[22]

6.7. Attention, inner speech, consciousness, and control

For James, attention's effects extended down to the most basic and biologically prepared forms of perception, upward to the most conscious and endogenously controlled mental actions. Having considered the lower bounds of attention, we might now consider its upper bounds in rational cognition. In particular, after having reviewed the ability

---

[22] Compare Smolensky et al. (2022).

of certain DNN architectures like transformers to produce grammatically and conceptually complex language, we might consider how the addition of a language module to the DoGMA might provide an additional form of control and coordination between other modules.

Prominent deep learning researchers—most especially Bengio (Goyal and Bengio 2020) and Chollet (Chollet 2019), but even major participants in the previous wave of connectionist research, such as Smolensky (1988)—have looked ahead to consider how language models might help implement "System II" (which we introduced at the end of Chapter 3) in a DNN-based architecture. This is a reference to dual-system or dual-process architectures from human psychology literature (Sloman 1996). In this standard division, System II (or "2") has more of the properties ascribed to a classical computer in reasoning, and it lies on top of and directs the effects of many different System I modules. System II is controlled, effortful, slow, serial, and conscious, in comparison to the automatic, effortless, fast, parallel, and mostly nonconscious operations of System I. Thus, we should expect there is a tight relationship between top-down attention and System II. There should also be a close relationship between System II and consciousness. This is often captured through the idea that conscious experience reflects the contents of a shared "global workspace" that allows the sharing of information between different modular subsystems (Baars 2005; Dehaene, Kerszberg, and Changeux 1998; Dehaene, Lau, and Kouider 2017; Prinz 2012; Van Gulick 2004).

There are many variants on this package of influential ideas and many reasons for skepticism. Moving quickly over rocky terrain here—without worrying about other approaches to consciousness, or skeptical concerns about the distinctiveness or interactions between the two systems, for example (Keren and Schul 2009)—we are now in position to consider an obvious and specific advance toward this long-term, widely shared goal of adding a conscious, serial, rule-interpreter type system to a DNN-based architecture. Namely, we could add a module corresponding to a language model which produces inner speech. The speech produced by this model could be used to modulate and coordinate the behavior of the other modules, simulating the role of inner speech in conscious, controlled thought. This may not be the only way to achieve System-II-type thinking—some people claim to think more in images than words—but inner speech plays some such role in this kind of thinking in a great many humans (Carruthers 2002, 2011, 2018; Martínez-Manrique and Vicente 2010; Morin 2005). In particular, the inner speech module could direct the behavior of other modules by globally broadcasting information in a low-dimensional format to influence their processing in an efficient, attention-like way (Antonello et al. 2021).[23]

Anyone who has raised or observed the development of young children will be familiar with the important coordinating role that speech can play in developing and directing the cognitive resources of children (Berk 1992; Clark 1998; Vygotsky 2012). Young children often have a difficult time maintaining sustained attention on a task or remembering the components of a complex, multistep activity. Learning to tie shoelaces is a common developmental milestone around the world. A child typically first learns by being explicitly guided via verbal instructions provided by a caregiver, coupled with embodied demonstration of the skill. The instructions for this complex, multistep motor activity are often provided in the form of a rhyme or song featuring topics that are intrinsically interesting to the child, such as rabbits and bows. Here is one variant commonly used in the United States, for example:

> Bunny ears, Bunny ears, playing by a tree.
> Criss-crossed the tree, trying to catch me.
> Bunny ears, Bunny ears, jumped into the hole,
> Popped out the other side beautiful and bold.

The language here plays many roles; it helps the child direct attention to ways of classifying the perceptual input (recognizing the crossover and loops of the knot as essential features), remember the order of the sequences, and insulate their focus from outside distractions until the activity is complete. It also eventually helps transfer intrinsic interest in the topic of the rhyme and fun of reciting the poem to derived interest

---

[23] Compare Piccinini (2020b:268–84) on how a language system might enable non-natural mental representation useful in offline simulations. For an early practical exploration of related ideas, see Huang et al. (2022).

in the mundane activity of tying shoelaces. After memorizing the rhyme, children then overtly recite it to themselves while performing the activity. The more surprising transition for most parents will be the so-called subvocalizing stage that many children pass through, where instead of explicitly vocalizing this speech, they begin muttering to themselves and eventually just silently moving their lips. Finally, they often show no outward signs of vocalization when aware of rehearsing "inner speech," but the internally simulated language—now thought to involve activation in many of the same motor areas responsible for the producing and auditory processing areas responsible for perceiving actual outer speech—still continues to play the same functional role.

Notably, such a language model would produce many of the effects associated with System II and attentional awareness simply by its standard mode of operation. Its deliverances are sequential and serial. They are, by definition, linguistically vehicled and grammatically structured in a way that could be exploited by other systems, even if the transformer that produces them itself lacks explicit grammatical production rules as it generates them. It could coordinate "grounded" simulations with richer representations of these objects, their properties, and their relations stored in other modules, even if the transformer itself lacked grounded representations (Patel and Pavlick 2021) and even when the referents of those representations were absent from current input (Piccinini 2020b). When linked with DCNNs, perceptual input can be represented in a way that not only records the locations of abstracted features of a stimulus but also the long-distance, holistic, compositional relations that hold among those features; this abstracted, relationally annotated image can in turn be used to generate even more coherent novel stimuli when paired with a GAN-like module (Colas et al. 2020; Esser, Rombach, and Ommer 2021). The course of inner speech production could in turn be directed by a winner-take-all competition between the influences of the other modules when taken as input, or more ambitiously by further reinforcement or meta-reinforcement learning algorithms that bias its parameters toward the production of language which is relevant to current goals or would be deemed appropriate by other speakers.[24] To

---

[24] Indeed, one of the most promising paradigms for training transformers involves reinforcement learning on human feedback, or RLHF (Bai et al. 2022; Ouyang et al.

be clear, this all remains highly speculative at present, but we can expect to see more systems experimenting with such modules in the next five to ten years. The use of transformers (or other sequence-learning architectures) with and for reinforcement learning is currently a hot topic of research (Chen et al. 2021; Parisotto et al. 2020), as is the use of meta-reinforcement learning to control and stabilize the cognitive activities of an agent architecture, by directing the trajectories of internal simulations of past, present, or future experience to implement roles attributed to internal conscious experience (Langdon et al. 2021). By forcing the centralized processing of the model through the textual bottleneck, it would also induce a domain-general bias toward representational "sparsity" that prominent researchers like Bengio have highlighted as a role for consciousness in DNN-based cognitive architectures (Bengio 2017).

Pairing a text-production transformer with some of the high-quality text-to-image Generative Adversarial Network (GAN) techniques described in the previous chapter might even allow AI to approach some of James's most ambitious ideas about attention as "preperceptive imagination." Specifically, the sequences of language tokens can be fed to multimodal GANs to generate an evolving, movie-like experience of the contents of the global workspace. Hobbyists and computational artists have already produced a number of compelling demonstrations of this method, by, for example, feeding poetry or famous literature excerpts to a multimodal GAN and visualizing the results of its ongoing exploration of the model's latent space into an evolving movie. Perceptual discrimination and recognition modules could then be directed at this simulation, to categorize its contents for other purposes and to compare its deliverances to occurrent perceptual signals (Gershman 2019; Lau 2019).

While it is clear that inner speech plays such roles in many humans, this alluring proposal raises as many questions as it answers. One major concern is about translating the representational format of

2022; Stiennon et al. 2020). RLHF-trained models outperformed other state-of-the-art transformers on a variety of criteria according to a "holistic" analysis performed by Stanford's Human-Centered Artificial Intelligence group (Liang et al. 2022). I discuss this at more length in section 7.4.

inner speech to the representational formats of other modules in a way that could be useful for controlling cognition (Langland-Hassan 2014). Fortunately, deep learning has recently been exploring a variety of "multimodal" text models which can combine information from sensory and linguistic representations in a single encoding (Xu, Zhu, and Clifton 2022). Systems could also develop their own decoders to translate the products of globally broadcast inner speech into their own vector space. Research on ways to model these control functions of inner speech to achieve goal-directed regulation of modular DNN-based architectures has only just begun (Goyal and Bengio 2020; Granato et al. 2021; Granato, Borghi, and Baldassarre 2020), but doubtless there will be more research pursuing this alluring idea in the near future now that we have models which can actually produce voluminous amounts of richly structured speech.[25]

6.7.1. A caveat: Mind-wandering and control

Before moving on to the final chapter, we should temper some of the Jamesian enthusiasm for controlled, focused cognition with a caveat. In particular, recent empirical work in psychology, neuroscience, and philosophy has suggested that mind-wandering may play an important role in our cognitive economy. This is contrary to the attitude of James, who seems to regard mind-wandering as a weakness that is antithetical to rationality and intelligence. "Sustained attention," James writes, is "easier, and [richer] in acquisitions the fresher and more original the mind," and "geniuses [. . .] excel other [people] in sustained attention" (*PP* 423). James has the highest praise for attention sustained on abstract topics, where one element seems to follow one another according to rational relations:

> When we come down to the root of the matter, we see that [the genius] differ[s] from ordinary [people] less in the character of their

---

[25] For older computational models attempting to capture the relationship between inner speech and cognition, see Cangelosi, Greco, and Harnad (2000); Garagnani and Pulvermüller (2013); and Lupyan (2005).

attention than in the nature of the objects upon which it is succes-
sively bestowed. In the genius, these form a concatenated series,
suggesting each other mutually by some rational law. (*PP* 423–24)[26]

The genius, James supposes, manages this by finding a greater degree
of intrinsic interest in abstract topics, whereas for common people,
"the series is for the most part incoherent, the objects having no rational bond, and we call the attention wandering and unfixed" (*PP*
424). Concerned for the nongeniuses among us, James suggests that
this lack of intrinsic interest in abstract topics can be compensated by
learned habits of attention. He praises the voluntary ability to bring
the wandering mind continually back to the same topic as "the very
root of judgment, character, and will" (*PP* 424). He seems to have only
laments for those who cannot manage either voluntary or automatic
sustained attention, noting that their work, "to the end of life, gets done
in the interstices of their mind-wandering" (*PP* 417). This can leave us
with the impression that mind-wandering is the enemy of intelligence
and rationality, a biological foible that artificial rational agents would
be better without.

On the contrary, recent research suggests that mind-wandering
may play an important role in solving the Control Problem, one that
has been neglected in AI research. A new wave of empirical research
has suggested that "not all minds who wander are lost" (Smallwood
and Andrews-Hanna 2013). In other words, mind-wandering—which
can comprise up to half of our conscious thought (Klinger and Cox
1987)—plays a central role in coordinating rational cognitive activity.
It can allow us to connect past and future selves, juggle multiple tasks
and goals, and uncover creative insights that could not be obtained
through more focused search. The particular thoughts which occur
during mind-wandering episodes, while unrelated to the current task,
are often relevant to other important goals in the past or future. For example, we may wonder while mind-wandering whether we answered

---

[26] In footnotes, James provides further historical and literary opinion linking attention and genius: " 'Genius,' says Helvetius, is nothing but a continued attention
[...] 'Genius,' says Buffon, 'is only a protracted patience. [...] And Chesterfield has also
observed that 'the power of applying an attention, steady and undissipated, to a single
object, is the sure mark of a superior genius' " (*PP* 423).

that important e-mail, locked the front door, or will hit that dangerous pothole on the way to work (Smallwood et al. 2011). Though James catalogues the benefits of directedness, an equally compelling list of famous anecdotes could be collected documenting cases when insightful solutions to problems arose spontaneously during mind-wandering, including such mental malingerers as Newton, Darwin, and Einstein (Baird et al. 2012). Neurologically, mind-wandering has been linked to the "default mode network," a system of interactions among brain areas that seems to play a critical role in regulating wide-scale brain activity (Buckner, Andrews-Hanna, and Schacter 2008). Daydreaming—which generally overlaps with mind-wandering—has long been linked to memory consolidation (Dudai, Karni, and Born 2015; O'Callaghan, Walpola, and Shine 2021), which may help us discover new representations through offline interleaved learning as described in Chapter 4.

On the philosophical side, Zac Irving (2016) has recently theorized that mind-wandering should be understood as unguided attention. This view is offered as a solution to the puzzle which faces previous theories of mind-wandering in light of this new research. On the one hand, it seems purposeless (psychologists have even frequently defined it as "task-unrelated thought"), but on the other hand it often seems to advance our goals and projects. Irving dissolves this tension by noting that mind-wandering is purposeless in the sense that the thoughts that succeed one another during mind-wandering need bear no obvious semantic or logical relation to one another; yet it is purposeful in the sense that the thoughts explored are related to our goals and interests. Indeed, the thoughts that occur during mind-wandering can often provide critical reminders or discoveries that prove essential to solving problems with which we are tasked, even or especially when more sustained attention has proven fruitless. This approach can provide guidance for AI modelers here, a helpful counter to James's stricter attitude.

Thinking of mind-wandering as unguided attention also helps unite it with the other Jamesian proposals in this chapter. In particular, we might want our agent architecture to afford "knobs" that allow it to relax the degree of control exerted over attentional resources when "frustrated" by a lack of progress from directed problem search. It has long been known that dynamically adjusting particular hyperparameters in a network to suit task characteristics can allow a wider exploration of activation space than a more focused search, potentially revealing important new solutions to problems (Duchi, Hazan, and Singer 2011; Ruder 2017), and this general insight can apply to attention as well. Allowing the mind to wander during periods of inactivity can also allow the agent to juggle multiple goals and tasks simultaneously, by for example recalling neglected alternative goals or forestalling problems that may arise from pursuing the current policy. It might thus help address the Control Problem by freeing up various modules to operate in parallel in an uncoordinated manner, and then allow one to seize control if it produces an output which is sufficiently interesting—by suggesting a solution to a vexing problem, for instance—to reclaim control of central attentional resources and dominate successive cycles. Further meta-reinforcement learning could be used to help the agent learn how to adjust these knobs to produce more successful, abstract, and rational patterns of behavior—developing James's ideas that attentional control is a "habit" to be cultivated much like others, through learning and deliberate practice.

6.8. Summary

In this chapter, I argued that Control Problems are likely to emerge as more perception, memory, and imagination-like DNN-based modules are combined into a coherent architecture, and that an additional attention-like module may help solve these issues. I reviewed theories of attentional selection from cognitive psychology and the work of William James, whose theory of attention as ideational preparation both systematizes many of the roles ascribed to attention by these psychological theories and fits well with trends in predictive approaches to learning in neuroscience and AI. I explained how many recent attempts to model attention in deep learning can be seen to realize aspects of this theory, and I suggested that much more may soon be achieved by using attention-based language models to capture aspects of inner speech in human thought. I finally cautioned that we should not neglect the benefits of unguided attention such as mind-wandering when attempting to solve complex coordination problems in AI.

In noting the promise that language models hold in solving Control Problems, we will also quickly realize that much of the linguistic input and training signals for such a control system would come from other language users—implicating social cognition. However, successfully interacting with other language users in a human-like way remains challenging for even state-of-the-art language models—in part perhaps because these models are often trained exclusively on noninteractive textual input and lack modules corresponding to the other faculties (such as memory—though see Ryoo et al. 2022), but also because they do not model aspects of human social cognition such as theory of mind, moral sentiments, and emotional responses. In the final chapter, I tackle these topics, completing an argument for the DoGMA by sketching a future research trajectory toward more human-like social cognition in deep learning.

7

Social Cognition

A child with enough intelligence to distinguish the
symptoms of suffering will sympathize with the person
who displays such symptoms, how the sight of pain can
affect her to the point of making her cry out, and cause
her to run away from it; how she may be more or less
moved, depending on how well she is acquainted with the
symptoms of suffering, and has more or less sensibility,
imagination, and memory.

—Sophie De Grouchy (2019), Letter I

To account for the sympathy we feel for the moral suffering that is common to all members of our species, we
need to go back to the cause of our private sympathies
[. . .] Each person finds herself, for all necessities—her
well-being and life's comforts—in a particular dependence
on many others [. . .] This particular dependence on a few
individuals begins in the crib; it is the first tie binding us to
our fellow creatures.

—Sophie de Grouchy (2019), Letter I

7.1. From individual to social cognition

Turning to social cognition, which here broadly involves the activity
of thinking about and with other rational agents, is timely in our over-
arching argument for the new empiricist DoGMA, as many of the remaining forms of abstract knowledge and rational decision-making
that have not yet been tackled in previous chapters are socially and

From Deep Learning to Rational Machines. Cameron J. Buckner, Oxford University Press.
© Oxford University Press 2024. DOI: 10.1093/oso/9780197653302.003.0007

culturally scaffolded. Examples include explicit theorizing about unobservable posits and relations in subjects as diverse as mathematics, logic, or science (including logical concepts of valid argument forms like DISJUNCTIVE SYLLOGISM and scientific posits like QUARK); the discovery, transmission, and maintenance of technology (from ARROWHEADS to CARBURETORS); and especially reasoning about other agents, subsuming both moral decision-making, which involves following norms and rules (including BELIEFS and DESIRES), and political coordination, which involves the ability to understand the goals and beliefs of others and cooperate with others toward normative ideals (such as MORAL WORTH, VIRTUE, or RATIONALITY itself). These concepts are essentially theoretical or social, and they are often thought to be uniquely human in nature—that is, beyond the learning capabilities of nonhuman animals. Most of these concepts are learned directly through interaction with other agents, and so are not themselves plausible candidates for innate knowledge. They are learned through explicit instruction by peers or teachers, and many of the theoretical or technological concepts were discovered through deliberate scientific theorizing and experimentation, which crucially involves critical interaction with other theorists.

Nativists often argue that the ability to learn through social interaction presupposes at least a basic start-up kit of domain-specific mechanisms specialized for tracking the mental states of other rational agents, though these claims have also been convincingly challenged by empiricists. As with other nativist hypotheses, there are disagreements as to what exactly must be packed into this social start-up kit; some think it will consist of a series of laws or generalizations (like an innate theoretical psychology concerning unobservable psychological relations, the so-called theory-theory; Penn and Povinelli 2007b), whereas more moderate nativist views require only biases toward animate or social agents (such as attentional biases toward faces or biological motion), from which the rest of the system can be bootstrapped through learning (Versace et al. 2018). Some views distinguish an implicit and an explicit social reasoning system, with the implicit system specialized for the ability to track and register the perceptual states of others, and a secondary explicit system covering basic theoretical principles like an ability to attribute false beliefs (Apperly and Butterfill 2009). In the realm of moral cognition, researchers emphasize altruistic emotional reactions like empathy, which we may or may not share with animals (De Waal 2012; Preston and De Waal 2002), or an ability to distinguish helpful from harmful agents (Hamlin 2013). In the area of cultural and technological transmission, there has been interest in an innate ability to imitate others (Meltzoff and Moore 1983). Notably, all of these findings have been subject to controversy over replication failures or competing empiricist or "neuroconstructivist" explanations, which argue that the innate biases, where they exist at all, are more domain-general and experience-dependent than the nativists suppose (Kulke et al. 2018; Margoni and Surian 2018; Ray and Heyes 2011; Simion and Leo 2010—and see Fig. 7.1).

Several established areas in computer science investigate artificial models of various aspects of social cognition, but research from these areas has not yet been well-integrated into deep learning research. For instance, the area of "human-aware AI" broadly attempts to create artificial agents that track and respond to the mental states of others, often by adding explicit symbols for mental states and rules for reasoning about them, or "mental models," which are drawn explicitly from the "theory of mind" tradition in psychology (Kambhampati 2019; Zahedi, Sreedharan, and Kambhampati 2022). "Swarm intelligence" approaches instead study the forms of collective decision-making that can emerge from relatively simple artificial agents interacting dynamically in larger groups, such as flocks of birds or colonies of ants (Kennedy 2006). The area of "affective computing" focuses on the emotional aspects of human sociality, by attempting to create robots that can detect, respond appropriately to, and simulate the affective states of humans (Picard 2000). Insights from these established areas are not commonly integrated into deep neural network (DNN)-based agents, perhaps because deep learning has developed so rapidly in such a short period of time, or perhaps because many of the methods for modeling social cognition in these other areas more closely resemble the rules-and-symbols, GOFAI-based approach that is more difficult to integrate with empiricist deep learning modeling techniques. Regardless, I argue that affective computing is the most promising area for the next round of breakthroughs in empiricist DoGMA, for both technical and

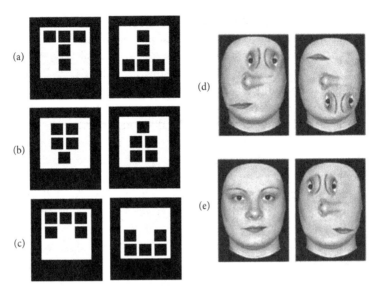

Figure 7.1 Stimuli used to assess the facial preferences of newborns. Simion et al. (2011) marshal diverse lines of psychological and neurological evidence to conclude that a general preference for top-heavy stimuli explains the preference that older infants show for face-like over non-face-like stimuli. Newborns prefer top-heavy to bottom-heavy stimuli even when schematic and not especially face-like, showing a preference in looking times to the left over right stimuli in (a)–(c) (reproduced by author from Simion et al. 2002). Newborns also show a preference for top-heavy versus bottom-heavy faces, even when the features are irregular or scrambled (preferring the left image over the right image in d) and show no preference for top-heavy versus veridical faces, with no significant differences observed in looking times between the left and right image in e) (Macchi Cassia, Turati, and Simion 2004). Simion et al. (2006) further found that newborns prefer to look at top-loaded but scrambled faces to veridical faces. The authors reason that the most parsimonious explanation for the pattern of findings that have been taken to support an innate representation of faces in infants is a more domain-general attentional bias (of the sort discussed in the last chapter) toward top-heavy stimuli, caused by greater processing of the top half of the visual field by the superior colliculus (which coordinates gaze shifts and head movements, among other functions). (Figures recreated by author or reproduced with permission from original sources cited herein.)

philosophical reasons—in particular, because of its fit with the empiricist sentimentalist tradition of theorizing about social cognition.

Before turning to that argument, it is important to point out that the DoGMA offers some reasons for optimism that affectively enhanced DNN-based agents can overcome the behavioral limitations of previous rule-and-symbol-based approaches to social intelligence. Specifically, I will explain how behaviors like gaze-tracking, behavioral prediction, imitation, and norm-following, from which more sophisticated social cognition can be scaffolded, might soon be mastered by DNN-based agents without the use of innate domain-specific concepts. Such optimism derives from ideas about social cognition from historical sentimentalists like Adam Smith and Sophie de Grouchy. Of course, exploring these ideas will uncover reasons for concern that some deep learning researchers are starting off in the wrong direction, perhaps because they have taken on board too many rationalist assumptions about the nature of social cognition without subjecting them to sufficient scrutiny. Rationalists tend to assume a solipsistic framing of the problems of social cognition; more specifically, many rationalists assume that agents begin life as selfish egoists—with only reliable introspective knowledge of their own minds and egoistic regard for their own welfare. These solipsistic agents then require some form of theoretical inference to bridge the self-other gap into the distinctively human forms of social and moral learning mentioned earlier. Indeed, leaping over this self-other gap—whether through an innate set of psychological principles like Theory of Mind (ToM), or through a universalizable moral rule like Kant's Categorical Imperative—is seen by some rationalists as the defining feature of distinctively human cognition (McCarty 1993; Penn et al. 2008). Again, as soon as the problem is defined in this way, a rationalist model equipped with innate, domain-specific social rules or concepts seems inevitable price to pay for human-like artificial social cognition.

Many empiricists have even accepted this solipsistic framing of the problem, to the degree that, over the centuries, vast swathes of moral philosophy have been devoted to understanding how human moral development normally overcomes a chasm between selfish regard for one's own welfare and altruistic regard for others. As a result, many empiricists have posited innate mechanisms for social cognition as their one domain-specific innate indulgence—usually a mechanism for sympathy/empathy, which enables us to "put ourselves in others' shoes" to understand how they might think and feel about aspects of our shared environment.

Sophie de Grouchy's work can be a particularly useful guidebook toward a more promising and distinctively empiricist agenda, because her theory eschews this concession to nativism through a strikingly simple and audacious idea: that a regard for others might emerge in the earliest stages of infancy, before we have developed a distinctive conception of our own self and hence before the self-other gap exists in the first place. From this perspective, selfish egoism is the distinctively theoretical attitude requiring special explanation, because it necessitates an ability to distinguish our own bodies, beliefs, and values from those of others. Newborns on De Grouchy's picture start valuing cues as to their own and their caregivers' emotional states on equal ground, only later progressing to a distinctive sense of self, and then to a sense of self-regard, and finally to reintegrating their other-directed emotional responses into a more mature system that represents regard for both self and other, with abilities to balance tensions between them.[1] This more mature system is built out of the other domain-general faculties we have already reviewed—perception, memory, and imagination, in particular. De Grouchy's simple inversion of the problem thus provides an alluring alternative to the puzzles that have long plagued rationalist and empiricist philosophers alike. It also suggests that both self- and other-regard might be acquired by basic reinforcement learning systems in ways that are fully consistent with the empiricist DoGMA and the Transformation Principle, provocatively suggesting potential implementation in terms of deep reinforcement learning.[2]

---

[1] Here as elsewhere, there is a nativist and an empiricist take on the evidence from developmental psychology. Rochat, for example, marshals evidence that the development of a sense of self emerges in stages and depends upon developmental experience (Rochat 2009), whereas nativists provide evidence that some of the most basic forms of self-awareness like body ownership are present from birth (Filippetti et al. 2013). These two perspectives may not ultimately be in tension if infants have access to developmental experience of invariant relationships between sensation and perception of their own body in the womb.

[2] This thus might be seen to address the concerns of Julia Haas, who has also sought to build social cognition into DNN-based agents on a foundation of reinforcement learning. Haas worries that sentimentalism sets up an opposition between reason and

It is an open empirical question whether this "Grouchean" perspective on social cognition is correct as a matter of developmental psychology, or useful as a foundation for engineering research, but there are recent reasons for confidence. In particular, current breakthroughs in deep learning have been achieved by providing relatively generic DNN-based agents with the same kinds of structured early experiences as newborn animals, allowing them to demonstrate some of the same inductive biases toward social behavior that rationalists have supposed must be innate (Lee, Gujarathi, et al. 2021; Lee, Wood, et al. 2021). The benefits of further pursuing this hypothesis are, again, numerous and interdisciplinary: it can help us obtain a more accurate understanding of the difference-making aspects of our own distinctively human forms of social cognition, but it can also help us create better artificial agents that are both more efficient and that can interact with us in more successful and natural ways. We already know that proceeding in the top-heavy, solipsistic tradition can have serious costs: by creating agents with social and moral reasoning systems that are not grounded in affective underpinnings, we create a hollow simulacrum of sociality which, similar to the grounding problems faced by GOFAI in other areas of inquiry, is more akin to the reasoning of psychopaths. They may correctly identify moral transgressions, but not be motivated by them in the right way (Aharoni, Sinnott-Armstrong, and Kiehl 2014).

The Grouchean perspective recommends instead replicating early developmental aspects of human social cognition in artificial agents, which would allow them to interact with us and one another more successfully—better anticipating our actions and concerns, learning from us and teaching us some of their insights, and reasoning in distinctively moral ways about our welfare—because their other faculties and representations would be more naturally linked to the more sophisticated social abilities they scaffold. To make this case, I begin this chapter by reviewing the more Machiavellian tradition, which approaches social cognition as competition among solipsistic egoists.

---

the emotions, and reinforcement-learning-based methods offer a third approach which bridges this gap (Haas 2019, 2020). On my view, the Smith/De Grouchy view bridges this gap in a way that is consistent with deep learning and the DoGMA specifically, by using domain-general faculties to control for social nuisance variables in empathetic simulation.

I then sketch a research program for social artificial intelligence based instead upon De Grouchy's more promising empiricist foundations. I conclude by reviewing early evidence in favor of the latter approach and end with speculative comments about the practical benefits of pursuing this tradition further.

7.2. Social cognition as Machiavellian struggle

Before considering the brighter alternative, let us first review the traditional solipsistic approach. On this view, one of the major developmental transitions in mental life occurs with the ability to understand that other rational beings are also agents with internal mental lives and intrinsic moral worth. This transition allows agents to treat other agents not as just one more complex kind of physical event whose behavior should be predicted on the basis of external circumstances according to regular laws, but rather as separate mental agents with their own complex and idiosyncratic internal organization. In particular, these other agents are taken to be rational, representational systems; they perceive, believe, and desire, and the contents of these mental states predict the behaviors that they will perform.[3] Unlike two members of the same physical class of object, which should generally behave the same way whenever placed in the same circumstances, two agents may react to the same external situation very differently as a result of having different internal "takes" on that situation. This can be useful not only for predicting the behaviors of different agents but also for the purposes of deception, as one agent might be able to use another's false beliefs to their advantage, whether by hiding information or producing misleading evidence in intentional deception. Such social competition has been hypothesized to be a general driver of human cognitive complexity in the "Machiavellian Intelligence Hypothesis," which suggests that the arms race to form and maintain alliances, as well as to deceive and manipulate others to defeat one's social competitors, caused a general increase not only in the sophistication of ToM in our closest

---

[3] To this somewhat stunted picture, we might also add the attribution of character traits and emotional states (Westra 2018).

primate ancestors but also in general cognitive resources (Byrne and Whiten 1994).

ToM has even been considered a distinctively human trait, or at least one shared only with our closest primate relatives like chimpanzees. This claim of human uniqueness is of great importance to artificial intelligence (AI), for if correct, ToM may lie at the heart of many other distinctively human cognitive achievements such as language use, technology, political organization, and culture. For example, some cognitive scientists have hypothesized that it would be impossible to learn language without a ToM, because we must know what other speakers are thinking about in order to disambiguate the reference of new words they use. For example, suppose I utter the word 'blicket' in a cluttered environment; there are a potentially infinite number of different objects, properties, or actions I might be referring to with the unknown word, and it will be difficult or impossible to disambiguate its reference without some hypothesis about the speaker's mental state. Similarly, there are obvious ties between ToM and the creation of technology; it is difficult to learn how to manufacture complex tools simply by observation without understanding the intended goal of elaborate physical movements performed in a long sequence. In politics, complex alliances or long-term relationships would be difficult to maintain without a sophisticated understanding of other agents' wants, desires, fears, hopes, and grievances. And much of our human understanding of the world—including the "common sense" that we began with in Chapters 1 and 2—may be thought to be a product of human cultural transmission, which is premised on the possibility of one generation of social beings transmitting their novel cognitive achievements to the next generation via directed instruction. Effective cultural instruction involves all of the previously mentioned components—linguistic communication, students understanding the teacher's pedagogical intentions, the teacher understanding the learner's ignorance or false beliefs, and more. If this were all correct, then ToM might be thought of as the key to unlocking distinctively human cognition, and it would be of great importance to build ToM modules into AI agents if we wished them to achieve human-like intelligence.

For much of the last two decades, ToM was also one of the strongest candidates for an innate, domain-specific module in humans. The attribution of mental states to others is considered a developmental milestone hit reliably by neurotypical children. In particular, the attribution of false belief came to be regarded as a particularly important empirical yardstick for the maturation of ToM. This research tradition can be seen as starting off with an influential article in *Behavior and Brain Sciences* by the primatologists Premack and Woodruff, which questioned whether chimpanzees might also have a ToM, and whether this question could be answered experimentally (1978). A trio of philosophers responded in commentary to this article that the attribution of false beliefs was particularly important here (Bennett 1978; D. Dennett 1978; Harman 1978), an insight which was turned into experimental paradigms by Wimmer and Perner (1983). The problem is that it would be difficult to determine experimentally whether a nonhuman animal like a chimpanzee could attribute beliefs to other agents unless it took those beliefs to be false; for the hypotheses of attributing a true belief to another agent and predicting the agent's behavior on the basis of one's own belief would seem to always make the same predictions in experimental designs. This led to emphasis on the socalled false-belief task as the arbiter of ToM possession.

A standard experimental design derived from this intuition is called the Sally-Anne task (Baron-Cohen, Leslie, and Frith 1985). In this design, a child watches an experimenter tell a story with two puppets (or actors), one introduced as "Sally" and another as "Anne." The task involves a toy object like a marble and two locations in which the toy can be hidden, such as a basket or a box. In the design, the child watches as the experimenter explains that Sally places the toy in the first location while Anne watches. Sally then departs the scene, and Anne moves the toy from the first location to the second. Sally then returns, and the child is asked by the experimenter where Sally will begin searching for the toy. The aspect of this design which implicates a false belief can be appreciated by considering the alternative, confounded scenario in which Sally was present to see the toy being moved; in that case, children will answer with the same location whether they are attributing a belief to Sally or simply answering in terms of where they know the marble to be in reality. When Sally does not witness the toy being moved, however, the attribution of a false belief makes a different prediction; if the child in the experiment says that Sally will look in the location where

Sally last saw the toy, they must be suppressing their tendency to answer that Sally will look in the toy's true location. This test (and numerous variants) came to be regarded as a standard benchmark for ToM development in neurotypical children, nearly all of whom would reliably pass it between four and six years of age, across differences in language, culture, and education (Wellman, Cross, and Watson 2001).

Neurotypical children tend to hit this standard developmental milestone for verbal false-belief understanding between the ages of four and six years, which leaves open whether it is the maturation of an innate mechanism or a learned ability; however, over the last two decades, nativist psychologists introduced innovative experimental designs that seemed to push the emergence of ToM even earlier, all the way back to early infancy. These designs relied on nonlinguistic versions of the false-belief task and nonverbal measures of understanding to determine whether infants had passed the test. Looking time is the most popular metric in these studies on young infants; in even simpler versions of false-belief tasks, infants as young as six months old have been reported to look first at expected outcomes (e.g., when they predict Sally will look where she last saw the toy) or longer at "surprising" outcomes (e.g., if Sally were observed searching for the toy where it actually is rather than where she had last observed it). A series of experimental failures seemed to show that even our closest relatives like chimpanzees lacked similar abilities (Penn et al. 2008; Penn and Povinelli 2007b). This research is often championed by nativists in the context of debates over AI, for it would seem to push the origins of human social cognition—often considered one of the main "Core Knowledge" systems—back to an age before which it could plausibly be learned through experience, language, or culture (Skerry, Carey, and Spelke 2013; Marcus 2018b; Mitchell 2019; Spelke 1998).

Perhaps for these reasons, simple false-belief tests have been one of the few aspects of social cognition empirically investigated using deep learning agents. The so-called ToM-Net system from DeepMind was directly inspired by this tradition in developmental psychology (Rabinowitz et al. 2018), as well as another tradition of thinking about ToM as a problem of inverse planning. The "inverse planning" approach suggests a similar maneuver to the one worked between abstraction in deep convolutional neural networks (DCNNs) and specification in generative adversarial networks (GANs)—perhaps an inferential procedure that takes the behaviors of others as input and outputs a hypothesis regarding their mental states could be achieved by simply inverting the processes that the observing agent already uses to produce its own behavior from its own plans. This approach has been pursued from the perspective of Bayesian planning (Baker, Saxe, and Tenenbaum 2009; Baker and Tenenbaum 2014) and reinforcement learning theory (Jara-Ettinger 2019).

These methods are often tested on simple toy problems, like Baker et al.'s "Food Truck" task. In the Food Truck setup, an observing agent is provided with information about the perceptual inputs (e.g., "line of sight") and moment-to-moment behaviors of observed agents moving around in a two-dimensional landscape (Fig. 7.2). The landscape contains one of several kinds of "food trucks"—labeled "Korean," "Lebanese," or "Mexican"—and opaque occluders blocking the line of sight. On the Bayesian approach, the observing agent begins with some options for representational primitives about different agents' movements and food preferences, using inverse Bayesian modeling to hypothesize agents' perceptual and goal states that would make the observed outputs most likely. The observing agent seemed to show that it developed hypotheses regarding an observed agent's motivations and goal states, hypotheses that were then revised as the agent produced behavior that was compatible or incompatible with the hypothesized goals (e.g., observing an agent backtracking to the Lebanese food truck after turning the corner of the occluder and detecting the Korean food truck as the other option caused the observing agent to revise the hypothesis of the observed agent's preference for Lebanese over Korean food).

Inverse reinforcement learning (IRL) works a similar trick, but it relies on algorithms designed to derive a reinforcement function that could produce some particular series of behaviors on the basis of observations. For instance, upon observing the behavior described in the previous paragraph, it would try to devise a reward function on which this backtracking would be predicted by the observed agent to be the most rewarding policy given the evidence the observing agent saw it collect. Both methods can produce promising results in Food Trucks–type tasks, but the Bayesian inference and inverse

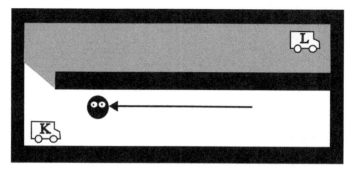

Figure 7.2 Example of training input in the "food trucks" theory of mind inference task (reproduced by author from Baker et al. 2009). The observing agent is provided with successive movements from the target agent (circle with "eyes") as it moves around looking for a desired food truck around an occluding obstacle; the shaded area indicates what is outside the viewpoint of the observed agent, and the "trucks" labeled 'K' and 'L' correspond to Korean and Lebanese food trucks, respectively. By observing where the agent goes and how it behaves (e.g., back-tracking after turning a corner and observing the "wrong" truck), the observing agent can develop hypotheses about the desires of the observed agent (what kind of food it prefers) and its beliefs (where it believes each type of food is located with respect to occluding barriers). Inverse planning or inverse reinforcement learning can be used to develop hypotheses about perceptual inputs and goal-state preferences that would predict (and retrodict) the behavior of the observed agent.

reinforcement learning are both regarded as too computationally expensive to model the neural mechanisms that implement social cognition.

State-of-the-art results on toy tasks inspired by the Food Truck experiment were achieved by Rabinowitz et al.'s ToMNet, a DNN-based architecture more biologically plausible than the Bayesian or IRL models in its computational demands. This architecture included two new "innate" DNN modules that were not derived from learning: a "character state net" and a "mental state net" (Fig. 7.3). The character state net develops a general model of each observed agent—called a "character embedding"—by observing and compressing previous

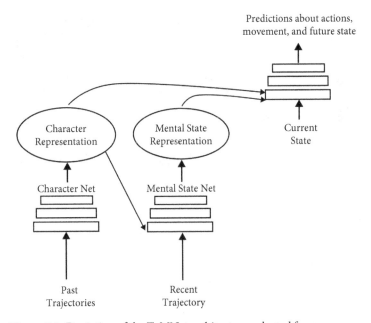

Figure 7.3 Depiction of the ToMNet architecture, adapted from Rabinowitz et al. (2018). The architecture has three basic networks, a "character net" that attributes stable characters to individuals on the basis of multiple past trajectories, a "mental state net" that attributes current mental states to agents on the basis of the observations in the current episode, and a "prediction net" that integrates the character, mental state, and current state representations to generate predictions about the next behavior of the agent (and successor representations regarding its subsequent states).

trajectories of that agent's interactions with its environment. The mental state net takes these character embeddings together with information about the current situation to form embeddings specific to the current episode trajectory. The model's authors hypothesize that this allows the architecture to "mentalize" about the current agent in the current episode, based on its stable character and recent behavior in the current episode, and outputs a mental state embedding for the agent in its current trajectory. The character embedding, the mental state embedding, and inputs from the current environment are passed to the overall prediction net, which then forecasts the agent's future behaviors. Like the Bayesian and IRL-based solutions to the task, the trajectory of the ToMNet's learning appeared to demonstrate revision of mental state hypotheses in response to the observation of inconsistent behavioral trajectories. The authors even created a situation where the observing agent could only correctly predict the observed agents' behavior by attributing false beliefs, by introducing "swap events" modeled on the Sally-Anne task in which "desired" objects were moved when outside of the observed agents' line of sight. The ToMNet was able to succeed on this task, though not at optimal levels of reliability.

According to key empiricist desiderata, the ToMNet is notably better off than more nativist approaches to ToM. In particular, the system does not include a hand-crafted model of other agents as rational planners; instead, agents learned to predict the behavior patterns of other agents purely by observing their past behavior. Further, and as already noted, its reliance on DNNs for mentalizing attributions is more computationally feasible than other algorithmic alternatives. It also demonstrates a "learning to learn" effect, in that it improves at predicting the behavior of agents in general and of individual agents in particular (given their distinctive "characters") over time. Crucially, this means that it eventually learns to predict the behavior of novel agents on the basis of very small amounts of observed behavior, often thought a key efficiency payoff of human-like ToM. This kind of approach might be especially promising as an interpretability method in XAI, as ToM-equipped DNN-based interpreters might provide some of the best tools to explain the behaviors of other DNN-based agents. It does, however, require two new innate modules that are more domain-specific in their application to social attributions than anything we have considered so far.

Despite the tendency of some deep learning critics to treat them as consensus findings in cognitive science, the innateness of false-belief understanding and its centrality to human social cognition remain unsettled and controversial. The first problem is that one of the main dependent variables assessed in the early infant research—looking times—is notoriously difficult to interpret. Infants displaying the same pattern of preferential or longer looking behavior may be driven by different underlying cognitive processes—longer looking can either indicate the detection of familiarity or of novelty, and experimenters must use diachronic monitoring of the microstructure of looks to determine their correct interpretation (Aslin 2007).[4] The various causes of looking behaviors often have contrary implications for experimental hypotheses, and in many of the standard designs, it can be difficult to determine which interpretation is correct (Rubio-Fernández 2019). Additionally, all theories of early infant ToM must make sense of the long gap between the purported manifestation of implicit nonverbal ToM and of explicit verbal ToM between two and five years of age, during which children possess much of the linguistic precursors to understanding the minds of others, but repeatedly fail linguistic versions of the false-belief task. Various proposals have been floated to explain the delay of explicit ToM ability, but they all incur additional empirical burden, such as the need to provide independent evidence for performance constraints on linguistic tasks (Fenici 2017; Westra 2017). In addition, the replication crisis in developmental psychology has hit its nonverbal false-belief designs hardest, with numerous replication failures and several prominent researchers in the area reporting that they have failed to reproduce some of their most famous results (Baillargeon, Buttelmann, and Southgate 2018; Kampis et al. 2020; Kulke et al. 2018; Powell et al. 2018; Sabbagh and Paulus 2018). Even the standard story that ToM emerges universally among neurotypical humans between the ages of four and six years has recently been challenged by new evidence of cultural variability. Of particular relevance is the finding that explicit mental attributions seem to be more common and emerge earlier in Western cultures that place greater emphasis on individuality and autonomy (Moore 2021; Warnell and Redcay 2019).

A more constructive empiricist response has also been simmering in the background. This counterargument emphasizes the (underestimated) amount and quality of social experience available to infants (Smith and Slone 2017). Researchers argue that this experience

---

[4] And, even when it is agreed that the longer looking indicates novelty detection, there is disagreement about how to interpret the regularity which is violated in a nonverbal false-belief task (Apperly and Butterfill 2009; Heyes 2014). I am grateful to Evan Westra for discussion of this and other points in this paragraph.

is sufficient to acquire competence on social cognition tasks without innate knowledge, often basing their conclusions on data recorded by infant headcams, which can then be used as input to train associative models that can be assessed for specific social skills (Smith et al. 2015; Yu and Smith 2013). A variety of other studies have found similar nonverbal evidence for ToM in nonhuman animals, even in nonprimates such as ravens (Bugnyar, Reber, and Buckner 2016; Karg et al. 2016; Krupenye et al. 2016; Tomasello, Call, and Hare 2003), which challenges claims of human uniqueness—at least if we accept nonverbal measures of ToM (though often the behavioral variables assessed in nonverbal ToM experiments on animals are less ambiguous than looking times). Recent surveys of social cognition research have also concluded that the attributions of beliefs and desires specifically, and of behavioral prediction more generally, comprise only a small part of our other-directed cognitive abilities. The abilities to understand others' perceptual states, character traits, emotions, and norms are perhaps even more important to our social lives (Spaulding 2018b). This more complete picture of our mentalizing abilities typically implicates imagination and emotional understanding to a much greater degree than has been supposed in the ToM debate (Nichols 2001; Nichols and Stich 2003; Spaulding 2018a; Westra 2018), further straining the "cold Machiavellian competitor" approach to rational cognition in humans. Ultimately, buyers in AI should beware of nativists in psychology selling innate, false-belief-centric ToM as a consensus and empirically established view; recent trends even within these psychological literatures recommend a more empiricist, pluralistic, affectively grounded take on social cognition, even when just considering humans.

7.3. Smith and De Grouchy's sentimentalist approach to social cognition

The experimenters working on the Food Trucks–style toy problems just discussed would readily admit that these tasks reflect a simplified and idealized approach to social cognition. We might wonder at this point whether further refinements in this tradition would eventually converge on human-like social cognition, or whether (instead) DNN-based social cognition is heading down the wrong track. There is, however, an alternative path to explore. In this subsection, I sketch a course for the DoGMA that recommends backtracking to an earlier point in the bootstrapping exercise—to the topic of emotion. Returning to the empiricist tradition defended in earlier chapters yields useful insights about the relevance of domain-general faculties, such as memory, imagination, and attention, often minimized or disparaged by rationalists. In fact, empiricists emphasize that particular emotional reactions in particular circumstances—not abstract epistemic inferences—first allow us to recognize that other humans are also agents with internal mental lives full of meaning and significance. On this view, personal attachments and particular sentiments such as love, camaraderie, shame, and regret—rather than impersonal propositional attitude ascriptions or universal rules—form the bedrock of human-like social understanding.

Of course, mature moral and social decision-making also involve balancing emotional reactions against more abstract considerations like justice and fairness. For this reason, two-systems views of social cognition have been popular in recent moral psychology, particularly views holding that adult humans can navigate social problems using an intuitive, affective, slow-learning, automatic emotional system and a reflective, abstract, fast-learning rule-based reasoning system (Greene 2014). But problems quickly result from glossing the two systems in this way, especially a gulf separating Kirk- and Spock-like angels on our shoulders, whose interactions and weighted negotiations in practical decision-making become mysterious (Cushman 2020; Pessoa 2008). A particular strain of empiricism found in Adam Smith and Sophie de Grouchy is exceedingly well-placed to provide solutions. Sarah Songhorian (2022), for instance, has argued that the "reflective sentimentalism" developed by Smith (and later De Grouchy) can bridge this gulf by adopting a diachronic, developmental perspective on moral cognition, allowing us to see how the rule-based system develops out of the affective system, and thus can interact and communicate with it in a common language, especially over longer timescales.

On Smith's reflective sentimentalism, agents actively develop a capacity for more rule-like social cognition by reflectively directing their powers of abstraction toward tensions and idiosyncrasies that emerge from the use of their initial, affective reactions as they are engaged across a range of diverse situations. Just as positional nuisance variables challenge our detection of abstract object categories like triangles and chairs, we may eventually abstract away from the idiosyncrasies of these personal attachments and social positions to form more general ideas of affective characters, mental states, and social situations.[5] As in previous chapters, the domain-general faculties of perception, memory, imagination, and attention play key roles in the abstractive process. Just as our imaginative powers enable us to explore novel values of nuisance parameters for abstract categories in visual perception, we might learn to envision novel social situations by plugging different agents or attitudes into slots in social contexts, allowing us to see how things look "in other people's shoes" (Buckner 2018b).[6] The starting point of this abstractive exercise, however, is located in the humbler, domain-general beginnings that help us navigate the nonsocial world, such as our basic affective responses and reinforcement learning.

There are other empiricist starting points, of course, but, following the strategy of earlier chapters, I focus on a particular route through empiricist territory that is most germane to the development of the DoGMA, using the work of Adam Smith and Sophie de Grouchy as

---

[5] Compare to Gordon (2021) on "agent-neutral coding."

[6] There have been a number of other empiricist-friendly trends in contemporary research on social cognition. One of the traditional alternatives to innate, theory-like ToM, for example, is called "simulation theory"; it operates on the assumption that we predict the behavior of other social agents by using our domain-general resources for imaginative simulation. In these simulations, we simply plug the perceptual and situational inputs of others into our own motivational architecture and imagine what we would do in their shoes (Goldman 2006). This led to standard debate between "theory-theory" and "simulation theory" camps (Stich and Nichols 1992); though most recent appraisals suggest that adult human social cognition is really a complex mixture of simulation- and theory-like elements (Nichols and Stich 2003; Spaulding 2018b). Another line of critique suggests that explaining the behavior of others might be just as important as predicting it, recommending a shift away from the obsession with competition characteristic of Machiavellian frames (Andrews 2005, 2012). Yet another but related perspective emphasizes the more engaged, collaborative aspects of social cognition, suggesting that our other-directed cognitive capacities might be more about "shaping" or enactively engaging one another's minds in a cooperative and interactive fashion (Gallagher 2001; Martens and Schlicht 2018; Zawidzki 2008, 2013).

guideposts.[7] Smith and De Grouchy are largely working within and extending the Lockean/Humean approach to empiricist faculty psychology discussed in previous chapters. Both locate the roots of adult social cognition in formative learning experiences early in childhood. This is particularly significant, given the emphasis we have placed in earlier chapters on the importance of structured early experiences to achieving human-like machine learning. Rather than an antiquated view of the origins of our social understanding, this kind of developmental approach is today considered a cutting-edge theoretical option in social psychology (Theriault, Young, and Barrett 2021). Indeed, the primary point of dispute between Smith and De Grouchy concerns how far back we must go in childhood to locate the first scaffolding experiences. While both of these thinkers highlight sympathy as the primary bridge between self-regarding and other-regarding mental capacities, Smith locates the origins of sympathy in the experience of being judged by others in childhood, whereas De Grouchy locates its origins in the first days of life, in the particular attachments and reciprocal interactions between an infant and its initial caregivers.

The sentimentalist tradition argues that at least some of our earliest affective responses are nonspecific to our own pains and pleasures, and thus generalize to others. This approach has many advantages. For one, it locates the origins of moral reasoning in natural psychological properties, such as the tendency to pursue pleasure and avoid pain in general reinforcement learning. Contrary to more rationalist approaches like that of Kant, sentimentalism requires no special contributions from pure rationality or from innate moral rules; the origins of moral sense and moral reasoning can be located, instead, in the emotions we feel when we observe the pleasure or suffering of others (Prinz 2007).[8] The sentimentalist approach is also more conducive to an evolutionary story about the origin of social cognition and morality, for we can find the precursors of moral emotions in our

---

[7] I am grateful to Olivia Bailey and Eric Schliesser for discussions on these topics.

[8] Prinz famously or notoriously takes a Humean approach to sentimentalism into the domain of normative theory, supposing that with the right empirical method we could read off the right normative theory from data such as functional magnetic resonance imaging (fMRI) scans. In eschewing normative sentimentalism, I am not taking that final leap here.

nearest primate relatives (De Waal 2012; Piccinini and Schulz 2018; Preston and De Waal 2002). However, sentimentalists tend to agree that only humans are capable of full moral reflection and reasoning, so there must be something still missing from the altruistic emotions that can be found in our nearest primate relatives.

For reflective sentimentalists, this is where reflective sympathy comes into the story, to bootstrap these social emotions to more mature moral decision-making. These sentimentalists highlight "sympathy" (which we would today call "empathy") as the fundamental bridge between self-regarding and other-regarding cognition. For Hume, sympathy in one way or another involves feeling what another feels, as though through a kind of emotional contagion (Fleischacker 2019; Wilson and Sober 1998). Hume describes it by comparison with phys- ically coupled systems: "As in strings equally wound up, the motion of one communicates itself to the rest; so all the affections pass readily from one person to another, and beget correspondent movements in every human creature" (*T* 3.3.1.7). Such contagion would provide a bridge for our inductive learning of the minds of others; we would learn that other persons are different from rocks because the former but not the latter arouse in us sympathetic emotions that provide good evidence for predictions, explanations, and evaluations of their be- havior. Yet commentators have observed that Hume seems to presume rather than explain how our affective responses become coupled to those of others, and this seems to leave a hole in the middle of his so- cial and moral psychology (Kim 2019). It is toward this gap that Smith directs much of his theorizing in *The Theory of Moral Sentiments*.

Even outside the empiricist tradition, philosophers and psychologists have wondered how we ever locate the evidence to cross the Rubicon from believing that we have internal mental lives with meaningful thoughts to believing that others also have minds with meaningful internal thoughts. It has long been treated as one of the foundational problems of philosophy (Sober 2000). The rationalist tradition—often taking Descartes's lead—assumes that we must start from the knowledge that we have minds (e.g., in the famous "I think therefore I am") and then find some sort of evidence that grounds an inference to the conclusion that others have minds as well. Empiricists in the sentimentalist tradition treat awareness of the emotional states

of others as something more like noninferential immediate perception, triggered by sentiments like sympathy. However, this incurs for
them the burden of explaining the origins of these other-regarding
emotions. Some of the fanciest footwork in twentieth-century philosophy has sought to dance around or invert the problem—such as
Sellars's "Myth of Jones," which speculates that introspective awareness
of our own mental states might grow out of theorizing that others have
minds with inner mental episodes that predict and explain their complex behavior (Sellars 1956).

Both Adam Smith and De Grouchy can be seen to pick up Humean
sentimentalism, but they both attempt to offer better answers to this
developmental riddle. For Smith, the origins of sympathy are to be
found in our early childhood interactions with others. As Fleischacker
(2019) notes, Smith offers a more "projective" account of sympathy (in
contrast to Hume's contagion account) which draws upon the imagination to simulate what we would feel if in another's circumstances.
According to Smith, this ability emerges out of experiences of judging
and being judged by others in early childhood, where we must learn
to understand and approximate one another's emotional reactions to
situations to judge their appropriateness. We come to realize that some
emotional reactions are appropriate to circumstances and others are
not, by seeing how children and adults react to acts of anger or kind-
ness displayed by ourselves and our peers.

Drawing on ideas in earlier chapters, we might liken this process
or moral abstraction to that by which nuisance variation is controlled
for via abstraction in perception. Just as we learn to recognize and
abstract away from differences in pose or location in the visual field
when solving object categorization tasks, we also learn that some of
our attitudes and starting points are idiosyncratic or disapproved of by
our community in social cognition, and so seek to abstract away from
them as sources of variation in practical judgment. Smith's most significant contribution to sentimentalist discourse here is his idea that
this process of abstraction will eventually equilibrate on a "concord"
with the perspective of others, whereby social agents "continually" and
"constantly" try to place themselves in one another's shoes—for if we
attempt to judge ourselves or others by a skewed standard, others will
call us out and point out the deviation.

At the limit of such equilibration, this concord should allow each of us to achieve the perspective of an "impartial spectator" for our culture, who would judge whether the affective responses in some situation are generally deemed appropriate (Songhorian 2022). Social behavior—whether pertaining to moral issues or nonmoral ones (such as etiquette)—arises from our implicit or explicit attempts to cultivate character traits and affective habits that this impartial spectator would deem appropriate. Smith, in essence, here sketches a method by which the abstractness and impartiality favored by the rationalist can be learned using affective and imaginative forms of cognition through an iterative process of reflective abstraction like those already discussed.[9]

De Grouchy, in commenting on Smith's view in her esteemed translation of his *Theory of Moral Sentiments*, provides even further developmental grounding for this sentimentalist approach to empathy, most especially by tracing its origins all the way back to the earliest experiences in infancy. While generally working within Smith's Humean empiricist psychology, De Grouchy registers several disagreements. For one, sympathy for De Grouchy is a more complex emotion: it consists of what she calls natural "sensibility" for the emotions of others (which is closer to Hume's emotional contagion), but, as it is developed over successive stages of moral education and experience, it also subsumes more abstract and theoretical components like Smith's abstract reflective concord. The earliest roots of sympathy, for De Grouchy, arise in the affective states that newborns experience in response to pleasurable or painful stimuli. According to De Grouchy, these affective states have both localized and nonlocalized dimensions; there is the pain perceived as occurring in a particular body part that is injured but also a nonspecific negative affect which is general and nonlocalized. The nonspecific affective component, she argues, remains motivationally significant even without the localized component; this is why the mere memory or imagination of a pain can remain affectively significant, though usually to a lesser degree. This nonspecific affective component is the keystone of the bridge that De Grouchy builds across the self-other gap in early developmental

---

[9] For a related view with some critical disagreements with the Impartial Spectator view, see Maibom (2022).

cognition—for she argues that, due to the lack of an established borderline between infant and nurse in neonates, the nonspecific component can be triggered by a caregiver's fortunes as well.

De Grouchy defends a natural empiricist progression, as Schliesser explains (De Grouchy 2019; Schliesser 2019), which can be cultivated by experience and education, from the innate sensibility of the infant to her own pains and pleasures to the most abstract moral propositions. This progression begins in the complete dependency of the infant on the caregiver; because of the link between the caregiver's visible signs of affect and the character of their responses to the dependent infant, the infant quickly learns that the caregiver's obstacles are her obstacles, and the caregiver's joys are her joys. Infants *start out* coupled in dependency with their caregivers; as developmental psychologists have observed, it is only later—via an important cognitive milestone—that they manage to think of themselves as separate beings. Newborns do not even have a developed body schema that would allow them to determine where their body ends and the caregiver's begins—and recent neuroscientific research has even suggested that the infant's own body map might develop contemporaneously with maps of the bodies of others, which could be relevant to the emergence of imitation (Rochat 2009; Rochat and Botto 2021). Infants thus noninferentially share the joys and sorrows of their caregivers, because they are not yet capable of drawing a distinction between their own body and the body of their caregiver in the first place.

As parents of newborns often learn, this development is very gradual, beginning with separation anxiety, which often manifests between the age of six months to one year (Battaglia et al. 2017), and culminating in the selfish egocentricity of Piaget's "preoperational" stage of development, which occurs from the age of two to seven years (Steinbeis 2016). It is after this stage that we begin to see the more typical pattern of human mentalizing associated with mature ToM. At that stage, perhaps, more inferential mechanisms might be introduced for more theory-like social cognitive capacities; but on the sentimentalist picture these will be laid on top of the much deeper framework of affective other-regarding scaffolding, which has been gradually constructed beginning in the first days of life. The infant, moreover, learns to modify the caregiver's affect through communication, which further strengthens reciprocal coupling between the infant and caregiver's well-being at an age before the infant can conceive of itself as a separate self. For instance, crying or cooing causes the caregiver to become distressed or affectionate, which in turn helps the infant alleviate her hungers or pains. Dependency upon and affective interaction with others is thus the emotional origin of social cognition, rather than the conclusion of a theoretical argument.

As the infant develops an understanding of her own body, she further learns to associate pains and pleasures in her own body parts to the causes of pains and pleasures in the body of the caregiver. These links are sufficient to trigger the nonspecific component of affective sensibility upon seeing the caregiver's joy or distress, just as a memory or imagined scenario of our own pleasures or pains can trigger the nonspecific affective component in the absence of the localized one. As De Grouchy puts it:

> All physical pleasure, as all physical pain, produces in us a sensation composed of a particular sensation of pleasure in the organ that receives it immediately, and a general sensation of well-being. And the latter can be renewed at the sight of pleasure, as a painful one can at the sight of pain. We are, therefore, susceptible to feeling sympathy for physical pleasures that others experience, just as we are for their pains. (De Grouchy 2019, *Letter I*)

At this point, De Grouchy's account generally links up with Smith's. As our imaginative faculties develop, and we obtain more experience with the appropriateness or inappropriateness of various sympathetic and mentalizing attributions in our society, we learn and master more social nuisance variables, allowing us to modulate our other-directed affective associations acquired in childhood to suit the diverse circumstances of observed agents, even when their circumstances differ from our own.[10]

---

[10] This learning-based account, for what it's worth, also comes with an attractive account of moral error—reflective sympathy is likely to go wrong when we attempt to imagine what things are like for forms of social variation that our learning history has not prepared us to imaginatively simulate.

330 FROM DEEP LEARNING TO RATIONAL MACHINES

Empiricists in general, and De Grouchy in particular, have a great deal more to say about the transition from these generalized affective responses to more mature moral reasoning. The faculties we have discussed in previous chapters play key roles in these explanations. For example, De Grouchy emphasizes the roles of memory and imagination in cultivating and calibrating the sentiment of remorse. Merely imagining a misfortune of our own can be motivational, she reminds us, and given the affective projection from self-to-other which is presumed to emerge in infancy, the same goes for imagining the misfortunes of others that result from our own actions:

> Just as knowing that we have done something good becomes tied to our existence and makes it more pleasurable, the consciousness that we have caused some harm troubles our existence by causing us to experience feelings of regret and remorse that are upsetting, distressful, disturbing, and painful, even when the painful memory of the harm we caused is no longer distinct in our minds. (De Grouchy 2019, *Letter V*)

According to De Grouchy, these pangs of remorse for remembered or imagined harms done to others—rather than impersonal or abstract moral rules—form the grounds of moral reasoning in humans.

As the child cultivates greater sensibility to the affective responses of others and builds attachments to a larger and more diverse set of individuals, she obtains a greater understanding of her own self and of human psychology in general. De Grouchy invokes the standard mechanisms of Lockean abstraction to explain how children develop these more impersonalized ideas about the causes and consequences of affect. As De Grouchy puts it:

> Fear of remorse is enough to keep all men away from evil, either because all are at least a little acquainted with remorse, even for a small misdeed, or because imagination alone suffices to give an idea of all of the torments that result from remorse even to a person who has only ever done good—if indeed such a person even existed. The satisfaction that comes with good deeds and the terror of the memory of bad ones are both efficacious causes of behavior. Both are universal

sentiments and they are part of the principles and grounds of human morality. (De Grouchy 2019, *Letter V*)

By subtracting out the idiosyncrasies of individual situations leading to positive or negative affect in different individuals, we formulate abstract ideas of pleasure and pain. Like Smith, De Grouchy frequently invokes reflection as the process by which our empathetic processing becomes more abstract, where reflection is the act of repeatedly considering, prospectively and retrospectively, whether our take on a situation was appropriate. We might suppose that this is like repeatedly reimagining some set of social variables from different background contexts, to see whether our affective responses still derive the same verdicts. Though De Grouchy notes that not all humans advance to the final stages of moral development, fortunate education and theoretical scaffolding can help people attune these sentimental responses to still more abstract moral ideas like those of justice, fairness, and even the abstract concepts of good or evil that we find in the most intellectualized moral theory. This is the sense in which De Grouchy says that while "it is reason that teaches us what is just and unjust," this reason must be built on a foundation of sentiment that "asserts and ratifies it," and it is "originally from sentiment that reason acquires moral ideas and derives principles" (126).

Throughout the process, we never require a theoretical leap via a faculty of pure rationality in order to see the worth in others and to be (morally) motivated by their pain or suffering. Though our regard for others can be suppressed through miseducation or hostile social circumstances, its normal development is a maturation of the initial spark of affective sensibility formed between the infant and her first caregivers, combined with domain-general tendencies toward abstraction and reflection. Contrary to the rationalist tradition and attitudes, our individual sentiments and attachments are not countervailing concerns which must be held at bay by facts and reason,[11] but rather the soil in which to cultivate our more mature regard for moral behavior and the good of humanity in the abstract, or as we might put it

---

[11] For a recent version of a rationalist approach applied to AI ethics, see Leben (2017, 2018).

today, the sources of nuisance variation from which we extract invariant moral considerations in the first place.

To summarize, the genius of De Grouchy's sentimentalist approach is that it dries up the self-other Rubicon that obstructed other theories by locating the origins of social cognition in a developmental period before the gap exists. Furthermore, a certain degree of social or cultural variability is built into the approach. Because our affected responses are socially shaped by the culture of our upbringing and education, they can be tailored through learning into different refined sentiments and virtues that are appropriate to different cultures and traditions. For instance, Western children schooled on the virtues of autonomy and personal responsibility can be expected to structure their moral reasoning around virtues like sympathy, fairness, and justice, whereas other cultural traditions might cultivate other sentiments and values. Liu has argued, in fact, that although the Confucian moral tradition can also be understood in sentimentalist terms, it emphasizes different sentiments, such as commiseration, shame/disgust, and respect/deference (Liu 2017). We may also expect that a Grouchean approach to ethics is more flexible and self-correcting than formal rule-based approaches, as agents will self-correct their ethical behavior based on the affective responses of other agents to which they are attuned. The approach thus seems to offer numerous attractions among empiricist theories of moral psychology, which are directly related to its promise as a framework for developmentally serious AI.

7.4. A Grouchean developmentalist framework for modeling social cognition in artificial agents

While the reflective sentimentalist approach offers many benefits to contemporary moral psychology, it also offers productive guidance on how deep learning methods could be used to model more human-like social cognition. In practical terms, this could allow DNN-based agents to interact with humans more successfully, especially by learning from and reasoning about them in a more responsive and sensitive way. The approach would differ markedly in its initial stages from the more false-belief-centric, Machiavellian alternatives; specifically, we should backtrack further in cognitive development to the emergence of the affective and emotional responses emphasized by the sentimentalists in early infancy, and reboot from there with a more developmental robotics approach—an approach recommended recently and persuasively by the ethicist Peter Railton (2020), by developmental psychologists (Smith and Slone 2017), and by engineers in the area of developmental robotics (Cangelosi and Schlesinger 2015). This revised program can draw upon several more mature traditions in social robotics and affective computing, though the lessons will be applied in a new environment and put toward new goals. In particular, we must revisit the points made about reinforcement learning in Chapter 4 to consider how a sentimentalist approach to affect can inform a more multidimensional approach to valuation. To reprise, one of the biggest challenges in developing reinforcement learning–trained agents is the lack of a single objective reinforcement proxy (such as game score) for many domains. A sentimentalist approach would allow us to translate language about sentiments from the empiricist philosophy into reinforcement valuation signals in the artificial models. This could allow more flexible learning in new training domains by allowing novice agents to improve their affective responses by comparing them to the appraisals evinced by other, more experienced agents.

Such an adaptation of the sentimentalist/affective story fits well with the role of "intentions" in Ibn Sina's account of estimation explored in Chapter 4; in this case, the sentiments are understood in terms of innate and derived reward signals processed in response to social stimuli. Just as empiricists should be allowed to assume that certain environmental signals are rewarding from birth, it should also be granted that certain generic social cues could be rewarding from a very early age, such as body heat or the feeling of gentle caresses. To scaffold these innate attunements to social stimuli, it may be that we need only very domain-general tweaks to perception and interoception (of states like pain, pleasure, hunger, boredom, etc.)—the sorts of "interests" that we discussed in the adaptation of James on attention in Chapter 6. Together with other more generic biases such as an aversion to boredom and attraction to novel stimuli and successful predictions, agents might quickly scaffold more advanced social sentiments, such as a bias toward triadic gaze with caregivers (which could render learned attentional selection much more efficient via social guidance) or social acclaim (which often comes with hugs or other more basic rewards). In short, we may already have ample empiricist resources to draw upon, potentially allowing us to endow artificial agents with a richer repertoire of affective responses which could be quickly tailored to distinctively social stimuli through reinforcement learning and eventually developed into mature adult moral and social cognition, such as a sense of fairness and ability to engage in the simulation of a wide variety of perceptual and affective mental states, via cultural instruction and shaping by humans or other artificial agents.[12]

The first area that could be mined by a sentimentalist approach to deep social learning is the "affective computing" tradition, which is most associated with the work of Rosalind Picard. Affective computing has generally broader goals than those that concern us here; the area encompasses a wide variety of attempts to create machines that "recognize, express, model, communicate, and respond to emotional information" (Picard 2000:55). Many of these efforts, though not explicitly implemented in an artificial neural network (ANN)-based situation, could be borrowed or serve as inspiration for similar-performing tweaks to the developing DoGMA. As with some of the caveats made in Chapter 1, the goal is generally to "model" emotion and emotion detection rather than create artificial agents that actually "feel" emotions themselves—a goal about which Picard herself has often expressed skepticism. Even if it were physically possible, there may also be ethical reasons to avoid attempting to create artificial agents capable of experiencing affectively laden conscious states, as the experimentation process might involve a great deal of unavoidable artificial suffering (Metzinger 2021). The important goal for present purposes is modeling enough of the important difference-makers behind human (and animal) sentiments to allow us to create artificial agents that can learn and interact with other agents in a human-like way.

To enable artificial agents to learn these sentiments and forms of social cognition in a human-like way, it is again essential to provide them with the kind of ecologically structured experience characteristic

---

[12]   I am grateful for discussions with my student Martin Wally Wallace on this topic.

of human and animal development. This suggests a quite different approach to artificial moral agents than those adopted in the past. Rather than programming agents to recognize emotions using special sensors like skin conductance detectors or symbolic inferential rules, we should create agents that recognize emotions using only the same sorts of cues available to humans; rather than training machines to recognize emotions for their own sake, using an annotated training set, they should learn to identify emotional states in others as a side effect of the fact that they depend upon others to satisfy basic goals, which are best achieved by identifying the emotions of potential collaborators and competitors; rather than aiming to create agents that should react to social cues adaptively "out of the box," these artificial agents should, like humans and other intelligent animals, have rather longer "artificial neoteny," during which they are helpless and spend a great deal of their time merely observing the actions and interactions of caregivers (Bufill, Agustí, and Blesa 2011).

We may need to provide agents with artificial social cues like gaze direction, facial expressions, and gestures, but we probably do not need to give them innate domain-specific representations for them to display the appropriate behaviors with human-like learning sets. To return to the example of early preferences for faces, domain-general biases like a bias toward top-heavy visual patterns discussed at the beginning of this chapter, when combined with early and structured exposure to human faces, may be sufficient to scaffold a preference for human faces (Macchi Cassia, Turati, and Simion 2004). This is not to say that we should be raising robo-infants with human foster parents, but rather that we need to take seriously the role played by early interactions in scaffolding the social cognition of humans and animals, and attempt to replicate important aspects of those early experiences in artificial environments and structured training curricula.

Crucially, vanilla DNNs could be supplemented with a variety of multidimensional affective and emotional responses corresponding to empiricist "passions," enhancing the performance of reinforcement learning–trained agents. According to a powerful idea in the neuroscience and psychology of the emotions, emotional responses serve as "somatic markers," helping organisms detect and learn from the motivational significance of basic biological situations (Damasio 1996).

Antonio Damasio, in particular, has argued that these somatic markers can be elicited simply by the prospective consideration of an outcome and can guide decision-making and planning. This theory dovetails nicely with the general points made in earlier chapters about the role possibly played by Ibn Sina–like intentions in guiding reinforcement learning–based decision-making. Similar to intrinsic interests in the empiricism of William James, a basic suite of affective responses to situations like pain, pleasure, boredom, curiosity, fear, hunger, and physical comfort has always been considered among the "passions" on which empiricists have drawn to explain more sophisticated emotional responses that nativists might suppose are driven by innate ideas. Some empiricists have more recently argued that even these basic somatic markers are more shaped by previous experience than we might have supposed (Maia and McClelland 2004). Regardless, even if we take some set of somatic markers as basic, so long as they do not require innate ideas or concepts to be triggered, they are consistent with the Transformation Principle and would not be out of place in the empiricist tradition of reflective sentimentalism.

The field of deep learning faces challenges in productively exploiting these insights, however. In particular, agents may need intricately shaped bodies to compute responses effectively. Here again, nativism tempts with special allure, as proponents prioritize the role of evolution in ensuring organisms will tend to efficiently produce behaviors well-adapted to their typical range of natural environments. But empiricists have not and need not deny the importance of evolution, nor do they need to deny that organisms typically end up well-adapted to their environments. To reprise the theme of Chapter 1, the disagreement between nativism and origin empiricism concerns whether this tendency toward adaptedness is best secured through innate domain-specific ideas and learning rules. If it turns out that the domain-specific evolutionary tuning needed to secure reliable, efficient adaptiveness comes from specializations of the body to produce certain types of experiences—through greater sensory acuity to some range of signals (as with intrinsic interests, such as toward loud sounds or certain frequencies of light) or through automatic affective responses (such as toward physical caresses or against boredom)—then experience shaped that outcome, rather than innate ideas or domain-specific rules. Regardless, the sorts of solutions suggested here require machine learning theorists to take the sensory organs and the body more generally much more seriously in future modeling. They might, for example, explore evolutionary parameter search to configure artificial bodies that shape artificial agents' input experiences in ways that make reliable adaptedness to particular environments more likely. Such an approach was recently recommended by roboticists Emma Hart and Léni Le Goff, among others, as an effective way to bootstrap cultural learning in artificial agents (Hart and Le Goff 2022). Some social roboticists are in fact already investigating how modeling the affect of other agents can allow artificial agents to model sympathy, making them, in turn, more effective caregivers and social companions for human users (Paiva et al. 2017).

Applying these insights in a deep-learning-focused research program might begin as a continuation of controlled rearing studies, in which artificial agents driven by DNN-based architectures can interact with one another to pursue goals in simulated environments by sending social cues to one another. Such a program could begin by endowing these agents with more robust artificial sensory organs and bodies that produce affective responses according to relatively generic environmental circumstances. The agents could then be fine-tuned on more specific social situations through social learning. Variants of this approach might be pursued by scaffolding the Wood-style artificial chick experiments mentioned in the previous chapter to higher levels of ontogeny in richer virtual environments, perhaps in tandem with research on raising reinforcement-based or self-supervised learning in virtual environments. Indeed, both approaches, with social-learning agents in virtual environments, are already being pursued at DeepMind by separate research teams (Christiano et al. 2017; DeepMind Interactive Agents Team et al. 2022). Combining these efforts with those using early tests of social cognition from infant and animal cognition research areas as enhancements of systematic testing in virtual environments, such as the Animal-AI Olympics platform (Beyret et al. 2019; Crosby et al. 2019), might yield further insights.

We might then return to some of the most advanced social behaviors highlighted by rationalists, but now with a toolkit containing more powerful building materials to draw upon. The kinds of false-belief attributions modeled by ToMNet could be set as a goal which we would expect to emerge from such agents, but only relatively late in artificial development, perhaps as a result of the affective experiences of being fooled or seeing others react to being fooled by deceptive situations and agents. The replication crisis in early infant ToM research suggests that false-belief attribution really does only emerge around age four to six years in human children, around the time that explicit linguistic resources to describe mental states are mastered (Rakoczy 2017). In other words, we would expect these capacities to be learned only through the scaffolding provided by many earlier capacities like affect identification, triadic gaze, and possibly even linguistic communication involving propositional attitude words like 'belief', 'desire', and 'intent'.

Ultimately, the approach to social cognition suggested earlier sets up an empiricist response to the nativist challenge to create artificial agents that learn like humans. Whereas nativists hope to create more human-like learning by packing in more innate theories or domain-specific learning rules and representational primitives, the empiricist perspective suggests instead that this high-level knowledge is derived from social interaction with other agents, especially through imitation and cultural instruction. It is true, empiricists hold, that explicit symbols play an important role in scaffolding human-like learning; however, as empiricists such as Hume and Locke long maintained, those explicit symbols are provided by linguistic and cultural interaction with other agents rather than an innate endowment. Artificial agents bootstrapped to acquire an ability to track the gaze, sentiment, and mental states of others could potentially use their interactive communication to scaffold a deeper understanding of new representations and problem-solving strategies through imitation and explicit instruction. According to this empiricist perspective, the uniquely human reservoir of knowledge that explains our ability to speak complex languages, discover and continuously improve scientific theories, create intricate technology, and form large social groups and political structures is not the product of innate endowment, but rather our distinctive ability to attune affectively to, acquire, and extend human culture.

This empiricist proposal regarding the cultural origins of social cognition raises a host of other questions. In particular, do our nearest non-human relatives, such as chimpanzees, have similar cultural-learning abilities (Toth et al. 1993)? If not, what then makes humans so uniquely effective at culture-based learning? Human culture is often described in this context as enjoying a distinctive and powerful "ratchet effect"; each generation of humans can use their associative learning abilities to modestly improve the concepts and strategies passed on to them by their caregivers and teachers; this boost can then be locked into place like a ratcheting wrench, and passed on, in turn, to the next generation for further improvement (Tennie, Call, and Tomasello 2009). A corollary research program has focused extensively on some of the earliest examples of uniquely human cultural transmission, such as flint-knapping to create arrowheads and stone knives, to try to determine whether these skills can be acquired by nonhuman animals, as well as which aspects of our ability to manufacture these technologies (if any) might be uniquely human. These authors' recent recommendation of "artificial flint-knapping" models, which use GANs to model key aspects of the human flint-knapping process, stands as an illustration of such focus and its extension to AI. Though these experiments are also in their earliest stages, a proof of concept has already been developed in a three-dimensional artificial environment; by programming in key variables involved in the flint-knapping process, the GAN-based model accurately predicted the length, width, volume, and shape of stone flakes removed in the actual knapping process (Orellana Figueroa et al. 2021). These initial steps point the way toward more ambitious experiments in artificial cultural transmission that are consistent with and can in turn further support the DoGMA's ascent into the most abstract forms of culturally transmitted human knowledge.

The stakes here are high. If we could create artificial agents that could learn from one another and from humans in a cultural, ratchet-like manner, then we might be able to create agents that could not only learn from us in the way that human children do, but that could also reverse the direction of learning, by using their superior powers for perceptual abstraction to push beyond the limits of human knowledge and teach us to see fundamentally new patterns, as well. Some degree of this is already happening, if indirectly, through AlphaZero and

MuZero; humans are reverse-engineering the strategies these systems use to trounce humans to derive fundamentally new strategies and integrate them into the cultural theory of Go and chess (Sadler and Regan 2019). Although we are, in essence, already using this turbo-powered ratchet ourselves, this method of applying deep learning to augment our own body of culturally derived knowledge still depends upon the flexibility of human ratcheting and creative reverse-engineering. Imagine if these networks could model our own understanding of a problem, drawing our attention toward aspects of the situation most salient for the acquisition of new and more powerful problem-solving strategies. We can, in fact, already imagine how simple versions of this could be implemented with existing technology: AlphaGo's smaller policy network in some sense modeled the likelihood that a human player would make a particular move; it would be trivial to estimate differences between likely human moves and what AlphaGo regarded as the optimal strategy, or to add a coaching subroutine on top that coached the human player's attention toward more promising moves. Actually explaining why these moves were superior in terms of gameplay principles exceeds the limits of current technology, but with recent advances in large language models such as the GPT series and PaLM, it is no longer absurd to suppose that passable verbal explanations for novel strategies might be just over the horizon.

In particular, the role of "chain-of-thought" prompting in PaLM's breakthrough performance on a variety of verbal tasks thought to be difficult or impossible for DNNs suggests that we are on the cusp of a breakthrough here. In particular, PaLM did markedly better on arithmetic word problems of the sort given to elementary school children when provided with chain-of-thought prompts. For example, when the model was given arithmetic word problems without any hints or structural advice, it tended to give incorrect answers. However, when it was given prompts suggesting which quantities were relevant and structuring the order of operations in which the problem could be solved—in the way one might guide a human child to complete more complex math problems using scaffolding from simpler problems earlier in the curriculum—its answers become much more accurate. Even more impressively, the model could then generate its own novel chain-of-thought prompts for answers in later experiments, which continued to enjoy the subsequent accuracy benefits. Importantly, if the process could be replicated for other types of problem-solving—and perhaps even laid on top of another faculty model that used a memory or imagination-like module to solve a problem—then the models might have the ability to scaffold human performance with explicit linguistic guidance in a ratchet-like way.

Even more suggestively, some of the strongest-performing language models at the time of this chapter's composition are fine-tined using reinforcement learning on human feedback (RLHF). This includes ChatGPT from OpenAI as well as a new RLHF-trained system from AnthropicAI, both of which outperform previously impressive language models on a host of metrics (Bai et al. 2022; Glaese et al. 2022; Liang et al. 2022; Stiennon et al. 2020). Even though the feedback sources on which these models are trained are much less sophisticated and multidimensional than the ones I proposed in this chapter—they tend to rely on simple binary evaluations like a thumbs up or thumbs down, or scales of how helpful and harmless a response has been—the improvements in performance, especially in interactive dialogue with human agents, are impressive. These breakthroughs suggest that the next steps to take in the development of more human-like AI would be to find ways to leverage a wider range of qualitatively distinct valences of human feedback. For example, we might hope that language models could be attuned to a variety of pragmatic implicatures from human agents as to ways in which its output was suitable or unsuitable on a range of different attributes that could be used for more multidimensional reinforcement learning: whether the feedback was truthful or misleading, pleasant or unpleasant, brief or verbose, aesthetically pleasing or clunky, and so on.[13] A system that could extract these forms of trainable feedback directly from the text of dialogue with human agents—perhaps by having certain words trigger certain affective markers, which in turn modulated subsequent learning, in the way that shame, surprise, or social praise modulates learning in humans—would have a limitless and powerful source of cultural training data available to improve its performance.

---

[13] I am grateful to Susanne Riehemann for discussion on these points.

To conclude by considering our ability to model distinctively moral decision-making, the empiricist hopes that agents endowed with a suite of affective responses, with language-mediated cultural engagement with other agents, and with the other domain general faculties discussed in previous chapters will be well-placed to bootstrap their own abstract, rule-like moral decision-making by controlling for differences in each agent's individual social positions. Specifically, differences in preferences, origins, or demographic factors would be treated as social nuisances that must be abstracted away from and controlled for in more abstract social simulations, thereby enabling artificial moral agents to model the human capacity for "impartial observer" type judgments of the sort emphasized by Smith and De Grouchy as the pinnacle of moral development.[14] For too long we have been building artificial moral agents as though they were solipsists growing up in isolation, adding moral reasoning as an afterthought. However, social learning should be seen as the bedrock of experience from which moral abstractions are derived.

To summarize this approach to human moral development, Songhorian states Smith's attitude expertly:

> If a person were to grow up in isolation, her original passions and desires—although present—would not occupy her thoughts (*TMS*, III.1.3) and she would have neither the need nor the spur to develop her conscience. It is only within a given community that human beings can both experience their sympathy toward others (*TMS*, I.i.1.3–4) and understand that others view them from the same kind of standpoint (*TMS*, II.ii.2.2). From such experiences, as we have seen, one can start to abstract and to judge herself according to how real spectators would judge her. It is by abstraction that the impartial spectator emerges as a figure of conscience. And yet, the ability

---

[14] Recent work in psychology and neuroscience suggests that animals and humans might represent their own and others' abstract locations in "social space" by repurposing some of the same psychological or neural structures which we discussed in previous chapters as performing roles attributed in perception, spatial navigation, and episodic memory (Gordon 2021; Omer et al. 2018; Schafer and Schiller 2018). The multipurpose function of these structures for spatial, temporal, memorial, and social reasoning is another piece of evidence that domain-general computations can accomplish many specialized domain-specific functions.

to abstract and to reason upon one's emotions is not as primitive as emotions themselves are. (2022:671)

Put another way, the other domain-general faculties previously discussed—such as memory, imagination, and attention—already provide sufficient resources to help complete the final bootstrapping toward the "disentanglement" of moral positions and the achievement of an impartial perspective on moral situations. The moral philosopher Antti Kauppinen in particular has argued that the impartial observer perspective in Smith's reflective sentimentalism should be understood as a specialization of the faculty of the imagination, of a learned ability to refocus attention on only the aspects of a situation which would be regarded as morally relevant by an impartial observer (Kauppinen 2010, 2017). An agent that could, while representing particular attachments to the affectively-significant aspects of a situation, also learn to modulate its attentional resources toward the abstract aspects of the situation that an impartial observer would regard as morally relevant, could be said to model the tension between our intuitive and reflective moral decision-making systems in a rich way indeed.

7.5. Summary

In this final chapter, I reviewed debates in social and moral cognition in psychology and AI, drawing a contrast between Machiavellian "cold calculation" approaches that have been popular in rationalist circles and sentimentalist approaches more popular in the empiricist camp. I reviewed progress that had been made on the rationalist side, but suggested that backtracking to model affects and more multidimensional reinforcement learning may be a more promising approach to model more aspects of human-like social and moral reasoning in DNN-based agents. I argued that the sentimentalist theories of Adam Smith and especially Sophie de Grouchy are well-suited to provide inspiration and ideological guidance to such research programs, and I reviewed early indicators that cultural feedback from humans, as found in chain-of-thought prompting and RLHF, already demonstrate the promise of this empiricism-inspired research agenda. Though these are only early and simple forms of learning from human social interaction and cultural instruction, they should inspire optimism that empiricist approaches will continue to make steady and astounding progress on modeling even the most complex forms of human social and cultural cognition in the years to come.

Epilogue

Deep learning's skeptics hold that empiricists, in attempting to model the rational mind, are entitled to begin with only one or two learning rules, and their models must learn everything else from experience. Whatever the merits of this radical empiricist view, I hope to have illustrated that it does not capture the dominant perspective of researchers in deep learning. Instead, much of the most successful research in deep learning is motivated by and in turn bolsters a more moderate empiricist view—one shared by the majority of philosophical empiricists from the history of philosophy—which holds that abstract knowledge is derived through the cooperation and interaction of active, domain-general faculties. Like the historical empiricists, they eschew innate ideas, rather than innate faculties. Indeed, there are so many examples of this moderate empiricism alive and well in deep learning research today that one could fill an entire book with examples.

I hope to also have illustrated that quite a bit more abstraction and rational decision-making can be captured by such faculty-inspired models than we might have supposed. Indeed, they can model some aspects of the loftiest heights of human rationality, and we should expect much more rapid progress in the years to come. However, most of the examples of faculty-inspired models reviewed in this book were one-offs—they only demonstrated the gains that can be obtained by the introduction of one or two faculty-like modules to an architecture. Rather than the next steps in artificial intelligence requiring more domain-specific innate knowledge, the next breakthroughs are likelier to be achieved by integrating more of these domain-general faculty modules into a coherent and cooperative faculty architecture of the sort envisioned by the historical empiricists. As we attempt to do so, we should expect that Control Problems will become more pressing, and engineers should begin preparing countermeasures now. I discussed

From Deep Learning to Rational Machines. Cameron J. Buckner, Oxford University Press.
© Oxford University Press 2024. DOI: 10.1093/oso/9780197653302.003.0008

some early ideas in this direction especially in Chapters 6 and 7, in the discussion of attention and social cognition.

None of this should imply that I think that we are on the precipice of achieving full human-like intelligence and rationality in an artificial system. While we should not downplay the rapid and astounding progress that has been achieved over the last decade, there are still two fundamental causes for concern that I have not fully addressed here. First, we might think that deep learning agents will need a fundamental change of course to model causal reasoning, a charge pressed most strongly by Judea Pearl. I reviewed throughout the chapters early moves toward modeling causal knowledge in deep neural networks (DNNs), and we might expect that much of the solution will depend upon using imagination-like modules to simulate future and counterfactual situations. Nevertheless, I think the empirical jury is still out on whether these scattered successes imply that more thorough solutions are on the horizon. Indeed, I think a whole book of similar length and complexity could be dedicated to causal inference in DNNs, so I have avoided passing strong verdicts on this subject here.

Second, I pressed in Chapter 7 that modeling social and moral cognition accurately will require deep learning to backtrack toward modeling more emotional and affective responses. The dominant empiricist line on social and moral cognition has always tended toward sentimentalism, emphasizing the role of affect and emotion in bootstrapping a mature faculty of empathy, which in turn would allow more abstract and theory-like moral and social cognition. It is unlikely that we can model this system in its full flexibility without first modeling the embodied, affective, and emotional reactions that bootstrap these processes in humans. And until we can model these processes more accurately, there should be safety and alignment concerns about some of the most ambitious ideas for deploying these machines in high-stakes contexts or in situations where they would socially interact with humans. I have not focused on those practical safety and alignment concerns here, but I hope that the discussion in Chapters 6 and 7 will be useful to researchers who want to focus on more specific use cases and dangers.

On the whole, I hope that the book has illustrated that rather than running out of ideas and hitting a wall, deep learning is just hitting its stride. I hope to have also illustrated to engineers that the history of philosophy, interpreted and applied to present debates with care, can be a useful source of challenge and inspiration for the next generation of technical achievements. The ideas of many philosophers may be dismissed as wild speculation, but I have provided numerous examples in this book of cases where, for the first time in history, it seems like we have the engineering prowess to turn their wildest fancies into useful tools. Although I focused mostly on Western European philosophers here, as there is a direct link of descent from their empiricism to contemporary machine learning theory and their names appear most often in the computer science debates, I look forward to additional cycles of this conversation, and I especially hope that scholars will mine lessons from other philosophical traditions for future engineering achievements.

References

Abdou, Mostafa, Ana Valeria Gonzalez, Mariya Toneva, Daniel Hershcovich, and Anders Søgaard. 2021. "Does Injecting Linguistic Structure into Language Models Lead to Better Alignment with Brain Recordings?" *ArXiv Preprint ArXiv:2101.12608.*

Achille, Alessandro, and Stefano Soatto. 2018. "Emergence of Invariance and Disentanglement in Deep Representations." *Journal of Machine Learning Research* 19(50):1–34.

Aharoni, Eyal, Walter Sinnott-Armstrong, and Kent A. Kiehl. 2014. "What's Wrong? Moral Understanding in Psychopathic Offenders." *Journal of Research in Personality* 53:175–81. doi: 10.1016/j.jrp.2014.10.002.

Aizawa, Kenneth. 2003. *The Systematicity Arguments.* Amsterdam: Kluwer Academic.

Alexander, Scott. 2022. "My Bet: AI Size Solves Flubs." *Astral Codex Ten.* Retrieved June 20, 2022. https://astralcodexten.substack.com/p/my-bet-ai-size-solves-flubs.

Allport, Alan. 1993. "Attention and Control: Have We Been Asking the Wrong Questions? A Critical Review of Twenty-Five Years." *Attention and Performance* 14:183–218.

AlQuraishi, Mohammed. 2019. "AlphaFold at CASP13." *Bioinformatics* 35(22):4862–65. doi: 10.1093/bioinformatics/btz422.

Alzantot, Moustafa, Yash Sharma, Ahmed Elgohary, Bo-Jhang Ho, Mani Srivastava, and Kai-Wei Chang. 2018. "Generating Natural Language Adversarial Examples." *ArXiv Preprint ArXiv:1804.07998.*

Amodei, Dario, and Jack Clark. 2016. "Faulty Reward Functions in the Wild." *OpenAI.* Retrieved October 14, 2019 (https://openai.com/blog/faulty-reward-functions/).

Anderson, John R., and Christian J. Lebiere. 2014. *The Atomic Components of Thought.* New York: Psychology Press.

Anderson, Michael L. 2010. "Neural Reuse: A Fundamental Organizational Principle of the Brain." *The Behavioral and Brain Sciences* 33(4):245–66; discussion 266–313. doi: 10.1017/S0140525X10000853.

Anderson, Michael L. 2014. *After Phrenology: Neural Reuse and the Interactive Brain.* Cambridge, MA: MIT Press.

Andreoli, Jean-Marc. 2019. "Convolution, Attention and Structure Embedding." *ArXiv Preprint ArXiv:1905.01289.*

Andrews, K. 2005. "Chimpanzee Theory of Mind: Looking in All the Wrong Places?" *Mind & Language* 20(5):521–36.

Andrews, K. 2012. *Do Apes Read Minds?: Toward a New Folk Psychology.* MIT Press.

Antonelli, G. Aldo. 2010. "Notions of Invariance for Abstraction Principles." *Philosophia Mathematica* 18(3):276–92.

Antonello, Richard, Javier S. Turek, Vy Vo, and Alexander Huth. 2021. "Low-Dimensional Structure in the Space of Language Representations Is Reflected in Brain Responses." Pp. 8332–44 in *Advances in Neural Information Processing Systems.* Vol. 34. Curran Associates. https://proc eedings.neurips.cc/paper_files/paper/2021/hash/464074179972cbbd75a39 abc6954cd12-Abstract.html.

Apperly, Ian A., and Stephen A. Butterfill. 2009. "Do Humans Have Two Systems to Track Beliefs and Belief-like States?" *Psychological Review* 116(4):953–70. doi: 10.1037/a0016923.

Ariew, Andre. 1996. "Innateness and Canalization." *Philosophy of Science* 63:S19–27.

Aronowitz, Sara, and Tania Lombrozo. 2020. *Learning through Simulation.* Ann Arbor: University of Michigan.

Aslin, Richard N. 2007. "What's in a Look?" *Developmental Science* 10(1):48–53.

Baars, Bernard J. 2005. "Global Workspace Theory of Consciousness: Toward a Cognitive Neuroscience of Human Experience." *Progress in Brain Research* 150:45–53.

Bachmanov, Alexander, Natalia P. Bosak, Cailu Lin, Ichiro Matsumoto, Makoto Ohmoto, Danielle R. Reed, and Theodore M. Nelson. 2014. "Genetics of Taste Receptors." *Current Pharmaceutical Design* 20(16):2669–83.

Bahdanau, Dzmitry, Kyunghyun Cho, and Yoshua Bengio. 2014. "Neural Machine Translation by Jointly Learning to Align and Translate." *ArXiv Preprint ArXiv:1409.0473.*

Bahdanau, Dzmitry, Harm de Vries, Timothy J. O'Donnell, Shikhar Murty, Philippe Beaudoin, Yoshua Bengio, and Aaron Courville. 2020. "CLOSURE: Assessing Systematic Generalization of CLEVR Models." *ArXiv:1912.05783 [Cs].*

Bai, Yuntao, Andy Jones, Kamal Ndousse, Amanda Askell, Anna Chen, Nova DasSarma, Dawn Drain, Stanislav Fort, Deep Ganguli, and Tom Henighan. 2022. "Training a Helpful and Harmless Assistant with Reinforcement Learning from Human Feedback." *ArXiv Preprint ArXiv:2204.05862.*

Baier, Annette C. 1993. "Hume: The Reflective Women's Epistemologist?" Pp. 35–50 in *A Mind of One's Own: Feminist Essays on Reason and Objectivity,* edited by L. Antony and C. Witt. Boulder, CO: Westview Press.

Baier, Annette C. 2010. "Hume's Touchstone." *Hume Studies* 36(1):51–60.

Baillargeon, Renée, David Buttelmann, and Victoria Southgate. 2018. "Invited Commentary: Interpreting Failed Replications of Early False-Belief Findings: Methodological and Theoretical Considerations." *Cognitive Development* 46:112–24.

Baird, Benjamin, Jonathan Smallwood, Michael D. Mrazek, Julia W. Y. Kam, Michael S. Franklin, and Jonathan W. Schooler. 2012. "Inspired by Distraction: Mind Wandering Facilitates Creative Incubation." *Psychological Science* 23(10):1117–22.

Baker, Chris L., Rebecca Saxe, and Joshua B. Tenenbaum. 2009. "Action Understanding as Inverse Planning." *Cognition* 113(3):329–49.

Baker, Chris L., and Joshua B. Tenenbaum. 2014. "Modeling Human Plan Recognition Using Bayesian Theory of Mind." *Plan, Activity, and Intent Recognition: Theory and Practice* 7:177–204.

Baldi, Pierre, Peter Sadowski, and Daniel Whiteson. 2014. "Searching for Exotic Particles in High-Energy Physics with Deep Learning." *Nature Communications* 5(1):1–9.

Baldwin, Dare A. 1993. "Early Referential Understanding: Infants' Ability to Recognize Referential Acts for What They Are." *Developmental Psychology* 29(5):832–43. doi: 10.1037/0012-1649.29.5.832.

Balestriero, Randall, Jerome Pesenti, and Yann LeCun. 2021. "Learning in High Dimension Always Amounts to Extrapolation." *ArXiv Preprint ArXiv:2110.09485.*

Banino, Andrea, Caswell Barry, Benigno Uria, Charles Blundell, Timothy Lillicrap, Piotr Mirowski, Alexander Pritzel, Martin J. Chadwick, Thomas Degris, and Joseph Modayil. 2018. "Vector-Based Navigation Using Grid-Like Representations in Artificial Agents." *Nature* 557(7705):429–33.

Baron-Cohen, Simon, Alan M. Leslie, and Uta Frith. 1985. "Does the Autistic Child Have a 'Theory of Mind'?" *Cognition* 21(1):37–46.

Barrett, David, Felix Hill, Adam Santoro, Ari Morcos, and Timothy Lillicrap. 2018. "Measuring Abstract Reasoning in Neural Networks." Pp. 511–20 in *International Conference on Machine Learning.* PMLR. http://proceedings. mlr.press/v80/barrett18a.html.

Barry, Daniel N., and Bradley C. Love. 2023. "A Neural Network Account of Memory Replay and Knowledge Consolidation." *Cerebral Cortex* 33(1):83–95. doi: 10.1093/cercor/bhac054.

Barsalou, Lawrence W. 1999. "Perceptual Symbol Systems." *Behavioral and Brain Sciences* 22(4):577–660.

Bartlett, F. C. 1932. *Remembering: A Study in Experimental and Social Psychology.* Cambridge: Cambridge University Press.

Bateson, Patrick, and Gabriel Horn. 1994. "Imprinting and Recognition Memory: A Neural Net Model." *Animal Behaviour* 48(3):695–715. doi: 10.1006/anbe.1994.1289.

Battaglia, Marco, Gabrielle Garon-Carrier, Sylvana M. Côté, Ginette Dionne, Evelyne Touchette, Frank Vitaro, Richard E. Tremblay, and Michel Boivin. 2017. "Early Childhood Trajectories of Separation Anxiety: Bearing on Mental Health, Academic Achievement, and Physical Health from Mid-Childhood to Preadolescence." *Depression and Anxiety* 34(10):918–27.

Battaglia, Peter W., Jessica B. Hamrick, Victor Bapst, Alvaro Sanchez-Gonzalez, Vinicius Zambaldi, Mateusz Malinowski, Andrea Tacchetti, David Raposo, Adam Santoro, and Ryan Faulkner. 2018. "Relational Inductive Biases, Deep Learning, and Graph Networks." *ArXiv Preprint ArXiv:1806.01261.*

Bechtel, William. 2008. *Mental Mechanisms: Philosophical Perspectives on Cognitive Neuroscience.* Mahwah, NJ: Lawrence Erlbaum Associates.

Bechtel, William, and Adele Abrahamsen. 2002. *Connectionism and the Mind: Parallel Processing, Dynamics, and Evolution in Networks.* Malden, MA: Blackwell.

Bender, Emily M., Timnit Gebru, Angelina McMillan-Major, and Shmargaret Shmitchell. 2021. "On the Dangers of Stochastic Parrots: Can Language Models Be Too Big?." Pp. 610–23 in *Proceedings of the 2021 ACM Conference on Fairness, Accountability, and Transparency.* https://aclanthology.org/2020.acl-main.463/.

Bender, Emily M., and Alexander Koller. 2020. "Climbing towards NLU: On Meaning, Form, and Understanding in the Age of Data." Pp. 5185–98 in *Proceedings of the 58th Annual Meeting of the Association for Computational Linguistics.*

Bengio, Yoshua. 2009. "Learning Deep Architectures for AI." *Foundations and Trends® in Machine Learning* 2(1):1–127.

Bengio, Yoshua. 2017. "The Consciousness Prior." *ArXiv Preprint ArXiv:1709.08568.*

Bengio, Yoshua, and Olivier Delalleau. 2011. "On the Expressive Power of Deep Architectures." Pp. 18–36 in *International Conference on Algorithmic Learning Theory.* Springer.

Bengio, Yoshua, Yann Lecun, and Geoffrey Hinton. 2021. "Deep Learning for AI." *Communications of the ACM* 64(7):58–65.

Bengio, Yoshua, Gregoire Mesnil, Yann Dauphin, and Salah Rifai. 2013. "Better Mixing via Deep Representations." Pp. 552–60 in *International Conference on Machine Learning.* PMLR.

Bennett, Jonathan. 1978. "Some Remarks about Concepts." *Behavioral and Brain Sciences* 1(4):557–60.

Ben-Younes, Hedi, Rémi Cadene, Matthieu Cord, and Nicolas Thome. 2017. "Mutan: Multimodal Tucker Fusion for Visual Question Answering." Pp. 2612–20 in *Proceedings of the IEEE International Conference on Computer Vision.*

Berk, Laura E. 1992. "Children's Private Speech: An Overview of Theory and the Status of Research." Pp. 17–53 in *Private Speech: From Social*

Interaction to Self-Regulation, edited by R. M. Diaz and L. E. Berk. New York: Psychology Press.

Berkeley, George. 1710. *A Treatise Concerning the Principles of Human Knowledge*. Dublin: RS Bear.

Bermúdez, José Luis. 2003. *Thinking without Words*. Oxford: Oxford University Press.

Bernardi, Silvia, Marcus K. Benna, Mattia Rigotti, Jérôme Munuera, Stefano Fusi, and C. Daniel Salzman. 2020. "The Geometry of Abstraction in the Hippocampus and Prefrontal Cortex." *Cell* 183(4):954–67.e21. doi: 10.1016/j.cell.2020.09.031.

Berns, Karsten, and Jochen Hirth. 2006. "Control of Facial Expressions of the Humanoid Robot Head ROMAN." Pp. 3119–24 in *2006 IEEE/RSJ International Conference on Intelligent Robots and Systems*. IEEE.

Berwick, Robert C., and Noam Chomsky. 2016. *Why Only Us: Language and Evolution*. Cambridge, MA: MIT Press.

Berwick, Robert C., and Noam Chomsky. 2017. "Why Only Us: Recent Questions and Answers." *Journal of Neurolinguistics* 43:166–77. doi: 10.1016/j.jneuroling.2016.12.002.

Beyret, Benjamin, José Hernández-Orallo, Lucy Cheke, Marta Halina, Murray Shanahan, and Matthew Crosby. 2019. "The Animal-Ai Environment: Training and Testing Animal-Like Artificial Cognition." *ArXiv Preprint ArXiv:1909.07483*.

Blakemore, S. J., D. Wolpert, and C. Frith. 2000. *Why Can't You Tickle Yourself? NeuroReport: For Rapid Communication of Neuroscience Research* 11(11):R11–R16.

Block, Ned. 1980. "Troubles with Functionalism." *Readings in Philosophy of Psychology* 1:268–305.

Block, Ned. 1995. "How Heritability Misleads about Race." *Cognition* 56(2):99–128.

Blundell, Charles, Benigno Uria, Alexander Pritzel, Yazhe Li, Avraham Ruderman, Joel Z. Leibo, Jack Rae, Daan Wierstra, and Demis Hassabis. 2016. "Model-Free Episodic Control." *ArXiv Preprint ArXiv:1606.04460*.

Boesch, C. 2007. "What Makes Us Human (Homo Sapiens)? The Challenge of Cognitive Cross-Species Comparison." *Journal of Comparative Psychology* 121(3):227–40.

Boesch, Christophe. 2010. "Away from Ethnocentrism and Anthropocentrism: Towards a Scientific Understanding of 'What Makes Us Human.'" *Behavioral and Brain Sciences* 33(2–3):86–87.

BonJour, Laurence, and Ernest Sosa. 2003. *Epistemic Justification: Internalism vs. Externalism, Foundations vs. Virtues*. Oxford: Wiley-Blackwell.

Bonnen, Tyler, Daniel L. K. Yamins, and Anthony D. Wagner. 2021. "When the Ventral Visual Stream Is Not Enough: A Deep Learning Account of Medial Temporal Lobe Involvement in Perception." *Neuron* 109(17):2755–66.e6. doi: 10.1016/j.neuron.2021.06.018.

Boone, Worth, and Gualtiero Piccinini. 2016. "Mechanistic Abstraction." *Philosophy of Science* 83(5):686–97.

Botvinick, Matthew, David G. T. Barrett, Peter Battaglia, Nando de Freitas, Darshan Kumaran, Joel Z. Leibo, Timothy Lillicrap, Joseph Modayil, Shakir Mohamed, and Neil C. Rabinowitz. 2017. "Building Machines That Learn and Think for Themselves." *Behavioral and Brain Sciences* 40:26–28.

Botvinick, Matthew, Jane X. Wang, Will Dabney, Kevin J. Miller, and Zeb Kurth-Nelson. 2020. "Deep Reinforcement Learning and Its Neuroscientific Implications." *Neuron* 107(4):603–16. doi: 10.1016/j.neuron.2020.06.014.

Bowers, Jeffrey S., Gaurav Malhotra, Marin Dujmović, Milton Llera Montero, Christian Tsvetkov, Valerio Biscione, Guillermo Puebla, Federico Adolfi, John E. Hummel, and Rachel F. Heaton. 2022. "Deep Problems with Neural Network Models of Human Vision." *Behavioral and Brain Sciences* 1–74. https://www.cambridge.org/core/journals/behavioral-and-brain-sciences/article/abs/deep-problems-with-neural-network-models-of-human-vision/ABCE483EE95E80315058BB262DCA26A9.

Bowman, Samuel R. 2022. *The Dangers of Underclaiming: Reasons for Caution When Reporting How NLP Systems Fail.* arXiv:2110.08300. doi: 10.48550/arXiv.2110.08300.

Boyd, Richard. 1991. "Realism, Anti-Foundationalism and the Enthusiasm for Natural Kinds." *Philosophical Studies* 61(1):127–48.

Boyd, Richard. 1999. "Kinds, Complexity and Multiple Realization." *Philosophical Studies* 95(1):67–98.

Bracci, Stefania, J. Brendan Ritchie, Ioannis Kalfas, and Hans P. Op de Beeck. 2019. "The Ventral Visual Pathway Represents Animal Appearance over Animacy, Unlike Human Behavior and Deep Neural Networks." *Journal of Neuroscience* 39(33):6513–25. doi: 10.1523/JNEUROSCI.1714-18.2019.

Broadbent, D. E. 1958. *Perception and Communication.* Elmsford, NY: Pergamon Press.

Brown, Tom, Benjamin Mann, Nick Ryder, Melanie Subbiah, Jared D. Kaplan, Prafulla Dhariwal, Arvind Neelakantan, Pranav Shyam, Girish Sastry, Amanda Askell, Sandhini Agarwal, Ariel Herbert-Voss, Gretchen Krueger, Tom Henighan, Rewon Child, Aditya Ramesh, Daniel Ziegler, Jeffrey Wu, Clemens Winter, Chris Hesse, Mark Chen, Eric Sigler, Mateusz Litwin, Scott Gray, Benjamin Chess, Jack Clark, Christopher Berner, Sam McCandlish, Alec Radford, Ilya Sutskever, and Dario Amodei. 2020. "Language Models Are Few-Shot Learners." Pp. 1877–1901 in *Advances in Neural Information Processing Systems.* Vol. 33. Curran Associates.

Bruna, Joan, and Stéphane Mallat. 2011. "Classification with Scattering Operators." Pp. 1561–66 in *CVPR 2011.* IEEE.

Buckner, Cameron. 2013. "Morgan's Canon, Meet Hume's Dictum: Avoiding Anthropofabulation in Cross-Species Comparisons." *Biology & Philosophy* 28(5):853–71.

Buckner, Cameron. 2015. "A Property Cluster Theory of Cognition." *Philosophical Psychology* 28(3):307–36.

Buckner, Cameron. 2017. "Understanding Associative and Cognitive Explanations in Comparative Psychology." Pp. 409–18 in *The Routledge Handbook of Philosophy of Animal Minds*, edited by Kristin Andrews and Jacob Beck. London: Routledge.

Buckner, Cameron. 2018a. "Empiricism without Magic: Transformational Abstraction in Deep Convolutional Neural Networks." *Synthese* 195(12):5339–72.

Buckner, Cameron. 2018b. "Scaffolding Intuitive Rationality." Pp. 821–42 in *The Oxford Handbook of 4E Cognition*, edited by A. Newen, L. De Bruin, and S. Gallagher. London: Oxford University Press.

Buckner, Cameron. 2019a. "Deep Learning: A Philosophical Introduction." *Philosophy Compass* 14(10):e12625.

Buckner, Cameron. 2019b. "Rational Inference: The Lowest Bounds." *Philosophy and Phenomenological Research* 98(3):697–724.

Buckner, Cameron. 2020a. "Black Boxes or Unflattering Mirrors? Comparative Bias in the Science of Machine Behaviour." *British Journal for the Philosophy of Science*. https://www.journals.uchicago.edu/doi/10.1086/714960.

Buckner, Cameron. 2020b. "Understanding Adversarial Examples Requires a Theory of Artefacts for Deep Learning." *Nature Machine Intelligence* 2(12):731–36.

Buckner, Cameron. 2022. "A Forward-Looking Theory of Content." *Ergo* 8(37):367–401.

Buckner, Cameron, and James Garson. 2018. "Connectionism and Post-Connectionist Models." Pp. 76–91 in *The Routledge Handbook of the Computational Mind*, edited by M. Sprevak and M. Columbo. London: Routledge University Press.

Buckner, Randy L., Jessica R. Andrews-Hanna, and Daniel L. Schacter. 2008. "The Brain's Default Network." *Annals of the New York Academy of Sciences* 1124(1):1–38. doi: 10.1196/annals.1440.011.

Bufill, Enric, Jordi Agustí, and Rafael Blesa. 2011. "Human Neoteny Revisited: The Case of Synaptic Plasticity." *American Journal of Human Biology* 23(6):729–39.

Bugnyar, Thomas, Stephan A. Reber, and Cameron Buckner. 2016. "Ravens Attribute Visual Access to Unseen Competitors." *Nature Communications* 2(1):136–38.

Burghardt, Gordon M. 2007. "Critical Anthropomorphism, Uncritical Anthropocentrism, and Naïve Nominalism." *Comparative Cognition & Behavior Reviews* 2.

Byrne, Richard, and Andrew Whiten. 1994. *Machiavellian Intelligence*. Oxford: Oxford University Press.

Camp, Elisabeth. 2015. "Logical Concepts and Associative Characterizations." Pp. 591–621 in *The Conceptual Mind: New Directions in the Study of Concepts*, edited by E. Margolis and S. Laurence. Cambridge, MA: MIT Press.

Campbell, Murray. 1999. "Knowledge Discovery in Deep Blue." *Communications of the ACM* 42(11):65–67. doi: 10.1145/319382.319396.

Canaan, Rodrigo, Christoph Salge, Julian Togelius, and Andy Nealen. Unpublished. "Leveling the Playing Field-Fairness in AI Versus Human Game Benchmarks." *ArXiv Preprint ArXiv:1903.07008.*

Cangelosi, Angelo, Alberto Greco, and Stevan Harnad. 2000. "From Robotic Toil to Symbolic Theft: Grounding Transfer from Entry-Level to Higher-Level Categories1." *Connection Science* 12(2):143–62.

Cangelosi, Angelo, and Matthew Schlesinger. 2015. *Developmental Robotics: From Babies to Robots*. Cambridge, MA: MIT Press.

Cao, Rosa, and Daniel Yamins. 2021a. "Explanatory Models in Neuroscience: Part 1—Taking Mechanistic Abstraction Seriously." *ArXiv Preprint ArXiv:2104.01490.*

Cao, Rosa, and Daniel Yamins. 2021b. "Explanatory Models in Neuroscience: Part 2–Constraint-Based Intelligibility." *ArXiv Preprint ArXiv:2104.01489.*

Carey, Susan, and Elizabeth Spelke. 1996. "Science and Core Knowledge." *Philosophy of Science* 63(4):515–33.

Carroll, Lewis. 1895. "What the Tortoise Said to Achilles." *Mind* 4(14):278–80.

Carruthers, Peter. 2002. "The Cognitive Functions of Language." *The Behavioral and Brain Sciences* 25(6):657–74; discussion 674–725.

Carruthers, Peter. 2006. *The Architecture of the Mind*. Oxford: Oxford University Press.

Carruthers, Peter. 2011. *The Opacity of Mind: An Integrative Theory of Self-Knowledge*. Oxford: Oxford University Press.

Carruthers, Peter. 2018. "The Causes and Contents of Inner Speech." Pp. 31–52 in *Inner Speech: New Voices*, edited by A. Vicente and P. Langland-Hassan. Oxford: Oxford University Press.

Casasanto, Daniel, and Lera Boroditsky. 2008. "Time in the Mind: Using Space to Think about Time." *Cognition* 106(2):579–93.

Caucheteux, Charlotte, Alexandre Gramfort, and Jean-Rémi King. 2021. "GPT-2's Activations Predict the Degree of Semantic Comprehension in the Human Brain." *BioRxiv.*

Chatterjee, Anjan. 2010. "Disembodying Cognition." *Language and Cognition* 2(1):79–116.

Chatterjee, Anjan. 2011. "Neuroaesthetics: A Coming of Age Story." *Journal of Cognitive Neuroscience* 23(1):53–62.

Chen, Lili, Kevin Lu, Aravind Rajeswaran, Kimin Lee, Aditya Grover, Michael Laskin, Pieter Abbeel, Aravind Srinivas, and Igor Mordatch. 2021. "Decision Transformer: Reinforcement Learning via Sequence Modeling." *ArXiv Preprint ArXiv:2106.01345.*

Chen, Xi, Yan Duan, Rein Houthooft, John Schulman, Ilya Sutskever, and Pieter Abbeel. 2016. "Infogan: Interpretable Representation Learning by Information Maximizing Generative Adversarial Nets." *ArXiv Preprint ArXiv:1606.03657.*

Cherniak, Christopher. 1990. *Minimal Rationality.* Cambridge, MA: MIT Press.

Childers, Timothy, Juraj Hvorecký, and Ondrej Majer. 2023. "Empiricism in the Foundations of Cognition." *AI & Society* 38:67–87. doi: 10.1007/s00146-021-01287-w.

Chirimuuta, Mazviita. 2018. "Explanation in Computational Neuroscience: Causal and Non-Causal." *The British Journal for the Philosophy of Science* 69(3):849–80.

Chollet, François. 2019. "On the Measure of Intelligence." *ArXiv Preprint ArXiv:1911.01547.*

Chollet, Francois. 2021. *Deep Learning with Python.* New York: Simon and Schuster.

Chomsky, Noam. 1966. *Cartesian Linguistics: A Chapter in the History of Rationalist Thought.* New York: Cambridge University Press.

Chomsky, Noam. 1980. "A Review of BF Skinner's Verbal Behavior." *Readings in Philosophy of Psychology* 1:48–63.

Chomsky, Noam. 1986. *Knowledge of Language: Its Nature, Origin, and Use.* Westport, CT: Greenwood.

Chomsky, Noam. 1993. "A Minimalist Program for Linguistic Theory." Pp. 1–53 in *The View from Building 20: Essays in Linguistics in Honor of Sylvain Bromberger,* edited by K. Hale and S. J. Keyser. Cambridge, MA: MIT Press.

Chowdhery, Aakanksha, Sharan Narang, Jacob Devlin, Maarten Bosma, Gaurav Mishra, Adam Roberts, Paul Barham, Hyung Won Chung, Charles Sutton, and Sebastian Gehrmann. 2022. "Palm: Scaling Language Modeling with Pathways." *ArXiv Preprint ArXiv:2204.02311.*

Christiano, Paul F., Jan Leike, Tom Brown, Miljan Martic, Shane Legg, and Dario Amodei. 2017. "Deep Reinforcement Learning from Human Preferences." *Advances in Neural Information Processing Systems* 30.

Christiansen, Morten H., and Nick Chater. 2016. *Creating Language: Integrating Evolution, Acquisition, and Processing.* Cambridge, MA: MIT Press.

Churchland, Patricia Smith. 1989. *Neurophilosophy: Toward a Unified Science of the Mind-Brain.* Cambridge, MA: MIT Press.

Churchland, Paul M. 1989. *A Neurocomputational Perspective: The Nature of Mind and the Structure of Science* Cambridge, MA: MIT Press.

Churchland, Paul M. 2012. *Plato's Camera: How the Physical Brain Captures a Landscape of Abstract Universals.* Cambridge, MA: MIT Press.

Clark, Andy. 1989. *Microcognition: Philosophy, Cognitive Science, and Parallel Distributed Processing.* Vol. 6. Cambridge, MA: MIT Press.

Clark, Andy. 1998. "Magic Words: How Language Augments Human Computation." Pp. 162–83 in *Language and Meaning in Cognitive Science,* edited by A. Clark and J. Toribio. London: Routledge.

Clark, Andy. 2013. "Whatever Next? Predictive Brains, Situated Agents, and the Future of Cognitive Science." *Behavioral and Brain Sciences* 36(03):181–204.

Clark, Andy. 2015. *Surfing Uncertainty: Prediction, Action, and the Embodied Mind*. Oxford: Oxford University Press.

Clark, Kevin, Urvashi Khandelwal, Omer Levy, and Christopher D. Manning. 2019. "What Does Bert Look at? An Analysis of Bert's Attention." *ArXiv Preprint ArXiv:1906.04341*.

Clatterbuck, Hayley. 2016. "Darwin, Hume, Morgan, and the Verae Causae of Psychology." *Studies in History and Philosophy of Science Part C: Studies in History and Philosophy of Biological and Biomedical Sciences* 60:1–14.

Clayton, Nicola S., and James Russell. 2009. "Looking for Episodic Memory in Animals and Young Children: Prospects for a New Minimalism." *Neuropsychologia* 47(11):2330–40.

Coghill, George Ellett. 1929. *Anatomy and the Problem of Behaviour*. Cambridge: Cambridge University Press.

Colas, Cédric, Tristan Karch, Nicolas Lair, Jean-Michel Dussoux, Clément Moulin-Frier, Peter Dominey, and Pierre-Yves Oudeyer. 2020. "Language as a Cognitive Tool to Imagine Goals in Curiosity Driven Exploration." *Advances in Neural Information Processing Systems* 33:3761–74.

Colton, Simon, and Geraint A. Wiggins. 2012. "Computational Creativity: The Final Frontier?" Pp. 21–26 in *ECAI 2012*. Vol. 12. Montpelier.

Constantinescu, Alexandra O., Jill X. O'Reilly, and Timothy EJ Behrens. 2016. "Organizing Conceptual Knowledge in Humans with a Gridlike Code." *Science* 352(6292):1464–68.

Conze, Edward. 1963. "Spurious Parallels to Buddhist Philosophy." *Philosophy East and West* 13(2):105–15.

Copeland, B. Jack, and Diane Proudfoot. 1996. "On Alan Turing's Anticipation of Connectionism." *Synthese* 108(3):361–77.

Cordonnier, Jean-Baptiste, Andreas Loukas, and Martin Jaggi. 2019. "On the Relationship between Self-Attention and Convolutional Layers." *ArXiv Preprint ArXiv:1911.03584*.

Costelloe, Timothy M. 2018. *Imagination in Hume's Philosophy: The Canvas of the Mind*. Edinburgh: Edinburgh University Press.

Cowie, Fiona. 1998. "Mad Dog Nativism." *The British Journal for the Philosophy of Science* 49(2):227–52.

Craver, C. F. 2007. *Explaining the Brain: Mechanisms and the Mosaic Unity of Neuroscience*. Clarendon Press.

Chicago Craver, C. F. 2009. "Mechanisms and Natural Kinds." *Philosophical Psychology* 22(5):575–94. doi: 10.1080/09515080903238930.

Craver, Carl F., and David M. Kaplan. 2020. "Are More Details Better? On the Norms of Completeness for Mechanistic Explanations." *The British Journal for the Philosophy of Science* 71(1):287–319.

Crosby, Matthew. 2020. "Building Thinking Machines by Solving Animal Cognition Tasks." *Minds and Machines* 30:589–615. doi: 10.1007/s11023-020-09535-6.

Crosby, Matthew, Benjamin Beyret, and Marta Halina. 2019. "The Animal-AI Olympics." *Nature Machine Intelligence* 1(5):257. doi: 10.1038/s42256-019-0050-3.

Cross, Logan, Jeff Cockburn, Yisong Yue, and John P. O'Doherty. 2021. "Using Deep Reinforcement Learning to Reveal How the Brain Encodes Abstract State-Space Representations in High-Dimensional Environments." *Neuron* 109(4):724–738.e7. doi: 10.1016/j.neuron.2020.11.021.

Cueva, Christopher J., and Xue-Xin Wei. 2018. "Emergence of Grid-Like Representations by Training Recurrent Neural Networks to Perform Spatial Localization." *ArXiv Preprint ArXiv:1803.07770*.

Cummins, Robert. 1996. "Systematicity." *The Journal of Philosophy* 93(12):591–614.

Cushman, Fiery. 2020. "Rationalization Is Rational." *Behavioral and Brain Sciences* 43:e28.

Dąbrowska, Ewa. 2015. "What Exactly Is Universal Grammar, and Has Anyone Seen It?" *Frontiers in Psychology* 6:852.

Dally, Joanna M., Nathan J. Emery, and Nicola S. Clayton. 2006. "Food-Caching Western Scrub-Jays Keep Track of Who Was Watching When." *Science* 312(5780):1662–65.

Damasio, Antonio R. 1996. "The Somatic Marker Hypothesis and the Possible Functions of the Prefrontal Cortex." *Philosophical Transactions of the Royal Society of London. Series B: Biological Sciences* 351(1346):1413–20.

Danks, David. 2009. "The Psychology of Causal Perception and Reasoning." Pp. 447–70 in *Oxford Handbook of Causation*, edited by H. Beebee, C. Hitchcock, and P. Menzies. Oxford: Oxford University Press.

Darwin, Charles. 1871. *The Descent of Man and Selection in Relation to Sex*. 1st ed. London: John Murray.

Dasgupta, Ishita, Andrew K. Lampinen, Stephanie C. Y. Chan, Antonia Creswell, Dharshan Kumaran, James L. McClelland, and Felix Hill. 2022. "Language Models Show Human-like Content Effects on Reasoning." *ArXiv Preprint ArXiv:2207.07051*.

Davidson, Guy, and Brenden Lake. 2021. "Examining Infant Relation Categorization through Deep Neural Networks." *Proceedings of the Annual Meeting of the Cognitive Science Society* 43(43):258–64.

Davis, Ernest. 2017. "Logical Formalizations of Commonsense Reasoning: A Survey." *Journal of Artificial Intelligence Research* 59:651–723.

Davis, Ernest, and Gary Marcus. 2015. "Commonsense Reasoning and Commonsense Knowledge in Artificial Intelligence." *Communications of the ACM* 58(9):92–103.

Dayer, Alex, and Carolyn Dicey Jennings. 2021. "Attention in Skilled Behavior: An Argument for Pluralism." *Review of Philosophy and Psychology* 12(3):615–38.

De Brigard, Felipe. 2014. "Is Memory for Remembering? Recollection as a Form of Episodic Hypothetical Thinking." *Synthese* 191(2):155–85.

De Brigard, Felipe, and Natasha Parikh. 2019. "Episodic Counterfactual Thinking." *Current Directions in Psychological Science* 28(1):59–66. doi: 10.1177/0963721418806512.

De Grouchy, Sophie. 2019. *Letters on Sympathy*. Oxford: Oxford University Press.

De Waal, Frans BM. 2012. "Empathy in Primates and Other Mammals." Pp. 87–106 in *Empathy from Bench to Bedside*, edited by J. Decety. Cambridge, MA: MIT Press.

DeepMind Interactive Agents Team, Josh Abramson, Arun Ahuja, Arthur Brussee, Federico Carnevale, Mary Cassin, Felix Fischer, Petko Georgiev, Alex Goldin, Mansi Gupta, Tim Harley, Felix Hill, Peter C. Humphreys, Alden Hung, Jessica Landon, Timothy Lillicrap, Hamza Merzic, Alistair Muldal, Adam Santoro, Guy Scully, Tamara von Glehn, Greg Wayne, Nathaniel Wong, Chen Yan, and Rui Zhu. 2022. "Creating Multimodal Interactive Agents with Imitation and Self-Supervised Learning." *ArXiv:2112.03763 [Cs]*.

Dehaene, Stanislas, Michel Kerszberg, and Jean-Pierre Changeux. 1998. "A Neuronal Model of a Global Workspace in Effortful Cognitive Tasks." *Proceedings of the National Academy of Sciences* 95(24):14529–34.

Dehaene, Stanislas, Hakwan Lau, and Sid Kouider. 2017. "What Is Consciousness, and Could Machines Have It?" *Science* 358(6362):486–92.

Delius, Juan. 1994. "Comparative Cognition of Identity." Pp. 25–40 in *International Perspectives on Psychological Science, Vol. 1: Leading Themes*, edited by P. Bertelson and P. Eelen. Hillsdale, NJ: Erlbaum.

Demeter, Tamás. 2021. "Fodor's Guide to the Humean Mind." *Synthese* 199(1):5355–75.

Deng, Zhipeng, Hao Sun, Shilin Zhou, Juanping Zhao, Lin Lei, and Huanxin Zou. 2018. "Multi-Scale Object Detection in Remote Sensing Imagery with Convolutional Neural Networks." *ISPRS Journal of Photogrammetry and Remote Sensing* 145:3–22. doi: 10.1016/j.isprsjprs.2018.04.003.

Dennett, Daniel C. 1978. "Why Not the Whole Iguana?" *Behavioral and Brain Sciences* 1(1):103–4.

Dennett, DC. 1978. "Beliefs about Beliefs." *Behavioral and Brain Sciences* 4(568–70).

Deutsch, J. A., and D. Deutsch. 1963. "Attention: Some Theoretical Considerations." *Psychological Review* 70(1):80–90. doi: 10.1037/h0039515.

Dhariwal, Prafulla, Heewoo Jun, Christine Payne, Jong Wook Kim, Alec Radford, and Ilya Sutskever. 2020. "Jukebox: A Generative Model for Music." *ArXiv Preprint ArXiv:2005.00341*.

DiCarlo, James J., and David D. Cox. 2007. "Untangling Invariant Object Recognition." *Trends in Cognitive Sciences* 11(8):333–41. doi: 10.1016/j.tics.2007.06.010.

DiCarlo, James J., Davide Zoccolan, and Nicole C. Rust. 2012. "How Does the Brain Solve Visual Object Recognition?" *Neuron* 73(3):415–34.

Dragoi, George, and Susumu Tonegawa. 2013. "Distinct Preplay of Multiple Novel Spatial Experiences in the Rat." *Proceedings of the National Academy of Sciences* 110(22):9100–105. doi: 10.1073/pnas.1306031110.

Driver, Jon. 2001. "A Selective Review of Selective Attention Research from the Past Century." *British Journal of Psychology* 92(1):53–78.

Dubey, Rachit, Pulkit Agrawal, Deepak Pathak, Thomas L. Griffiths, and Alexei A. Efros. 2018. "Investigating Human Priors for Playing Video Games." *ArXiv Preprint ArXiv:1802.10217.*

Duchi, John, Elad Hazan, and Yoram Singer. 2011. "Adaptive Subgradient Methods for Online Learning and Stochastic Optimization." *Journal of Machine Learning Research* 12(7):2121–59.

Dudai, Yadin, Avi Karni, and Jan Born. 2015. "The Consolidation and Transformation of Memory." *Neuron* 88(1):20–32.

Dujmović, Marin, Gaurav Malhotra, and Jeffrey S. Bowers. 2020. "What Do Adversarial Images Tell Us about Human Vision?" edited by G. J. Berman, R. L. Calabrese, and C. Firestone. *ELife* 9:e55978. doi: 10.7554/eLife.55978.

Dusek, Jeffery A., and Howard Eichenbaum. 1997. "The Hippocampus and Memory for Orderly Stimulus Relations." *Proceedings of the National Academy of Sciences of the United States of America* 94(13):7109–14.

Duvelle, É., and K. J. Jeffery. 2018. "Social Spaces: Place Cells Represent the Locations of Others." *Current Biology* 28(6):R271–73.

Eichenbaum, Howard. 2014. "Time Cells in the Hippocampus: A New Dimension for Mapping Memories." *Nature Reviews Neuroscience* 15(11):732–44.

Eichenbaum, Howard, and Neal J. Cohen. 2004. *From Conditioning to Conscious Recollection: Memory Systems of the Brain.* Oxford: Oxford University Press on Demand.

Elgammal, Ahmed, Bingchen Liu, Mohamed Elhoseiny, and Marian Mazzone. 2017. "Can: Creative Adversarial Networks, Generating 'Art' by Learning about Styles and Deviating from Style Norms." *ArXiv Preprint ArXiv:1706.07068.*

Elhage, Nelson, Neel Nanda, Catherine Olsson, Tom Henighan, Nicholas Joseph, Benn Mann, Amanda Askell, Yuntao Bai, Anna Chen, Tom Conerly, Nova DasSarma, Dawn Drain, Deep Ganguli, Zac Hatfield-Dodds, Danny Hernandez, Andy Jones, Jackson Kernion, Liane Lovitt, Kamal Ndousse, Dario Amodei, Tom Brown, Jack Clark, Jared Kaplan, Sam McCandlish, and Chris Olah. 2021. "A Mathematical Framework for Transformer Circuits." *Transformer Circuits.* https://transformer-circuits.pub/2021/framework/index.html.

Elizabeth S. Spelke, Emily P. Bernier, and Amy E. Skerry. 2013. "Core Social Cognition." Pp. 11–16 in *Navigating the Social World: What Infants, Children, and Other Species Can Teach Us*, edited by M. R. Banaji and S. A. Gelman. New York: Oxford University Press.

Elman, Jeffrey L. 1992. "Grammatical Structure and Distributed Representations." Pp. 138–78 in *Connectionism. Theory and Practice*, edited by Steven Davis. Oxford, UK: Oxford University Press.

Elman, Jeffrey L., Elizabeth A. Bates, and Mark H. Johnson. 1998. *Rethinking Innateness: A Connectionist Perspective on Development*. Vol. 10. Cambridge, MA: MIT Press.

Elsayed, Gamaleldin, Shreya Shankar, Brian Cheung, Nicolas Papernot, Alexey Kurakin, Ian Goodfellow, and Jascha Sohl-Dickstein. 2018. "Adversarial Examples That Fool Both Computer Vision and Time-Limited Humans." Pp. 3910–20 in *Advances in Neural Information Processing Systems 31*.

Engstrom, Logan, Justin Gilmer, Gabriel Goh, Dan Hendrycks, Andrew Ilyas, Aleksander Madry, Reiichiro Nakano, Preetum Nakkiran, Shibani Santurkar, Brandon Tran1, Dimitris Tsipras, and Eric Wallace. 2019. "A Discussion of 'Adversarial Examples Are Not Bugs, They Are Features.'" *Distill* 4(8):e19. doi: 10.23915/distill.00019.

Esser, Patrick, Robin Rombach, and Bjorn Ommer. 2021. "Taming Transformers for High-Resolution Image Synthesis." Pp. 12873–83 in *Proceedings of the IEEE/CVF Conference on Computer Vision and Pattern Recognition*.

Evans, Richard. 2020. "Kant's Cognitive Architecture." PhD Thesis, Imperial College London.

Richard Evans, José Hernández-Orallo, Johannes Welbl, Pushmeet Kohli, and Marek Sergot. 2021. "Making Sense of Sensory Input." *Artificial Intelligence* 293:103438.

Eykholt, Kevin, Ivan Evtimov, Earlence Fernandes, Bo Li, Amir Rahmati, Chaowei Xiao, Atul Prakash, Tadayoshi Kohno, and Dawn Song. 2018. "Robust Physical-World Attacks on Deep Learning Visual Classification." Pp. 1625–34 in *Proceedings of the IEEE Conference on Computer Vision and Pattern Recognition*.

Feinman, Reuben, and Brenden M. Lake. 2018. "Learning Inductive Biases with Simple Neural Networks." *ArXiv Preprint ArXiv:1802.02745*.

Fenici, Marco. 2017. "What Is the Role of Experience in Children's Success in the False Belief Test: Maturation, Facilitation, Attunement or Induction?" *Mind & Language* 32(3):308–37.

Ferrucci, David, Eric Brown, Jennifer Chu-Carroll, James Fan, David Gondek, Aditya A. Kalyanpur, Adam Lally, J. William Murdock, Eric Nyberg, and John Prager. 2010. "Building Watson: An Overview of the DeepQA Project." *AI Magazine* 31(3):59–79.

Filippetti, Maria Laura, Mark H. Johnson, Sarah Lloyd-Fox, Danica Dragovic, and Teresa Farroni. 2013. "Body Perception in Newborns." *Current Biology* 23(23):2413–16. doi: 10.1016/j.cub.2013.10.017.

Fine, Kit. 2002. *The Limits of Abstraction*. Oxford: Clarendon Press.

Finke, Ronald A., Steven Pinker, and Martha J. Farah. 1989. "Reinterpreting Visual Patterns in Mental Imagery." *Cognitive Science* 13(1):51–78.

Firestone, Chaz. 2020. "Performance vs. Competence in Human-AI Comparisons." *Proceedings of the National Academy of Sciences* 117(43): 26562–71.

Fitch, W. Tecumseh. 2010. *The Evolution of Language*. Cambridge: Cambridge University Press.

Fitzsimonds, Reiko Maki, Hong-jun Song, and Mu-ming Poo. 1997. "Propagation of Activity-Dependent Synaptic Depression in Simple Neural Networks." *Nature* 388:439–48.

Fleischacker, Samuel. 2019. *Being Me Being You: Adam Smith and Empathy*. Chicago: University of Chicago Press.

Fodor, Janet Dean. 2001. "Setting Syntactic Parameters." Pp. 730–68 in *The Handbook of Contemporary Syntactic Theory*, edited by M. Baltin and C. Collins. Malden, MA: Blackwell.

Fodor, Jerry A. 1975. *The Language of Thought*. Cambridge, MA: Harvard University Press.

Fodor, Jerry A. 1983. *The Modularity of Mind: An Essay on Faculty Psychology*. Cambridge, MA: MIT Press.

Fodor, Jerry A. 2000. *The Mind Doesn't Work That Way: The Scope and Limits of Computational Psychology*. Cambridge, MA: MIT Press.

Fodor, Jerry A. 2003. *Hume Variations*. Oxford: Oxford University Press.

Fodor, Jerry A. 2008. *LOT 2: The Language of Thought Revisited*. Oxford: Oxford University Press on Demand.

Fodor, Jerry A., and Zenon W. Pylyshyn. 1988. "Connectionism and Cognitive Architecture: A Critical Analysis." *Cognition* 28(1–2):3–71.

Foster, David J., and Matthew A. Wilson. 2006. "Reverse Replay of Behavioural Sequences in Hippocampal Place Cells during the Awake State." *Nature* 440(7084):680–83.

Frank, Michael C., Elika Bergelson, Christina Bergmann, Alejandrina Cristia, Caroline Floccia, Judit Gervain, J. Kiley Hamlin, Erin E. Hannon, Melissa Kline, Claartje Levelt, Casey Lew-Williams, Thierry Nazzi, Robin Panneton, Hugh Rabagliati, Melanie Soderstrom, Jessica Sullivan, Sandra Waxman, and Daniel Yurovsky. 2017. "A Collaborative Approach to Infant Research: Promoting Reproducibility, Best Practices, and Theory-Building." *Infancy* 22(4):421–35. doi: 10.1111/infa.12182.

Frankenhuis, Willem E., and Annemie Ploeger. 2007. "Evolutionary Psychology versus Fodor: Arguments for and against the Massive Modularity Hypothesis." *Philosophical Psychology* 20(6):687–710.

Fridland, Ellen. 2017. "Automatically Minded." *Synthese* 194(11):4337–63.

Friston, Karl. 2010. "The Free-Energy Principle: A Unified Brain Theory?" *Nature Reviews Neuroscience* 11(2):127–38. doi: 10.1038/nrn2787.

Fukushima, Kunihiko. 1979. "Neural Network Model for a Mechanism of Pattern Recognition Unaffected by Shift in Position-Neocognitron." *IEICE Technical Report, A* 62(10):658–65.

Fukushima, Kunihiko, and Sei Miyake. 1982. "Neocognitron: A Self-Organizing Neural Network Model for a Mechanism of Visual Pattern Recognition." Pp. 267–85 in *Competition and Cooperation in Neural Nets*. Springer.

Funke, Christina M., Judy Borowski, Karolina Stosio, Wieland Brendel, Thomas SA Wallis, and Matthias Bethge. 2021. "Five Points to Check When Comparing Visual Perception in Humans and Machines." *Journal of Vision* 21(3):16, 1–23.

Gaines, R. 1975. "Developmental Perception and Cognitive Styles: From Young Children to Master Artists." *Perceptual and Motor Skills* 40(3):983–98.

Gainza, P., F. Sverrisson, F. Monti, E. Rodolà, D. Boscaini, M. M. Bronstein, and B. E. Correia. 2019. "Deciphering Interaction Fingerprints from Protein Molecular Surfaces Using Geometric Deep Learning." *Nature Methods* 17:184–92. doi: 10.1038/s41592-019-0666-6.

Gallagher, S. 2001. "The Practice of Mind. Theory, Simulation or Primary Interaction?" *Journal of Consciousness Studies* 8(5–6):83–108.

Garagnani, Max, and Friedemann Pulvermüller. 2013. "Neuronal Correlates of Decisions to Speak and Act: Spontaneous Emergence and Dynamic Topographies in a Computational Model of Frontal and Temporal Areas." *Brain and Language* 127(1):75–85.

Gärdenfors, Peter. 2004. *Conceptual Spaces: The Geometry of Thought*. Cambridge, MA: MIT Press.

Garrett, Aaron. 2017. "Hume's 'Original Difference': Race, National Character and the Human Sciences." Pp. 241–66 in *David Hume*, edited by Knud Haakonssen and Richard Whatmore. London: Routledge.

Gatys, Leon A., Alexander S. Ecker, and Matthias Bethge. 2016a. "Image Style Transfer Using Convolutional Neural Networks." Pp. 2414–23 in *Proceedings of the IEEE Conference on Computer Vision and Pattern Recognition*.

Gatys, Leon A., Alexander S. Ecker, and Matthias Bethge. 2016b. "Image Style Transfer Using Convolutional Neural Networks." Pp. 2414–23 in *Proceedings of the IEEE Conference on Computer Vision and Pattern Recognition*.

Gauker, Christopher. 2013. *Words and Images: An Essay on the Origin of Ideas*. Reprint ed. Oxford: Oxford University Press.

Gauthier, Isabel, Pawel Skudlarski, John C. Gore, and Adam W. Anderson. 2000. "Expertise for Cars and Birds Recruits Brain Areas Involved in Face Recognition." *Nature Neuroscience* 3(2):191–97.

Gelfert, Axel. 2016. *How to Do Science with Models: A Philosophical Primer*. Cham: Springer.

Gentry, Hunter. 2023. "Special Attention to the Self: A Mechanistic Model of Patient RB's Lost Feeling of Ownership." *Review of Philosophy and Psychology* 14:57–85.

Gentry, Hunter, and Cameron Buckner. 2019. "Locating Animals with Respect to Landmarks in Space-Time." *Behavioral and Brain Sciences* 42:e251.

Gershman, Samuel J. 2019. "The Generative Adversarial Brain." *Frontiers in Artificial Intelligence* 2:18. doi: 10.3389/frai.2019.00018.

Gigerenzer, Gerd, and Henry Brighton. 2009. "Homo Heuristicus: Why Biased Minds Make Better Inferences." *Cognitive Science* 1:107–43. doi: 10.1111/j.1756-8765.2008.01006.x.

Gigerenzer, Gerd, Peter M. Todd, and ABC Research Group. 1999. *Simple Heuristics That Make Us Smart.* Oxford: Oxford University Press.

Gilovich, T., D. W. Griffin, and D. Kahneman. 2002. *Heuristics and Biases: The Psychology of Intuitive Judgement.* Cambridge: Cambridge University Press.

Girshick, Ross, Jeff Donahue, Trevor Darrell, and Jitendra Malik. 2014. "Rich Feature Hierarchies for Accurate Object Detection and Semantic Segmentation." Pp. 580–87 in *Proceedings of the IEEE Conference on Computer Vision and Pattern Recognition.*

Glaese, Amelia, Nat McAleese, Maja Trębacz, John Aslanides, Vlad Firoiu, Timo Ewalds, Maribeth Rauh, Laura Weidinger, Martin Chadwick, Phoebe Thacker, Lucy Campbell-Gillingham, Jonathan Uesato, Po-Sen Huang, Ramona Comanescu, Fan Yang, Abigail See, Sumanth Dathathri, Rory Greig, Charlie Chen, Doug Fritz, Jaume Sanchez Elias, Richard Green, Soňa Mokrá, Nicholas Fernando, Boxi Wu, Rachel Foley, Susannah Young, Iason Gabriel, William Isaac, John Mellor, Demis Hassabis, Koray Kavukcuoglu, Lisa Anne Hendricks, and Geoffrey Irving. 2022. "Improving Alignment of Dialogue Agents via Targeted Human Judgements." *ArXiv Preprint.* doi: 10.48550/arXiv.2209.14375.

Glausser, Wayne. 1990. "Three Approaches to Locke and the Slave Trade." *Journal of the History of Ideas* 51(2):199–216.

Glimcher, Paul W. 2011. "Understanding Dopamine and Reinforcement Learning: The Dopamine Reward Prediction Error Hypothesis." *Proceedings of the National Academy of Sciences* 108(Suppl. 3):15647–54. doi: 10.1073/pnas.1014269108.

Gluck, Mark A., and Catherine E. Myers. 1993. "Hippocampal Mediation of Stimulus Representation: A Computational Theory." *Hippocampus* 3(4):491–516.

Gluck, Mark A., and Catherine E. Myers. 2001a. *Gateway to Memory: An Introduction to Neural Network Modeling of the Hippocampus.* Cambridge, MA: MIT Press.

Gluck, Mark A., and Catherine E. Myers. 2001b. *Gateway to Memory: An Introduction to Neural Network Modeling of the Hippocampus and Learning.* Cambridge, MA: MIT Press.

Glymour, Clark. 1997. "Social Statistics and Genuine Inquiry: Reflections on the Bell Curve." Pp. 257–80 in *Intelligence, Genes, and Success*, edited by Devlin, Bernie, Stephen E. Fienberg, Daniel P. Resnick, and Kathryn Roeder. New York: Springer.

Goldman, Alvin I. 2006. *Simulating Minds: The Philosophy, Psychology, and Neuroscience of Mindreading*. Oxford: Oxford University Press on Demand.

Godfrey-Smith, P. 2006. "The Strategy of Model-Based Science." *Biology and Philosophy* 21:725–740.

Goldstein, Ariel, Zaid Zada, Eliav Buchnik, Mariano Schain, Amy Price, Bobbi Aubrey, Samuel A. Nastase, Amir Feder, Dotan Emanuel, and Alon Cohen. 2021. "Thinking Ahead: Prediction in Context as a Keystone of Language in Humans and Machines." *BioRxiv* 2020–12.

Goodale, Melvyn A., and A. David Milner. 1992. "Separate Visual Pathways for Perception and Action." *Trends in Neurosciences* 15(1):20–25.

Goodfellow, Ian. 2016. "NIPS 2016 Tutorial: Generative Adversarial Networks." *ArXiv Preprint ArXiv:1701.00160*.

Goodfellow, Ian, Yoshua Bengio, and Aaron Courville. 2016. *Deep Learning*. Cambridge, MA: MIT Press.

Goodfellow, Ian, Jean Pouget-Abadie, Mehdi Mirza, Bing Xu, David Warde-Farley, Sherjil Ozair, Aaron Courville, and Yoshua Bengio. 2014. "Generative Adversarial Nets." Pp. 2672–80 in *Advances in Neural Information Processing Systems*.

Goodman, Nelson. 1972. "Seven Strictures on Similarity." Pp. 437–47 in *Problems and Projects*, edited by Nelson Goodman. Indianapolis: Bobbs-Merrill.

Gopnik, Alison. 2009. "Could David Hume Have Known about Buddhism?: Charles François Dolu, the Royal College of La Flèche, and the Global Jesuit Intellectual Network." *Hume Studies* 35(1/2):5–28.

Gorchetchnikov, Anatoli, and Stephen Grossberg. 2007. "Space, Time and Learning in the Hippocampus: How Fine Spatial and Temporal Scales Are Expanded into Population Codes for Behavioral Control." *Neural Networks* 20(2):182–93.

Gordon, Robert M. 2021. "Simulation, Predictive Coding, and the Shared World." Pp. 237–55 in *The Neural Basis of Mentalizing*, edited by M. Gilead and K. N. Ochsner. Cham: Springer.

Gould, Stephen Jay, and Steven James Gold. 1996. *The Mismeasure of Man*. New York: WW Norton & Company.

Goyal, Anirudh, and Yoshua Bengio. 2020. "Inductive Biases for Deep Learning of Higher-Level Cognition." *ArXiv Preprint ArXiv:2011.15091*.

Granato, Giovanni, Anna M. Borghi, and Gianluca Baldassarre. 2020. "A Computational Model of Language Functions in Flexible Goal-Directed Behaviour." *Scientific Reports* 10(1):21623. doi: 10.1038/s41598-020-78252-y.

Granato, Giovanni, Anna M. Borghi, Andrea Mattera, and Gianluca Baldassarre. 2021. "Autism and Inner Speech: A Computational Model of Language Functions in Autistic Flexible Behaviour." https://www.researc hsquare.com/article/rs-744730/v1.

Grauman, Kristen, Michael Wray, Adriano Fragomeni, Jonathan P. N. Munro, Will Price, Pablo Arbelaez, David Crandall, Dima Damen, Giovanni Maria Farinella, Bernard Ghanem, C. V. Jawahar, Kris Kitani, Aude Oliva, Hyun Soo Park, James M. Rehg, Yoichi Sato, Mike Zheng Shou, Antonio Torrallba, and Jitendra Malik. 2022. "Ego4D: Computer Vision and Pattern Recognition (CVPR)." *2022 IEEE/CVF Conference on Computer Vision and Pattern Recognition (CVPR)* 18973–90. doi: 10.48550/arXiv.2110.07058.

Graves, Alex, Greg Wayne, and Ivo Danihelka. 2014. "Neural Turing Machines." *ArXiv Preprint ArXiv:1410.5401.*

Greene, Joshua. 2014. *Moral Tribes: Emotion, Reason, and the Gap between Us and Them.* London: Penguin.

Greenwood, John D. 1999. "Understanding the 'Cognitive Revolution' in Psychology." *Journal of the History of the Behavioral Sciences* 35(1):1–22.

Greff, Klaus, Sjoerd van Steenkiste, and Jürgen Schmidhuber. 2020. "On the Binding Problem in Artificial Neural Networks." *ArXiv Preprint ArXiv:2012.05208.*

Griffiths, Paul E., and Edouard Machery. 2008. "Innateness, Canalization, and 'Biologicizing the Mind.'" *Philosophical Psychology* 21(3):397–414.

Griffiths, Paul E., and James Tabery. 2013. "Developmental Systems Theory: What Does It Explain, and How Does It Explain It?" Pp. 65–94 in *Advances in Child Development and Behavior*, edited by Janette Benson . Vol. 44. Elsevier.

Griffiths, Thomas L., Charles Kemp, and Joshua B. Tenenbaum. 2008. "Bayesian Models of Cognition." Pp. 59–100 in *The Cambridge Handbook of Computational Psychology*, edited by R. Sun. Cambridge: Cambridge University Press.

Grover, Aditya, Manik Dhar, and Stefano Ermon. 2018. "Flow-Gan: Combining Maximum Likelihood and Adversarial Learning in Generative Models." In *Proceedings of the AAAI Conference on Artificial Intelligence.* Vol. 32.

Guo, Chong, Michael J. Lee, Guillaume Leclerc, Joel Dapello, Yug Rao, Aleksander Madry, and James J. DiCarlo. 2022. "Adversarially Trained Neural Representations May Already Be as Robust as Corresponding Biological Neural Representations." *Proceedings of the 39th International Conference on Machine Learning*, PMLR 162:8072–81.

Gutas, Dimitri. 2012. "The Empiricism of Avicenna." *Oriens* 40(2):391–436.

Haas, Julia. 2019. "Valuation Mechanisms in Moral Cognition." *Behavioral and Brain Sciences* 42:e155.

Haas, Julia. 2020. "Moral Gridworlds: A Theoretical Proposal for Modeling Artificial Moral Cognition." *Minds and Machines* 30(2):219–46.

Hamlin, J. Kiley. 2013. "Moral Judgment and Action in Preverbal Infants and Toddlers: Evidence for an Innate Moral Core." *Current Directions in Psychological Science* 22(3):186–93.

Hamrick, Jessica B. 2019. "Analogues of Mental Simulation and Imagination in Deep Learning." *Current Opinion in Behavioral Sciences* 29:8–16.

Hamrick, Jessica B., Andrew J. Ballard, Razvan Pascanu, Oriol Vinyals, Nicolas Heess, and Peter W. Battaglia. 2017. "Metacontrol for Adaptive Imagination-Based Optimization." *ArXiv Preprint ArXiv:1705.02670.*

Harman, G. 1978. "Studying the Chimpanzee's Theory of Mind." *Behavioral and Brain Sciences* 4:576–77.

Hart, Emma, and Léni K. Le Goff. 2022. "Artificial Evolution of Robot Bodies and Control: On the Interaction between Evolution, Learning and Culture." *Philosophical Transactions of the Royal Society B* 377(1843):20210117.

Hassabis, Demis, Dharshan Kumaran, Christopher Summerfield, and Matthew Botvinick. 2017. "Neuroscience-Inspired Artificial Intelligence." *Neuron* 95(2):245–58.

Hasselmo, ME. 2006. "The Role of Acetylcholine in Learning and Memory." *Current Opinion in Neurobiology* 16(6):710–15.

Hasson, Uri, Samuel A. Nastase, and Ariel Goldstein. 2020. "Direct Fit to Nature: An Evolutionary Perspective on Biological and Artificial Neural Networks." *Neuron* 105(3):416–34.

Haugeland, John. 1985. *Artificial Intelligence: The Very Idea.* Cambridge, MA: MIT Press.

Hauser, Marc, and Justin Wood. 2010. "Evolving the Capacity to Understand Actions, Intentions, and Goals." *Annual Review of Psychology* 61:303–24.

Heider, Fritz, and Marianne Simmel. 1944. "An Experimental Study of Apparent Behavior." *The American Journal of Psychology* 57(2):243–59.

Hernández-Orallo, José. 2017. *The Measure of All Minds: Evaluating Natural and Artificial Intelligence.* Cambridge: Cambridge University Press.

Hernández-Orallo, Jose, Marco Baroni, Jordi Bieger, Nader Chmait, David L. Dowe, Katja Hofmann, Fernando Martínez-Plumed, Claes Stranneg\aard, and Kristinn R. Thórisson. 2017. "A New AI Evaluation Cosmos: Ready to Play the Game?" *AI Magazine* 38(3):66–69.

Hernández-Orallo, José, Bao Sheng Loe, Lucy Cheke, Fernando Martínez-Plumed, and Seán Ó hÉigeartaigh. 2021. "General Intelligence Disentangled via a Generality Metric for Natural and Artificial Intelligence." *Scientific Reports* 11(1):22822. doi: 10.1038/s41598-021-01997-7.

Hespos, Susan J., and Kristy VanMarle. 2012. "Physics for Infants: Characterizing the Origins of Knowledge about Objects, Substances, and Number." *Wiley Interdisciplinary Reviews: Cognitive Science* 3(1):19–27.

Heyes, Cecilia. 2014. "Submentalizing: I Am Not Really Reading Your Mind." *Perspectives on Psychological Science* 9(2):131–43.

Higgins, Irina, Loic Matthey, Arka Pal, Christopher Burgess, Xavier Glorot, Matthew Botvinick, Shakir Mohamed, and Alexander Lerchner. 2022. "Beta-VAE: Learning Basic Visual Concepts with a Constrained Variational Framework." International Conference on Learning Representations.

Hill, Felix, Andrew Lampinen, Rosalia Schneider, Stephen Clark, Matthew Botvinick, James L. McClelland, and Adam Santoro. 2020. "Environmental Drivers of Systematicity and Generalization in a Situated Agent." *ArXiv:1910.00571 [Cs]*.

Hinton, Geoffrey E., and James McClelland. 1988. "Learning Representations by Recirculation." Pp. 358–66 in *Neural Information Processing Systems*, edited by D. Z. Anderson. New York: American Institute of Physics.

Hoerl, Christoph, and Teresa McCormack. 2019. "Thinking in and about Time: A Dual Systems Perspective on Temporal Cognition." *Behavioral and Brain Sciences* 42:e244.

Hohwy, Jakob. 2013. *The Predictive Mind*. Oxford: Oxford University Press.

Hommel, Bernhard, Craig S. Chapman, Paul Cisek, Heather F. Neyedli, Joo-Hyun Song, and Timothy N. Welsh. 2019. "No One Knows What Attention Is." *Attention, Perception, & Psychophysics* 81(7):2288–303.

Honig, Barry. 1999. "Protein Folding: From the Levinthal Paradox to Structure Prediction." *Journal of Molecular Biology* 293(2):283–93. doi: 10.1006/jmbi.1999.3006.

Hornstein, Norbert. 2012. "Faculty of Language: Poverty of Stimulus Redux." *Faculty of Language*. Retrieved February 2, 2022. http://facultyoflanguage.blogspot.com/2012/11/poverty-of-stimulus-redux.html.

Htut, Phu Mon, Jason Phang, Shikha Bordia, and Samuel R. Bowman. 2019. "Do Attention Heads in BERT Track Syntactic Dependencies?" *ArXiv Preprint ArXiv:1911.12246*.

Huang, Wenlong, Fei Xia, Ted Xiao, Harris Chan, Jacky Liang, Pete Florence, Andy Zeng, Jonathan Tompson, Igor Mordatch, and Yevgen Chebotar. 2022. "Inner Monologue: Embodied Reasoning through Planning with Language Models." *ArXiv Preprint ArXiv:2207.05608*.

Hubel, David H., and Torsten N. Wiesel. 1962. "Receptive Fields, Binocular Interaction and Functional Architecture in the Cat's Visual Cortex." *The Journal of Physiology* 160(1):106–54.

Hubel, David H., and Torsten N. Wiesel. 1967. "Cortical and Callosal Connections Concerned with the Vertical Meridian of Visual Fields in the Cat." *Journal of Neurophysiology* 30(6):1561–73.

Hutchinson, John M. C., and Gerd Gigerenzer. 2005. "Simple Heuristics and Rules of Thumb: Where Psychologists and Behavioural Biologists Might Meet." *Behavioural Processes* 69(2):97–124. doi: 10.1016/j.beproc.2005.02.019.

Ilyas, Andrew, Shibani Santurkar, Dimitris Tsipras, Logan Engstrom, Brandon Tran, and Aleksander Madry. 2019. "Adversarial Examples Are Not Bugs, They Are Features." *Advances in Neural Information Processing Systems* 32.

Irpan, Alex. 2018. "Deep Reinforcement Learning Doesn't Work Yet." *Sorta Insightful*. Retrieved May 6, 2019. https://www.alexirpan.com/2018/02/14/rl-hard.html.

Irving, Zachary C. 2016. "Mind-Wandering Is Unguided Attention: Accounting for the 'Purposeful' Wanderer." *Philosophical Studies* 173(2):547–71.

Iyer, Abhiram, Karan Grewal, Akash Velu, Lucas Oliveira Souza, Jeremy Forest, and Subutai Ahmad. 2021. "Avoiding Catastrophe: Active Dendrites Enable Multi-Task Learning in Dynamic Environments." *ArXiv Preprint ArXiv:2201.00042*.

Jackendoff, Ray. 1987. *Consciousness and the Computational Mind*. Cambridge, MA: MIT Press.

Jacobson, Anne Jaap. 2010. *Feminist Interpretations of David Hume*. University Park, PA: Penn State Press.

Jain, Sarthak, and Byron C. Wallace. 2019. "Attention Is Not Explanation." *ArXiv Preprint ArXiv:1902.10186*.

James, William. 1890. *The Principles of Psychology*. Vol. 1. New York: Henry Holt and Company.

Janiak, Andrew. 2020. *Space: A History*. New York: Oxford University Press.

Jara-Ettinger, Julian. 2019. "Theory of Mind as Inverse Reinforcement Learning." *Current Opinion in Behavioral Sciences* 29:105–10.

Jennings, Carolyn Dicey. 2012. "The Subject of Attention." *Synthese* 189(3):535–54.

Jetley, Saumya, Nicholas A. Lord, Namhoon Lee, and Philip H. S. Torr. 2018. "Learn to Pay Attention." *ArXiv Preprint ArXiv:1804.02391*.

Jitsumori, Masako, and Juan D. Delius. 2001. "Object Recognition and Object Categorization in Animals." Pp. 269–93 in *Primate Origins of Human Cognition and Behavior*, edited by T. Matsuzawa. Tokyo: Springer Japan.

Johnson, Kent. 2004. "On the Systematicity of Language and Thought." *The Journal of Philosophy* 101(3):111–39.

Jumper, John, Richard Evans, Alexander Pritzel, Tim Green, Michael Figurnov, Olaf Ronneberger, Kathryn Tunyasuvunakool, Russ Bates, Augustin Žídek, and Anna Potapenko. 2021. "Highly Accurate Protein Structure Prediction with AlphaFold." *Nature* 596(7873):583–89.

Jurafsky, Daniel, and James Martin. 2020. *Speech and Language Processing: An Introduction to Natural Language Processing, Computational Linguistics, and Speech Recognition*. 3rd ed. Hoboken NJ: Prentice Hall.

Kahneman, Daniel, and Shane Frederick. 2005. *A Model of Heuristic Judgment*. Cambridge: Cambridge University Press.

Kahneman, Daniel, and Amos Tversky. 1996. "On the Reality of Cognitive Illusions." *Psychological Review* 103(3):582–91.

Kaiser, Mary Kister, John Jonides, and Joanne Alexander. 1986. "Intuitive Reasoning about Abstract and Familiar Physics Problems." *Memory & Cognition* 14(4):308–12.

Kambhampati, Subbarao. 2019. "Challenges of Human-Aware AI Systems." *ArXiv Preprint ArXiv:1910.07089.*

Kampis, Dora, Petra Karman, Gergely Csibra, Victoria Southgate, and Mikolaj Hernik. 2020. "A Two-Lab Direct Replication Attempt of Southgate, Senju, & Csibra (2007)." Royal Society Open Science 8:210190.

Kansky, Ken, Tom Silver, David A. Mély, Mohamed Eldawy, Miguel Lázaro-Gredilla, Xinghua Lou, Nimrod Dorfman, Szymon Sidor, Scott Phoenix, and Dileep George. 2017. "Schema Networks: Zero-Shot Transfer with a Generative Causal Model of Intuitive Physics." *ArXiv Preprint ArXiv:1706.04317.*

Karg, Katja, Martin Schmelz, Josep Call, and Michael Tomasello. 2016. "Differing Views: Can Chimpanzees Do Level 2 Perspective-Taking?" *Animal Cognition* 19(3):555–64.

Karin-D'Arcy, M. 2005. "The Modern Role of Morgan's Canon in Comparative Psychology." *International Journal of Comparative Psychology* 18(3): 179–201.

Karras, Tero, Samuli Laine, Miika Aittala, Janne Hellsten, Jaakko Lehtinen, and Timo Aila. 2020. "Analyzing and Improving the Image Quality of Stylegan." Pp. 8110–19 in *Proceedings of the IEEE/CVF Conference on Computer Vision and Pattern Recognition.*

Kathryn Tabb. 2018. "Madness as Method: On Locke's Thought Experiments about Personal Identity." *British Journal for the History of Philosophy* 26(5):871–89. doi: 10.1080/09608788.2017.1350936.

Katsuno, Hirofumi, and Daniel White. 2023. "Engineering Robots with a Heart in Japan: The Politics of Cultural Difference in Artificial Emotional Intelligence." Pp. 295–318 in *Imagining AI: How the World Sees Intelligent Machines,* edited by S. Cave and K. Dihal. Oxford: Oxford University Press.

Kauppinen, Antti. 2010. "What Makes a Sentiment Moral?" Pp. 225–56 in *Oxford Studies in Metaethics,* Vol. 5, edited by R. Shafer-Landau. Oxford: Oxford University Press.

Kauppinen, Antti. 2017. "Empathy and Moral Judgment." Pp. 215–26 in *The Routledge Handbook of Philosophy of Empathy,* edited by Heidi Maibom. London: Routledge.

Ke, Nan Rosemary, Silvia Chiappa, Jane Wang, Anirudh Goyal, Jorg Bornschein, Melanie Rey, Theophane Weber, Matthew Botvinic, Michael Mozer, and Danilo Jimenez Rezende. 2022. "Learning to Induce Causal Structure." *arXiv Preprint arXiv:2204.04875.*

Kędzierski, Jan, Robert Muszyński, Carsten Zoll, Adam Oleksy, and Mirela Frontkiewicz. 2013. "EMYS—Emotive Head of a Social Robot." *International Journal of Social Robotics* 5(2):237–49.

Keil, Frank C. 1992. *Concepts, Kinds, and Cognitive Development.* Cambridge, MA: MIT Press.

Kemp, Simon, and Garth J. O. Fletcher. 1993. "The Medieval Theory of the Inner Senses." *The American Journal of Psychology* 106(4):559–76.

Kennedy, James. 2006. "Swarm Intelligence." Pp. 187–219 in *Handbook of Nature-Inspired and Innovative Computing: Integrating Classical Models with Emerging Technologies*, edited by A. Y. Zomaya. Boston: Springer.

Keren, Gideon, and Yaacov Schul. 2009. "Two Is Not Always Better Than One: A Critical Evaluation of Two-System Theories." *Perspectives on Psychological Science* 4(6):533–50. doi: 10.1111/j.1745-6924.2009.01164.x.

Khalidi, Muhammad Ali. 2001. "Innateness and Domain Specificity." *Philosophical Studies* 105(2):191–210.

Khalidi, Muhammad Ali. 2013. *Natural Categories and Human Kinds: Classification in the Natural and Social Sciences*. Cambridge: Cambridge University Press.

Khalidi, Muhammad Ali. 2016. "Innateness as a Natural Cognitive Kind." *Philosophical Psychology* 29(3):319–33.

Khaligh-Razavi, Seyed-Mahdi, and Nikolaus Kriegeskorte. 2014. "Deep Supervised, but Not Unsupervised, Models May Explain IT Cortical Representation." *PLoS Computational Biology* 10(11):e1003915. doi: 10.1371/journal.pcbi.1003915.

Kieval, Phillip Hintikka. 2022. "Mapping Representational Mechanisms with Deep Neural Networks." *Synthese* 200(3):1–25.

Kim, Byoungjae. 2019. "Hume on the Problem of Other Minds." *British Journal for the History of Philosophy* 27(3):535–55.

Kim, Junkyung, Matthew Ricci, and Thomas Serre. 2018. "Not-So-CLEVR: Learning Same–Different Relations Strains Feedforward Neural Networks." *Interface Focus* 8(4):20180011.

Kim, Kuno, Megumi Sano, Julian De Freitas, Nick Haber, and Daniel Yamins. 2020. "Active World Model Learning with Progress Curiosity." Pp. 5306–15 in *International Conference on Machine Learning*. Proceedings of Machine Learning Research 119.

Kingma, Durk P., and Prafulla Dhariwal. 2018. "Glow: Generative Flow with Invertible 1x1 Convolutions." *Advances in Neural Information Processing Systems* 31.

Kirsh, David. 1998. "When Is Information Explicitly Represented?" Pp. 240–67 in *Machine Intelligence*, edited by A. Clark and J. Toribio. Routledge.

Kitamura, Takashi, Sachie K. Ogawa, Dheeraj S. Roy, Teruhiro Okuyama, Mark D. Morrissey, Lillian M. Smith, Roger L. Redondo, and Susumu Tonegawa. 2017. "Engrams and Circuits Crucial for Systems Consolidation of a Memory." *Science* 356(6333):73–78. doi: 10.1126/science.aam6808.

Klein, Colin, Jakob Hohwy, and Tim Bayne. 2020. "Explanation in the Science of Consciousness: From the Neural Correlates of Consciousness (NCCs) to the Difference Makers of Consciousness (DMCs)." *Philosophy and the Mind Sciences* 1(II).

Klein, Stanley B. 2016. "Autonoetic Consciousness: Reconsidering the Role of Episodic Memory in Future-Oriented Self-Projection." *Quarterly Journal of Experimental Psychology* 69(2):381–401.

Klinger, Eric, and W. Miles Cox. 1987. "Dimensions of Thought Flow in Everyday Life." *Imagination, Cognition and Personality* 7(2):105–28.

Koch, Christof. 2016. "How the Computer Beat the Go Master." *Scientific American* 27(4):20–23.

Kojima, Takeshi, Shixiang Shane Gu, Machel Reid, Yutaka Matsuo, and Yusuke Iwasawa. 2022. "Large Language Models Are Zero-Shot Reasoners." *ArXiv Preprint ArXiv:2205.11916.*

Kong, Nathan, and Anthony Norcia. 2021. "Are Models Trained on Temporally-Continuous Data Streams More Adversarially Robust?" In *SVRHM 2021 Workshop@ NeurIPS.*

Konkel, Alex, and Neal J. Cohen. 2009. "Relational Memory and the Hippocampus: Representations and Methods." *Frontiers in Neuroscience* 3:23.

Korsgaard, Christine M. 1986. "The Right to Lie: Kant on Dealing with Evil." *Philosophy & Public Affairs* 15(4):325–49.

Köster, Raphael, and Martin J. Chadwick. 2021. "What Can Classic Atari Video Games Tell Us about the Human Brain?" *Neuron* 109(4):568–70. doi: 10.1016/j.neuron.2021.01.021.

Kramer, Mark A. 1991. "Nonlinear Principal Component Analysis Using Autoassociative Neural Networks." *AIChE Journal* 37(2):233–43.

Kriegel, Uriah. 2013. *Phenomenal Intentionality.* Oxford: Oxford University Press.

Krizhevsky, Alex, Ilya Sutskever, and Geoffrey E. Hinton. 2012. "Imagenet Classification with Deep Convolutional Neural Networks." Pp. 1097–105 in *Advances in Neural Information Processing Systems.*

Krueger, David, Nicolas Ballas, Stanislaw Jastrzebski, Devansh Arpit, Maxinder S. Kanwal, Tegan Maharaj, Emmanuel Bengio, Asja Fischer, and Aaron Courville. 2017. "Deep Nets Don't Learn via Memorization." In *ICLR 2017.*

Krupenye, Christopher, Fumihiro Kano, Satoshi Hirata, Josep Call, and Michael Tomasello. 2016. "Great Apes Anticipate That Other Individuals Will Act According to False Beliefs." *Science* 354(6308):110–14.

Kruschke, John K. 1992. "ALCOVE: An Exemplar-Based Connectionist Model of Category Learning." *Psychological Review* 99(1):22.

Kubricht, James R., Keith J. Holyoak, and Hongjing Lu. 2017. "Intuitive Physics: Current Research and Controversies." *Trends in Cognitive Sciences* 21(10):749–59.

Kulke, Louisa, Britta von Duhn, Dana Schneider, and Hannes Rakoczy. 2018. "Is Implicit Theory of Mind a Real and Robust Phenomenon? Results from a Systematic Replication Study." *Psychological Science* 29(6):888–900.

Kumaran, Dharshan, and Eleanor A. Maguire. 2005. "The Human Hippocampus: Cognitive Maps or Relational Memory?" *Journal of Neuroscience* 25(31):7254–59.

Kunst-Wilson, William R., and Robert B. Zajonc. 1980. "Affective Discrimination of Stimuli That Cannot Be Recognized." *Science* 207(4430):557–58.

Kuo, Zing Yang. 1932a. "Ontogeny of Embryonic Behavior in Aves. III. The Structural and Environmental Factors in Embryonic Behavior." *Journal of Comparative Psychology* 13(2):245.

Kuo, Zing Yang. 1932b. "Ontogeny of Embryonic Behavior in Aves: V. The Reflex Concept in the Light of Embryonic Behavior in Birds." *Psychological Review* 39(6):499.

Kuo, Zing Yang. 1932c. "Ontogeny of Embryonic Behavior in Aves. IV. The Influence of Embryonic Movements upon the Behavior after Hatching." *Journal of Comparative Psychology* 14(1):109.

Kuo, Zing Yang. 1933. "Ontogeny of Embryonic Behavior in Aves. VI. Relation between Heart Beat and the Behavior of the Avian Embryo." *Journal of Comparative Psychology* 16(3):379.

Kusner, Matt J., Brooks Paige, and José Miguel Hernández-Lobato. 2017. "Grammar Variational Autoencoder." *ArXiv Preprint ArXiv:1703.01925*.

Laird, John E. 2019. *The Soar Cognitive Architecture*. Cambridge, MA: MIT Press.

Laird, John E., Christian Lebiere, and Paul S. Rosenbloom. 2017. "A Standard Model of the Mind: Toward a Common Computational Framework across Artificial Intelligence, Cognitive Science, Neuroscience, and Robotics." *Ai Magazine* 38(4):13–26.

Lake, Brenden, and Marco Baroni. 2018. "Generalization without Systematicity: On the Compositional Skills of Sequence-to-Sequence Recurrent Networks." Pp. 2873–82 in *International Conference on Machine Learning*. PMLR.

Lake, Brenden M. 2014. "Towards More Human-like Concept Learning in Machines: Compositionality, Causality, and Learning-to-Learn." PhD Thesis, Massachusetts Institute of Technology.

Lake, Brenden M. 2019. "Compositional Generalization through Meta Sequence-to-Sequence Learning." Pp. 9791–801 in *Advances in Neural Information Processing Systems 32*.

Lake, Brenden M., Tal Linzen, and Marco Baroni. 2019. "Human Few-Shot Learning of Compositional Instructions." *ArXiv Preprint ArXiv:1901.04587*.

Lake, Brenden M., Tomer D. Ullman, Joshua B. Tenenbaum, and Samuel J. Gershman. 2016. "Building Machines That Learn and Think Like People." *Behavioral and Brain Sciences* 40:e253. doi: 10.1017/S0140525X16001837.

Lake, Brenden M., Tomer D. Ullman, Joshua B. Tenenbaum, and Samuel J. Gershman. 2017. "Ingredients of Intelligence: From Classic Debates to an Engineering Roadmap." *Behavioral and Brain Sciences* 40:e281.

Landy, David. 2017. *Hume's Science of Human Nature: Scientific Realism, Reason, and Substantial Explanation*. London: Routledge.

Langdon, Angela, Matthew Botvinick, Hiroyuki Nakahara, Keiji Tanaka, Masayuki Matsumoto, and Ryota Kanai. 2021. "Meta-Learning, Social Cognition and Consciousness in Brains and Machines." *Neural Networks* 145:80–89.

Langland-Hassan, Peter. 2014. "Inner Speech and Metacognition: In Search of a Connection." *Mind & Language* 29(5):511–33. doi: 10.1111/mila.12064.

Larochelle, Hugo, and Geoffrey E. Hinton. 2010. "Learning to Combine Foveal Glimpses with a Third-Order Boltzmann Machine." *Advances in Neural Information Processing Systems* 23:1243–51.

Lasnik, Howard, and Terje Lohndal. 2010. "Government–Binding/Principles and Parameters Theory." *Wiley Interdisciplinary Reviews: Cognitive Science* 1(1):40–50.

Lassiter, G. Daniel, Andrew L. Geers, Patrick J. Munhall, Robert J. Ploutz-Snyder, and David L. Breitenbecher. 2002. "Illusory Causation: Why It Occurs." *Psychological Science* 13(4):299–305. doi: 10.1111/j.0956-7976.2002.x.

Lau, Hakwan. 2019. "Consciousness, Metacognition, and Perceptual Reality Monitoring." *PsyArXiv*. https://doi.org/10.31234/osf.io/ckbyf.

Laurence, Stephen, and Eric Margolis. 2002. "Radical Concept Nativism." *Cognition* 86(1):25–55.

Laurence, Stephen, and Eric Margolis. 2012. "Abstraction and the Origin of General Ideas." *Philosopher's Imprint* 12(19).

Laurence, Stephen, and Eric Margolis. 2015. "Concept Nativism and Neural Plasticity." Pp. 117–47 in *The Conceptual Mind: New Directions in the Study of Concepts*, edited by S. Laurence and E. Margolis. Cambridge, MA: MIT Press.

Leben, Derek. 2017. "A Rawlsian Algorithm for Autonomous Vehicles." *Ethics and Information Technology* 19(2):107–15.

Leben, Derek. 2018. *Ethics for Robots: How to Design a Moral Algorithm*. London: Routledge.

LeCun, Yann. 2018. "The Power and Limits of Deep Learning." *Research-Technology Management* 61(6):22–27. doi: 10.1080/08956308.2018.1516928.

LeCun, Yann, Bernhard Boser, John S. Denker, Donnie Henderson, Richard E. Howard, Wayne Hubbard, and Lawrence D. Jackel. 1989. "Backpropagation Applied to Handwritten Zip Code Recognition." *Neural Computation* 1(4):541–51.

Lee, Donsuk, Pranav Gujarathi, and Justin N. Wood. 2021. "Controlled-Rearing Studies of Newborn Chicks and Deep Neural Networks." *ArXiv Preprint ArXiv:2112.06106*.

Lee, Donsuk, Denizhan Pak, and Justin N. Wood. 2021. "Modeling Object Recognition in Newborn Chicks Using Deep Neural Networks." *ArXiv Preprint ArXiv:2106.07185*.

Lee, Donsuk, Samantha M. W. Wood, and Justin N. Wood. 2021. "Development of Collective Behavior in Newborn Artificial Agents." *ArXiv Preprint ArXiv:2111.03796*.

Legg, Shane, and Marcus Hutter. 2007. "A Collection of Definitions of Intelligence." *Frontiers in Artificial Intelligence and Applications* 157:17.

Lehrman, Daniel S. 1953. "A Critique of Konrad Lorenz's Theory of Instinctive Behavior." *The Quarterly Review of Biology* 28(4):337–63.

Lewkowycz, Aitor, Anders Andreassen, David Dohan, Ethan Dyer, Henryk Michalewski, Vinay Ramasesh, Ambrose Slone, Cem Anil, Imanol Schlag, and Theo Gutman-Solo. 2022. "Solving Quantitative Reasoning Problems with Language Models." *ArXiv Preprint ArXiv:2206.14858.*

Li, Belinda Z., Maxwell Nye, and Jacob Andreas. 2021. "Implicit Representations of Meaning in Neural Language Models." *ArXiv Preprint ArXiv:2106.00737.*

Li, Linyang, Ruotian Ma, Qipeng Guo, Xiangyang Xue, and Xipeng Qiu. 2020. "Bert-Attack: Adversarial Attack against Bert Using Bert." *ArXiv Preprint ArXiv:2004.09984.*

Liang, Percy, Rishi Bommasani, Tony Lee, Dimitris Tsipras, Dilara Soylu, Michihiro Yasunaga, Yian Zhang, Deepak Narayanan, Yuhuai Wu, and Ananya Kumar. 2022. "Holistic Evaluation of Language Models." *ArXiv Preprint ArXiv:2211.09110.*

Liley, A. W. 1972. "3 - Disorders of Amniotic Fluid." Pp. 157–206 in *Fetal-Placental Disorders*, edited by N. S. Assali. New York: Academic Press.

Lillicrap, Timothy P., Daniel Cownden, Douglas B. Tweed, and Colin J. Akerman. 2016. "Random Synaptic Feedback Weights Support Error Backpropagation for Deep Learning." *Nature Communications* 7:13276. doi: 10.1038/ncomms13276.

Lin, Long-Ji. 1992. *Reinforcement Learning for Robots Using Neural Networks.* Pittsburgh: Carnegie Mellon University.

Lindsay, Grace W. 2020. "Attention in Psychology, Neuroscience, and Machine Learning." *Frontiers in Computational Neuroscience* 14:29.

Lindsay, Grace W. 2021. "Convolutional Neural Networks as a Model of the Visual System: Past, Present, and Future." *Journal of Cognitive Neuroscience* 33(10):2017–31.

Lipton, Zachary C. 2018. "The Mythos of Model Interpretability: In Machine Learning, the Concept of Interpretability Is Both Important and Slippery." *Queue* 16(3):31–57.

Liu, J. 2017. "Confucian Robotic Ethics." In *International Conference on the Relevance of the Classics under the Conditions of Modernity: Humanity and Science*. Hong Kong: The Hong Kong Polytechnic University.

Liu, JeeLoo. 2021. "Why We Need Emotional Intelligence in the Design of Autonomous Social Robots and How Confucian Moral Sentimentalism Can Help." Pp. 229–46 in *International Conference on Social Robotics*. Springer.

Lloyd, Genevieve. 1993. *The Man of Reason: "Male" and "Female" in Western Philosophy*. 2nd ed. London: Routledge.

Loftus, Elizabeth F. 1996. *Eyewitness Testimony*. Cambridge, MA: Harvard University Press.

Logan, Gordon D. 1994. "Spatial Attention and the Apprehension of Spatial Relations." *Journal of Experimental Psychology: Human Perception and Performance* 20(5):1015.

Lorenz, Konrad. 1935. "Der Kumpan in Der Umwelt Des Vogels. Der Artgenosse Als Auslösendes Moment Sozialer Verhaltungsweisen." *Journal Für Ornithologie. Beiblatt.(Leipzig)* 83:137–213.

Lotter, William, Gabriel Kreiman, and David Cox. 2017. "Deep Predictive Coding Networks for Video Prediction and Unsupervised Learning." *arXiv preprint arXiv:1605.08104.*

Lowe, E. J. 1993. "Rationality, Deduction and Mental Models." Pp. 211–30 in *Rationality: Psychological and Philosophical Perspectives*, International Library of Psychology, edited by K. I. Manktelow and D. E. Over. Florence, KY: Taylor & Frances.

Luc, Pauline, Natalia Neverova, Camille Couprie, Jakob Verbeek, and Yann LeCun. 2017. "Predicting Deeper into the Future of Semantic Segmentation." In *IEEE International Conference on Computer Vision (ICCV)*. Vol. 1.

Lupyan, Gary. 2005. "Carving Nature at Its Joints and Carving Joints into Nature: How Labels Augment Category Representations." Pp. 87–97 in *Modeling Language, Cognition and Action*, edited by Angelo Cangelosi, Guido Bugmann, and Roman Burisyuk. Singapore: World Scientific.

Macchi Cassia, Chiara Turati, and Francesca Simion. 2004. "Can a Nonspecific Bias toward Top-Heavy Patterns Explain Newborns' Face Preference?" *Psychological Science* 15(6):379–83.

Machamer, P., L. Darden, and C. Craver. 2000. "Thinking about Mechanisms." *Philosophy of Science* 67(1):1–25.

Machery, Edouard. 2006. "Two Dogmas of Neo-Empiricism." *Philosophy Compass* 1(4):398–412.

Machery, Edouard. 2008. "Massive Modularity and the Flexibility of Human Cognition." *Mind & Language* 23(3):263–72.

Machery, Edouard. 2009. *Doing without Concepts*. Oxford: Oxford University Press.

Macmillan, N. A. 2002. "Signal Detection Theory." Pp. 43–90 in *Stevens' Handbook of Experimental Psychology*, edited by S. Yantis. Mankato: Coughlan.

Mag Uidhir, Christy, and Cameron Buckner. 2014. "A Portrait of the Artist as an Aesthetic Expert." In *Aesthetics and the Sciences*, edited by Gregory Currie, Matthew Kieran, and Aaron Meskin. Oxford University Press.

Mahadevan, Sridhar. 2018. "Imagination Machines: A New Challenge for Artificial Intelligence." In *Proceedings of the AAAI Conference on Artificial Intelligence*. Vol. 32.

Maia, Tiago V., and James L. McClelland. 2004. "A Reexamination of the Evidence for the Somatic Marker Hypothesis: What Participants Really Know in the Iowa Gambling Task." *Proceedings of the National Academy of Sciences* 101(45):16075–80. doi: 10.1073/pnas.0406666101.

Maibom, Heidi L. 2022. *The Space Between: How Empathy Really Works.* New York: Oxford University Press.

Maier, N. R. F., and T. C. Schneirla. 1964. *Principles of Animal Psychology.* Oxford: Dover.

Malcolm, Noel. 1996. *Thomas Hobbes: Leviathan.* Oxford: Oxford University Press.

Mallon, Ron, and Jonathan M. Weinberg. 2006. "Innateness as Closed Process Invariance." *Philosophy of Science* 73(3):323–44.

Mameli, Matteo, and Patrick Bateson. 2006. "Innateness and the Sciences." *Biology and Philosophy* 21(2):155–88.

Mandelbaum, Eric. 2016. "Attitude, Inference, Association: On the Propositional Structure of Implicit Bias." *Noûs* 50(3):629–58.

Mandler, George. 1990. "William James and the Construction of Emotion." *Psychological Science* 1:179–80. doi: 10.1111/j.1467-9280.1990.tb00193.x.

The ManyBabies Consortium. 2020. "Quantifying Sources of Variability in Infancy Research Using the Infant-Directed-Speech Preference." *Advances in Methods and Practices in Psychological Science* 3(1):24–52. doi: 10.1177/2515245919900809.

Marcus, Gary. 2018a. "Deep Learning: A Critical Appraisal." *ArXiv Preprint ArXiv:1801.00631.*

Marcus, Gary. 2018b. "Innateness, Alphazero, and Artificial Intelligence." *ArXiv Preprint ArXiv:1801.05667.*

Marcus, Gary F. 2003. *The Algebraic Mind: Integrating Connectionism and Cognitive Science.* Cambridge, MA: MIT Press.

Margoni, Francesco, and Luca Surian. 2018. "Infants' Evaluation of Prosocial and Antisocial Agents: A Meta-Analysis." *Developmental Psychology* 54(8):1445.

Martens, J., and T. Schlicht. 2018. "Individualism versus Interactionism about Social Understanding." *Phenomenology and the Cognitive Sciences* 17:245–66.

Martínez-Manrique, Fernando, and Agustín Vicente. 2010. "What the . . . !' The Role of Inner Speech in Conscious Thought." *Journal of Consciousness Studies* 17(9–10):141–67.

Martinho, Antone, and Alex Kacelnik. 2016. "Ducklings Imprint on the Relational Concept of 'Same or Different.'" *Science* 353(6296):286–88.

Matsuyama, Takashi. 1993. "Expert Systems for Image Processing, Analysis, and Recognition: Declarative Knowledge Representation for Computer Vision." *Advances in Electronics and Electron Physics* 86:81–171.

Matuszek, Cynthia, Michael Witbrock, John Cabral, and John DeOliveira. 2006. "An Introduction to the Syntax and Content of Cyc." Pp. 44–49 in *UMBC Computer Science and Electrical Engineering Department Collection.* AAAI Spring Symposium: Formalizing and Compiling Background Knowledge and Its Applications to Knowledge Representation and Question Answering.

McCarthy, John, Marvin L. Minsky, Nathaniel Rochester, and Claude E. Shannon. 2006. "A Proposal for the Dartmouth Summer Research Project on Artificial Intelligence, August 31, 1955." *AI Magazine* 27(4):12–12.

McCarty, Richard R. 1993. "Kantian Moral Motivation and the Feeling of Respect." *Journal of the History of Philosophy* 31(3):421–35.

McClelland, J., B. McNaughton, and Randall C. O'Reilly. 1995. "Why There Are Complementary Learning Systems in the Hippocampus and Neocortex: Insights from the Successes and Failures of Connectionist Models of Learning and Memory." *Psychological Review* 102(3):419–57.

McClelland, James L. 1995. "Constructive Memory and Memory Distortions: A Parallel-Distributed Processing Approach." Pp. 69–90 in *Memory Distortions: How Minds, Brains, and Societies Reconstruct the Past*, edited by Daniel Schacht. Cambridge, MA: Harvard University Press.

McClelland, James L., Matthew M. Botvinick, David C. Noelle, David C. Plaut, Timothy T. Rogers, Mark S. Seidenberg, and Linda B. Smith. 2010. "Letting Structure Emerge: Connectionist and Dynamical Systems Approaches to Cognition." *Trends in Cognitive Sciences* 14(8):348–56.

McClelland, James L., David E. Rumelhart, and PDP Research Group. 1986. "Parallel Distributed Processing." *Explorations in the Microstructure of Cognition* 2:216–71.

McClelland, James L., David E. Rumelhart, and Geoffrey E. Hinton. 1986. *The Appeal of Parallel Distributed Processing*. Cambridge, MA: MIT Press.

McCloskey, Michael, Alfonso Caramazza, and Bert Green. 1980. "Curvilinear Motion in the Absence of External Forces: Naïve Beliefs about the Motion of Objects." *Science* 210(4474):1139–41. doi: 10.1126/science.210.4474.1139.

McCloskey, Michael, and Neal J. Cohen. 1989. "Catastrophic Interference in Connectionist Networks: The Sequential Learning Problem." Pp. 109–65 in *Psychology of Learning and Motivation*. Vol. 24. Elsevier.

McCulloch, Warren S., and Walter Pitts. 1943. "A Logical Calculus of the Ideas Immanent in Nervous Activity." *The Bulletin of Mathematical Biophysics* 5(4):115–33.

Meltzoff, Andrew N., and M. Keith Moore. 1983. "Newborn Infants Imitate Adult Facial Gestures." *Child Development* 54(3):702–9. doi: 10.2307/1130058.

Mendelovici, Angela A. 2018. *The Phenomenal Basis of Intentionality*. Oxford: Oxford University Press.

Mennella, Julie A. 2014. "Ontogeny of Taste Preferences: Basic Biology and Implications for Health." *The American Journal of Clinical Nutrition* 99(3):704S–11S.

Mennella, Julie A., and Nuala K. Bobowski. 2015. "The Sweetness and Bitterness of Childhood: Insights from Basic Research on Taste Preferences." *Physiology & Behavior* 152:502–7. doi: 10.1016/j.physbeh.2015.05.015.

Metzinger, Thomas. 2021. "Artificial Suffering: An Argument for a Global Moratorium on Synthetic Phenomenology." *Journal of Artificial Intelligence and Consciousness* 8(1):43–66.

Millican, Peter. 2009. "Hume on Induction and the Faculties." *Draft Article.* https://davidhume.org/scholarship/papers/millican/2009%20Hume%20In duction%20Faculties.pdf.

Minsky, Marvin, and Seymour A. Papert. 1969. *Perceptrons: An Introduction to Computational Geometry.* Cambridge, MA: MIT Press.

Miracchi, Lisa. 2017. "Generative Explanation in Cognitive Science and the Hard Problem of Consciousness." *Philosophical Perspectives* 31(1):267–91.

Miracchi, Lisa. 2019. "A Competence Framework for Artificial Intelligence Research." *Philosophical Psychology* 32(5):588–633.

Mitchell, Melanie. 2019. *Artificial Intelligence: A Guide for Thinking Humans.* London: Penguin.

Mnih, Volodymyr, Adria Puigdomenech Badia, Mehdi Mirza, Alex Graves, Timothy Lillicrap, Tim Harley, David Silver, and Koray Kavukcuoglu. 2016. "Asynchronous Methods for Deep Reinforcement Learning." Pp. 1928–37 in *International Conference on Machine Learning.* PMLR.

Mnih, Volodymyr, Nicolas Heess, Alex Graves, and koray kavukcuoglu. 2014. "Recurrent Models of Visual Attention." Pp. 2204–12 in *Advances in Neural Information Processing Systems 27.*

Mnih, Volodymyr, Koray Kavukcuoglu, David Silver, Alex Graves, Ioannis Antonoglou, Daan Wierstra, and Martin Riedmiller. 2013. "Playing Atari with Deep Reinforcement Learning." *ArXiv Preprint ArXiv:1312.5602.*

Mnih, Volodymyr, Koray Kavukcuoglu, David Silver, Andrei A. Rusu, Joel Veness, Marc G. Bellemare, Alex Graves, Martin Riedmiller, Andreas K. Fidjeland, and Georg Ostrovski. 2015. "Human-Level Control through Deep Reinforcement Learning." *Nature* 518(7540):529.

Mole, Christopher. 2011a. *Attention Is Cognitive Unison: An Essay in Philosophical Psychology.* Oxford: Oxford University Press.

Mole, Christopher. 2011b. "Nineteen Fifty-Eight: Information Technology and the Reconceptualisation of Creativity." *The Cambridge Quarterly* 40(4):301–27.

Mole, Christopher. 2021. "Attention." In *The Stanford Encyclopedia of Philosophy*, edited by E. N. Zalta. Metaphysics Research Lab, Stanford University.

Momennejad, Ida, Evan M. Russek, Jin H. Cheong, Matthew M. Botvinick, Nathaniel Douglass Daw, and Samuel J. Gershman. 2017. "The Successor Representation in Human Reinforcement Learning." *Nature Human Behaviour* 1(9):680–92.

Montagrin, Alison, Catarina Saiote, and Daniela Schiller. 2018. "The Social Hippocampus." *Hippocampus* 28(9):672–79.

Montalvo, David. 1999. "The Buddhist Empiricism Thesis: An Extensive Critique." *Asian Philosophy* 9(1):51–70.

Moore, Andrew W., and Christopher G. Atkeson. 1993. "Prioritized Sweeping: Reinforcement Learning with Less Data and Less Time." *Machine Learning* 13(1):103–30.

Moore, Richard. 2021. "The Cultural Evolution of Mind-Modelling." *Synthese* 199(1):1751–76.

Moosavi-Dezfooli, Seyed-Mohsen, Alhussein Fawzi, Omar Fawzi, and Pascal Frossard. 2017. "Universal Adversarial Perturbations." Pp. 1765–73 in *Proceedings of the IEEE Conference on Computer Vision and Pattern Recognition*.

Morgan, Conwy Lloyd. 1903. *An Introduction to Comparative Psychology*. London: W. Scott.

Morin, Alain. 2005. "Possible Links between Self-Awareness and Inner Speech Theoretical Background, Underlying Mechanisms, and Empirical Evidence." *Journal of Consciousness Studies* 12(4–5):115–34.

Moser, Edvard I., Emilio Kropff, and May-Britt Moser. 2008. "Place Cells, Grid Cells, and the Brain's Spatial Representation System." *Annual Review of Neuroscience* 31:69–89.

Moustafa, Ahmed A., Catherine E. Myers, and Mark A. Gluck. 2009. "A Neurocomputational Model of Classical Conditioning Phenomena: A Putative Role for the Hippocampal Region in Associative Learning." *Brain Research* 1276:180–95.

Müller, Jörn. 2015. "Memory as an Internal Sense: Avicenna and the Reception of His Psychology by Thomas Aquinas." *Quaestio* 15:497–506.

Mura, Emi, Akiyuki Taruno, Minako Yagi, Kohei Yokota, and Yukako Hayashi. 2018. "Innate and Acquired Tolerance to Bitter Stimuli in Mice." *PLOS ONE* 13(12):e0210032. doi: 10.1371/journal.pone.0210032.

Murphy, Sheila T., and Robert B. Zajonc. 1993. "Affect, Cognition, and Awareness: Affective Priming with Optimal and Suboptimal Stimulus Exposures." *Journal of Personality and Social Psychology* 64(5):723.

Nader, Karim, and Oliver Hardt. 2009. "A Single Standard for Memory: The Case for Reconsolidation." *Nature Reviews Neuroscience* 10(3):224–34.

Nagel, Jennifer. 2012. "Gendler on Alief." *Analysis* 72(4):774–88.

Nanay, Bence. 2016. "The Role of Imagination in Decision-Making." *Mind & Language* 31(1):127–43.

Nayebi, Aran, Javier Sagastuy-Brena, Daniel M. Bear, Kohitij Kar, Jonas Kubilius, Surya Ganguli, David Sussillo, James J. DiCarlo, and Daniel L. K. Yamins. 2022. "Recurrent Connections in the Primate Ventral Visual Stream Mediate a Tradeoff Between Task Performance and Network Size During Core Object Recognition." *Neural Computation* 34(8):1652–75. doi: 2021.02.17.431717.

Neisser, Ulric. 1967. *Cognitive Psychology*. New York: Appleton-Century-Crofts.

Neisser, Ulric. 1976. *Cognition and Reality: Principles and Implications of Cognitive Psychology*. New York: W H Freeman.

von Neumann, J. 1993. "First Draft of a Report on the EDVAC." *IEEE Annals of the History of Computing* 15(4):27–75. doi: 10.1109/85.238389.

Newell, Allen, J. Clifford Shaw, and Herbert A. Simon. 1962. "The Processes of Creative Thinking." Pp. 63–119 in *Contemporary Approaches to Creative Thinking*, edited by H. E. Gruber, G. Terrell, and M. Wertheimer. New York: Atherton Press.

Newell, Allen, and Herbert A. Simon. 1976. "Computer Science as Empirical Inquiry: Symbols and Search." *Communications of the ACM* 19(3):113–26.

Nguyen, Anh, Jason Yosinski, and Jeff Clune. 2015. "Deep Neural Networks Are Easily Fooled: High Confidence...Google Scholar." *IEEE Conference on Computer Vision and Pattern Recognition* 427–36.

Nguyen, C. Thi. 2021. "The Seductions of Clarity." *Royal Institute of Philosophy Supplements* 89:227–55.

Nichols, Shaun. 2001. "Mindreading and the Cognitive Architecture Underlying Altruistic Motivation." *Mind & Language* 16(4):425–55.

Nichols, Shaun, and Stephen P. Stich. 2003. *Mindreading: An Integrated Account of Pretense, Self-Awareness, and Understanding Other Minds.* London: Clarendon Press.

Nisbett, RE, and TD Wilson. 1977. "Telling More Than We Can Know: Verbal Reports on Mental Processes." *Psychological Review* 84(3):231–57.

Noether, Emmy. 1971. "Invariant Variation Problems." *Transport Theory and Statistical Physics* 1(3):186–207.

Northcott, Robert, and Gualtiero Piccinini. 2018. "Conceived This Way: Innateness Defended." *Philosophers' Imprint* 18(18).

Northcutt, Curtis G., Anish Athalye, and Jonas Mueller. 2021. "Pervasive Label Errors in Test Sets Destabilize Machine Learning Benchmarks." *ArXiv Preprint ArXiv:2103.14749.*

Nosofsky, Robert M. 1992. "Exemplar-Based Approach to Relating Categorization, Identification, and Recognition." Pp. 363–93 in *Multidimensional Models of Perception and Cognition*, edited by F. Gregory Ashby. Scientific psychology series. Hillsdale, NJ: Lawrence Erlbaum Associates.

Oakes, Lisa M. 2017. "Sample Size, Statistical Power, and False Conclusions in Infant Looking-Time Research." *Infancy: The Official Journal of the International Society on Infant Studies* 22(4):436–69. doi: 10.1111/infa.12186.

O'Callaghan, Claire, Ishan C. Walpola, and James M. Shine. 2021. "Neuromodulation of the Mind-Wandering Brain State: The Interaction between Neuromodulatory Tone, Sharp Wave-Ripples and Spontaneous Thought." *Philosophical Transactions of the Royal Society B* 376(1817):20190699.

Odegard, Douglas. 1965. "Locke as an Empiricist." *Philosophy* 40(153):185–96.

Odena, Augustus, Vincent Dumoulin, and Chris Olah. 2016. "Deconvolution and Checkerboard Artifacts." *Distill* 1(10):e3.

O'Keefe, J., and J. Dostrovsky. 1971. "The Hippocampus as a Spatial Map: Preliminary Evidence from Unit Activity in the Freely-Moving Rat." *Brain Research* 34:171–75. doi: 10.1016/0006-8993(71)90358-1.

O'Keefe, John, and Lynn Nadel. 1978. *The Hippocampus as a Cognitive Map.* London: Clarendon Press.

Olsson, Catherine, Elhage Nelson, Neel Nanda, Nicholas Joseph, Nova DasSarma, Tom Henighan, Ben Mann, Amanda Askell, Yuntao Bai, Anna Chen, Tom Conerly, Dawn Drain, Deep Ganguli, Zac Hatfield-Dodds, Danny Hernandez, Scott Johnston, Andy Jones, Jackson Kernion, Liane Lovitt, Kamal Ndousse, Dario Amodei, Tom Brown, Jack Clark, Jared Kaplan, Sam McCandish, and Chris Olah. 2022. "In-Context Learning and Induction Heads." *Transformer Circuits.* https://transformer-circuits.pub/2022/in-context-learning-and-induction-heads/index.html

Omer, David B., Shir R. Maimon, Liora Las, and Nachum Ulanovsky. 2018. "Social Place-Cells in the Bat Hippocampus." *Science* 359(6372):218–24.

O'Reilly, Randall C. 1996. "Biologically Plausible Error-Driven Learning Using Local Activation Differences: The Generalized Recirculation Algorithm." *Neural Computation* 8(5):895–938.

Orellana Figueroa, Jordy Didier, Jonathan Scott Reeves, Shannon P. McPherron, and Claudio Tennie. 2021. "A Proof of Concept for Machine Learning-Based Virtual Knapping Using Neural Networks." *Scientific Reports* 11(1):19966. doi: 10.1038/s41598-021-98755-6.

Orhan, Emin, Vaibhav Gupta, and Brenden M. Lake. 2020. "Self-Supervised Learning through the Eyes of a Child." *Advances in Neural Information Processing Systems* 33:9960–71.

Ouyang, Long, Jeff Wu, Xu Jiang, Diogo Almeida, Carroll L. Wainwright, Pamela Mishkin, Chong Zhang, Sandhini Agarwal, Katarina Slama, Alex Ray, John Schulman, Jacob Hilton, Fraser Kelton, Luke Miller, Maddie Simens, Amanda Askell, Peter Welinder, Paul Christiano, Jan Leike, and Ryan Lowe. 2022. "Training Language Models to Follow Instructions with Human Feedback." *Advances in Neural Information Processing Systems* 35:27730–44.

Paiva, Ana, Iolanda Leite, Hana Boukricha, and Ipke Wachsmuth. 2017. "Empathy in Virtual Agents and Robots: A Survey." *ACM Transactions on Interactive Intelligent Systems (TiiS)* 7(3):1–40.

Parisotto, Emilio, Francis Song, Jack Rae, Razvan Pascanu, Caglar Gulcehre, Siddhant Jayakumar, Max Jaderberg, Raphael Lopez Kaufman, Aidan Clark, and Seb Noury. 2020. "Stabilizing Transformers for Reinforcement Learning." Pp. 7487–98 in *International Conference on Machine Learning.* PMLR.

Patel, Ankit B., Minh Tan Nguyen, and Richard Baraniuk. 2016. "A Probabilistic Framework for Deep Learning." Pp. 2558–66 in *Advances in Neural Information Processing Systems.*

Patel, Roma, and Ellie Pavlick. 2021. "Mapping Language Models to Grounded Conceptual Spaces." In *International Conference on Learning Representations.*

Pearce, John M. 2002. "Evaluation and Development of a Connectionist Theory of Configural Learning." *Animal Learning & Behavior* 30(2):73–95.

Pearce, John M., and Mark E. Bouton. 2001. "Theories of Associative Learning in Animals." *Annual Review of Psychology* 52(1):111–39.

Pearl, Judea. 1984. *Heuristics: Intelligent Search Strategies for Computer Problem Solving.* Cambridge: Addison-Wesley Longman.

Pearl, Judea. 2009. *Causality.* Cambridge: Cambridge University Press.

Pearl, Judea. 2019. "The Seven Tools of Causal Inference, with Reflections on Machine Learning." *Communications of the ACM* 62(3):54–60.

Pearl, Judea. 2021. "Radical Empiricism and Machine Learning Research." *Journal of Causal Inference* 9(1):78–82.

Penn, Derek C., Keith J. Holyoak, and Daniel J. Povinelli. 2008. "Darwin's Mistake: Explaining the Discontinuity between Human and Nonhuman Minds." Edited by B. Smith and D. Woodruff Smith. *Behavioral and Brain Sciences* 31(2):109–30; discussion 130–78.

Penn, Derek C., and Daniel J. Povinelli. 2007a. "Causal Cognition in Human and Nonhuman Animals: A Comparative, Critical Review." *Annual Review of Psychology* 58(1):97–118. doi: 10.1146/annurev.psych.58.110405.085555.

Penn, Derek C., and Daniel J. Povinelli. 2007b. "On the Lack of Evidence That Non-Human Animals Possess Anything Remotely Resembling a 'Theory of Mind.'" *Philosophical Transactions of the Royal Society of London - Series B: Biological Sciences* 362(1480):731–44.

Perea-García, Juan Olvido, Mariska E. Kret, Antónia Monteiro, and Catherine Hobaiter. 2019. "Scleral Pigmentation Leads to Conspicuous, Not Cryptic, Eye Morphology in Chimpanzees." *Proceedings of the National Academy of Sciences* 116(39):19248–50.

Perfors, Amy, Joshua B. Tenenbaum, and Terry Regier. 2011. "The Learnability of Abstract Syntactic Principles." *Cognition* 118(3):306–38.

Perry, Carolyn Jeane, and Mazyar Fallah. 2014. "Feature Integration and Object Representations along the Dorsal Stream Visual Hierarchy." *Frontiers in Computational Neuroscience* 8. doi: 10.3389/fncom.2014.00084.

Pessoa, Luiz. 2008. "On the Relationship between Emotion and Cognition." *Nature Reviews Neuroscience* 9(2):148–58.

Pessoa, Luiz, Loreta Medina, and Ester Desfilis. 2022. "Refocusing Neuroscience: Moving Away from Mental Categories and towards Complex Behaviours." *Philosophical Transactions of the Royal Society B* 377(1844):20200534.

Pfeiffer, Brad E., and David J. Foster. 2013. "Hippocampal Place Cell Sequences Depict Future Paths to Remembered Goals." *Nature* 497(7447):74–79. doi: 10.1038/nature12112.

Phillips, Webb, Maya Shankar, and Laurie R. Santos. 2010. "Essentialism in the Absence of Language? Evidence from Rhesus Monkeys (Macaca Mulatta)." *Developmental Science* 13(4):F1–7. doi: 10.1111/j.1467-7687.2010.00982.x.

Picard, Rosalind W. 2000. *Affective Computing*. Cambridge, MA: MIT Press.

Picard, Rosalind W. 2003. "Affective Computing: Challenges." *International Journal of Human-Computer Studies* 59(1–2):55–64.

Piccinini, Gualtiero. 2015. *Physical Computation: A Mechanistic Account*. Oxford: Oxford University Press.

Piccinini, Gualtiero. 2020a. *Neurocognitive Mechanisms: Explaining Biological Cognition*. Oxford: Oxford University Press.

Piccinini, Gualtiero. 2020b. "Nonnatural Mental Representation." Pp. 254–86 in *What Are Mental Representations*, edited by Joulia Smortchkova, Tobias Schlicht, and Krzysztof Dolega. New York: Oxford Unviersity Press.

Piccinini, Gualtiero, and Carl Craver. 2011. "Integrating Psychology and Neuroscience: Functional Analyses as Mechanism Sketches." *Synthese* 183(3):283–311. doi: 10.1007/s11229-011-9898-4.

Piccinini, Gualtiero, and Armin Schulz. 2018. "The Evolution of Psychological Altruism." *Philosophy of Science* 85(5):1054–64. doi: 10.1086/699743.

Pinker, Steven. 2003. *The Blank Slate: The Modern Denial of Human Nature*. Penguin.

Pinker, Steven. 2005. "The Blank Slate." *The General Psychologist* 41(1):1–8.

Plunkett, Kim, and Patrick Juola. 1999. "A Connectionist Model of English Past Tense and Plural Morphology." *Cognitive Science* 23(4):463–90. doi: https://doi.org/10.1207/s15516709cog2304_4.

Podzimek, Š., M. Dušková, Z. Broukal, B. Racz, L. Starka, and J. Dušková. 2018. "The Evolution of Taste and Perinatal Programming of Taste Preferences." *Physiological Research* 67:S421–S429.

Poole, David, Alan Mackworth, and Randy Goebel. 1998. *Computational Intelligence: A Logical Approach*. New York: Oxford University Press.

Povinelli, D. J., and T. J. Eddy. 1996. "What Young Chimpanzees Know about Seeing." *Monographs of the Society for Research in Child Development* 61(3):i–vi, 1–152; discussion 153–91.

Powell, Lindsey J., Kathryn Hobbs, Alexandros Bardis, Susan Carey, and Rebecca Saxe. 2018. "Replications of Implicit Theory of Mind Tasks with Varying Representational Demands." *Cognitive Development* 46:40–50.

Powers, John. 1994. "Empiricism and Pragmatism in the Thought of Dharmakīrti and William James." *American Journal of Theology & Philosophy* 15(1):59–85.

Premack, D., and G. Woodruff. 1978. "Does the Chimpanzee Have a Theory of Mind?" *Behavioral and Brain Sciences* 1(04):515–26. doi: 10.1017/S0140525X00076512.

Preston, Stephanie D., and Frans BM De Waal. 2002. "Empathy: Its Ultimate and Proximate Bases." *Behavioral and Brain Sciences* 25(1):1–20.

Prinz, Jesse. 2000. "A Neurofunctional Theory of Visual Consciousness." *Consciousness and Cognition* 9(2):243–59.

Prinz, Jesse. 2007. *The Emotional Construction of Morals*. Oxford: Oxford University Press.

Prinz, Jesse. 2012. *The Conscious Brain*. Oxford: Oxford University Press.

Prinz, Jesse. 2022. "James and Attention: Reactive Spontaneity." In *The Oxford Handbook of William James*, edited by A. Klein. New York: Oxford University Press. https://academic.oup.com/edited-volume/34712.

Prinz, Jesse J. 2002. *Furnishing the Mind: Concepts and Their Perceptual Basis*. Cambridge, MA: MIT Press.

Prinz, Jesse J. 2004. *Gut Reactions: A Perceptual Theory of Emotion*. Oxford: Oxford University Press.

Prinz, Jesse J. 2005. "A Neurofunctional Theory of Consciousness." Pp. 381–96 in *Cognition and the Brain: The Philosophy and Neuroscience Movement*, edited by Andrew Brook and Kathleen Akins. Cambridge: Cambridge University Press.

Proudfoot, Diane. 2011. "Anthropomorphism and AI: Turing's Much Misunderstood Imitation Game." *Artificial Intelligence* 175(5–6):950–57.

Quine, W. V. 1951. "Two Dogmas of Empiricism." *The Philosophical Review* 60(1):20–43.

Quine, Willard Van Orman. 1969. "Linguistics and Philosophy." Pp. 95–98 in *Language and Philosophy*, edited by S. Hook. New York University Press.

Rabinowitz, Neil C., Frank Perbet, H. Francis Song, Chiyuan Zhang, S. M. Eslami, and Matthew Botvinick. 2018. "Machine Theory of Mind." *ArXiv Preprint ArXiv:1802.07740*.

Racanière, Sébastien, Théophane Weber, David Reichert, Lars Buesing, Arthur Guez, Danilo Jimenez Rezende, Adrià Puigdomènech Badia, Oriol Vinyals, Nicolas Heess, and Yujia Li. 2017. "Imagination-Augmented Agents for Deep Reinforcement Learning." *Advances in Neural Information Processing Systems* 30.

Radford, Alec, Luke Metz, and Soumith Chintala. 2015. "Unsupervised Representation Learning with Deep Convolutional Generative Adversarial Networks." *ArXiv Preprint ArXiv:1511.06434*.

Rahwan, Iyad, Manuel Cebrian, Nick Obradovich, Josh Bongard, Jean-François Bonnefon, Cynthia Breazeal, Jacob W. Crandall, Nicholas A. Christakis, Iain D. Couzin, Matthew O. Jackson, Nicholas R. Jennings, Ece Kamar, Isabel M. Kloumann, Hugo Larochelle, David Lazer, Richard McElreath, Alan Mislove, David C. Parkes, Alex 'Sandy' Pentland, Margaret E. Roberts, Azim Shariff, Joshua B. Tenenbaum, and Michael Wellman. 2019. "Machine Behaviour." *Nature* 568(7753):477–86. doi: 10.1038/s41586-019-1138-y.

Railton, Peter. 2020. "Ethical Learning, Natural and Artificial." Pp. 45–70 in *Ethics of Artificial Intelligence*, edited by S. M. Liao. Oxford: Oxford University Press.

Rakoczy, Hannes. 2017. "In Defense of a Developmental Dogma: Children Acquire Propositional Attitude Folk Psychology around Age 4." *Synthese* 194(3):689–707. doi: 10.1007/s11229-015-0860-8.

Ramesh, Aditya, Prafulla Dhariwal, Alex Nichol, Casey Chu, and Mark Chen. 2022. "Hierarchical Text-Conditional Image Generation with Clip Latents." *ArXiv Preprint ArXiv:2204.06125.*

Ranzini, Mariagrazia, Matteo Lisi, and Marco Zorzi. 2016. "Voluntary Eye Movements Direct Attention on the Mental Number Space." *Psychological Research* 80(3):389–98.

Ravfogel, Shauli, Grusha Prasad, Tal Linzen, and Yoav Goldberg. 2021. "Counterfactual Interventions Reveal the Causal Effect of Relative Clause Representations on Agreement Prediction." *ArXiv Preprint ArXiv:2105.06965.*

Ray, Elizabeth, and Cecilia Heyes. 2011. "Imitation in Infancy: The Wealth of the Stimulus." *Developmental Science* 14(1):92–105.

Reali, Florencia, and Morten H. Christiansen. 2005. "Uncovering the Richness of the Stimulus: Structure Dependence and Indirect Statistical Evidence." *Cognitive Science* 29(6):1007–28.

Reath, Andrews. 1989. "Kant?S Theory of Moral Sensibility. Respect for the Moral Law and the Influence of Inclination." *Kant Studien* 80(1–4):284–302. doi: 10.1515/kant.1989.80.1-4.284.

Reilly, Steve, and Radmila Trifunovic. 2001. "Lateral Parabrachial Nucleus Lesions in the Rat: Neophobia and Conditioned Taste Aversion." *Brain Research Bulletin* 55(3):359–66.

Ren, Shaoqing, Kaiming He, Ross Girshick, and Jian Sun. 2015. "Faster R-Cnn: Towards Real-Time Object Detection with Region Proposal Networks." Pp. 91–99 in *Advances in Neural Information Processing Systems.*

Rescorla, Robert A. 1972. "A Theory of Pavlovian Conditioning: Variations in the Effectiveness of Reinforcement and Nonreinforcement." Pp. 64–99 in *Classical Conditioning II: Current Research and Theory*, edited by A. H. Black and W. F. Prokasy. New York: Appleton-Century-Crofts.

Reynolds, Laria, and Kyle McDonell. 2021. "Prompt Programming for Large Language Models: Beyond the Few-Shot Paradigm." Pp. 1–7 in *Extended Abstracts of the 2021 CHI Conference on Human Factors in Computing Systems.*

Ricci, Matthew, Rémi Cadène, and Thomas Serre. 2021. "Same-Different Conceptualization: A Machine Vision Perspective." *Current Opinion in Behavioral Sciences* 37:47–55.

Richardson, Ken. 2002. "What IQ Tests Test." *Theory & Psychology* 12(3):283–314. doi: 10.1177/0959354302012003012.

Ritchie, J. Brendan. 2021. "What's Wrong with the Minimal Conception of Innateness in Cognitive Science?" *Synthese* 199(1):159–76.

Ritchie, J. Brendan, David Michael Kaplan, and Colin Klein. 2019. "Decoding the Brain: Neural Representation and the Limits of Multivariate Pattern

Analysis in Cognitive Neuroscience." *The British Journal for the Philosophy of Science* 70(2):581–607.

Ritchie, J. Brendan, Astrid A. Zeman, Joyce Bosmans, Shuo Sun, Kirsten Verhaegen, and Hans P. Op de Beeck. 2021. "Untangling the Animacy Organization of Occipitotemporal Cortex." *Journal of Neuroscience* 41(33):7103–19.

Robbins, Philip. 2009. "Modularity of Mind." In *The Stanford Encyclopedia of Philosophy*, edited by E. N. Zalta.

Robins, Sarah K. 2019. "Confabulation and Constructive Memory." *Synthese* 196(6):2135–51.

Rochat, Philippe. 2009. *Others in Mind: Social Origins of Self-Consciousness.* Cambridge: Cambridge University Press.

Rochat, Philippe, and Sara Valencia Botto. 2021. "From Implicit to Explicit Body Awareness in the First Two Years of Life." Pp. 181–93 in *Body Schema and Body Image: New Directions*, edited by P. Rochat and S. V. Botto. Oxford University Press.

Rogers, Anna, Olga Kovaleva, and Anna Rumshisky. 2020. "A Primer in Bertology: What We Know about How Bert Works." *Transactions of the Association for Computational Linguistics* 8:842–66.

Rogers, Timothy T., and James L. McClelland. 2004. *Semantic Cognition: A Parallel Distributed Processing Approach*. Cambridge, MA: MIT Press.

Rogers, Timothy T., and James L. McClelland. 2014. "Parallel Distributed Processing at 25: Further Explorations in the Microstructure of Cognition." *Cognitive Science* 38(6):1024–77.

Ronacher, Bernhard. 2019. "Innate Releasing Mechanisms and Fixed Action Patterns: Basic Ethological Concepts as Drivers for Neuroethological Studies on Acoustic Communication in Orthoptera." *Journal of Comparative Physiology. A, Neuroethology, Sensory, Neural, and Behavioral Physiology* 205(1):33–50. doi: 10.1007/s00359-018-01311-3.

Rosa-Salva, Orsola, Uwe Mayer, Elisabetta Versace, Marie Hébert, Bastien S. Lemaire, and Giorgio Vallortigara. 2021. "Sensitive Periods for Social Development: Interactions between Predisposed and Learned Mechanisms." *Cognition* 213:104552. doi: 10.1016/j.cognition.2020.104552.

Rosenblatt, Frank. 1958. "The Perceptron: A Probabilistic Model for Information Storage and Organization in the Brain." *Psychological Review* 65(6):386.

Rosenbloom, Paul S. 2013. "The Sigma Cognitive Architecture and System." *AISB Quarterly* 136:4–13.

Rosenstein, Diana, and Harriet Oster. 1988. "Differential Facial Responses to Four Basic Tastes in Newborns." *Child Development* 59(6):1555–68.

Rosker, Jernej, and Ziva Majcen Rosker. 2021. "Correlations between Gaze Fixations to Different Areas of Interest Are Related to Tennis Serve Return Performance in Two Different Expert Groups." *International*

Journal of Performance Analysis in Sport 21(6):1–13. doi: 10.1080/24748668.2021.1979840.

Roskies, Adina L. 2021. "Representational Similarity Analysis in Neuroimaging: Proxy Vehicles and Provisional Representations." *Synthese* 199(3):5917–35.

Rubin, David C., and Sharda Umanath. 2015. "Event Memory: A Theory of Memory for Laboratory, Autobiographical, and Fictional Events." *Psychological Review* 122(1):1–23. doi: 10.1037/a0037907.

Rubio-Fernández, Paula. 2019. "Publication Standards in Infancy Research: Three Ways to Make Violation-of-Expectation Studies More Reliable." *Infant Behavior and Development* 54:177–88.

Ruder, Sebastian. 2017. *An Overview of Gradient Descent Optimization Algorithms.* arXiv:1609.04747. arXiv. doi: 10.48550/arXiv.1609.04747.

Rudin, Cynthia. 2019. "Stop Explaining Black Box Machine Learning Models for High Stakes Decisions and Use Interpretable Models Instead." *Nature Machine Intelligence* 1(5):206–15.

Rugani, Rosa, Giorgio Vallortigara, Konstantinos Priftis, and Lucia Regolin. 2015. "Number-Space Mapping in the Newborn Chick Resembles Humans' Mental Number Line." *Science* 347(6221):534–36. doi: 10.1126/science.aaa1379.

Russakovsky, Olga, Jia Deng, Hao Su, Jonathan Krause, Sanjeev Satheesh, Sean Ma, Zhiheng Huang, Andrej Karpathy, Aditya Khosla, and Michael Bernstein. 2015. "Imagenet Large Scale Visual Recognition Challenge." *International Journal of Computer Vision* 115(3):211–52.

Russell, Stuart, and Peter Norvig. 2003. *Artificial Intelligence: A Modern Approach.* Second Edition. Upper Saddle River, NJ: Pearson Education.

Russin, Jacob, Roland Fernandez, Hamid Palangi, Eric Rosen, Nebojsa Jojic, Paul Smolensky, and Jianfeng Gao. 2021. "Compositional Processing Emerges in Neural Networks Solving Math Problems." *CogSci ... Annual Conference of the Cognitive Science Society. Cognitive Science Society (U.S.). Conference* 2021:1767–73.

Russin, Jake, Jason Jo, Randall C. O'Reilly, and Yoshua Bengio. 2019. "Compositional Generalization in a Deep Seq2seq Model by Separating Syntax and Semantics." *ArXiv Preprint ArXiv:1904.09708.*

Rusu, Andrei A., Neil C. Rabinowitz, Guillaume Desjardins, Hubert Soyer, James Kirkpatrick, Koray Kavukcuoglu, Razvan Pascanu, and Raia Hadsell. 2016. "Progressive Neural Networks." *ArXiv Preprint ArXiv:1606.04671.*

Ryoo, Michael S., Keerthana Gopalakrishnan, Kumara Kahatapitiya, Ted Xiao, Kanishka Rao, Austin Stone, Yao Lu, Julian Ibarz, and Anurag Arnab. 2022. "Token Turing Machines." *ArXiv Preprint ArXiv:2211.09119.*

Sabbagh, Mark A., and Markus Paulus. 2018. "Replication Studies of Implicit False Belief with Infants and Toddlers." *Cognitive Development* 46:1–3.

Sadler, Matthew, and Natasha Regan. 2019. *Game Changer: AlphaZero's Groundbreaking Chess Strategies and the Promise of AI*. Amsterdam: New In Chess.

Saharia, Chitwan, William Chan, Saurabh Saxena, Lala Li, Jay Whang, Emily Denton, Seyed Kamyar Seyed Ghasemipour, Burcu Karagol Ayan, S. Sara Mahdavi, Rapha Gontijo Lopes, Tim Salimans, Jonathan Ho, David J. Fleet, and Mohammad Norouzi. 2022. "Photorealistic Text-to-Image Diffusion Models with Deep Language Understanding." *Advances in Neural Information Processing Systems* 35: 36479–94.

Salvadori, Eliala, Tatiana Blazsekova, Agnes Volein, Zsuzsanna Karap, Denis Tatone, Olivier Mascaro, and Gergely Csibra. 2015. "Probing the Strength of Infants' Preference for Helpers over Hinderers: Two Replication Attempts of Hamlin and Wynn (2011)." *PLOS ONE* 10(11):e0140570. doi: 10.1371/journal.pone.0140570.

Samuels, Richard. 2000. "Massively Modular Minds: Evolutionary Psychology and Cognitive Architecture." Pp. 13–46 in *Evolution and the Human Mind: Modularity, Language and Meta-Cognition*, edited by P. Carruthers and A. Chamberlain. Cambridge: Cambridge University Press.

Samuels, Richard. 2004. "Innateness in Cognitive Science." *Trends in Cognitive Sciences* 8(3):136–41.

Samuels, Richard. 2007. "Is Innateness a Confused Notion?" Pp. 17–36 in *The Innate Mind: Foundations and the Future*, edited by P. Carruthers, S. Laurence, and S. Stich. Oxford University Press. Oxford: Oxford University Press.

Samuels, Richard, Stephen Stich, and Michael Bishop. 2002. "Ending the Rationality Wars: How to Make Disputes About Human Rationality Disappear." Pp. 236–68 in *Common Sense, Reasoning and Rationality*, edited by R. Elio. Oxford: Oxford University Press.

Santos, L. R., J. I. Flombaum, and W. Phillips. 2007. "The Evolution of Human Mindreading: How Non-Human Primates Can Inform Social Cognitive Neuroscience." Pp. 433–56 in *Evolutionary Cognitive Neuroscience*, edited by S. Platek, J. Keenan, and T. Shackleford. Cambridge, MA: MIT Press.

Saxe, Andrew, Stephanie Nelli, and Christopher Summerfield. 2020. "If Deep Learning Is the Answer, What Is the Question?" *Nature Reviews Neuroscience* 22(1):55–67.

Sayer, Peter. 2017. "Twenty Years after Deep Blue, What Can AI Do for Us?" *Computerworld*. https://www.computerworld.com/article/3196407/twenty-years-after-deep-blue-what-can-ai-do-for-us.html.

Scellier, Benjamin, and Yoshua Bengio. 2017. "Equilibrium Propagation: Bridging the Gap between Energy-Based Models and Backpropagation." *Frontiers in Computational Neuroscience* 11. doi: 10.3389/fncom.2017.00024.

Schacter, Daniel L. 1987. "Implicit Memory: History and Current Status." *Journal of Experimental Psychology: Learning, Memory, and Cognition* 13(3):501.

Schacter, Daniel L., and Donna Rose Addis. 2007. "The Cognitive Neuroscience of Constructive Memory: Remembering the Past and Imagining the Future." *Philosophical Transactions of the Royal Society B: Biological Sciences* 362(1481):773–86. doi: 10.1098/rstb.2007.2087.

Schacter, Daniel L., and Endel Tulving. 1982. "Memory, Amnesia, and the Episodic/Semantic Distinction." Pp. 33–65 in *The Expression of Knowledge*, edited by Robert L. Isaacson and Norman E. Spear. New York: Springer.

Schafer, Matthew, and Daniela Schiller. 2018. "Navigating Social Space." *Neuron* 100(2):476–89.

Schliesser, Eric. 2019. "Sophie de Grouchy, Adam Smith, and the Politics of Sympathy." Pp. 193–219 in *Feminist History of Philosophy: The Recovery and Evaluation of Women's Philosophical Thought*. New York: Springer.

Schmidhuber, Jürgen. 2015. "Deep Learning in Neural Networks: An Overview." *Neural Networks* 61:85–117.

Schrimpf, Martin, Idan Asher Blank, Greta Tuckute, Carina Kauf, Eghbal A. Hosseini, Nancy Kanwisher, Joshua B. Tenenbaum, and Evelina Fedorenko. 2021. "The Neural Architecture of Language: Integrative Modeling Converges on Predictive Processing." *Proceedings of the National Academy of Sciences* 118(45): e2105646118.

Schwarz, Wolf, and Inge M. Keus. 2004. "Moving the Eyes along the Mental Number Line: Comparing SNARC Effects with Saccadic and Manual Responses." *Perception & Psychophysics* 66(4):651–64.

Sellars, Wilfrid. 1956. "Empiricism and the Philosophy of Mind." *Minnesota Studies in the Philosophy of Science* 1(19):253–329.

Shalizi, Cosma. 2007. "G, a Statistical Myth." *The Three-Toed Sloth*. Retrieved November 18, 2020. http://bactra.org/weblog/523.html

Shallue, Christopher J., and Andrew Vanderburg. 2018. "Identifying Exoplanets with Deep Learning: A Five-Planet Resonant Chain around Kepler-80 and an Eighth Planet around Kepler-90." *The Astronomical Journal* 155:94.

Shanahan, Murray, Matthew Crosby, Benjamin Beyret, and Lucy Cheke. 2020b. "Artificial Intelligence and the Common Sense of Animals." *Trends in Cognitive Sciences* 24(11):862–72. doi: 10.1016/j.tics.2020.09.002.

Shapiro, Stewart. 2004. "The Nature and Limits of Abstraction." Edited by K. Fine. *The Philosophical Quarterly (1950-)* 54(214):166–74.

Shevlin, Henry, and Marta Halina. 2019. "Apply Rich Psychological Terms in AI with Care." *Nature Machine Intelligence* 1:165–67.

Silver, David, Aja Huang, Chris J. Maddison, Arthur Guez, Laurent Sifre, George van den Driessche, Julian Schrittwieser, Ioannis Antonoglou, Veda Panneershelvam, Marc Lanctot, Sander Dieleman, Dominik Grewe, John Nham, Nal Kalchbrenner, Ilya Sutskever, Timothy Lillicrap, Madeleine

Leach, Koray Kavukcuoglu, Thore Graepel, and Demis Hassabis. 2016. "Mastering the Game of Go with Deep Neural Networks and Tree Search." *Nature* 529(7587):484–89. doi: 10.1038/nature16961.

Silver, David, Julian Schrittwieser, Karen Simonyan, Ioannis Antonoglou, Aja Huang, Arthur Guez, Thomas Hubert, Lucas Baker, Matthew Lai, and Adrian Bolton. 2017. "Mastering the Game of Go without Human Knowledge." *Nature* 550(7676):354–59.

Simion, Francesca, and Irene Leo. 2010. "A Neoconstructivistic Approach to the Emergence of a Face Processing System." Pp. 314–32 in *Neoconstructivism: The New Science of Cognitive Development*, edited by Scott P. Johnson. Oxford: Oxford University Press.

Simion, Francesca, Chiara Turati, Eloisa Valenza, and Irene Leo. 2006. "The Emergence of Cognitive Specialization in Infancy: The Case of Face Preference." Pp. 189–208 in *Attention and Performance XXI, Processes of Change in Brain and Cognitive Development*, edited by M. H. Johnson and M. Munakata. Oxford: Oxford University Press.

Simion, Francesca, E. Di Giorgio, I. Leo, and L. Bardi. 2011. "The Processing of Social Stimuli in Early Infancy: From Faces to Biological Motion Perception." *Progress in Brain Research* 189:173–93.

Simion, Francesca, Eloisa Valenza, Viola Macchi Cassia, Chiara Turati, and Carlo Umiltà. 2002. "Newborns' Preference for up–down Asymmetrical Configurations." *Developmental Science* 5(4):427–34.

Simon, Jon. 2021. "What Does Transformer Self-Attention Actually Look At?" Retrieved September 16, 2022. https://scribe.froth.zone/what-does-tran sformer-self-attention-actually-look-at-5318df114ac0.

Simons, Daniel J., and Daniel T. Levin. 1997. "Change Blindness." *Trends in Cognitive Sciences* 1(7):261–67.

Singer, Charles Joseph. 1952. *Vesalius on the Human Brain: Introduction, Translation of Text, Translation of Descriptions of Figures, Notes to the Translations, Figures.* Oxford: Oxford University Press.

Skinner, Burrhus Frederic. 1957. *Verbal Behavior.* New York: Appleton-Century-Crofts.

Skerry, A. E., S. E. Carey, and E. S. Spelke. 2013. "First-Person Action Experience Reveals Sensitivity to Action Efficiency in Prereaching Infants." *Proceedings of the National Academy of Sciences* 110(46):18728–33.

Sloman, Steven A. 1996. "The Empirical Case for Two Systems of Reasoning." *Psychological Bulletin* 119(1):3–22. doi: 10.1037/0033-2909.119.1.3.

Smallwood, Jonathan, and Jessica Andrews-Hanna. 2013. "Not All Minds That Wander Are Lost: The Importance of a Balanced Perspective on the Mind-Wandering State." *Frontiers in Psychology* 4:441.

Smallwood, Jonathan, Jonathan W. Schooler, David J. Turk, Sheila J. Cunningham, Phebe Burns, and C. Neil Macrae. 2011. "Self-Reflection and the Temporal Focus of the Wandering Mind." *Consciousness and Cognition* 20(4):1120–26.

Smith, Linda B. 2000. "Avoiding Associations with It's Behaviorism You Really Hate." Pp. 169–74 in *Becoming a Word Learner: A Debate on Lexical Acquisition*, edited by R. Golinkoff. Oxford: Oxford University Press.

Smith, Linda B., and Lauren K. Slone. 2017. "A Developmental Approach to Machine Learning?" *Frontiers in Psychology* 8:2124.

Smith, Linda B., Chen Yu, Hanako Yoshida, and Caitlin M. Fausey. 2015. "Contributions of Head-Mounted Cameras to Studying the Visual Environments of Infants and Young Children." *Journal of Cognition and Development* 16(3):407–19.

Smith, Linda, and Chen Yu. 2008. "Infants Rapidly Learn Word-Referent Mappings via Cross-Situational Statistics." *Cognition* 106(3):1558–68. doi: 10.1016/j.cognition.2007.06.010.

Smithies, Declan. 2012. "The Mental Lives of Zombies." *Philosophical Perspectives* 26:343–72.

Smolensky, Paul. 1987. "The Constituent Structure of Connectionist Mental States: A Reply to Fodor and Pylyshyn." *Southern Journal of Philosophy* 26(Supplement):137–63.

Smolensky, Paul. 1988. "On the Proper Treatment of Connectionism." Edited by A. Goldman. *Behavioral and Brain Sciences* 11(1):1–74.

Smolensky, Paul. 1990. "Tensor Product Variable Binding and the Representation of Symbolic Structures in Connectionist Systems." *Artificial Intelligence* 46(1–2):159–216.

Smolensky, Paul, R. Thomas McCoy, Roland Fernandez, Matthew Goldrick, and Jianfeng Gao. 2022. *Neurocompositional Computing: From the Central Paradox of Cognition to a New Generation of AI Systems*. arXiv:2205.01128.

Soatto, Stefano, and Alessandro Chiuso. 2014. "Visual Representations: Defining Properties and Deep Approximations." *ArXiv Preprint ArXiv:1411.7676*.

Sober, Elliott. 1998. "Black Box Inference: When Should Intervening Variables Be Postulated?" *The British Journal for the Philosophy of Science* 49(3):469–98. doi: 10.1093/bjps/49.3.469.

Sober, Elliott. 2000. "Evolution and the Problem of Other Minds." *The Journal of Philosophy* 97(7):365–86. doi: 10.2307/2678410.

Songhorian, Sarah. 2022. "Adam Smith's Relevance for Contemporary Moral Cognition." *Philosophical Psychology* 35(5): 662–83.

Sorabji, Richard. 1993. *Animal Minds and Human Morals: The Origins of the Western Debate*. Ithaca, NY: Cornell University Press.

Spackman, Kent A. 1989. "Signal Detection Theory: Valuable Tools for Evaluating Inductive Learning." Pp. 160–63 in *Proceedings of the Sixth International Workshop on Machine Learning*. Ithaca, NY: Elsevier.

Spaulding, Shannon. 2018a. *How We Understand Others: Philosophy and Social Cognition*. London: Routledge.

Spaulding, Shannon. 2018b. "Mindreading beyond Belief: A More Comprehensive Conception of How We Understand Others." *Philosophy Compass* 13(11):e12526.

Spelke, Elizabeth. 1994. "Initial Knowledge: Six Suggestions." *Cognition* 50(1–3):431–45.

Spelke, Elizabeth S. 1998. "Nativism, Empiricism, and the Origins of Knowledge." *Infant Behavior and Development* 21(2):181–200.

Squire, Larry R. 2004. "Memory Systems of the Brain: A Brief History and Current Perspective." *Neurobiology of Learning and Memory* 82(3):171–77.

Srivastava, Aarohi, Abhinav Rastogi, Abhishek Rao, Abu Awal Md Shoeb, Abubakar Abid, Adam Fisch, Adam R. Brown, Adam Santoro, Aditya Gupta, and Adrià Garriga-Alonso. 2022. "Beyond the Imitation Game: Quantifying and Extrapolating the Capabilities of Language Models." *ArXiv Preprint ArXiv:2206.04615.*

Stachenfeld, Kimberly L., Matthew M. Botvinick, and Samuel J. Gershman. 2017. "The Hippocampus as a Predictive Map." *Nature Neuroscience* 20(11):1643–53.

Staddon, J. E. R. 1989. "Animal Psychology: The Tyranny of Anthropocentrism." Pp. 123–35 in *Perspectives in Ethology, Vol. 8: Whither Ethology?*, edited by P. P. G. Bateson and P. H. Klopfer. New York: Plenum Press.

Steinbeis, Nikolaus. 2016. "The Role of Self–Other Distinction in Understanding Others' Mental and Emotional States: Neurocognitive Mechanisms in Children and Adults." *Philosophical Transactions of the Royal Society B: Biological Sciences* 371(1686):20150074.

Stephenson, C., J. Feather, S. Padhy, O. Elibol, H. Tang, J. McDermott, and S. Chung. 2019. "Untangling in Invariant Speech Recognition." *Advances in Neural Information Processing Systems* 32. https://proceedings.neurips.cc/paper_files/paper/2019/hash/e2db7186375992e729165726762cb4c1-Abstract.html.

Sterelny, Kim. 1989. "Fodor's Nativism." *Philosophical Studies* 55(2):119–41.

Sterrett, Susan G. 2012. "Bringing up Turing's 'Child-Machine.'" Pp. 703–13 in *Conference on Computability in Europe.* Springer.

Stich, S., and S. Nichols. 1992. "Folk Psychology: Simulation or Tacit Theory?." *Mind & Language* 7(1–2):35–71.

Stiennon, Nisan, Long Ouyang, Jeffrey Wu, Daniel Ziegler, Ryan Lowe, Chelsea Voss, Alec Radford, Dario Amodei, and Paul F. Christiano. 2020. "Learning to Summarize with Human Feedback." Pp. 3008–21 in *Advances in Neural Information Processing Systems.* Vol. 33.

Stinson, Catherine. 2018. "Explanation and Connectionist Models." Pp. 120–34 in *The Routledge Handbook of the Computational Mind*, edited by M. Sprevak and M. Colombo. London: Routledge.

Stinson, Catherine. 2020. "From Implausible Artificial Neurons to Idealized Cognitive Models: Rebooting Philosophy of Artificial Intelligence." *Philosophy of Science* 87(4):590–611.

Stork, David G. 1989. "Is Backpropagation Biologically Plausible." Pp. 241–46 in *International Joint Conference on Neural Networks.* Vol. 2. Washington, DC: IEEE.

Stroud, Barry. 1979. "Inference, Belief, and Understanding." *Mind* 88(1):179–96.

Su, Jiawei, Danilo Vasconcellos Vargas, and Kouichi Sakurai. 2019. "One Pixel Attack for Fooling Deep Neural Networks." *IEEE Transactions on Evolutionary Computation* 25(5):828–41.

Suddendorf, T., and M. Corballis. 2008. "New Evidence for Animal Foresight?" *Animal Behaviour* 75(5):e1–3. doi: 10.1016/j.anbehav.2008.01.006.

Suddendorf, Thomas, Donna Rose Addis, and Michael C. Corballis. 2009. "Mental Time Travel and Shaping of the Human Mind." *Philosophical Transactions of the Royal Society B: Biological Sciences* 364(1521):1317–24.

Sullivan, Emily. 2022. "Understanding from Machine Learning Models." *The British Journal for the Philosophy of Science* 73(1):109–33. doi: 10.1093/bjps/axz035.

Sullivan, Jessica, Michelle Mei, Andrew Perfors, Erica Wojcik, and Michael C. Frank. 2022. "SAYCam: A Large, Longitudinal Audiovisual Dataset Recorded from the Infant's Perspective." *Open Mind* 5:20–29.

Sutton, Richard. 2019. "The Bitter Lesson." *Incomplete Ideas*. Retrieved November 3, 2020. http://www.incompleteideas.net/IncIdeas/BitterLesson.html

Sutton, Richard S., and Andrew G. Barto. 2018. *Reinforcement Learning: An Introduction*. Cambridge, MA: MIT Press.

Talmor, Alon, Yanai Elazar, Yoav Goldberg, and Jonathan Berant. 2020. "OLMpics—On What Language Model Pre-Training Captures." *Transactions of the Association for Computational Linguistics* 8:743–58. doi: 10.1162/tacl_a_00342.

Tarski, Alfred, and John Corcoran. 1986. "What Are Logical Notions?" *History and Philosophy of Logic* 7(2):143–54.

Tay, Yi, Mostafa Dehghani, Jai Gupta, Dara Bahri, Vamsi Aribandi, Zhen Qin, and Donald Metzler. 2021. "Are Pre-Trained Convolutions Better Than Pre-Trained Transformers?" *ArXiv Preprint ArXiv:2105.03322*.

Taylor, Alex H., Amalia P. M. Bastos, Rachael L. Brown, and Colin Allen. 2022. "The Signature-Testing Approach to Mapping Biological and Artificial Intelligences." *Trends in Cognitive Sciences* 26(9):738–50. doi: 10.1016/j.tics.2022.06.002.

Taylor, Kenneth. 2003. *Reference and the Rational Mind*. Stanford: CSLI.

Tennie, Claudio, Josep Call, and Michael Tomasello. 2009. "Ratcheting Up the Ratchet: On the Evolution of Cumulative Culture." *Philosophical Transactions of the Royal Society of London B: Biological Sciences* 364(1528):2405–15.

Theriault, Jordan E., Liane Young, and Lisa Feldman Barrett. 2021. "The Sense of Should: A Biologically-Based Framework for Modeling Social Pressure." *Physics of Life Reviews* 36:100–136.

Tillemans, Tom. 2021. "Dharmakīrti." In *The Stanford Encyclopedia of Philosophy*, edited by E. N. Zalta. Metaphysics Research Lab, Stanford University.

Tomasello, Michael, Josep Call, and Brian Hare. 2003. "Chimpanzees Understand Psychological States – the Question Is Which Ones and to What Extent." *Trends in Cognitive Sciences* 7(4):153–56. doi: 10.1016/ S1364-6613(03)00035-4.

Tomasello, Michael, Brian Hare, Hagen Lehmann, and Josep Call. 2007. "Reliance on Head versus Eyes in the Gaze Following of Great Apes and Human Infants: The Cooperative Eye Hypothesis." *Journal of Human Evolution* 52(3):314–20.

Toneva, Mariya, and Leila Wehbe. 2019. "Interpreting and Improving Natural-Language Processing (in Machines) with Natural Language-Processing (in the Brain)." In *Advances in Neural Information Processing Systems*. Vol. 32.

Toth, Nicholas, Kathy D. Schick, E. Sue Savage-Rumbaugh, Rose A. Sevcik, and Duane M. Rumbaugh. 1993. "Pan the Tool-Maker: Investigations into the Stone Tool-Making and Tool-Using Capabilities of a Bonobo (Pan Paniscus)." *Journal of Archaeological Science* 20(1):81–91.

Treisman, Anne M. 1960. "Contextual Cues in Selective Listening." *Quarterly Journal of Experimental Psychology* 12(4):242–48.

Treisman, Anne M., and Garry Gelade. 1980. "A Feature-Integration Theory of Attention." *Cognitive Psychology* 12(1):97–136.

Tulving, Endel. 1972. "Episodic and Semantic Memory." Pp. 381–403 in *Organization of Memory*, edited by E. Tulving and W. Davidson. New York: Academic Press.

Tulving, Endel. 2001. "Origin of Autonoesis in Episodic Memory." Pp. 17–34 in *The Nature of Remembering: Essays in Honor of Robert G. Crowder*, edited by Henry L. Roediger, James S. Nairne, Ian Neath, and Aimée M. Surprenant. Science conference series. Washington, DC: American Psychological Association.

Tulving, Endel. 2005. "Episodic Memory and Autonoesis: Uniquely Human?" Pp. 3–56 in *The Missing Link in Cognition: Origins of Self-Reflective Consciousness*, edited by Herbert S. Terrace and Janet Metcalfe. New York: Oxford University Press.

Turing, Alan Mathison. 1948. *Intelligent Machinery*. Technical report. Teddington, England: National Physical Laboratory. Mathematics Division.

Turing, Allen M. 1950. "Computing Machinery and Intelligence." *Mind* 59(236):433.

Tversky, A., and D. Kahneman. 1974. "Judgment under Uncertainty: Heuristics and Biases." *Science* 185(4157):1124–31.

Uzgalis, William. 2020. "John Locke." In *The Stanford Encyclopedia of Philosophy*, edited by E. N. Zalta. Metaphysics Research Lab, Stanford University.

Van Gelder, Tim. 1990. "Compositionality: A Connectionist Variation on a Classical Theme." *Cognitive Science* 14(3):355–84.

Van Gulick, Robert. 2004. "Higher-Order Global States (HOGS): An Alternative Higher-Order Model." Pp. 67–93 in *Higher-Order Theories of Consciousness*, edited by R. Gennaro. New York: John Benjamins.

Van Leeuwen, Neil. 2013. "The Meanings of 'Imagine' Part I: Constructive Imagination." *Philosophy Compass* 8(3):220–30.

Vaswani, Ashish, Noam Shazeer, Niki Parmar, Jakob Uszkoreit, Llion Jones, Aidan N. Gomez, Lukasz Kaiser, and Illia Polosukhin. 2017. "Attention Is All You Need." Pp. 5998–6008 in *Advances in Neural Information Processing Systems*.

Versace, Elisabetta, Antone Martinho-Truswell, Alex Kacelnik, and Giorgio Vallortigara. 2018. "Priors in Animal and Artificial Intelligence: Where Does Learning Begin?" *Trends in Cognitive Sciences* 22(11):963–65.

Versace, Elisabetta, Michelle J. Spierings, Matteo Caffini, Carel Ten Cate, and Giorgio Vallortigara. 2017. "Spontaneous Generalization of Abstract Multimodal Patterns in Young Domestic Chicks." *Animal Cognition* 20(3):521–29.

Vidyasagar, Trichur Raman. 2013. "Reading into Neuronal Oscillations in the Visual System: Implications for Developmental Dyslexia." *Frontiers in Human Neuroscience* 7:e811. doi: 10.3389/fnhum.2013.00811.

Viganò, Simone, and Manuela Piazza. 2021. "The Hippocampal-Entorhinal System Represents Nested Hierarchical Relations between Words during Concept Learning." *Hippocampus* 31(6):557–68.

Vigo, Ronaldo. 2009. "Categorical Invariance and Structural Complexity in Human Concept Learning." *Journal of Mathematical Psychology* 53(4):203–21.

Vigo, Ronaldo. 2011. "Towards a Law of Invariance in Human Concept Learning." Pp. 2580–85 in *Proceedings of the 33rd Annual Meeting of the Cognitive Science Society*. Cognitive Science Society.

Vinyals, Oriol, Igor Babuschkin, Junyoung Chung, Michael Mathieu, Max Jaderberg, Wojciech Czarnecki, Andrew Dudzik, Aja Huang, et al. 2019. "AlphaStar: Mastering the Real-Time Strategy Game StarCraft II." *DeepMind*. Retrieved April 5, 2019. https://www.deepmind.com/blog/alphastar-mastering-the-real-time-strategy-game-starcraft-ii.

Voita, Elena, David Talbot, Fedor Moiseev, Rico Sennrich, and Ivan Titov. 2019. "Analyzing Multi-Head Self-Attention: Specialized Heads Do the Heavy Lifting, the Rest Can Be Pruned." Pp. 5797–5808 in *Proceedings of the 57th Annual Meeting of the Association for Computational Linguistics*. Florence, Italy: Association for Computational Linguistics.

Vygotsky, Lev S. 2012. *Thought and Language*. Cambridge, MA: MIT Press.

de Waal, F. B. M. 2000. "Anthropomorphism and Anthropodenial: Consistency in Our Thinking about Humans and Other Animals." *Philosophical Topics* 27:255–80.

Wagner, Allan R., and Robert A. Rescorla. 1972. "Inhibition in Pavlovian Conditioning: Application of a Theory." Pp. 301–36 in *Inhibition and Learning*, edited by R. A. Boakes and M. S. Halliday. New York: Academic Press.

Wang, Zhangyang, Ding Liu, Shiyu Chang, Florin Dolcos, Diane Beck, and Thomas Huang. 2017. "Image Aesthetics Assessment Using Deep Chatterjee's Machine." Pp. 941–48 in *2017 International Joint Conference on Neural Networks (IJCNN)*. IEEE.

Warnell, Katherine Rice, and Elizabeth Redcay. 2019. "Minimal Coherence among Varied Theory of Mind Measures in Childhood and Adulthood." *Cognition* 191:103997.

Warstadt, Alex, and Samuel R. Bowman. 2022. "What Artificial Neural Networks Can Tell Us about Human Language Acquisition." Pp. 17–60 in *Algebraic Structures in Natural Language*, edited by Shalom Lappin and Jean-Phillipe Bernardy. Boca Raton, FL: CRC Press.

Wason, Peter Cathcart, and Philip Nicholas Johnson-Laird. 1972. Psychology of Reasoning: Structure and Content. Vol. 86. Cambridge, MA: Harvard University Press.

Watanabe, S. 2011. "Discrimination of Painting Style and Quality: Pigeons Use Different Strategies for Different Tasks." *Animal Cognition* 14:797–808. https://doi.org/10.1007/s10071-011-0412-7.

Webb, Barbara. 2009. "Animals Versus Animats: Or Why Not Model the Real Iguana?" *Adaptive Behavior* 17(4):269–86. doi: 10.1177/1059712309339867.

Weiskopf, D. A. 2011. "Models and Mechanisms in Psychological Explanation." *Synthese* 183(3):313–38.

Wellman, Henry M., David Cross, and Julanne Watson. 2001. "Meta-Analysis of Theory-of-Mind Development: The Truth about False Belief." *Child Development* 72(3):655–84. doi: 10.1111/1467-8624.00304.

Werbos, Paul. 1974. "Beyond Regression:" New Tools for Prediction and Analysis in the Behavioral Sciences." PhD dissertation, Harvard University.

Werning, M. 2020. "Predicting the Past from Minimal Traces: Episodic Memory and Its Distinction from Imagination and Preservation." *Review of Philosophy and Psychology* 11:301–33. https://doi.org/10.1007/s13 164-020-00471-z.

Westra, Evan. 2017. "Pragmatic Development and the False Belief Task." *Review of Philosophy and Psychology* 8(2):235–57.

Westra, Evan. 2018. "Character and Theory of Mind: An Integrative Approach." *Philosophical Studies* 175(5):1217–41.

Whittington, J. C., Joseph Warren, and Timothy E. J. Behrens. 2021. "Relating Transformers to Models and Neural Representations of the Hippocampal Formation." *arXiv* preprint arXiv:2112.04035.

Wieczorek, Martyna N., Michał Walczak, Marzena Skrzypczak-Zielińska, and Henryk H. Jeleń. 2018. "Bitter Taste of Brassica Vegetables: The Role of Genetic Factors, Receptors, Isothiocyanates, Glucosinolates, and Flavor

Context." *Critical Reviews in Food Science and Nutrition* 58(18):3130–40. doi: 10.1080/10408398.2017.1353478.

Wilson, David Sloan, and Elliott Sober. 1998. *Unto Others: The Evolution and Psychology of Unselfish Behavior Harvard University Press, Cambridge* .

Wimmer, Heinz, and Josef Perner. 1983. "Beliefs about Beliefs: Representation and Constraining Function of Wrong Beliefs in Young Children's Understanding of Deception." *Cognition* 13(1):103–28.

Winston, Andrew S. 2020. "Scientific Racism and North American Psychology." In *Oxford Research Encyclopedia of Psychology*, edited by I. Johnsrude.

Wood, Justin N., Aditya Prasad, Jason G. Goldman, and Samantha MW Wood. 2016. "Enhanced Learning of Natural Visual Sequences in Newborn Chicks." *Animal Cognition* 19(4):835–45.

Woodfield, Andrew. 1991. "Conceptions." *Mind* 100(4):547–72.

Wu, Wayne. 2011a. "Confronting Many-Many Problems: Attention and Agentive Control." *Noûs* 45(1):50–76.

Wu, Wayne. 2011b. "What Is Conscious Attention?" *Philosophy and Phenomenological Research* 82(1):93–120.

Wu, Zhirong, Yuanjun Xiong, Stella X. Yu, and Dahua Lin. 2018. "Unsupervised Feature Learning via Non-Parametric Instance Discrimination." Pp. 3733–42 in *Proceedings of the IEEE Conference on Computer Vision and Pattern Recognition*.

Xu, Kelvin, Jimmy Ba, Ryan Kiros, Kyunghyun Cho, Aaron Courville, Ruslan Salakhudinov, Rich Zemel, and Yoshua Bengio. 2015. "Show, Attend and Tell: Neural Image Caption Generation with Visual Attention." Pp. 2048–57 in *International Conference on Machine Learning*.

Xu, Peng, Xiatian Zhu, and David A. Clifton. 2022. "Multimodal Learning with Transformers: A Survey." IEEE Transactions on Pattern Analysis and Machine Intelligence. https://ieeexplore.ieee.org/abstract/document/10123038.

Xu, Weilin, David Evans, and Yanjun Qi. 2017. "Feature Squeezing: Detecting Adversarial Examples in Deep Neural Networks." *ArXiv Preprint ArXiv:1704.01155*.

Yamins, Daniel L. K., and James J. DiCarlo. 2016. "Using Goal-Driven Deep Learning Models to Understand Sensory Cortex." *Nature Neuroscience* 19(3):356.

Yang, Li-Chia, Szu-Yu Chou, and Yi-Hsuan Yang. 2017. "MidiNet: A Convolutional Generative Adversarial Network for Symbolic-Domain Music Generation." *ArXiv Preprint ArXiv:1703.10847*.

Yorzinski, Jessica L., Amy Harbourne, and William Thompson. 2021. "Sclera Color in Humans Facilitates Gaze Perception during Daytime and Nighttime." *PLOS ONE* 16(3):e0249137. doi: 10.1371/journal.pone.0249137.

Yorzinski, Jessica L., and Jacob Miller. 2020. "Sclera Color Enhances Gaze Perception in Humans." *PLOS ONE* 15(2):e0228275. doi: 10.1371/journal.pone.0228275.

Yousefzadeh, Roozbeh. 2021. "Deep Learning Generalization and the Convex Hull of Training Sets." *ArXiv Preprint ArXiv:2101.09849.*

Yu, Chen, and Linda B. Smith. 2013. "Joint Attention without Gaze Following: Human Infants and Their Parents Coordinate Visual Attention to Objects through Eye-Hand Coordination." *PloS One* 8(11):e79659.

Zaadnoordijk, Lorijn, Tarek R. Besold, and Rhodri Cusack. 2020. "The Next Big Thing (s) in Unsupervised Machine Learning: Five Lessons from Infant Learning." *ArXiv Preprint ArXiv:2009.08497.*

Zaadnoordijk, Lorijn, Tarek R. Besold, and Rhodri Cusack. 2022. "Lessons from Infant Learning for Unsupervised Machine Learning." *Nature Machine Intelligence* 4(6):510–20.

Zador, Anthony M. 2019. "A Critique of Pure Learning and What Artificial Neural Networks Can Learn from Animal Brains." *Nature Communications* 10(1):1–7. doi: 10.1038/s41467-019-11786-6.

Zahedi, Zahra, Sarath Sreedharan, and Subbarao Kambhampati. 2022. "A Mental-Model Centric Landscape of Human-AI Symbiosis." *ArXiv Preprint ArXiv:2202.09447.*

Zarepour, Mohammad Saleh. 2020. "Avicenna's Notion of Fiṭrīyāt: A Comment on Dimitri Gutas' Interpretation." *Philosophy East and West* 70(3):819–33.

Zawidzki, Tadeusz W. 2013. *Mindshaping: A New Framework for Understanding Human Social Cognition.* MIT Press.

Zawidzki, Tadeusz W. 2008. "The Function of Folk Psychology: Mind Reading or Mind Shaping?" *Philosophical Explorations* 11(3):193–210.

Zeki, Semir. 2002. "Inner Vision: An Exploration of Art and the Brain." *Journal of Aesthetics and Art Criticism* 60(4):365–66.

Zerilli, John, Alistair Knott, James Maclaurin, and Colin Gavaghan. 2019. "Transparency in Algorithmic and Human Decision-Making: Is There a Double Standard?" *Philosophy & Technology* 32(4):661–83. doi: 10.1007/s13347-018-0330-6.

Zhang, Aston, Zachary C. Lipton, Mu Li, and Alexander J. Smola. 2021. "Dive into Deep Learning." *ArXiv Preprint ArXiv:2106.11342.*

Zhang, Chiyuan, Samy Bengio, Moritz Hardt, Benjamin Recht, and Oriol Vinyals. 2017. "Understanding Deep Learning Requires Rethinking Generalization." *ArXiv:1611.03530 [Cs].*

Zhang, Chiyuan, Samy Bengio, Moritz Hardt, Benjamin Recht, and Oriol Vinyals. 2021. "Understanding Deep Learning (Still) Requires Rethinking Generalization." *Communications of the ACM* 64(3):107–15.

Zhang, Muhan, Shali Jiang, Zhicheng Cui, Roman Garnett, and Yixin Chen. 2019. "D-Vae: A Variational Autoencoder for Directed Acyclic Graphs." Pp. 1588–1600 in *Advances in Neural Information Processing Systems.*

Zhang, Yan, Jonathon Hare, and Adam Prügel-Bennett. 2018. "Learning to Count Objects in Natural Images for Visual Question Answering." *ArXiv:1802.05766 [Cs]*.

Zhou, Zhenglong, and Chaz Firestone. 2018. "Taking a Machine's Perspective: Human Deciphering of Adversarial Images." *ArXiv Preprint ArXiv:1809.04120*.

Zhou, Zhenglong, and Chaz Firestone. 2019. "Humans Can Decipher Adversarial Images." *Nature Communications* 10(1):1334. doi: 10.1038/s41467-019-08931-6.

Zhu, Shengyu, Ignavier Ng, and Zhitang Chen. 2019. "Causal Discovery with Reinforcement Learning." *ArXiv Preprint ArXiv:1906.04477*.

Złotowski, Jakub, Diane Proudfoot, Kumar Yogeeswaran, and Christoph Bartneck. 2015. "Anthropomorphism: Opportunities and Challenges in Human–Robot Interaction." *International Journal of Social Robotics* 7(3):347–60.

Index

For the benefit of digital users, indexed terms that span two pages (e.g., 52–53) may, on occasion, appear on only one of those pages.

Tables and figures are indicated by *t* and *f* following the page number